THE FURY ARCHIVES

MODERNIST LATITUDES

MODERNIST LATITUDES

Jessica Berman and Paul Saint-Amour, Editors

Modernist Latitudes aims to capture the energy and ferment of modernist studies by continuing to open up the range of forms, locations, temporalities, and theoretical approaches encompassed by the field. The series celebrates the growing latitude ("scope for freedom of action or thought") that this broadening affords scholars of modernism, whether they are investigating little-known works or revisiting canonical ones. Modernist Latitudes will pay particular attention to the texts and contexts of those latitudes (Africa, Latin America, Australia, Asia, Southern Europe, and even the rural United States) that have long been misrecognized as ancillary to the canonical modernisms of the global North.

For a complete list of books in the series, see page 331

THE FURY ARCHIVES

Female Citizenship, Human Rights, and the International Avant-Gardes

Jill Richards

Columbia University Press
New York

Columbia University Press gratefully acknowledges the generous support for this book provided by a Publisher's Circle member.

Columbia University Press
Publishers Since 1893
New York   Chichester, West Sussex
cup.columbia.edu
Copyright © 2020 Columbia University Press
All rights reserved

Library of Congress Cataloging-in-Publication Data
Names: Richards, Jill C., 1983– author.
Title: The fury archives : female citizenship, human rights, and the international avant-gardes / Jill Richards.
Description: New York : Columbia University Press, [2020] | Series: Modernist latitudes | Includes bibliographical references and index.
Identifiers: LCCN 2019058884 (print) | LCCN 2019058885 (ebook) | ISBN 9780231197106 (hardback) | ISBN 9780231197113 (paperback) | ISBN 9780231551984 (ebook)
Subjects: LCSH: Feminism—History. | Women political activists—History. | Women radicals—History. | Women's rights—History. | Citizenship—History.
Classification: LCC HQ1150 .R53 2020 (print) | LCC HQ1150 (ebook) | DDC 305.4209—dc23
LC record available at https://lccn.loc.gov/2019058884
LC ebook record available at https://lccn.loc.gov/2019058885

Cover images: Claude Cahun, *I am in training don't kiss me* (1927), photograph, courtesy of the Jersey Heritage Collection. Suzanne Malherbe manuscript (background image), Claude Cahun and Suzanne Malherbe Collection, courtesy of the Beinecke Library, Yale University.

Contents

Acknowledgments vii

Introduction 1

PART I SEX AND CITIZENSHIP IN THE ATLANTIC ARCHIVES

1. The Fury Archives: Afterlives of the Female Incendiary 31
2. The Long Middle: Militant Suffrage from Britain to South Africa 68

PART II THE REPRODUCTIVE ATLANTIC

3. The Art of Not Having Children: Birth Strike, Sabotage, and the Reproductive Atlantic 105
4. Rhineland Bastards, Queer Species: An Afro-German Case Study 144

PART III CONVERGENCES IN INSTITUTIONAL HUMAN RIGHTS

5. Surrealism's Inhumanities: Chance Encounter, Lesbian Crime, Queer Resistance 185
6. The Committee Form: Négritude Women and the United Nations 230

   Epilogue. Social Reproduction and the Midcentury Witch: Leonora Carrington in Mexico 254

Notes 271
Bibliography 297
Index 317

Acknowledgments

The questions driving this book emerged outside of or against the university, through the reading groups, committee meetings, and actions associated with the University of California Student Occupation Movement, Occupy Oakland, and associated anarchist, left-communist, feminist, queer, and antiracist organizing in the Bay Area from 2009 through 2014. I am so grateful for these communities, alongside the wider extra-academic political formations that have sustained and challenged me in the subsequent years spent on the East Coast, in New Haven, Philadelphia, and Brooklyn.

At the same time, this book was made possible through sustained institutional support on many fronts. In the Department of English at the University of California, Berkeley, I owe special thanks to my formidable advisors Charles Altieri, Dan Blanton, and Lyn Hejinian. I am particularly appreciative of this group for their continuous goodwill and encouragement when I changed the focus of my research midstream, from aesthetic theory to radical feminism. At Berkeley, I am also thankful for a number of excellent teachers and mentors in the English Department and beyond, including Kathleen Donegan, Eric Falci, Cecil Giscombe, Kevis Goodman, Celeste Langan, Colleen Lye, Maura Nolan, and Linda Williams. I want to send extra gratitude to Dan Blanton for his generous and devastatingly smart readings of my writing well after graduation. Lyn Hejinian was an invaluable source of inspiration for political, and especially feminist, organizing in the academy. I feel especially lucky to have as classmates the marvelous Sookyoung Lee, Lili Loofbourow, Batya Ungar-Sargon, and Mia You. My dissertation work was supported by grants from the Summer Mellon Dissertation Seminar Fund, taught by Michael Lucey and the Chernin Program, then headed up by Maura Nolan, who was an outstanding mentor when I needed one the most.

In Berkeley and Oakland but extending outside the strict context of institutional affiliation, thank you and love to my housemates at Casa Milvia, Sarah Chihaya and Jessica Crewe, who shared conversation, writing, and late-night movie trivia that sustained me through graduate school. Thanks to Jessie Hock and Alex Dubilet, not least for their sunny, book-filled apartment as a rest stop. I owe so much to my weekly television buddy and teargas hand-holder Callie Maidof. More widely, gratitude and love to an Oakland crew including but not limited to Jasper Bernes, Matt Bonal, Shane Boyle, Chris Chen, Joshua Clover, Chris Nealon, Dan Nemser, Oki Sogumi, Juliana Spahr, and Wendy Trevino. Tim Kreiner deserves special mention and thanks for many years of support. Thanks too to Meredith Wallis, for California activist lawyering and East Coast friendship over the phone. Finally, thank you and appreciation to the ACLU lawyers who argued a class-action lawsuit against the city of Oakland and Alameda County for the mass arrests on January 28, 2012. That settlement paid for a summer of writing this book, though it meant a lot more than that to many different people.

In turning from California to Connecticut, I am first struck by my vast good fortune to have joined the English Department at Yale the same year as the indomitable Marta Figlerowicz, who has provided years of witty commentary, last-minute read-throughs, and solidarity in friendship. Sunny Xiang joined us the next year, along with Rasheed Tazudeen, to form the reconstituted Berkeley network of my dreams. During this time, Briallen Hopper has been a fount of kindness and grace, Greta LaFleur an indefatigable joy, and Eda Pepi my dearest coconspirator. Big thanks to Jill Jarvis, for friendship, dog-walking company, and generous readings of this work when the writing was in the weeds. Lucia Hulsether deserves special thanks for her support during late-stage editing meltdowns. I am most grateful for the existence of my New Haven therapist, Isha Vela, who helped me keep mind and body together over the course of several years. Amid the morass of hasty revisions, Brandon Proia was an excellent developmental editor, offering key suggestions for concision and clarity throughout. In the English Department, Joe Cleary, Wai Chee Dimock, Ben Glaser, Jacqueline Goldsby, Langdon Hammer, Cajetan Iheka, David Kastan, Naomi Levine,

ACKNOWLEDGMENTS

Katja Lindskog, Priyasha Mukhopadhyay, Stephanie Newell, Catherine Nicholson, Joe North, Anthony Reed, and Katie Trumpener offered academic and extracurricular support. Extra thanks to Caleb Smith, for his generous reading of drafts and direction amid bureaucratic tangles. In Women, Gender, and Sexuality Studies, I am thankful to have worked with two brilliant, supportive chairs, Inderpal Grewal and Margaret Homans, and for the queer comradeship of Serena Bassi, Igor De Souza, Robin Dembroff, Joe Fischel, and Evren Savci. Katie Lofton deserves a sentence of her own of enthusiastic thanks, for mentorship and much-needed encouragement. I am thankful to have worked as a Mellon Dissertation Workshop fellow, particularly alongside Doug Rogers, who has taught me much about what mentorship can look like in the best of circumstances. At Yale, this book has been supported by the grants from the Fund for Lesbian and Gay Studies (FLAGS) Research Award, A. Whitney Griswold Faculty Research Fund, and the Frederick W. Hilles Publication Fund.

This book benefited from a manuscript workshop, and I am so thankful to participants Ann Cvetkovich, Michael Denning, Inderpal Grewal, and Paul Saint-Amour for their generous reading and suggestions. Over the years, I have given a number of presentations from these materials and am particularly indebted to the brilliant Elizabeth Anker for a wonderful experience at the Law and Humanities Colloquium at the Cornell Law School. Thank you to the people at MODS: Twentieth-Century Graduate Reading Group at the University of Pennsylvania, especially Jed Esty and Paul Saint-Amour, for their warm welcome and good cheer while I was living in Philadelphia. I had a great time and conversation with Lori Cole and the Center for Comparative Modernism Working Group at New York University. Particular gratitude goes to Sara Crangle and Natalia Cecire, as my hosts and interlocutors at the Center for Modernist Studies, Sussex University. Thank you to Melissa Zeiger and the Department of English at Dartmouth University for their interest in the history of feminist bureaucracies. At Columbia University Press, I am particularly thankful to be working for the second time with such a smart and kind editor, Philip Leventhal, alongside the fantastic editors for the Modernist Latitudes Series, Jessica Berman and Paul Saint-Amour.

The driving intellectual force for good in my life comes from Gina Patnaik and Kelly Rich, whose ongoing conversations, writing retreats, and friendship is inestimable. In Philadelphia, special thanks to Eli Kim, who kept me going during a year of no schedule and remains a dear friend and cheerful recipient of too many dog selfies. In New York, I am grateful for the comradeship of Michelle O'Brien, who keeps me hopeful about the prospect of queer communism. Emma Heaney has scraped me off the floor, read the worst of bad drafts, and answered the phone in the middle of the night, alongside other life-sustaining acts of friendship. Thank you too to my *Ferrante Letters* cowriters and brilliant friends, Sarah Chihaya, Merve Emre, and Katherine Hill, who worked through many of these ideas in other venues and remain my go-to sites for writerly inspiration. Left Coast beloveds Shu Dar Yao and Melani Baker, alongside my dearest born-again Texan, Kristin Nolan, deserve special thanks for their enduring care and encouragement in sickness and in health. My parents, Steve and Carol Richards, have been very patient over too many years of my writing-induced anxiety, slow progress, and job-precarity grumpiness. On both coasts, I have relied on their love and support from West Texas. This book should rightfully be dedicated to my parents, but I am sure they will understand if I extend the umbrella of gratitude to include Dave Bush, the best of best brothers-in-law, close to my heart for more than a decade now, and, finally, to the person in my life who does too many admirable things to name but is most regularly a sustaining force of gravity when the world goes upside-down, my sister, Dawn Michelle Bush.

THE FURY ARCHIVES

Introduction

This book assembles a transatlantic archive of female citizenship. It tracks women's arson campaigns, suffrage riots, birth strikes, illegal birth control clinics, industrial sabotage, antilynching activism, queer revolutionary cells, and the more daily work of committee meetings, sewing circles, and letter-writing campaigns. These actions were not always militant or righteous. They did not necessarily involve stated demands. Often enough the people involved did not use the language of action but instead took up the more diffuse terms of waiting, refusal, survival, practice, cooperation, and care. Many of these political tendencies wanted to abolish the nation-state or sought out modes of affiliation, recognition, and belonging across national boundaries. One of the more contradictory aspects of this history is the way that these efforts retained the language of rights and citizenship even while working toward more radical futures. How do we negotiate the disparities between demands for women's rights and the social worlds that emerged around these demands? In what ways did the construction of these social worlds exceed or transform the language of rights altogether?

In revising the terms of female citizenship and the perspectives from which we understand its import, *The Fury Archives* looks to unsettle what counts as the basis of knowledge in wider narratives of women's rights during the period most often referred to as feminism's first wave. In this sense, the "archive" of my title is not only a matter of recovery but also a more polemical intervention.[1] This intervention sets aside the articulated demand for the woman's vote and moves into the more daily life of organizing that emerged through and alongside this demand. In many cases, a more granular attention to the daily life of a political tendency, seen apart from the achievement of a stated demand, lands upon moments of impasse, boredom, and failure. It tracks threads never followed up on and political tangents broken off from more recognized or respectable currents. However, this perspective also allows for the destabilization of the category *woman* as a primary site of retrospective emphasis, revealing a more coalitional entanglement among socialist, syndicalist, anarchist, and anticolonial groups. This perspective sets aside the question of singular will to consider people acting together who might disagree about what their action means or why they are doing it. In considering these often peripheral or forgotten intersections as they play out in the field of political action, *The Fury Archives* assembles an alternative conceptual vocabulary for rights claims, moving beyond juridically defined freedoms and obligations understood in relation to the nation-state.

My consideration of the female citizen as a subject of action responds to a wide body of feminist scholarship that has traditionally focused on identity and injury. In these works, shared pain and suffering provide a foundation for the female citizen's felt sense of national belonging. In Wendy Brown's influential account, people who have been marginalized from the abstract claims of liberal humanist personhood establish a sense of political identity through their "wounded attachment" to shared histories of exclusion.[2] Lauren Berlant articulates this shared sense of injury as constitutive of modern citizenship, locating a sense of belonging in "the capacity for suffering and trauma at the citizen's core."[3] Building on and shifting these field-shaping debates, *The Fury Archives* approaches female citizenship from a different angle, setting aside the rubric of injured identity and the theorization of affect more generally to reconsider the daily life of collective action as a site of vast theoretical and aesthetic complexity. In this framing, female citizenship is constituted through ongoing practice and process, rather than a prior history of woundedness.[4]

This turn from injured identity to the daily life of feminist action necessitates a methodological shift. Scholars working at the intersection of literature, citizenship, and rights discourses most often consider a set of genres closely associated with traumatic injury, including testimony, witness, documentary, and the confession. In these accounts, realist narrative makes suffering legible to a wider audience through the reader's sympathetic identification.⁵ Narrative can "give suffering a human face" that reveals concealed or forgotten violence.⁶ For Lynn Hunt, the eighteenth-century epistolary novel gives rise to the sympathetic attachments necessary for a human rights framework; for Joseph Slaughter, the bildungsroman provides a model of the liberal individual incorporated by human rights discourses; for Elizabeth Anker, contemporary world literature offers an embodied alternative to the individualizing, abstract language of rights discourses.⁷ Whether celebratory or critical, these arguments rely on a realist model of narrative, one that offers readerly models of identification, recognition, sympathy, and attachment. But what about entirely abstract works of art that lack coherent subjects or plotlines? Moving beyond the questions of recognition and into an antimimetic and experimental tradition allows for a different set of questions: Why does the suffering subject need to be a subject that readers can recognize? What forms of likeness does this recognition impose or assume? First-wave feminism and institutional human rights came of age at the same time as the Dadaist word salad and the surrealist dreamscape. How might we understand these currents alongside one another, as part of the same historical moment?

This alternative history begins with the little-known but nevertheless extensive entanglement between women's rights movements and the international avant-gardes. In the early decades of the twentieth century, avant-garde and women's rights movements were in much closer contact than has been supposed. Part of this alignment emerged from a mutual dependence on a socialist international that financed the distribution of radical newspapers, journals, and pamphlets across the Atlantic. However, much of this archive exceeds the traditional confines of the socialist press or little magazine to include a more unorthodox set of genres, including parliamentary inquiries, police reports, mug shots, propaganda booklets, foreign policy notes, the *League of Nations News*, and the United Nations' *Yearbook*. Crossing oceans and continents, these print cultures ground the central claim of this book, that women's rights movements and the historical avant-gardes became intertwined in an often vexed but hugely influential relationship of reciprocal construction. Each offered the other a conceptual vocabulary to imagine forms of life excluded from the rights of man and citizen. Avant-garde experiments with fractured, collaged, or inhuman representations of modern personhood offered feminists a language for a paradoxical subject of rights: the woman who is active in the public sphere of politics but not recognized by the state as a citizen. At the same time, the paradoxical legal status of the female citizen provided the avant-gardes with a template for the utopian reimagination of the boundaries of the human and of human rights during moments of radical political upheaval. *The Fury Archives* follows this imagination through revolutionary currents peppering the late nineteenth and early twentieth centuries. The book ultimately locates, among women's movements, socialist tendencies, and the avant-gardes, a radical alternative to liberal human rights discourses in formation at the same historical moment. Toward this end, each chapter focuses on the intersection of a specific avant-garde movement, women's rights struggles, and the discursive formation of human rights in the years leading up to the Cold War.

This perspective contrasts to a more familiar Enlightenment genealogy of natural law, as cited in the *Universal Declaration of Human Rights* (*UDHR*). Rather than a survey of European political theory, I arrive at the establishment of the *UDHR* through a different path. This book assembles a counterarchive of rights practiced by female incendiaries, self-named terrorists, anticolonial insurgents, witches, cross-dressers, lesbian criminals, and queer resistance cells. In so doing, I follow the ways that the human emerged as a legal category for women and queers amid an international push for suffrage reform. But I also move outside the courtroom, to more vernacular imaginations of the human and human rights during moments of revolutionary upheaval. To set women's movements alongside this imagination of what is called human allows for a biopolitical theory of right, one that tracks the twentieth century's well-known gains in suffrage reform alongside increasing state control of fertility, particularly among nonwhite, colonial, and queer people.

In calling this book *The Fury Archives*, I do not mean to focus on anger as the prevailing emotional response across these disparate histories. "Fury" is a strange word, a marker for feelings in general and for a vengeful woman in particular. In these pages it primarily signals the legal imagination of the female citizen as an inhuman woman warped by her paradoxical relation to state recognition and the public sphere. But "fury" also occurs, in these settings, as a punitive adjective for irrational, unchecked emotion. In the military trials for female arsonists considered in the first chapter, the "fury" is one of many names for women who actively take part in a revolutionary struggle: "She was more enraged than a viper, she was a fury, she was bent in two under the weight of the stuff that she carried to feed the fire."[8] What interests me is the way that feminist political action, from the extremely mild-mannered to the militant, has historically been received as the work of angry or vengeful women. In this book, I turn to the ways that anger has been weaponized to delegitimize political claims under the rubrics of respectability, seriousness, and social worth. In the most classical literary sense, in the *Oresteia*, the Furies are the antithesis of democratic politics; their vengeful justice provides a counterpart to the procedural justice of legal institutions, where guilt is determined by evidence, argument, and citizen juries.[9] In considering this archive, I mean to excavate histories of feminist contestation not directly engaged with legal remedy, considered from the midst of day-to-day action, apart from any stated demand. This perspective sets aside the successes or failures we know to be true in order to inhabit a social world of action from the perspective of the persons involved. Here emphasis shifts from articulated demands to forms of world making, through people working together in the streets, the factories, and at home. This shift allows us to reconsider what might be asked for and who gets to ask; what kinds of spaces and labors are political; and the ways that forms of waiting, survival, and domestic care undergird more traditional accounts of the public sphere of politics.

Indeed, one of the main lines running through this book is that the narrative of human rights that foregrounds the League of Nations and the United Nations is not the only narrative to be had. Suspicious of juridical reform and discourses of universalism, a number of early women's movements sought out a more radical understanding of the human and of human rights beyond the confines of the nation-state. Tracing this counterhistory shifts our understanding of rights from a kind of boundary, between citizen and noncitizen, to a set of practices that dismantle such boundaries in the attempt to rebuild social relations and social life. For this reason, I take up the roughly one-hundred-year period between the mid-nineteenth and mid-twentieth centuries to reconsider a moment before the discourses of human rights became a dominant ethical language for multinational institutions. The chapters that follow move across three overlapping fields of extraterritorial scale: the rise of the socialist internationals as an early program for rights beyond the territorial limits of the nation-state, feminist internationalisms between metropole and the colonies, and the avant-garde formations that understood their art to be in the service of a global revolution. These formations are not internally consistent and certainly do not align in any neat or narratively coherent way. Instead, much of what follows highlights moments of rupture when these groups come into conflict with one another.

From our current perspective, many of these political tendencies might seem like blips and caesuras on the way to the inexorable rise of neoliberalism. However, I argue against this more fatalistic historical purview, focusing instead on the voices of nonstate actors and unofficial representatives, as indicative of political imaginations more varied, radical, and transformative than the versions that have since achieved canonical status in more standard histories of international justice. Finally, I also argue that any consideration of socialist internationalism must reckon with the "women question" as a central preoccupation, one animating yet another archive of rights, this time focused on public health, family, and reproduction. Most pointedly, my account foregrounds the unwaged reproductive labor of cooking, cleaning, pregnancy, child rearing, and elder care as an often overlooked foundation necessary for political mobilization and a significant site of feminist and queer politics in its own right. I collect this archive, for all its inconsistencies and ineffectuality, to argue that our current moment of human rights governmentality was not inevitable. These documents suggest other historical courses that might have been, as well as conjunctures for our present history.

Feminist Internationalisms and the Governance of Human Rights

There are many ways to narrate a history of human rights: as Enlightenment philosophy, as natural law, as postwar institutional doctrine, as universalizing morality. The most familiar account begins with the UN Charter in 1945 and continues into the present day, a moment when the language of human rights has solidified into the normative ethical discourse to address social justice across national boundaries. In the 1970s, the Czech jurist Karel Vasak proposed a generational model to understand this history as a gradual unfolding narrative of progress, from first-generation rights that protect the individual from the state, prominent in the eighteenth-century declarations, to second-generation social and economic liberties, like public health and education, included in the UN covenants.[10] However, this generational model does not attend to the ways that rights regimes emerged through and alongside the expansion of empire. One of the major debates shaping this field of study attends to the paradoxical quality of universal rights, often rendered as a gap between abstract claims for equality and the material fact of unequal people, subject to vastly different life chances, racialized forms of precarity, and vulnerability to premature death.

This scholarship informs much of the book to come. However, for now I want to mark a shift in emphasis away from theoretical considerations of what rights are, or even how our current human rights regime came to be, and instead toward the ways human rights language has been used as a vocabulary for freedoms and obligations beyond the territorial jurisdiction of the nation-state. That is to say, the governmentality of human rights will become my primary point of emphasis, and for this reason I forgo many of the more famous declarations to consider instead the ways human rights operated as both a tactic and a technology of power outside the field of sovereignty.[11] Rather than focus on the content of who is considered human or reject this category altogether, I am interested in the ways human rights claims were used, appropriated, or transformed to make demands for justice beyond the remedies provided by positive law. What follows tells a history of human rights that attends to this expanded juridical scope, beyond the nation and state actors traditionally cited by the laws of war.

To tell this story, I turn to an earlier historical moment, before the midcentury institutionalization of human rights through the United Nations. This account begins with what the legal historian Micheline Ishay has described as a major split between two opposing tendencies: first, the liberal internationalism of the League of Nations promoted by Woodrow Wilson, consistent with multinational capitalism, and, second, the supranational rights promised by the socialist internationals in the service of a global revolution.[12] When socialists and anarchists founded the First International, in 1864, their stated goals entailed collaboration across national lines, from organizations representing over one hundred countries, for social, political, and economic rights. Though the First International was short lived, the Second International proved more resilient, spanning the period between 1889 and 1916. After World War I and the Bolshevik Revolution, a Third International continued to challenge liberal visions of rights, often in friction with radical socialist parties that formed their own confederation of nations, including the Vienna International.

In Samuel Moyn's revisionary history, our current regime of human rights emerged in the 1970s, when these proliferating internationalisms collapsed at the same time that postcolonial statecraft came into crisis.[13] At this moment in the 1970s, the phrase "human rights" exploded as a commonplace term to talk about the protection of individual citizens from the state and to justify interventionist foreign policy on moral grounds. Rather than approach the period after the Enlightenment as a narrative leading up to this moment, I want to tease out a more speculative history, opening up space for competing claims on rights to proliferate into messier and more contradictory forms. This long middle between the Enlightenment and the Cold War, considered on its own terms, allows for a more improvisatory, more extravagant imagination of international justice, in part because the referential status of human rights had not yet calcified as an institutional norm.

This periodization stages the high-water mark of two linked internationalisms, one socialist, one feminist. In the roughly one hundred years that make up this study, these groups are more often in conflict than not.[14] This was often a question of prioritization. One of the long-standing debates between socialists and feminists during the Second International concerned the way questions relating to women's rights, particularly housework, might fit into a wider radical agenda. In 1901, the SPD member Lily Braun published a proposal for *Einküchenhäuser* (one-kitchen buildings) to collectivize housekeeping and childcare in her book *Frauenarbeit und Hauswirtschaft* (*Women and Housework*). Clara Zetkin, the leader of the women's movement in Germany and a member of the Women's International Congress, responded to this proposal as the "latest blossoming of Utopianism in its most dangerous, opportunistic form."[15] Zetkin's response holds fast to the International's party line: what might be desirable after the revolution could be counterproductive during earlier stages of the social struggle. For this reason, political platforms relating specifically to women's rights should only arise at the right moment, in the appropriate historical stage, to hasten a larger revolution of the proletariat.

At this time, the Socialist International was riven with a number of contradictory programs for revolution. For Lenin, in *What Is to Be Done?*, the correct path to revolution would be led by the party, who will bring class consciousness to the masses. In this infamously stagist account, the party becomes a kind of guiding star, one that channels the energy of the workers. Revolution can only occur at a future historical moment when the party has sufficiently grown, when the masses are prepared, and when the objective circumstances are ripe. What garners mistaken worshipful sentiment is the organic response of the workers or, in Lenin's paraphrase, "spontaneity, i.e. of that which exists at the present moment."[16]

What preoccupies Rosa Luxemburg, in her direct criticism of Lenin, is the possibility of spontaneous political action to produce new organizational structures among factory workers that moves from the bottom up rather than from the party down. Alongside Lenin, Luxemburg agrees that the masses need political education. But for Luxemburg, this education does not come from the party. Instead, for Luxemburg, spontaneous action in the present becomes the ground for political education that allows for the revolution in the future. In this way, revolution can be seen as a much longer process of gains and losses. For Luxemburg, it is not "pamphlets and leaflets" that prepare the masses but an ongoing "living political school, by the fight and in the fight, in the continuous course of the revolution" as a succession of smaller gains and losses.[17]

For our purposes, Luxemburg's theory is usefully extended by her ally, the Dutch Council communist Anton Pannekoek. Like Luxemburg, Pannekoek rejects what he sees, in the theories of Lenin and Kautsky, as a "dichotomy between day-to-day action and revolution." For Pannekoek, the process of workers organizing together in unions, through gains and losses, becomes the stuff of a longer revolution. This is not education through theory, handed out in pamphlets to the masses from above; rather, "it is only by the struggle for power itself that the masses can be assembled, drilled and formed into an organization capable of taking power." Pannekoek sees the formation of these new kinds of organizations and new bonds of solidarity among workers during the ongoing struggle as something that transforms individual subjects:

> They have become completely different persons from the old individualistic petty-bourgeois and peasants . . . the transformation of human nature in the proletariat is primarily the effect of the conditions under which the workers live, trained as they are to act collectively by the shared experience of exploitation in the same factory, and secondarily a *product of class struggle*, that is to say militant action on the part of the organization.[18]

We might note here as well that there is among these theories of revolution a narrative commonality. In each case, the program for revolution insists upon a protagonist and a path. For the reigning currents of the Second

International, this protagonist was the male industrial worker. Across these various programs, the status of the human protagonist, or the becoming-human of the protagonist through struggle, is a universal category that is also limited to the body of a male factory worker. In what follows, I take up these accounts of action "under the present conditions," in "the present time," apart from the party, as a vocabulary for the day-to-day forms of contestation for women living outside the wage relation, with no clear role in the stagist programs of the Socialist Internationals.

That said, the friction between socialist and feminist internationalisms allows for a more expansive vocabulary for extraterritorial rights, promoting an imagination of justice not limited to the nation-state. This approach draws on the work of a number of scholars, including Brent Hayes Edwards, Cheryl Higashida, and Aarthi Vadde, who have taken up Edward Said's early call to reckon with the formation of "adversarial internationalization" in the wake of empire.[19] These challenges to universalist Western paradigms restage the question of international alliance, this time centering populations and geographies often excluded from the "rights of man and citizen." Rather than dismiss internationalist ambitions as a purely imperial or homogenizing project, I want to consider how feminists appropriated and transformed this conceptual vocabulary to rethink feminist alliance, solidarity, and care beyond the nation. These efforts were often reformist or reactionary. However, tracing the day-to-day life of this internationalist tendency reveals the ways that women's rights and human rights have long been overlapping fields of inquiry.

Many of the case studies I go on to consider prefigure a major current in transnational feminist activism and legal scholarship that called for a recalibration of "women's rights as human rights."[20] Emerging in the 1990s, this tendency focused on the ways that the seemingly neutral language of human rights doctrine relies on a clear divide between public and private spheres. This division prioritized human rights concerns as the domain of men in the public sphere, rendering the rights of women and children in the home a matter of lesser consequence unrelated to the workings of foreign policy. Against this model, feminist legal scholars and activists argued for a reconsideration of women's experience in the field of human rights, along with increased attention to social and economic entitlements, including access to housing, education, and health care.

By turning to a historical moment many decades before the call for "women's rights as human rights," I argue that the public/private split has a more varied history than we might imagine. Feminists were making these claims well before the 1990s, before even the midcentury institutionalization of human rights. Attention to this history challenges the regnant model of international law as a doctrine focused on war and its aftermaths, making visible instead the ways that childbirth, housework, domestic violence, sex work, race hygiene, and public health were positioned as a matter for international justice. In some cases, these rights movements were productive of jurisprudence at a national or international level. However, more often in this history, the call to reclassify women's rights as human rights is better understood as a tactical maneuver, to call attention to gendered forms of injury often disregarded in the normative focus on war and revolution. *The Fury Archives* begins with the premise of women's action, but these actions can also be framed as a response to unlivable or precarious conditions of life, including state-sanctioned torture, routinized sexual assault, domestic violence, infanticide, eugenic sterilization, and the criminalization of nonnormative sexualities. To approach this history is not just a matter of legal categorization or recovery but also a more interventionist claim to reconsider whose rights are deemed important in the wider scope of international justice.

At the same time, postcolonial scholars have long noted the ways that white women invoked the language of humanity to justify their political inclusion in the British Empire. In the historian Antoinette Burton's account, British feminists imagined colonial women as their own particular burden, situating white women's enfranchisement as one step toward a wider civilizing process because enfranchised white women would then go on to liberate colonial populations.[21] From the 1860s to World War I, a wide variety of British feminists argued that it was their humanity, their ability to sympathize with and promote the well-being of colonial subjects, that made them particularly suitable for franchise. Here again, human rights work as a tactical language, this time asserting white women's citizenship through a racial hierarchy of social worth. This book looks to account for both these narratives, that is, the uses and abuses of the human in the practice of early women's rights movements. Rather than a narrative of women's progress, this is a double-sided movement, wherein the celebrated freedoms of some rest upon the subjugation of others. Here, at the crux of feminism's first wave, gains in white women's rights are contemporaneous and often intertwined with a new science of government directed at the management of colonial populations.

As a case in point and as an outline for the archival methodology to come, I turn now to a series of debates circa 1912 concerning wages for housework as a human rights issue. At this time, the London-based weekly *The Freewoman* published a series of articles on cooperative housekeeping and the motherhood endowment, a state subsidy that would be paid to unwed mothers.[22] What joins these articles is the wider sense that the burden of unpaid housework fetters the development of woman's human personality. In February, the front-page editorial, "The Drudge," staged this dilemma through the language of foreign politics: "It is quite true that the State interfered with the wife's empire over the children, and, at age of five years, has claimed the right to withdraw them also from the home. Even so; and here is the housewife's chance to regain her dignity as a wealth-producing individual. She can now cease to be a housewife, and become a human being."[23] Though suspicious of state power, the article argues for the establishment of a collective nursery for the maintenance of infants beginning five weeks after birth so that mothers might rejoin the waged workforce more quickly.

Marsden's editorial set off a wider debate not just on the motherhood endowment or a radical crèche but over the vexed relationships among dignity, freedom, housework, and the British Empire. What would it mean to consider the wider run of *The Freewoman* as an experimental form that responds and adapts to this configuration? How might we consider this paper as a technology that produces gendered subjects transnationally, as audience, authors, and objects of discipline? This question marks a shift in scale. Rather than a single article, the points of conflict between adjacent and unlike forms become the primary site of emphasis. Consider, for instance, the table of contents in *The Freewoman* from Thursday, March 7, 1912. There is the continuation of the motherhood endowment coverage, alongside three major conversations in the letters: the birthrate; the continuation of the housework debates; and the question of male homosexuality ("Who Are the 'Normal'"? "'The Normal' Again"). The "Foreign Affairs" news includes reporting on sex workers in Japan, a split in the South African suffrage movement over the question of universal suffrage for colonial subjects, and the expansion of the feminist press in southern China. From this perspective, the weekly run of *The Freewoman* is a material instance of a collage form that brings together widely divergent topics and sets them side by side. These currents emerge alongside an internationalist agenda, one that includes reporting on women's rights in China, Persia, India, New Zealand, and Australia.

Over the next six months, many of these articles on housework, motherhood, and eugenics look like typical opinion pieces of the period, voiced by experts. However, Dora Marsden and Mary Gawthorpe published their critique of the motherhood endowment in the form of a multipage questionnaire. The prospect of state payment for childbirth prompted an entire series of new questions on women and labor more generally: Is pregnancy like a disability? Should wives expect payment for companionship or sex? If wives and mothers are a class of workers, can they form a "trade union of wives" and mutiny? What if wives refused to work entirely?

The questionnaire is a strange political document for the ways that it sidesteps a program of action, instead offering points of inquiry, some reactionary, some radical. What is important here is the way that the questionnaire defamiliarizes established ways of thinking about women, labor, and the state. These questions leave open the possibility that unwaged workers can be imagined as a transnational public with political impact. The questions present what might have seemed like an open-and-shut case as a site of debate: first, the possibility that the domestic work of cleaning, cooking, and child rearing might be considered value-producing forms somehow linked to the reproduction of the nation; and second, the possibility that companionship might be seen as a kind of necessary labor for which a person, sex worker or wife, could be paid.

Marsden and Gawthorpe presented their questions as a rhetorical feat too absurd to be answered. However, many responses poured in, which *The Freewoman* published in turn. The science-fiction author and utopian socialist H. G. Wells took the form of the questionnaire quite seriously and provided an enumerated list of likely answers, beginning with the clarification: "It's not human beings we want to buy and enslave, it's a social service, a collective need, we want to sustain."[24] Though better known for his wartime manifesto *The Rights of Man, or What Are We Fighting For*, cited by the drafters of the *Universal Declaration of Human Rights*, Wells's writing in *The Freewoman* makes a prominent intervention in the gendering of early human rights claims, in that this writing foregrounds the private sphere, the family, and women's household labor.

However, Wells was not alone in this endeavor. For a weekly journal, *The Freewoman* dedicated an outsize portion of its pages to letters to the editor. "Correspondence" often occupied a third of the issue, and letters were presented as though they were articles, with titles and page numbers listed in the table of contents. In the summer of 1912 many of these letters offered their own thesis on wages for housework and childbirth. Letter writers argued that the status of motherhood should be considered alongside the collective maintenance required by the coal strikes; that state-organized, free crèche systems should be considered as a legal right; that all businesses that employ women should be required to provide on-site free childcare; that wives have a right to a proportion of their husband's earnings; that readers should publish a public list of employers that pay fair wages to women and those that do not; and that readers should start their own small-scale cooperative kitchens with other women in their neighborhoods. Often signed with initials or a pen name, the letters go on at length, describing the tasks involved in assembling meals or nursing infants, then comparing these labors with the paid work of clerks and factory workers. In some cases, the editorial staff offered a response keyed to Marden's original antistate, antiendowment program. However, in later weeks, this writing acknowledges that some women might prefer to work in their homes. "It is best of all to be an independent, self-supporting human being, because then you can choose whether you will be a machinist or a mother, or both or neither."[25]

In the spring of 1912, *The Freewoman* began advertising an evening "Discussion Circle" for readers on key topics of interest, including housework, eugenics, and the birthrate. The programs for the meeting were circulated in advance (see the table "Programme for Session"). More straightforward manifestos for the collectivization of housework and the abolition of the nuclear family can be found in a competing venue, *The Worker's Dreadnought*, at roughly the same period.[26] In *The Freewoman*, the schedule of discussion meetings is a different kind of archive, one that usually does not merit attention as a source of knowledge for rights claims or international politics. The meeting schedule suggests ties between topics of concern (eugenics, celibacy, housework, prostitution) but does not put forth a plan of action or a philosophy of right.

The meeting schedule does not offer a utopian program; it does not tell us what to do or make demands for the future. Alongside the questionnaire and the letters to the editor, the meeting schedule chronicles the kinds of social worlds that emerged from more daily configurations of trial and error. These worlds certainly extend beyond what can be found in the digitized archives of *The Freewoman*. In the years before publication, Gawthorpe and Marsden had already been arrested and jailed together a number of times.

Programme for Session, July–October 1912

Date	Subject	Speaker
July 3	Sex Oppression and the Way Out	Mr. Guy Aldred
July 17	Some Problems in Eugenics	Mrs. Havelock Ellis
July 31	The Problem of Celibacy	Mrs. Gallichan
Sept. 4	Neo-Malthusianism	Dr. Drysdale
Sept. 18	Prostitution	— —
Oct. 2	The Abolition of Domestic Drudgery	Mrs. Melvin and Miss Rona Robinson, M.Sc
Oct. 16	The Reform of the Divorce Laws	Mr. E. S. P. Haynes

Source: "'The Freewoman' Discussion Circle," *The Freewoman* 2, no. 32 (June 27, 1912): 115.

In 1910, along with Mabel Capper, they were assaulted during a suffragette protest and unsuccessfully brought charges against three men in a highly publicized trial. *The Freewoman* was largely Marsden's effort to break off from the mainstream suffrage movement, turning from a single-issue focus on the vote to wider issues of women's social and economic justice. In the years following its founding, the magazine had many lives and collaborators: it was rebranded as the *New Freewoman*, and then *The Egoist*, which would go on to publish some of the most famous contributors to high modernism and the European avant-gardes.

I want to highlight the strangeness of this adjacency: *The Egoist* serialized James Joyce's *Portrait of the Artist as a Young Man* and T. S. Eliot's "Tradition and the Individual Talent," alongside a more self-consciously avant-garde tendency that included the imagist manifestos. But only a few years earlier the same journal, under a different name, included a months-long debate on payment for childcare and housework as a human right, alongside reporting on eugenics, the birthrate, and women's foreign affairs. Across these years, the publication maintained its internationalist agenda, often using the language of human rights as a barometer for racial progress and the expansion of empire. I chart out these coordinates in part to mark a material adjacency, page facing page. However, more important is the way that meeting schedules and questionnaires here emerge alongside the manifesto as experimental forms to account for new kinds of action, subjects, and alliances during a moment of proliferating internationalisms.

Intimate Theory of the Avant-Garde

In the last section, *The Freewoman* and its successor, *The Egoist*, provide a material site of adjacency between women's rights movements, human rights claims, modernist literature, and the avant-garde manifesto. This section looks to add specificity and depth to this last term, "the avant-garde," in distinction to a wider literary modernism. Both high-modernist and avant-garde formations during this period were experimenting with traditional modes of realist representation through a turn to abstraction, fragmentation, disordered syntax, and collage. For most critics, what differentiates the avant-garde from a wider modernist tradition is a real or imagined alliance with radical political movements on the ground. However, the avant-garde is a notoriously tricky historical concept in part because it is often a retrospective label for artistic currents that understood themselves through more precise registers of symbolism, imagism, vorticism, Dada, surrealism, and Négritude. The chapters that follow hew to the particularities of these more local movements as they are happening. Rather than determine the precise relation between art and politics in the generalized phenomena retrospectively labeled avant-garde, I want to expand and complicate what counts as political labor during this historical moment. In so doing, I hope to show how the gendering of the political has shaped the theorization of the avant-garde more widely.

One of the earliest attempts at a retrospective consolidation, Renato Poggioli's *The Theory of the Avant-Garde*, was first published in four installments in the Italian-language literary journal *Inventario*, from 1949 to 1951.[27] With Italy in ruins and the horrors of Stalinism growing more and more visible, Poggioli had good reasons for deemphasizing the avant-garde's ties to radical political movements. He writes off surrealism's involvement with the Communist Party and futurism's nationalist fervor as somewhat naïve adventurism or merely superficial sympathy, never actually effective. In this way, Poggioli rejects the often spoken insistence that to be properly avant-garde artists have to be actively in league with the radical movements to which they lay claim. Instead, Poggioli charts out a history of convergence and separation. This begins with the French revolutions of 1830 and 1848 as the first moment the term "avant-garde" was commonly used in a nonmilitary context to describe radical political movements. In Poggioli's account, the category "avant-garde" begins to shift meaning during the uprising and repression of the Paris Commune. At this moment, "avant-garde" briefly signals an alliance between cultural and political groups working together. After that first moment of practical overlap during the Paris Commune, there are two avant-gardes, one cultural and one political. Their ties are rhetorical. The cultural avant-gardes imagine a new world that they, as a group, will herald through art in the service of revolution, not political activism on the ground. This art serves revolution through variants of antagonism, whether nihilistic, scandalous, eschatological, or messianic. In the broadest sense, for Poggioli, the avant-garde is a "movement formed in part or in whole to agitate *against* something or someone."[28]

When Poggioli posits a clear line between artistic vanguards and political vanguards, he has a specific version of political practice in mind. This practice might occur in the streets, at the barricades, in the midst of a worker's strike, or through the Socialist International. But these versions of politics hypothesize a European male political actor and center the identity of a largely male working class. In the following pages, I want to reconsider what counts as political practice and where this practice might occur, to accommodate other versions of politics and other kinds of subjects who are not necessarily waged, located in the factories, or members of a Socialist International. For many of the figures that I consider in this book, Poggioli's sense of a clear division between artistic and political avant-gardes does not hold fast. Rebecca West was a novelist and also rioted with the suffragettes. Angelina Weld Grimké was active in antilynching campaigns. During World War II, Claude Cahun and her partner, Marcel Moore, were sent to a prisoner of war camp for their participation in the French resistance. Hannah Höch was a Dadaist, recipient of two abortions, and advocate for birth control reform. Til Brugman joined the Dutch resistance. Paulette Nardal produced a black feminist periodical and served as an area expert for the newly formed United Nations. Better known as a British surrealist, Leonora

Carrington was also a refugee several times over who fled Mexico in fear of retribution for her participation in antigovernment protest meetings. Often left aside in the major theoretical formulations of the avant-garde, these figures necessitate a different conceptual schema, one that can account for the intersection of artistic forms and political action in a manner that is not purely deterministic. Regarding the cultural products themselves, I am not sure that art makes anything happen, to borrow Auden's phrase, and certainly don't think, alongside André Breton, that avant-garde art can sway the proletarian masses. However, it does seem reasonable to me that the strategies developed in collective social movements make their way as new forms or paradoxes into cultural objects, which then become sites to imagine personhood in ways not entirely constrained by force or necessity.

For this perspective, the first chapter of this book also turns to the Paris Commune but shifts Poggioli's account in two ways, first, to account for the gendering of citizenship for communard women and, second, to consider the racialization of both women's rights and human rights through contemporaneous anticolonial uprisings in Martinique. In reframing the import of the Paris Commune as an origin story, I join a growing group of scholars interested in expanding the geographies, races, genders, and sexualities that might be considered avant-garde more widely.[29] This expansion proceeds in part through transatlantic modes of comparison but more significantly through a reconsideration of intimate life as a site of gendered political labor and racialized discipline. In so doing, I respond to a wide body of work that has centered the role of sexuality, marriage, kinship, and reproductive labor in the wider arc of empire building and revolutionary upheavals across the nineteenth and twentieth centuries.[30] These accounts reject a clear division between the public sphere of politics and what Jürgen Habermas has called "that area where the experience of 'humanity' originated: in the humanity of the intimate relations between human beings who, under the aegis of the family, were nothing more than human."[31] In Habermas's account of the rise of the eighteenth-century public sphere, the bourgeois family becomes a "domain of pure humanity" that offers a counterpart to the political-economic realm of labor and commodity exchange. This book looks to cross this division, between the household and the political-economic realm, as part of a wider accounting for the gendering of the category "human" across legal, political, and aesthetic sites.

This mode of comparison looks to account for a wider historical conjecture that ties the late-nineteenth- and early-twentieth-century expansion of empire to gendered divisions of labor. Drawing these two currents together as part of an account of "patriarchy and accumulation on a world-scale," Maria Mies has argued that colonization should be understood as the counterpart to a simultaneous process of what she calls "housewifization" in Europe.[32] Mies thus tracks European attempts to impose the nuclear family upon colonial populations alongside "housewifization," which splits off unwaged reproductive labor performed by women in the home from the wider category of women's waged labor. As part of what a number of historians have called the normalization of the nuclear family among the working class, this gendered division of labor cements a spatial division between the private sphere of the family and the public sphere of politics. This transnational framework then has a much more local correlate through the politicization of reproductive labor as a site of political contestation. Inflected by a body of work broadly conceived of as social reproduction theory, my sense of social reproduction marks unwaged domestic labor in the home but also any number of affects, actions, and institutions devoted to care that form a racialized division in the global labor force and serve as part of the reproduction of people necessary for capitalist development.[33] As Silvia Federici, a key theorist of this tendency, has pointed out, feminists have demanded wages for housework and imagined forms of intimate care outside the heterosexual family form well before the more well-known currents of Marxist feminism in the 1970s.[34]

This book recovers this archive in order to situate what I call an "intimate theory of the avant-garde." My emphasis falls on the establishment of a social community rather than a set of aesthetic commitments or experimental forms shared between artists.[35] I focus on the social intimacy of salon cultures that nourish conversations between artistic and political circles. This turn to the salon begins, most simply, by taking up a host of material practices, both inside and outside the home. These forms of intimacy emerge from collaboration in the production of little magazines, manifestos, performances, or political meetings. Affiliation often involves a common language or a common enemy. This wider social nexus might involve lovers, friends, or family but does not necessarily cede to heterosexual models of kinship. Instead, the group form offers a politicized relation of care that does not necessarily entail shared goals or experience. This moves us away from the critical theories based on the positive affects associated with collectivity, including friendship, affinity, or romance, to a social tie without any determinate mood attached, geared less toward feeling for or with than the bare fact of working together. In this case, what matters is the imagination of a *we* that makes demands. In some cases, this *we* joins other versions of *us* and *ours* in the name of survival. This joining isn't necessarily cause for celebration or comfort. These modes of relation might include the ties between coauthors, collaborators, and lovers; between mothers and children; amid sewing circles; and inside queer salons. But these relations of care extend into the street as well, as a way of sustaining a more public social movement. These are the invisible labors of preparation, the organization of marches, cooking for insurgents, or tending wounds. Here feminized forms of labor connect different kinds of bodies that might lay claim to the category "woman," without necessitating a genital configuration. I follow these relations into prisons and among rioters at the docks, arsonists, hunger strikers, anarchists, exiles, and pamphleteers.

For the public cultures that named themselves avant-garde, this joining up was often ineffectual. The avant-garde imagined art to do all sorts of things that it did not do. Most fantastically, this was the artist provoking revolution or, in the darker case of Ezra Pound, inciting a new guild society of ruler-artists swaying the masses toward their autocratic demands. In hindsight, it is sometimes difficult to argue against Fredric Jameson's melancholic purview of "the determinate failure of all the revolutions that have taken place in human history."[36] Every radical political struggle in the following pages, on the Right and the Left, inarguably, indisputably, failed in terms of its stated ambitions. But that failure, seen from the present, tells us very little. It could not necessarily be foretold by the participants involved. It says nothing about the working existence of politics on the ground or aesthetic formations intertwined with them. To begin with tragedy constructs a narrative based upon the ending that was, as though each work of art and every political action were always already pointing to that ending. At our present moment, it seems more useful to take up the force of this antagonism rather than the tragedy of its failures. I want to consider the way that artists and activists said *no, not this*. This *against*, I will argue, changes people and communities in the present tense of its articulation. As a form of intimacy in the key of solidarity, this shared antagonism, as productive of a *we* or *us*, marks the boundaries of the art that I call avant-garde more so than the naming of an -ism, though the two categories certainly collide.

Documenting Woman, Human, and Homosexual

One of the challenges of this book has been locating methodologies adequate to the archives under discussion. For this reason, the methodology in this book often departs from more traditional modes of literary scholarship. This difference can be polarizing for readers expecting an area-studies approach or a formalist close reading of orthodox literary genres. A reading of an instruction manual or the notes from a birth-strike meeting will look different from a reading of a novel, potentially in ways that are unsettling or irritating. The readings of novels and poems in the wake of these archives will look different as well. But the avant-gardes were also interested in the unsettling or irritating, through the presentation of everyday found objects like toilets or trashcans as works of art. In aligning these contemporaneous traditions, this book asks: What kinds of archives can account for the daily life of feminist action? In what ways can this archive provide a basis for thinking about rights that moves beyond the sympathetic representations of personal suffering?

As one response to these questions, this book foregrounds what I call the long middle of women's rights movements as a perspective that can account for daily forms of world making as an ongoing process, set apart from any stated demand. To account for this perspective, I leave aside the avant-garde manifesto to focus instead on more incremental archives of practice, including journals, tables of contents, lists of names, meeting minutes, birth control manuals, and prison medical logs. A number of chapters offer theorizations of genres that emerge alongside and through these practices, including the instruction manual, the case study, and the committee meeting. Indeed, throughout this book, there are consistent returns to political meetings, in terms of not just what was collectively decided but also all the more banal processual details: the divisions of tasks; forming of committees; the arguments, heated and flagging; the inevitable boredom, bad behavior, or grandstanding; the compromises, defections, and collective moods. This archival method works to establish an archive of localized actions severed from the kinds of demands more forcefully stated in manifestos or declarations of right. Rather than foreground a singular subject of action, this perspective allows for a plurality of wills, intentions, and feelings that we might attribute to the people acting together. As a politics of the street or square, this perspective looks to foreground the bodily dimension of action and the material supports it requires: what different bodies need, what they can do or not do, and the ways that they are unequally vulnerable.[37]

For this reason, I situate feminist action as site of both freedom and injury, understood in conjunction with and often productive of disciplinary norms at an institutional level. That is to say, alongside these more local accounts of collective action, this book situates the governmentality of rights at the level of the state and within the transnational arc of empire. Rather than trace what some historians call a "woman to human transition," I want to put some pressure on the legal categories "woman" and "human" as shifting terrain, subject to sudden reversals, overlap, and incommensurability.[38] Part of this consideration includes a closer look at institutional practices of documentation, particularly through the rise of biological racism and the criminalization of homosexuality. Scholars have traditionally regarded such classifications according to a Foucauldian schema, as a means of subjugation that both controls and constitutes human subjects. I don't disagree with this view but want to consider other more varied effects of institutional classification beyond the more familiar terrain of discipline.

As one final case study in method, consider one of the stranger afterlives of the Paris Commune, the posthumous appearance of the *pétroleuse* Louise Michel in Magnus Hirschfeld's magnum opus, *Homosexuality in Men and Women*. First published in 1913, the diagnostic manual frequently cites from a book-length character study of Louise Michel written by Karl von Levetzow. Quoting liberally, Hirschfeld describes a number of unusual traits: as a child, Michel did not care for dolls or cooking; she played outdoors; as an adult, she disliked corsets and high heels; she enjoyed the music of Wagner; she was courageous, almost reckless; she was flat-chested and angular; she did not take much trouble with her appearance; her features were masculine, her demeanor, mannish.[39]

Somewhat infamously, Emma Goldman bristled at this retrospective classification and wrote a lengthy letter in defense of Michel's heterosexuality. Published in Hirschfeld's *Yearbook for Sexual Intermediate Types*, the letter involved some rhetorical contortions. Goldman assures Hirschfeld that she is not prejudiced against homosexuals and notes that she finds her own friends of Uranian disposition above average in terms of charm and intelligence. However, Goldman takes issue with the diagnosis, which presents unfeminine characteristics as evidence of a Uranian nature. Somewhat paradoxically, Goldman then argues von Levetzow point by point. ("As to her face, it is clear to me that von Levetzow never saw Louise smile. If he had done so he would no longer have seen the male in her.")[40]

Set side by side, Goldman's letter and the diagnostic manual muddle the familiar terms of archival recovery. Here the radical feminist letter of protest does not offer a more liberating definition of homosexual identity than the institutional diagnosis, only its inverse. This muddling becomes even more vexed amid the wider historical conjuncture between sexual science and the language of universal rights. At this moment in Germany, a number of early gay rights groups were using the rubric of human rights. In 1903, Johannes Holzmann founded the League for Human Rights (Bund für Menschenrecht) in Berlin, which hosted regular meetings for people interested in sexual freedom and anarchist politics. Inspired by Hirschfeld's Scientific-Humanitarian Committee, in 1924 Henry Gerber founded the first gay rights group in the United States, Chicago's Society for Human Rights.[41] It is tempting to posit the early existence of these human rights groups as a radical queer counterpart to the more conservative institutional history of human rights discourses. However, these organizations were not necessarily emancipatory for the subjects named. After the war, a mass homosexual rights movement in Germany included right-wing nationalists, anti-Semites, liberals, Social Democrats, and communists, all in favor of legal reform but of different minds about how to get there.[42] Among these currents we can locate a number of gay advocacy groups calling themselves "Human Rights Leagues," most prominently in Friedrich Raduzveit's popular journal *News for Human Rights (Blätter für Menschenrecht)*. However, the *Blätter* was deeply interested in its own project of classification. The journal argued for a distinction between good and bad citizens of the state: between manly homosexual men and the unfortunately swishy or deviant types, including cross-dressers, sex workers, and fairies.

This more conservative invocation of human rights, as a way to distinguish between good and bad homosexual citizens, offers one particular ruse of counterhistory: the implication that the recovery of a feminist, queer, or erased history will be more egalitarian than the dominant institutional narrative. To study the public reception and renegotiation of the categories "woman," "human," and "homosexual" does not necessarily result in a clear binary: the bad institutional narrative against its emancipatory avant-garde reconfiguration. Nor do I mean to dismiss the historical gains and efficacy of human rights language for grassroots activism ongoing at the present moment. Instead, as a methodological framework in my work more widely, I am interested in two related perspectives: first, the institutional configuration of identity-based rights as a vexed domain and, second, the movement from identity-based rights claims for recognition to collective practices of citizenship, in all their contradictions, lulls, and fracture.

This book is divided into three parts. The first locates early discourses of the human alongside the presumed inhumanity of the female citizen. Rather than endow these figures with full personhood after the fact, this section considers the ways that the juridical inhumanity of the female citizen allows for a reimagination of political change. Not recognized as part of the industrial proletariat or public sphere, the female citizen provides an opening for the reconstruction of who might participate in revolutionary struggle, what kinds of rights could be demanded, and where such struggles might take place. Toward this end, part 1, "Sex and Citizenship in the Atlantic Archives," repositions the hazy formation often referred to as first-wave feminism as an integral part of socialist and avant-garde radicalism in the early twentieth century.

Chapter 1 offers a study of two contemporaneous trials on either side of the Atlantic: for the *pétroleuse* of the Paris Commune and the female insurgents accused of arson in Martinique's Insurrection of the South. The military trials showcase the juridical construction of the female citizen as a paradox, active in the public sphere but not recognized by the state. This archive provides the groundwork for the rest of the book, through the historical gendering of citizenship and the formation of the juridical human amid the rise of positive law. A final section turns to Ina Césaire's play *Fire's Daughters (Rosanie Soleil)*, as an animation of the Martinican insurgency that offers new pathways to reconsider the entanglements between practices of sexual citizenship and avant-garde performativity. Césaire shifts the time and place of women's political practice by resituating reproductive labor as a practice of political contestation.

Chapter 2 builds an archive of female citizenship through the daily life of tactics in the militant suffragette movement. Through attention to a catalogue-heavy archive, including mug shots, arrest records, and prison medical reports, this chapter examines the textures of suffragette action as a world-building practice. In suffragette autobiography, feminist periodical cultures, and Rebecca West's *The Sentinel: An Incomplete Early Novel*, narrative does not develop toward some future gain, like the vote or revolution. Instead, recursive, often repetitive plots create a long middle of protest and police repression. Rather than an emphasis on demands for the future, here the content of the women's revolution is the transformation of public space and social relations in the present tense. The chapter ends with a reading of serialized accounts of the hunger strike, to take up the ways that this narrative framework coincided with the tactical use of human rights rhetoric in suffragette attempts to classify the force-feeding of hunger-striking prisoners as domestic torture.

While the first section of the book offers a narrative of feminist gains, part 2, "The Reproductive Atlantic," follows the ways that suffrage reform corresponded with increasing state regulation of sexuality, particularly along racial lines. Part 2 thus offers a biopolitical history of human rights and revolution, taking up birth control legislation, miscegenation, sexual violence, and larger questions of public health. Beginning with the early years of the transatlantic birth control movement, chapter 3 considers anarchosyndicalist tendencies that aligned the sex rights of women with social revolution. Rather than viewing reproductive freedom as a *right to privacy* to be granted by the state, these groups positioned birth control as a direct action, a *tactic for equality* in the larger struggle against capitalism. The first half of the chapter centers on a particular tactic generally left out of the wider birth control movement: the proletarian birth strike. Around the turn of the century, neo-Malthusians and anarchists argued that women should stop having children in order to fell capitalism through an undersupply of workers. The second half of the chapter traces the convergence between industrial production and female reproduction in a set of adjacent texts, including Angelina Weld Grimké's lynching stories for the *Birth Control Review* and the 1951 petition to the United Nations, *We Charge Genocide*. Moving beyond the

American birth control movement into what I call the reproductive Atlantic, this cluster of texts makes up a distinctly feminist theory of right. Rather than a focus on the agential subject—the "good female character" with access to birth control—this expanded field of feminist print culture turns to a more tactical practice of reproductive justice as a human right.

The interwar era also gave rise to a much more reactionary biopolitics, as I discuss in chapter 4. In the spring of 1920, E. D. Morel flooded the British socialist press with a series of articles on the French occupation of the Rhineland. Morel's pamphlets touched upon the conditions of the Versailles Treaty but focused particularly, and with particular hysteria, on the presence of black colonial soldiers on the Franco-German border. In what would become an international print sensation, the "Black Horror on the Rhine" propaganda aligned the sexual threat posed by the African troops with the metaphorical "rape" of Germany through an unfairly punitive foreign policy. The Berlin Dada artist Hannah Höch explicitly takes up the Rhineland controversy, but these works tie the fate of the "Rhineland bastards" to the sexual science of early gay rights movements. For Höch, experiments with the photographic image allow for inhuman combinations that literalize relations of enmity. In this way, Höch's work allows for a mapping of the intimate relationship between rights and injuries precisely at the moment these rights are becoming articulated through the biological determinism of a human subject.

Part 3, "Convergences in Institutional Human Rights," takes up a more direct interaction among avant-garde circles, feminist activism, and the formation of the United Nations at midcentury. Here the administrative processes of international law, seen through archives of the drafting process, offer a counterpoint to more grassroots forms of feminist and queer activism on the ground. Chapter 5 thus focuses on family law, beginning in the years leading up to World War II, when European legal practice began to regulate legal personhood against the specter of depopulation. The chapter takes up this juridical history alongside the surrealist work of Claude Cahun, a flamboyantly queer poet, actress, photographer, and activist in the French resistance. In Cahun's later work, experiments with chance shift registers, moving from a celebratory fracturing of the bourgeois subject to an uncanny reproduction of the unmaking of persons through juridical practice. In this way, Cahun's prison writing recodes the chance procedure, moving from aleatory mysticism to the purely contingent selection of people persecuted in Vichy France and National Socialist Germany. Departing from traditional accounts of Cahun's work as a drag performance, the chapter argues that the prison writings offer an inquiry into the boundaries of the human and inhuman, citizen and noncitizen, in light of wide-scale rights abuses during World War II.

Finally, the last chapter reconsiders the committee meeting as a form of social life, decision making, care work, and governmentally central to the early development of the United Nations. In contrast to a more traditional understanding of the public sphere as a space of rational-critical debate among equals, this turn to one of the less-celebrated technologies of social organization, the committee, highlights the daily practices of government among markedly unequal bodies. In so doing, I look to establish an alternative methodology for human rights critique, and open up a somewhat massive bureaucratic archive by reconsidering the daily life of the committee meeting. This shift in attention allows for a more flexible genealogy of the human and human rights, one that can pivot between UN bureaucracy and the working existence of black feminist organizing in the colonies. Here I turn to the Négritude author and UN ambassador Paulette Nardal, whose monthly periodical *La Femme dans la Cité* published regular updates on the United Nations, alongside editorials arguing that newly enfranchised Martinican women were particularly well adapted to continue the UN's "civilizing process" among the island's working poor. This little-known journal also participated in the wider context of Négritude print cultures, publishing poems, songs, short stories, and folktales of a quite different political stripe. Reading back and forth across the pages of *La Femme dans la Cité*, this chapter locates the emergence of a black counterpublic sphere rendered through the grassroots committee meeting as an alternative practice of sociality and care.

My epilogue turns to the development of social reproduction theory in the work of Silvia Federici and others, to offer a reading of the witches, crones, and fantastic beasts in Leonora Carrington's midcentury novel *The Hearing Trumpet*. Written in postrevolutionary Mexico in the 1950s, *The Hearing Trumpet* was not published until the 1970s, at what many consider to be the end of the avant-garde, the end of actually existing socialism, and the beginning of second-wave feminism. My reading of the text complicates these historical arcs from the perspective of Cold War Mexico, through Carrington's juxtaposition of the marvelous with the prospect of atomic devastation.

⁂

This book began in Oakland, during the Movement of Squares, as a way to think through the working existence of publicly reclaimed spaces. It was finished in New Haven, Philadelphia, and Brooklyn, amid the rise of Black Lives Matter, #MeToo, and the Trump presidency. From the vantage of our current moment, I don't turn to the historical past for lessons, so much as to sound out some of the narratives that have been erased or forgotten and understand why others have become so familiar to almost seem like truth. For this reason, I am skeptical of the stories of progress often attached to first-wave feminism or the defeatist summary of socialist revolutions past. Instead of drawing up a balance sheet of the twentieth century, seen through the lens of success or failure, I turn to what these formations might have looked like on the ground, while things were happening, before a decisive end could be determined.

Not that grand narratives don't have their functional place. It is true enough that in the salons and along the barricades, there were women who wanted everything, not just the parliamentary vote. By necessity this wanting involved rejection, antagonism, opposition, but it also took on other forms more casual, friendly, daily, or minute. Looking backward from the present, well after "a century of failed revolutions," I want to understand this period not from what we know to be true, now, but from what it might have looked like then, not knowing what the end of the story would be. This perspective is always a fiction, of course. It is a posture just as much as left-wing melancholy or the heroics of deeds. In many ways, this book is an attempt to exorcise those last two tendencies, of tragedy or heroism, as poses that suggest the history of attempts to change society, to manage it differently or start again, are all already over, finished for good. What the following pages attempt is a more modest effort, to capture what that antagonism looked like, what that wanting looked like, then, there, at what must have seemed like a beginning.

PART I

SEX AND CITIZENSHIP IN THE ATLANTIC ARCHIVES

1

The Fury Archives

Afterlives of the Female Incendiary

The women were ugly, to be sure, but not quite ugly enough, or not as ugly as one might have expected, a somewhat regretful Léonce Dupont recalled, in what would become a standard account of the fourth military tribunal of the Paris Commune, the first of the trials to be devoted to the female communards. Indeed, it seems that the five women produced by the court that day were quite a disappointment. For Dupont, the accused were "not hideous enough, not old enough, not criminal enough to inspire horror."[1] This overt lack of monstrosity did not stop the author from further elaboration. Schooled in the finer arts of physiognomy, Dupont paid special attention to the accused's facial deformities. Though he admitted it not very sporting to focus on the ugliness of women, Dupont allowed that Elizabeth Rétiffe had a large nose and "beast-like" grin. She perspired too much, having overdressed for the weather. Léontine Suétens's left cheek was scarred, as though someone had bitten her, most likely, Dupont suggests, in a brothel. The washerwoman Joséphine Marchais seemed dirty and withered, though still angry looking, "like a fury."[2] More gentle was twenty-four-year-old Eulalie Papavoine, unfortunately in possession of a large "flat face." Perhaps running out of steam, Dupont found the last defendant, the laundress Lucie Marris Bocquin, merely "sweet," though her mouth was too big.

The fourth military tribunal tried five women, all accused of arson during the final weeks of the Paris Commune. The history of the Commune will be treated at more length in the pages to come. For now, it is enough to know that this social experiment in working-class radicalism, what Marx called the first proletarian revolution, rejected the authority of the French Third Republic and governed Paris from March 18 to May 28, 1871. It wasn't until the last week in May, when the French army invaded the city, that the fires were set, burning down the Tuileries Palace, the Richelieu library of the Louvre, the Hotel de Ville, and dozens of smaller buildings near the Rue Royale and the Rue du Faubourg Saint-Honoré. In the months that followed, these fires were attributed to the female communards, named *pétroleuses*.

My focus in these first pages concerns the legal aftermath of the Commune for its female participants. Key to this framing is a problem of categorization, but not necessarily for what the women did. What takes center stage are the vengeful feelings that prompted such action and the ways these feelings might manifest in the body as a distortion of femininity that could be readily observed. Consider, for instance, the journalist for *Le Figaro*, René de Pont-Jest, who was also disappointed with the looks of the accused. That said, Pont-Jest makes a cleaner distinction between what was expected and what was seen. The crowd had awaited the trial with some excitement, no doubt, Pont-Jest writes, because the very word "*pétroleuse*" summoned the most sinister menace, that is to say, "savage hordes of she-devils."[3] However, to the audience's dismay, the persons led to the bench were "ruined girls, ragged, grown pale from their night watches or darkened by the sun, their voices hoarse, their eyes dull, no longer feminine or masculine, beings without sex, without morality, without conscience, without even cynicism."[4] Though he does not use the language of ugliness or beasts, Pont-Jest makes it clear that the accused women could not really be women, or men, or, one might surmise, altogether human.

In many ways, both journalists were merely taking cues from what had been a summer of political caricatures. Well before the trials began, the *pétroleuse* had become a fixation in the popular press. Cartoons show befouled ghouls carrying cans of petrol. There are mustachioed women and those rendered pig-like or insane. Propaganda postcards render the *pétroleuse* as witches or harpies grimly watering the fires of destruction. The conservative press invoked the language of she-wolves, hydra, and other monstrosities. In the months that followed, the prosecution took up that language of monstrosity in a slightly different key. What began as a somewhat unremarkable misogyny, likening radical women to fantastic beasts, became literalized through the quality of women's legal personhood. As the persons before the law, the female communards offered a particularly visible animation of the paradox between abstract rights and materially unequal subjects. The women were active within the public sphere of politics while formally excluded from universal political recognition, both within the Second Empire and the Commune's Central Committee. They were political actors but not citizens. They were human, but not subject to the rights of man. In some extreme cases, the *pétroleuses* seemed not quite human at all, but something else more difficult to name, "no longer feminine or masculine, but beings without sex." This chapter traces the afterlives of this legal imagination across the Atlantic, moving from metropolitan France to colonial Martinique.

According to the National Assembly's official report, 1,051 women were arrested and taken to Versailles.[5] It is harder to picture these other women. We do not know their names, the shapes of their faces, whether they were prone to nervous sweating, how often they were married or not, what children existed. Attempts were made to categorize these other women as outside agitators, foreigners, and prostitutes. They might be nihilists, atheists, murderesses, or communists, associated with Pierre-Joseph Proudhon's distrust of property and the utopian thought of Charles Fourier, proponent of free love and homosexuality. What is known about these nameless others are the sorts of extrajudicial punishments they suffered. Here is Georges Jenneret, using a pointed metaphor:

> As for the women who were shot, they treated them almost like the poor Arabs of an insurgent tribe: after they had killed them, they stripped them, while they were still in their death throes, of part of their clothing. Sometimes they went even further, as at the foot of the Faubourg Montmartre and in the place Vendôme, where some women were left naked and defiled on the sidewalks.[6]

Jenneret's comparison is one of many that likened the communard women to French colonial populations in North Africa.[7]

The colonial encounter provided a language for what appeared to be an entirely new sort of savagery, imported from afar. What Jenneret found barbaric might be the murder of women. It might be the military weaponization of rape. What is considered savage could be that this violence happens in public, rather than the less remarkable violence behind walls and in houses. Potentially, in this obscure grammar, it is the defilement of the body that is no longer living that seems exceptionally foreign. In any case, Jenneret's vocabulary for what is inhumane seizes upon what Alexis de Tocqueville would call a "new science" of government practiced in colonial North Africa.[8] In a series of reports on the region, Tocqueville reasons that a different sort of bureaucracy must be forged in the colonies because the enemy is "not a real army, but the population itself."[9] For this reason, subjugation would need to involve practices of war that might be discouraged in Europe. "I believe that the right of war authorizes us to ravage the country and that we must do it," writes Tocqueville in the 1841 "Essay on Algeria." "I think that all means of desolating these tribes must be employed."[10] It is a somewhat startling moment for the way that Tocqueville, champion of Enlightenment values, allows the rights of war to sanction all acts against combatants and civilians alike as a particular kind of freedom. Tocqueville does not go into much detail on what sorts of acts might subdue the enemy population, but others do. "Voilà, my brave friend, how you must wage war against the Arabs. Kill all men over the age of fifteen, take all the women and children, load them onto boats, send them to the Marquesas Islands or elsewhere," writes Lieutenant-Colonel de Montagnac, in a letter to a friend. "In one word, annihilate all who will not crawl beneath our feet like dogs."[11]

What is the relationship between this model of colonial governmentality and contemporaneous military trials of the female communards? This chapter assembles a critical genealogy, crossing between the trials of the *pétroleuse* and the racial biopolitics of a wider colonial legacy. In so doing, the chapter establishes three conceptual schemes that will be developed across the rest of the book. In this first section, I turn to the aftermath of the Paris Commune to frame the female citizen as a paradoxical legal category. Drawing on a long tradition of leftist legal critique, this section examines the renegotiation of citizenship, moving from state recognition to collective practices set in opposition to the authority of the state. The second section turns to an uprising contemporaneous with the Paris Commune but much less discussed: Martinique's Southern Insurrection of 1870. Assembling a very different history of the female incendiary through military transcripts, letters, and official reports, I frame colonial women's rights through the emergent juridical category of "the human." In this case, during the rise of modern positive law, colonial women are not excluded from the rights of man but incorporated into the category "human" as a wider process of colonial security. The military transcripts allow for a mapping of the intersection between women's rights and the state management of colonial populations.

Finally, the third section reconsiders the Southern Insurrection through its aesthetic afterlife in Ina Césaire's play *Fire's Daughters* (*Rosanie Soleil*). Césaire's work provides an opportunity to situate an intimate theory of the avant-garde, moving away from the more well-known programs of the European manifestos. In this case, it is not just a matter of making visible the women who burned the cane fields or fought alongside soldiers. *Fire's Daughters* politicizes the often invisible labors of social reproduction, including the care work, kinship, and affective labor necessary to support a wider mobilization. By staging the insurrection inside the home, amid the dishes dried and laundry hung, Césaire's play articulates the space of political action across the gendered division between public and private spheres. This restructuring of what counts as political labor and who counts as a political actor moves past the shop floor or the battlefield to include persons assembled and acting together wherever they happen to be.

The Gender of Citizenship: Paris 1871

As General Appert informed the National Assembly, women were "seen fighting in the ranks of the National Guard, lighting fires, slaughtering hostages, and killing officers and soldiers in cold blood in the streets of Paris."[12] However, Appert explained that many had escaped arrest and even more were freed because there were no witnesses that could place them at the scene of the crime. In most cases, testimonies could only place the accused near the barricades. ("She was dressed in a white blouse and red scarf, carrying a rifle.")[13] Left with such paltry evidence, Prosecutor Jouenne turned to science. The female incendiaries were unnatural women for leaving their hearths and entering the public sphere of political life. Proof of this unnatural biology might be found in sexual behavior. Rétiffe lived with a man for seven years, unmarried. Suétens had done the same. Marchais had served in the same battalion as her lover. Papavoine had a child out of wedlock. Bocquin was an adulteress who had abandoned her child to live with a soldier.

Conservative attempts to explain the *pétroleuse* were not always cartoonish or hysterical. Consider, for instance, this moment in the "Parliamentary Inquiry Into the May 18 Insurrection" compiled by the National Assembly.

The table "Role of Women During the Battle of the Commune" is the beginning of the report on the female communards arrested and held in Versailles. It bears the note: "*(Account of Capitan Briot, proxy of the 4th Military Tribunal)*. 1,051 women were defendants in the 4th military tribunal and belong to the following categories." The report goes on to enumerate professions, then nationalities, then final sentences. Though in the following pages there will be many claims about the horror and monstrosity of the female political subject, I find this chart more striking for its ordinariness. There is no effort to convince. There is no whipping up of frenzy or indignation. That a summary of the thousand-plus women arrested for their political crimes need begin with the sexual relation of these women to men for the purposes of the bureaucracy of the National Assembly is a fact that goes without saying.

Role of Women During the Battle of the Commune

Inventory	
Married, living with their husbands	221
Married, living as concubines	117
	338
Widows, living alone	7
Widows, living as concubines	76
	83
Single, living alone	82
Single, living as concubines	302
Single, surrendered to the police	246
	630
Total	1,051

Source: *Enquête parlementaire sur l'insurrection du 18 Mars 1871* (Paris: Librairie Législative, 1872), 548.

The parliamentary report is only one part of a much larger legal archive. Here at the beginning, I want some sense of scope, so that the reactions to the *pétroleuse*, ranging from hysterical to matter of fact, do not seem like the work of one lone crank. But it quickly becomes tedious to enumerate the ways that these women were hated and why. My point here, in tracking this archive, is to sound out the negative responses to the *pétroleuse* as a fearful, defensive, sometimes petty reaction to women who did not accord with the norms of traditional femininity. This negative response was not just about manners and beauty but about the way women's political actions might have economic consequences for the rest of the population. To make this point brutally clear, I'll pass briefly over an article by *Le Figaro*'s Francis Magnard, whose horror at the female communards, those "literary bitches, female novelists, free-thinkers, furious ugly women," is quite explicitly linked to the women's impractical professional goals:

> They wanted to share everything with us, universities, courts, hospitals; they demanded their place in universal suffrage; they were no longer happy to stay at home, that dear, little realm where their mothers had lived, loved their husbands and raised children. They wanted the big universe, the vast world to develop their talents and fashion a domain according to their reforms. [Elles voulaient tout partagés avec nous, académies, tribunaux, cliniques ; elles exigeaient leur place dans le suffrage universel; elles ne se contentaient plus de la maison, ce cher petit royaume intime où leurs mères avaient vécu, aimaient leurs maris et élevaient leurs enfants. Il leur fallait le grand univers, le vaste monde pour développer leurs talents et fournir un champ à leurs réformes.][14]

Such aspirations for "the big universe, the vast world," Magnard writes, will lead women to ruin. The article opens with a description of a female corpse seen on the street, "soiled with mud and blood. Her head, which had been pretty, almost distinguished, wore in death an expression of savage hatred."[15] It is not just that politics will make women ugly but that it will make them dead, Magnard reasons, with some cause, it should be said, one month after the "bloody week" of May. This coupling of ugliness and death, alongside the imagined overthrow of man's "big universe, the vast world," was the least interesting response to the women of the Paris Commune, so it is best to get it out of the way, here at the start.

Instead, I want to highlight the ways this writing situates the gender of citizenship as contested terrain. Magnard lists rights that are traditionally afforded to full citizens: education, employment, health care, the vote, access to the public sphere. If citizenship has been premised on its exclusions, on who is *not* a rights-bearing subject, to change the status of these exclusions also means changing what this term "citizen" signifies. The Paris Commune marks one occasion when the gendered status of the rights-bearing citizen was under revision. In other words, the Commune marks one occasion to move beyond a progressive story of state recognition and consider instead collective social practices. In this case, these are practices wielded *against the state*, as part of a wider experiment in the understanding of rights and citizenship more generally. During the spring of 1871, traditional programs for revolution were under revision, too. According to the tenets of what would later become scientific socialism, revolution must occur at the proper historical stage, when capitalism has ratcheted up its class contradictions to the appropriate level. In *The Civil War in France*, Marx argues that the Paris Commune is history's first proletarian revolution and therefore breaks the model of bourgeois revolutions past. The experiment of the Commune, for Marx, was something altogether new and unexpected. It did not require fidelity to older models and predictions. The life of the Commune marked, instead, the creation of new forms of politics. On one hand, Marx writes, "the working class cannot simply lay hold of the ready-made state machinery, and wield it for its own purposes."[16] The Commune's Central Committee may have laid hold of this state machinery—the army, police, bureaucracy, clergy, and judicature—but these bodies could not just continue on with new leaders. No longer appendages of capital, serving the propertied classes, this state machinery could be appropriated by the Commune, but this machinery could not, after that initial moment of seizure, continue to operate in the same manner. At the same time, the communards could not simply apply, as if wrested from thin air, "ready-made utopias to introduce *par décret du people*."[17]

Instead, the governmental form that was the Paris Commune became for Marx "the political form at last discovered under which to work out the economic emancipation of labour."[18] These new forms of social and political life did not entail a transfer of power from one class to another as in bourgeois revolutions past. What social and political life would look like could not be set out in advance to accord with the appropriate developmental stage or laid down from on high. This was a new kind of revolution, one against the state itself. In place of the state, as an instrument of repression, of capital over labor, emerged the antiparliamentary form of the Commune. In this way, the space occupied by the communards became a laboratory for politics. It was where political forms might be discovered in the working out of daily social life, in committees and camps, on the streets and in the clubs, through what Marx called the commune's "working existence."[19]

Kristin Ross's two books on the Commune focus on this "working existence" as a practice that generated its own critical theory, through what she calls "the displacement of the political onto seemingly peripheral areas of everyday life—the organization of space and time, changes in lived rhythms and social ambiences."[20] Rather than begin with the seizure of the cannons, on the night of March 31, Ross opens with a moment of invocation, in the Vaux-Hall ballroom, when the address *"Citoyennes et citoyens"* marks a "subject predicated on any number of disidentifications—from the state, the Empire, the police, and the world of the so-called 'honnêtes gens.'"[21] In the Vaux-Hall ballroom, the female *citoyennes* of the Paris Commune identified with a new form of political life by claiming an antagonistic relation to state belonging. What interests me is this moment of political transition, of claiming a right as a kind of collective practice that destroys and redefines what that right might have meant before. However, to linger on the scene of the *citoyenne* is also to note the ways that this claiming, a seemingly utopian moment of new forms of political life, could coexist with ongoing forms of domination.

Since this time, socialist, communist, and anarchist groups have argued about the legacy of the Commune as polestar or bad example. Over the next hundred-odd years, the Commune became the flashpoint for the European Left of the early Internationals and amid more contemporary ultraleft circles. I don't want to weigh into these conversations, or even begin to survey the wider bibliography, so much as present a different archive, one that looks at the working existence of women's political action as militant, but also as a matter of unwaged reproductive labor, of cooking, cleaning and looking after children, alongside the daily, entirely unspectacular experience of bodily vulnerability in public and behind closed doors. To look more closely at the day-to-day life of a working existence means to pause, sometimes uncomfortably, on the ways that the plaza or square might be the site of transformative social practices but not utopia for everyone through and through, day in and day out. To consider this working existence as a laboratory for theory means pausing too on the ways that older forms of inequality did not suddenly disappear at the commencement of revolutionary activity but continued into it, in warped and contradictory fashions. The working existence of the Commune was a laboratory for new theories of collective action, but this experimentation did not proceed without some stutters, nor did it abolish all that came before. Shifts in social relations were unbalanced, sometimes moving forward, sometimes reproducing familiar habits, as though nothing had changed.

From its beginning, the Central Committee had no female representatives. The universal suffrage that was praised by Marx did not include women. On its first day of existence, the Committee of Public Safety, an executive governing body of Blanquist and Jacobin persuasion, passed a resolution prohibiting women from the field of battle.[22] During the Prussian siege, a battalion of fighting women, or "Amazons," had been proposed and rejected, with some laughter. The new ateliers served working-class men but did not recognize the labor of working-class women. Yet women communards, lacking sanction from the new government, had been key participants all along. They were there blocking the cannons on March 31, fighting in the battles at Issy and Châtillon. There was the Légion des fédérées that trained women to fight at the barricades; the Filles du Pères Duchêne that guarded the city's gates; the woman's battalion that was the Club des femmes patriots; and the Union des femmes organizing *ambulancières* and *cantinières*, papering the walls of Paris with "An Appeal to the Working Women of Paris," demanding the recognition and reorganization of women's labor.[23]

More than one thousand women were arrested and taken to Versailles, but almost none of them appear in the extant documentary photographs. If one flips through the extensive archives of the Commune, there are not many images of women at all. Women are not in the photographs of the barricades, the portraits of the Central Committee, or shown standing beside the ruined architecture, among the cannons in the street. The exception to this tendency is a curious one. The photographer Eugène Appert, an anticommunard and propagandist for the realm, took a series of portraits of the female communards incarcerated at Versailles. These were later used in police files for the purposes of identification (figures 1.1–1.2). However, Appert also used the portraits for his own, more experimental art. Appert restaged a number of

FIGURE 1.1 Ernest Charles Appert, "Louise Frédérique Bonnefoy, French Communard and caretaker." 1871. Print on albumen paper.

Source: Paris, Musée Carnavalet.
© Ernest Charles Appert / Musée Carnavalet / Roger Viollet Ventes directes.

FIGURE 1.2 Ernest Charles Appert, "Eulalie Papavoine, Incendiary of Lille Street." No date. Photograph.

Source: Paris, Musée Carnavalet.
© Ernest Charles Appert / Musée Carnavalet / Roger Viollet Ventes directes.

the more pivotal moments of the Commune, particularly the executions, using actors. He then pasted the faces of known communards, taken from the Versailles prison portraits, onto the actors' bodies. These images were used for the purposes of propaganda, though perhaps too effectively. Eventually, the photomontages would be banned by the government for "disturbing the peace."[24]

So completely organized, no body blocking another, the photomontage of the female communards is uncanny (figure 1.3). It seems the photographer could not quite decide whether this was to be a formal portrait, with all the women in a line staring at the camera, hands demurely folded in their laps, or a scene taken from life, with people sewing, eating, drinking straight from the bottle, or reclining into sleep. Some of the heads are too small for the bodies onto which they are pasted. Some heads are pasted at the incorrect angle, as though the women had infinitely flexible necks. What I take to be the claim of the staged and collaged image is this: the female communards could not be simply recorded alongside the members of the National Guard. Instead, for the likes of Appert, these women had to be made anew, using older forms but tweaking them into something slightly monstrous, a technological feat. Taken in court or prison, then pasted onto the bodies of others, the photographic fragments, literally disembodied heads, reveal a presence and absence, an exclusion and inclusion that is the structural phenomenon I have been describing as the paradox of the female citizen.

The use of collage, by a failed painter no less, is particularly germane to our case. Here the new disjunctive technologies of the arts, just beginning to be termed avant-garde, bleed into political discourse. How we feel about this rendering may depend on the morbidity of the viewer. Do those oddly tilted necks look broken or merely fanciful? In any case, collage offers one way to think through the structural paradoxes of gendered citizenship: as a truth and its negation, an assertion that transcends its object, multiple claims that cancel one another out, presence and absence in the same space, a category and its exception at once. Much will depend on how these experiments with female personhood are turned to the light as punitive or utopian. It is possible to see these experiments with the female body in disassembled parts as a symptom of misogyny. However, it is also possible to see, in the experiments of what will come to be called the avant-garde, the recombinant possibilities of collage form as a template upon which to imagine new forms of personhood.

FIGURE 1.3 Ernest Charles Appert, "Prison des Chantiers à Versailles. Le 15 août 1871." 1871. Print on albumen paper.

Source: Paris, Musée Carnavalet. © Ernest Charles Appert / Musée Carnavalet / Roger Viollet Ventes directes.

Collage is the formal technology that represented the paradox of the female citizen in state-sponsored propaganda, but it can also be found in the contemporaneous poetry of Rimbaud. Though I will have more to say about the avant-gardes in the final section of this chapter, for now I want to pause a moment, to consider Rimbaud's ode to the female communard, "Marie Jeanne's Hands":

> These are shapers of spines
> Hands that do no harm
> More deadly than machines,
> Stronger than a horse!
>
> [Ce sont des casseuses d'échines
> Des mains que ne font jamais mal
> Plus fatales que des machines,
> Plus fortes que tout un cheval!][25]

Note first the way that the hands stand in for Marie Jeanne, who never appears as a complete body in the poem. These hands are tricky to pin down. They appear first as creators. They are named as harmless but then considered deadly. The hands are likened to machines and animals. But the thing that becomes somewhat thorny is the alien quality of these hands as actors on their own, perpetually defined, through action real or supposed, in contradictory ways. These hands can't quite be pictured, because they are machines and horses. They can't be pictured because they are harmless and deadly at the same time. The hands are a part of a whole that does not act the way that wholes are supposed to work. These hands are body parts personified, as a kind of alien presence, acting in inexplicable ways, beyond the reach of a coherent simile. Hands do not sing, nor do they shed. The disembodied hands, running around Paris and strangling evil women, are the locus of so many poetic feats: synecdoche, personification, and, of course, apostrophe, in that the poem speaks to these hands rather than to Marie Jeanne herself.

There is a certain family likeness between these hands, the face of the dead woman on the pages of *Le Figaro*, and the photomontage that places the heads of the communards on the bodies of actresses. However, unlike those other instances of the body in pieces—of the *pétroleuse* as a kind of inhuman entity beyond the pale of law and representation—here the very flexibility of the female citizen, in her working existence, offers the poem a much more utopian possibility. The hands of the poem disconnect from Jeanne-Marie to mark the status of poetic form itself, as what contours and creates: "These are shapers of spines." At the outset of a line, the unspecified "these" allows the referent to expand, to include Marie Jeanne's hands and the lines of the poem themselves, as forces that shape persons, disfigure them, and derange them into sensory categories that do not match up. For this reason, the predominance of the hands in the poem is not a dehumanization of the *pétroleuse* Marie Jeanne, though one might certainly read the lines in this manner. Those disembodied hands also signal the possibilities of the poetic form to create new modes of female personhood, infinitely recombinant, that can cycle through body parts, apostrophized objects, and machines, rendering their subject a location of impossibly mixed actions and a feeler of fantastic destinies. Here Rimbaud uses the contradictory category of the *pétroleuse* not as a symptom of the moral degeneration of women but as a template upon which to imagine a new kind of personhood that is brutal, somewhat disorienting, but also extremely flexible. Looking backward, from the collaged photographs of the Communard women to the poem, I want to note first the ways that collage disembodies the female form—in this case headless or all hands. The wider argument here and throughout this chapter is that the paradoxical rendering of citizenship in the Commune resulted in aesthetic experiments that depict the female body as warped, deformed, fragmented, or infinitely flexible. Though feminist writing on the avant-garde has traditionally positioned these experiments as a symptom of misogyny, revealing the avant-garde artists' hatred of women, I want to consider these experiments with inhuman women as a more utopian figuration for the plasticity of the female citizen's legal personhood in a moment of revolutionary change.

Colonial Insurgency and the Juridical Human: Martinique, 1870

Half a world away, on a small island in the Caribbean, the fall of the Second Empire sparked off another, less celebrated insurrection. The most detailed firsthand account comes from Charles Menche de Loisne, then the governor of Martinique. Loisne addresses his report, with some flourishes, to Vice-Admiral Pothuau, minister of the navy and the colonies. The report is some fifty pages long, with many key details missing. Loisne assumes that the reader has already encountered newspaper coverage of the military trials, brought to France by the American and British press. But Loisne considers himself apart from such journalists, who might be prone to theatricality. He modestly suggests that a brief, impartial account of Martinique's Insurrection of the South, the largest of its kind since the revolt in Haiti, might be of some interest or use to people on the mainland.

We might raise an eyebrow to this claim of impartiality, but Loisne's history begins correctly enough, with Léopold Lubin, a young and well-liked farmer of a good family, sentenced to five years of forced labor for striking a white man. Loisne allows that this was a particularly harsh sentence. He notes that, among the races of color, particularly the blacks, the trial stirred up long-standing anger. For those attending the trial, anger focused particularly around one juror, the overseer, a Mr. Codé, who was not, Loisne notes, particularly prudent in his speech. What further enflamed the black population of southern Martinique was that "by circumstance still unexplained, and by strange fortune, a kind of white flag had long flown from M. Codé's home."[26] Loisne clarifies: for Martinique's black population, such a flag would signal a desire for the reestablishment of slavery.

Loisne does not offer further commentary on this matter. He does not relay Codé's remarks that Lubin would serve as an example for "any negro that dared raise a hand to a white."[27] Loisne does not explain another mysterious circumstance, that two black men on the jury were replaced by whites before the start of the trial. Nor does Loisne's report fill in the wider cultural and social context of postemancipation Martinique. Certainly, the white flag would mark a very particular threat, among a population of former slaves freed by the Constituent Assembly in 1794, then enslaved again under Napoleon, then freed by the Schoelcher decree of 1848. However, the provocations of Codé were not the only source of Martinican unrest. At the time of the insurrection, twenty-two years after formal emancipation had awarded the rights of citizenship to black men, forced labor remained common.[28] The colonial government enforced rigid work contracts for black agricultural workers and limited movement between different parts of the island. A vast influx of Chinese, Indian, and African laborers kept wages precariously low and sparked interracial tensions between immigrants and former slaves. Shortages because of the ongoing Franco-Prussian War led to a spike in commodity prices. The national bank ran out of currency and began to give out vouchers, making it difficult for plantation owners to provide food and wages for their immigrant laborers.

Loisne writes with formal politeness, as a teacher might explain to a favorite student, that "in a country like Martinique, where the passions are strong, where the antagonism which so unhappily divides the races is always so violent, a light remark is taken well by some, soured by others."[29] All the same, Loisne claims that the general unrest surrounding the Lubin affair was calming down, until a packet boat arrived with news from across the Atlantic of the fall of the French Empire. At this news, two detachments of infantry were deployed by boat to southern Martinique, where the troops were garrisoned near the neighborhoods of Marin and Trinity. Taking all necessary precautions, the governor (Loisne, in a curious use of the third person), announced the new Republic of France to an assembled crowd. In Rivière-Pilot, the scene of the Lubin affair, this news was met with a riot. A crowd armed with stones and pikes marched to the plantation of Codé, who had fled with his family. The crowd set fire to the house, then set off after Codé, who was later found in the countryside and killed by the mob. Over the next three days, armed bands of men and women, farmers, artisans, city workers, and immigrant laborers set fire to twenty-five plantations across southern Martinique. There was widespread looting, particularly among the women insurgents, who gathered farm animals and grain from the burning properties. During the night, new fires spread across the horizon. According to Loisne, from sunset to dawn each night, it appeared as though the low-lying ground of the capital city was entirely encircled by flames.[30]

From here, the bulk of Loisne's report concerns the military organization involved in quelling the insurrection. However, the ex-governor devotes some space to the matter of political will. Loisne concludes that the insurgents wanted "the right to do anything, to take vengeance, to kill, to pillage, to set fires and divvy up property among themselves."[31] While the common people might have been blindly led by hatred, the chiefs of the bands of insurgents were cannier, Loisne argues. These chiefs took advantage of the defeat of the French army to establish their own independent island, their own Haiti, by any means necessary. In this vein, Loisne ends his report with a consideration of the military trials held that summer in Fort-de-France. With some disdain, the ex-governor notes that none of the accused admitted to their crimes. However, Loisne sees the depositions of witnesses as a source of overwhelming evidence:

> [The depositions] have put the full light on the double goal that followed the revolts: the extermination of whites and the independence of Martinique. They have equally proved that the women who took part in the fight have shown themselves more cruel than the men. There is a woman, Surprise, who, in setting fire to a property, said, "There is nothing to save. If the good Lord had a hut on this land I would burn it, because he must be an old *béqué* [white]." That's her who threatened to destroy the hut of a black man, if he did not take up arms and follow her, declaring this terrible blasphemy: "I will burn my mother and even God if it is necessary." [Elles ont mis en pleine lumière le double but que poursuivaient les révoltés : l'extermination des blancs et l'indépendance de Martinique. Elles ont également prouvé que les femmes qui avaient pris part à la lutte s'étaient montrées plus cruelles que les hommes. C'est une femme, Surprise, qui, en incendiant une propriété, disait : « Il ne faut rien épargner. Le bon Dieu aurait une case sur la terre que je la brûlerais, parce qu'il doit être un vieux béqué (blanc) » C'est elle qui menaçant un noir de détruite sa case, s'il ne s'armait pas pour la suivre, proférait cet épouvantable blasphème : « Je brûlerai ma mère et Dieu même s'il faut! »][32]

Loisne quotes from the second session of the military trials, which took place from May to June, 1871. The reports from the second session will be the focus of what follows, but I should note first that this is a highly unreliable historical archive. The prosecution's remarks are recorded in full, but there is no record of the defense. Many of the accused would not have spoken French, so their testimonies were given in Creole and then translated, with only the translation recorded.[33] Translators were also on hand for the accused immigrant workers from India and Africa, who would give their testimonies in their native dialects. The majority of the accused were agricultural laborers, many of them illiterate. First-person memoirs or letters detailing the insurrection, written by the insurrectionists themselves, do not exist. Finally, as Loisne notes, the accused all denied participating in insurrectionary activities or claimed they were forced into such actions on the pain of death.

However, the second session of the military trials went on for some time, for more than one hundred recorded pages, so the repetition of particular questions and answers suggests some sort of narrative, though it would be hasty to try to decode these answers for truth or untruth. What is certain is that the prosecution looked to uncover a race war and to lay this plot at the feet of a few key leaders, particularly the increasingly famous septuagenarian chief Eugène Lacaille. According to the testimony of Léonce Valoise, a dressmaker, Lacaille was heard saying that the whites should be exterminated, leaving the island to the blacks and mulattos. By other accounts, this plot looked to establish a new government, with shared governance among people of color. In some depositions, it was mere anarchy, a republic based on looting and riots. The prosecution pressed particularly hard on the anarchy plot, with focus on the disregard of private property as signaling a wider, communitarian politics also ravaging Paris. Noting Lacaille's alleged intention to redistribute and share property, the prosecution suggested an explicit comparison as insult: "That's what is said today by the people of the Commune in France."[34]

According to these depositions, we can see a distinct division of blame between the insurgent men and women. Leaders like Lacaille were charged with instigating a race war, while the court positioned women like Surprise as emotional beings without clear goals, driven by anger, revenge, and blind hatred. They were cruel for the sake of being cruel. This cruelty was imagined as revenge, though no one specifies what injuries the revenge aimed to address. By some accounts, including those of the insurgent women, they were tricked or forced into participation. This participation did not mark an equal standing with men like Lacaille or Louis Telga. The insurgent women marched behind the men, carrying stones in their skirts and vials of pepper water as a kind of Molotov cocktail to throw in the eyes of French soldiers.[35] The women were blamed for most of the looting of house furniture, farm animals, and other food supplies. Some were suspected of poisoning white plantation owners. As in France, only a tiny percentage of the women involved could be tried. According to what archives exist, fifteen women stood trial, most under thirty years old and some unsure of their exact age (see "Women on Trial for Participation in Martinique's Insurgency of the South"). It would be wrong to speak of this grouping as a women's rights movement. But it is also wrong to lump these women together with the male insurgents, who were treated differently by the courts and one another.

During the trial, prosecutors focused on the cruelty of the insurgent women as a fundamental character flaw, as though their feminine nature had

Women on Trial for Participation in Martinique's Insurgency of the South

Name	Age	Profession	Sentence	Crime
Lumina Sophie, aka "Surprise"	23	Seamstress	Forced labor in perpetuity	Arson
Asténie Boissonnet	21	Agricultural laborer	Forced labor in perpetuity	Arson and looting
Maria Bouchon	n/a*	Agricultural laborer	Twenty years forced labor	Arson and looting
Dame Jean-Louis Camille Cyrille	32	Agricultural laborer	Twenty years forced labor	Arson
Hortensia Châlon	n/a*	Maid	Fifteen years forced labor	Arson and looting
Robertine Geneviève	21	Agricultural laborer	Ten years forced labor	Arson and looting
Malvina Sylvain	21	Agricultural laborer	Ten years forced labor	Arson
Aline Ménage	n/a*	Agricultural laborer	Ten years forced labor	Arson
Rosanie Soleil	27	Seamstress	Five years prison	Presence near the murder of Codé
Adèle Frémont	n/a*	Agricultural laborer	Five years prison	Furnished flaming torches
Chériette Chérubin	17	Seamstress	Two years prison, 200 F fine	Looting
Louisine Chérubin	23	Seamstress	Two years prison, 200 F fine	Looting
Madeleine Clem	n/a	n/a	Condemned to death (in absentia)	Participation in the murder of Codé
Adèle Négrand	n/a	n/a	Forced labor in perpetuity (in absentia)	Furnished flaming torches
Sylvanie Sylvain	23	Seamstress	Acquitted	Presence near fire

* accused testifies that she does not know her age

Source: Gilbert Pago, *Lumina Sophie dit "Surprise" 1848–1879 insurgée et bagnarde* (Matoury, Guyana: Ibis Rouge Editions, 2008), 75–76.

spoiled. Most notorious among these women was Marie-Philomène Roptus, called Lumina Sophie, called "Surprise," who was named "queen of the company," the most savage of the savage women.[36] A number of witnesses testify to Surprise's poor character. ("She's a bad woman, she is very wicked. All of the neighborhood complains about her.")[37] Allegedly, the nineteen-year-old seamstress, then pregnant, incited reluctant men to action. ("I followed the group, because Surprise is a bad woman and she was capable of setting me on fire.")[38] Here is a version of the speech that Loisne quoted earlier, as it appears in one witness's testimony:

> **The Célina brother:** Then Surprise arrived at the plantation, I advised her to not burn the buildings because I had cane to make, she responded: I will burn everything, *if the good Lord had a plantation, I would burn it too, because he must be an old béqué* [white creole settler].
>
> **The Chairman, to Surprise:** It appears that you are more learned than the others. How do you know that *the Good Lord is a béqué.* You have already seen him then. The good Lord, you understand, is master to all, black and white.
>
> **Surprise:** I never said that. It's the first time I've heard myself blamed for that.
>
> [R:. . . . Lorsque Surprise est arrivé sur l'habitation, je lui ai conseillé de ne pas brûler les bâtiments parce que j'avais des cannes à faire, elle m'a répondu: je brûlerai tout, *si le bon Dieu avait une habitations je la brûlerais aussi, car ça doit être un vieux béqué.*
>
> **Le Président,** à **Surprise:** Il parait que vous êtes plus savant que les autres. Comment savez-vous que le *Bon Dieu est un béqué.* Vous l'avez donc déjà vu. Le bon Dieu entendez-vous est notre maître à tous blancs ou noirs.
>
> **Surprise:** Je n'ai jamais dit cela. C'est la première fois que j'entends me reprocher cela.][39]

(CG 79)

The witness is one of the brothers Célina (Emile, Octave, Astride), who are not always distinguished from one another. This is, in fact, the second time that a witness has blamed Surprise for threatening to burn down everything, including the plantations, her mother, and the Good Lord. In the closing arguments, some weeks later, the prosecution repeats Surprise's alleged threat, with some additional commentary. ("What horrible blasphemy in the mouth of a girl so young!!")[40] Meanwhile, at least a dozen other witnesses place Surprise at the scene of the crime, setting fire to the cane fields, the mill, the kitchens, and an old couch. Some saw Surprise with kerosene; another claims she was armed with a bottle of pepper water; others claimed she threatened their lives if they did not join her cause; a few did not see her there at all.

It would be possible to read these interactions more closely, with the assumption that the witness is telling the truth and that Surprise's denial is a lie. It would be possible to assume that the witness is a liar and to take Surprise's defense as the truth: "I never said that. It's the first time I've heard myself blamed for that." As legal evidence, the transcript does not offer a clear indication either way. It seems all leading questions and accusations of lies, transcribed with many errors across two languages. Different people say slightly mismatched versions of the same thing. The alleged threats are filtered through a network of other versions: I have heard it was said, I heard her say, my wife said she said, and so on. For these reasons, I want to tip the archive at a different angle. In this perspective, it is not the truth of what Surprise did or did not say while she was lighting the cane fields on fire that is most important. Rather, I want to highlight what her claims meant in the eyes of the court and how this way of meaning constructs a particular view of the world.

During the end of the second session, Surprise was often coupled with another woman known for her cruelty, Camille Jean Lois Cyrille, called "the woman Cyrille," to distinguish her from her husband. The women's infernal partnership is mentioned early on, during the opening remarks: "The one named Surprise and Camille Jean Louis Cyrille are noted for their exaltation in the midst of the conflagration."[41] According to the later testimony of Gersan, a former slave sympathetic to the French, Cyrille was "more enraged than a viper, she was a fury, she was bent in two under the weight of the stuff that she carried to feed the fire."[42] Watching this fire spread, Cyrille allegedly acquired cannibalistic tendencies. In what would become another case of nearly mythic rumor, a number of people claim to have heard Cyrille say, "What a beautiful fire. Where then is St. Pée, so that I can cut off a piece of his face to grill and eat it."[43] Over the second session of the military trials, we hear various renditions of this threat. The wording changes slightly, but what remains the same—and persistently denied by the woman Cyrille—is the intention to roast and eat the face of St. Pée. During the testimony of the plantation owner Jean David St. Pée himself, Cyrille's threat becomes a prelude to a wider set of intentions about the insurrection's future. Though not at the scene of the crime, having fled before the nights of insurrection, St. Pée conveys a secondhand account of the incident:

> **St. Pée:** Madame Cyrille said: That she regretted not finding me there, because she would have cut off a piece of my face to roast and eat it. . . . [Cyrille] said to St. Esprit *that they were not finished with the whites, that the prisoners would be set free, that everything was going to start again, that this time everything would be destroyed.*
> **Prosecution:** Always the hope of impunity; we expect then the liberation of all the prisoners.
> **St. Pée:** Why then, Mr. President, *we have even prepared a party for them on the first day of the year.*
> **The President to the woman Cyrille:** Who made you think they were going to set the prisoners free?
> **Cyrille:** I never said such a thing, it's by way of a great *exoneration* that St. Pée said that.
> **Prosecution:** Shut up, what *exoneration* could St. Pée have against a creature of your species.

> [**St. Pée.:** Mme. Cyrille a dit: Qu'elle avait regretté de ne m'avoir pas trouvé, car elle aurait coupé un morceau de ma gueule pour le rôtir et le manger. . . . Elle a dit au St. Esprit *qu'on n'avait pas fini avec les blancs, que les prisonniers allaient être mis en liberté, que tout allait recommencer, que cette fois-ci on allait tout raser.*
> **D:** Toujours l'espoir de l'impunité ; on s'attendait donc à la mise en liberté de tous ces prisonniers.
> **St. Pée.:** Comment donc, M. le Président, *on leur avant même préparé une fête pour le premier de l'an.*
> **Le Président à la femme Cyrille:** Qui vous faisait donc penser qu'on allait mettre les prisonniers en liberté ?

> **Cyrille:** Je n'ai jamais dit pareille chose, c'est par une grande *vindication* que M. St. Pée dit cela.
> **D:** Taisez-vous, quelle *vindication* St. Pée peut-il avoir contre une créature de votre espèce.]
>
> (*CG* 78)

"I never said such a thing," Cyrille responds. The truth or untruth of the allegation, as something that might be attached to the person Camille Cyrille, cannot be known. But it is important that her statement suggests a future to come through a return to the past, to the 1848 emancipation. According to the testimony in the military trials, in the days of the 1870 insurrection, "she said to St. Esprit *that they were not finished with the whites, that the prisoners would be set free, that everything was going to start again, that this time everything would be destroyed.*" The insurgency becomes, in this imagination, a repetition of formal emancipation that turns out differently, allowing not just for the formal end of slavery but for a total liberation, for prisoners and colonial subjects more widely. In some ways, this claim proposes a counterfactual history of emancipation, one that reworks 1848 all over again, so that liberty marks something more than the merely formal, merely abstract equality.

For St. Pée and the prosecutors, who are notably familiar with one another, this reworking of historical fact is a laughable ambition. Perhaps the sarcasm and jokes come from defensiveness—it is hard to tell without intonation. In any case, Cyrille's imagination of a repetition of the earlier days of revolts, this time with a different end, is something that, for the president of the proceedings, Cyrille could not have come up with by herself. Jean Louis Camille Cyrille was, according to the record, a thirty-two-year-old agricultural worker, only nine years old in 1848 when slavery was abolished. It is unlikely that Cyrille could read or write. Nor could she vote. It is not entirely surprising, then, that the prosecution was so startled with Cyrille's use of the legal term "exonerate." At the mention of this word, the prosecution loses face, for a moment, and reminds the woman Cyrille that she and St. Pée are not, in the eyes of the law or biology, on the same plane. Here is a question transcribed without a question mark. "Shut up, what *exoneration* could St. Pée have against a creature of your species."

If Cyrille has posited one version of a history that could be, the prosecution offers another. Moving from the case of individual citizens to a more nebulous object, the population, the prosecutor Mr. Fournier invokes the security of the colony as a whole. Fournier reminds the jury that, only nine months earlier, the accused spread hatred into the wider, formally peaceful population. Faced with this past unrest, Fournier councils, the jury can use the sentence of exile to a distant penal colony as a kind of antidote to save Martinique's colonized peoples from infection, thus preserving the security of the white creoles as well. M. Fournier implores the jury to take action: "The law has armed you with the power to throw back these incendiaries, plague [*fléau*] of our Society, do it if you want to spare our colony from new horrors."[44]

Here, then, is another future to come, in an if/then clause, wherein the expulsion of some ensures the survival of others. Here again is a scene of *making* legal subjects. Though we can read, in the cited words of Cyrille and others, different sorts of futures, of what might have happened or could be, these other futures would not be available to the women on trial. Four days after the closing remarks, Surprise received a life sentence of forced labor in French Guiana. She died there in 1879, at the age of thirty-one. At that time, Camille Jean Louis Cyrille would have been imprisoned on the penal colony too, eight years into a twenty-year sentence for arson. Theoretically, Cyrille was pardoned through the amnesty of 1880, though she never returned to Martinique. In the state archives, there is no record of her death.

The military trials animate two incommensurate theories of right—the settler colonialists' right to property and the insurgent's right to national sovereignty, though the debates do not explicitly take up these terms. Instead, what echoes through the trials are the speech acts attributed to Lumina Sophie and the woman Cyrille as evidence of a particular cruelty. These threats suggest sadist pleasure and latent cannibalism: "What a beautiful fire. Where then is St. Pée, so that I can cut off a piece of his face to grill and eat it." The persistent return to this speech suggests that the trial also staged a more epistemological conflict. The focus on Cyrille's speech, rather than her actions, begins to categorize her as a particular kind of legal subject on a spectrum of civilization. Cyrille is not outside of the law: her lawyer speaks for her, in court. But Cyrille is not in a position to make claims of her own against the exoneration of St. Pée. Cyrille's legal status thus appears in a twilight state: she is somehow "not yet" a rights-bearing subject but close enough to be considered guilty or innocent as a defendant on trial. Part of what is on trial here is her humanity, defined by the appropriate reactions to destruction and violence. That Surprise and Cyrille appear to enjoy the insurrection, to exalt amid the flames and even find the fire beautiful, is their most damning attribute. Beyond the matter of setting the fires or providing the matches, Surprise and Cyrille are categorized as vipers or Furies because their emotional reactions to the insurrection are the wrong reactions. These responses, repeated throughout the trial in slightly different variations, signal a departure from rational thought and a waning humanity.

In the courtroom, this categorization of the human extends and reworks what legal scholars cite as a major transition in juridical science from the transcendental principles of natural law to a more empiricist understanding of legal positivism.[45] At this point in the long nineteenth century, at the high-water mark of empire building and state formation, European jurists turned to legal positivism as a way to render law through acts of state rather than through universal principles of rationality or justice. Positivists emphasized their doctrine as scientific, precise, and practical, in contrast to the baggy romanticism of moral principles. Rather than a universal claim to rights as the essence of all men, modern positive law could recognize citizen-subjects differentially on a spectrum of civilization, so that some subjects might be caught in an incipient citizenship, a state of "not yet." In this case, legal personhood takes on a teleological dimension, so that some subjects are regarded as undergoing a civilizing process, with legal personhood its designated endpoint.

This transition entailed a host of other changes. If natural law was a given, positive law had to be created, often through an institutional process. Over the next fifty years, the rise of the European institutions as technologies of governance facilitated the racialization of the juridical personality, in terms of who is defined as the proper subject of the law. From the Berlin Conference's "scramble for Africa" to the Mandate System of the League of Nations, these institutions of international law determined the methods by which non-Western subjects might be incorporated into the framework of European law as a project of humanization, or a way to *make* human subjects. For Talal Asad, this *making* establishes the secular foundations of contemporary human rights discourses as always already wrapped up in a colonial history of violence. What is named as cruelty here takes on an oblique relation to suffering: "In their attempts to outlaw customs the European rulers considered cruel," Asad writes, "it was not concern with indigenous suffering that *dominated* their thinking, but the desire to impose what they considered civilized standards of justice and humanity on a subject population—that is, the desire to create new human subjects."[46]

This model of incorporation thus challenges a major tenet of anticolonial theory, that colonial law dehumanized its subjects by setting them outside or beyond the realm of law. In Asad's accounting of legal modernity as a site of transition, processes of so-called humanization act as a technology of governance through an increasingly elaborate taxonomy of what characteristics might constitute a rights-bearing subject. Rather than the development of international law as such, I want to focus on these mechanisms—the technologies of administration, categorization, recording, and inscription—surrounding our understanding of the human as a legal category. This sense of humanization as an administrative and legal process imposed on subject populations animates Samira Esmeir's historical accounting of modern colonial law. For Esmeir, the transition to positive law signals a moment when what is human is no longer a matter of birth but instead a juridical category conferred through the state. What is called human thus becomes the endpoint of a longer process of humanization as a technology of colonial governance. Esmeir thus shifts our focus from the extralegal status of persons not recognized by the law to the ways that recognition itself becomes a site of ongoing colonial violence "directed at prescribing new modern sensibilities toward pain and at delineating the sphere of useful, legal, and acceptable violence."[47]

Against the wider backdrop of an uneven positivization of natural law, Esmeir's turn to humanization as a juridical process allows for a reconsideration of the Paris Commune as one moment in a more biopolitical narrative. If the insurrections were reworkings of the appellation *"citoyenne"* as a potentially conflictual relationship to the state, the Martinican trials gravitate around the formation of a different legal category, the "juridical human," as a way to ensure the security of the settler-colonial population. While one term suggests an emancipatory narrative for rights-based discourses, the other begins to reveal the ways that identity-based rights can act as a vehicle for domination. In different ways, the trials and their associated reports function as a technology of classification for an increasingly wide spectrum of persons. The military trials can then be understood not just as an awarding of guilt or innocence; they function as a more systematic classificatory process of legal personhood across a spectrum of racialized humanity.

Intimate Theater and the Insurrectionary Archive

In a "Note" to the play *Fire's Daughters*, Ina Césaire clarifies her intentions. Although this work is set in 1870, during Martinique's Southern Insurrection, and though the title character, Rosanie Soleil, was a historical figure, what follows is not a historical drama but a chamber play, or, in the more literal French, "a play of intimate character [*une pièce à caractère intimiste*]."[48] This is a counterintuitive claim, here at the start. The play is about history, but not historical. It is intimate, or takes place inside, in the domestic sphere. Indeed, *Fire's Daughters* is a spare production, featuring four women, the revolution off stage. From the military trial reports, we know that the eponymous heroine Rosanie Soleil received a five-year sentence for her participation in the murder of Leopold Codé. Soleil was also suspected of sorcery. According to one witness's testimony, she carried a bowl of pepper and salt to the scene of the "crime, either as poison or for cannibalistic purposes to season the body" of Codé.[49] However, none of this information appears in Césaire's play. The audience never sees the riot, the fires, the mob murder, or the subsequent trials.

The entirety of *Fire's Daughters* takes place inside a simple home that the stage directions specify as fastidiously clean. The major characters are family: Rosanie is daughter to Mother Sun and twin to Annarose. One daughter is "chabine," or blond and light-skinned, while the other is dark-skinned. For this reason, the daughters' paternity is uncertain. A fourth character, the neighbor Sister Smoke (Fumée), suggests a white priest who has since left the island might be the father, but Mother Sun insists that her lover was the son of a black Haitian. The play does not specify which version of paternity is the truth. Rather, the light skin of one twin against the darkness of the other becomes an unspoken visual testament to the persistence of sexual violence past. At certain moments, the sisters question the possible violence of their conception, almost as a taunt: "Do you know who your father is, little one? Do you?" (28). But the play does not allow these questions to be answered. Instead, interracial sexual violence is a legacy perpetually in the air, obliquely referred to but never quite stated outright. Barely a moment in the wider narrative of the play, the question of Rosanie and Annarose's paternity only gestures toward a much wider set of familial relations in *Fire's Daughters* that could be called intimate. However, rather than trace these more thematic currents, I want to consider the ways that the play situates intimacy as an experimental form, in the spatial overlay of two traditionally separated fields, insurrectionary violence and reproductive labor.

Throughout the play, four women narrate the events leading up to the insurrection. But all the while, chores are getting done. Mother Sun waters plants, arranges a tablecloth, then fills a vase. Rosanie is outside, gathering herbs. The women cook and clear the table. There are dishes to be washed and put away. This labor is ongoing, not commented upon, and so largely appears in the stage directions. "*Roseanna and Annarose are clearing the table*" (12) while they argue about the direction of the insurrection to come. In the next scene, when we learn that Mother Sun is hiding a wanted man in her home, the stage direction punctuates a moment of surprise: "(*She drops the embroidery she's been working on*)" (15). Annarose serves *soupe zhabitants* while we learn about the mob murder of Codé, the plantation owner that hung a white flag outside his home to signal a wish for the return of slavery. In act II, "*Roseanna and Annarose are in the courtyard in front of their cabin hanging freshly-washed laundry out to dry*" while the sisters argue again about the course of revolution, revealing Roseanna's involvement in the murder of Codé (27). "*On the small front porch of the cabin the four women shell peas or pick through lentils*": This is the scene when Smoke tells the history of the incident that sparked off the insurrection, though she mixes up the details, confusing the Lubin affair with another violent encounter a century earlier, between the slave Lindoret and his white master, Augier de Maintenon (30). Toward the end of the play, Rosanie, Annarose, and the Mother sit alone; "*They are busy sewing or embroidering*" (37) when the French military comes looking for the escaped insurgent. "The fire is backing up on us!" says Smoke. "Armed men are searching the cabins on Wind Hill" (40).

These labors are noted in the stage directions but not discussed in the dialogue. When the play is performed, housework becomes a constant, embodied practice that accompanies all the other actions. It is difficult to describe these actions as singular: wiping, folding, putting away. Rather, the accumulated reproductive labor that is ongoing throughout the play creates a particular sense of the meanwhile. These are actions that establish their own kind of repetitive temporality. They offer an experience of space and the bodies of other people that is most often invisible or erased. Not quite a dance or a song but also not quite narrative, these ongoing labors create a particular texture of everyday care work that is often unmarked or erased. In some cases, these labors move from the backdrop to center stage, to punctuate the overlying narrative. For instance, when Rosanie and Annarose quarrel about the identity of their absent father, alongside a different kind of inheritance, the violence of the insurrection, the scene ends with their visual dissimilarity and physical proximity: "*Folding a sheet, they come closer. Face to face, they stop and look gravely at each other*" (29).

By situating reproductive labor as a perpetual, embodied backdrop to the insurrection, *Fire's Daughters* dramatizes an intimate space that is also a political space, making unremarkable the reproductive labors necessary to keep mind and body intact during political mobilization. What is intimate, in this context, is not only the feminized, domestic sphere of labor but the insurrectionary activity in the cane fields and plantations, as narrated back and forth between women. Though we are made to understand that the play takes place in 1870, just before the beginning of the insurrection, other periods infect the telling. The four women weave together discrete historical moments: the Middle Passage, the Haitian Revolution, the Lubin affair, the Southern Insurgency.

This jumbled timeline emerges through what I understand to be the play's primary formal modality, the creole tale. As others have noted, Césaire's use of the folktale aligns her with a number of avant-garde tendencies. On one hand, she is daughter to Aimé Césaire and Suzanne Roussi, so she might seem to possess a filial relation to Négritude. On the other, Ina Césaire's work is contemporaneous with a more recent turn to creolité, though it reverses a traditionally masculinist narrative of national identity. However, Césaire's interest in Antillean ethnography began years before the rise of creolité and departs from the all-male cohort of the movement's adherents in significant ways.[50] Césaire describes her work as a theatricalization of the creole tale that popularizes more gendered histories left out of the colonial record. In Césaire's words, popular theater thus recuperates "the speech of those who are silent, those who act, those who have always acted, without their thought and their actions exceeding the family circle."[51] In this account, popular theater situates an alternative history but also shifts our understanding of where history is made and who makes it.

Set inside the family circle, *Fire's Daughters* is full of stories, as what has been known or overheard in the past, then recirculated by these four women, then passed on again. The four women go through series of questions and answers, interrupting and finishing one another's sentences. They speak in riddles and songs. The stories are a refrain, repeating and cycling. But each repetition is an additive process, contributing different details and different tellers. This is information lived with, the familiar knowledge passed back and forth, joked about and cried over, twisted up into punning songs, code, and creole verse. The characters can finish one another's sentences, correct one another, or leave words out because these are stories that they have heard before. It is a history that is part of the atmosphere, unsensational as furniture, set among the dishes cleared and laundry hung. "Well, I see you already know it all. I don't have anything left to tell you" (34). In the course of this telling, the women add other narratives not found in the state archives. "Last year when, he raped a black woman and left her for dead, Codé only had to pay a fine" (35).

The telling of stories offers a historical narrative, but it also becomes a way to communicate what is happening in the play's present tense. In this case, circumlocution is a matter of necessity. What goes unsaid is the presence of a man never seen, the injured insurrectionary wanted by the law, hidden in the house. To avoid naming this man, the women's language becomes more and more opaque. Words become coded to refer to multiple sites: "Fire" is the burning sensation of rum in the throat and rum the product of the island, cultivated by slaves; fire is the pain of childbirth, such that the twins are "fire's daughters"; the burning torches of the Haitian revolution are "a kaleidoscopic gathering of human fireflies," as intimations of the Martinican insurrection to come.

As Césaire suggested, this kind of wordplay emerges from the histories of plantation slavery, when linguistic experimentation could be understood as a tactic for slaves to communicate among one another without being understood.[52] This sense of tactics, as a way of using language, broadens out into the play's wider treatment of the historical archive. *Fire's Daughters* animates this archive not just as historical knowledge to be revealed but more strategically, with an eye toward the present tense of each performance. The prologue opens with Mother Sun doing housework, while an offstage voice reads the civil status of the accused insurrectionaries. This is a moment when the archive, as a reality fragment, is mixed into the dramatic space of the play, rough edges showing. It is a monologue I have reproduced in full:

Fleurius René-Corail: twenty-seven years old, carpenter, born and domiciled in Rivière Pilote.
Léo Magloire: known as "Tamarind Tree," twenty-two years old, fisherman, born in Rivière Pilote; domiciled in Sainte Anne.

Eugène Marius: known as "John Bull Titote," thirty-one years old, farmer, born and domiciled in Rivière Pilote.

Sonson Lacaille: known as "Turiaf," twenty-three years old, farmer, born and domiciled in Rivière Pilote.

Alcide Gruau: known as "Flea Face," forty-three years old, farmer, born and domiciled in Rivière Pilote.

Augustin Lubin: known as "Devil," forty years old, born and domiciled in Rivière Pilote.

Massamba: Africa, age unknown, farmer, domiciled in Rivière Pilote.

Alcide Bolivar: thirty years old, farmer, born in Marin, domiciled in Rivière Pilote. Wanted.

Dimbo: known as "The Good Nigger," African, age unknown, domiciled in Rivière Pilote.

Louis Telgard: sixty-eight years old, farmer, born and domiciled in Rivière Pilote.

Jorite Moutoussamy: Indian, thirty-seven years old, farmer, domiciled in Rivière Pilote.

Roro: son of Saint Marie Maison, known as "Private Alexander," carpenter, born and domiciled in Rivière Pilote.

Portaly Lacaille: known as "Taly," twenty-two years old, farmer, born and domiciled in Rivière Pilote.

Magdeleine Clem: known as "Smoke," forty-five years old, marketwoman, born and domiciled in Rivière Pilote. Wanted.

Scholastic: Wife of Siméon, thirty-three years old, farmer, born and domiciled in Rivière Pilote.

Lumina Sophie: known as "Surprise," forty years old, seamstress, born in Vauclin, domiciled in Rivière Pilote.

Roseanna Sun: twenty-four years old, laundress, born and domiciled in Rivière Pilote.[53]

The pronouncing of names, one by one, takes some time. The names take on time, giving them a kind of heft in a theatrical space that otherwise obscures the likes of John Bull Titote and Tamarind Tree. Stage directions call for a "monotone voice—which signifies the official legal system." These are not voices of the accused, the accused given voice, speaking finally, back from the dead. The law only gives voice to the civic status of colonial subjects as seen by the court. What facts are there are paltry—age, place of birth, profession. Some of the details are incorrect. Lumina Sophie, called Surprise, was nineteen, not forty years old.

The naming of persons suggests a way to think each individual person within the wider group. The naming of the individual creates particularity out of generalized suffering, as a sort of mnemonic device, giving some detail to each person lost as the son or daughter of someone, as growing up in a town that can be located on a map. Most familiar in the aesthetic of memorials, this naming of names attempts to materialize the abstraction of many, as though doing so might bestow a retrospective humanity on the numberless dead. However, to bestow personhood upon the dead, as a literary retrospective, is a tricky kind of magic, as *Fire's Daughters* makes clear.

In the opening scene of *Fire's Daughters*, the list of names is not, in itself, any sort of remedy. This naming offers a different sort of magic, in that it overlays the sonic world of the courtroom onto the visual space of the home. Rather than the establishment of a fully finished world, here the names are an irritant to realism. The litany of names creates a mode of estrangement, as we take note of two timelines: the trial marked by the offstage voice, as an impersonal ceremony of justice, and the ongoing actions of Mother Sun, which take place just before the insurrection, well before the trial. The list of names comes from a future to the play's present tense and so cannot be heard by the characters on stage. The list of names can't help but invoke remembrance; but hearing it as a soundscape that does not accord with the action on stage disrupts our habits of narrative absorption, so that we cannot quite settle into a position of sympathy or mourning.

If we begin to think of the naming of names as a tactic rather than as a memorial, the questions with which we approach the play change. It is no longer so much a matter of identification or memorialization. We do not ask, *Who was the person named? What was she like? What did she feel? How do I feel with/as her?* Instead, questions become oriented to the present tense: *How is the naming of names a demand for something else? What does this demand ask? What does the naming of names look to accomplish? What kinds of social bonds are created in the moment of collective articulation?* These questions move us out of the binaries of the individual spectator, to remember/forget, reveal/conceal. This perspective moves away from a more common framework for human rights discourses, in which the recognition and sympathy for past injury suggests some form of restitution. The list of names only abstractly represents suffering and so refuses to display the injured or tortured body as evidence.[54]

Fire's Daughters animates only certain fragments of the archive, rather than the scenarios of suffering that this archive suggests. Read from off stage, the list of names throws a disembodied voice into the juridical apparatus as a way to make claims in the present tense of each performance. By the end, the play does not narrate a ghastly history so much as actively rewrite it, through the staging of an alternative theater of justice. My sense of the dynamic between historical archive and its performance owes a debt to Diana Taylor, who has formulated an epistemological basis for understanding these seemingly opposed categories. On one hand, Taylor argues for the reconsideration of documents, maps, and letters of the written archive as an unstable site of cultural knowledge, produced through institutional selection and classification. On the other, she expands our sense of the repertoire, a term covering a wide range of embodied acts, including theater, dance, and ritual. In Taylor's account, the repertoire is not merely an ephemeral space of embodied performance but a site for the transmission and production of cultural memory. Rather than replace what has been lost or forgotten with a preferable story, the archive and the repertoire work in tandem through "acts of transfer" that allow for the "doubling, replication, and proliferation" of historical antecedents.[55]

In *Fire's Daughters*, this sort of proliferation emerges through the play's multiple and conflicting endings. The final scene is in fact a number of scenes layered over one another, each coming from distinct historical moments. There is, first, a night rally at Bois Caiman, the gathering of slaves that marked the beginning of the Haitian Revolution, and, second, a Voodoo ceremony on the eve of Martinique's Southern Insurrection. At this moment, Mother Sun is still at home, in her living room, when she sweeps a cloth off the side table to reveal a giant drum. At this moment, Mother Sun enters a kind of trance:

> **The Mother:** And there they are, climbing up and rushing down, coming from all sides and from times long past . . . Hills and Valleys are invaded by the sudden sound of thousands of bare feet. If you listen hard, you hear the murmuring of those myriad callused feet demanding recognition from the land that tore them away—until it confesses, having been worked over by all their furious stomping. Grave hands are raised, brandishing flaming torches and the Haitian forest

becomes a kaleidoscopic gathering of human fireflies suing for justice. In the middle of the clearing, the Assotor, the great drum, reigns, and the inspired drummer brings forth from it sounds which set humans in motion! Leaving behind their rag-piled pallets, they come running from all the neighboring houses; and even far-away places go into action, apprehending the meaning of the singing drum.

(45)

[**La Mere:** Et les voilà qui, venant de tous côtés des millénaires, grimpent et dévalent... Mornes et fonds sont envahis de la rumeur soudaine de milliers de pieds nus. Si on tend l'oreille, on entend le bruissement de ces milliers de pieds calleux exigeant de la terre du déracinement la reconnaissance de sa paternité, jusqu'à ce qu'elle avoue, cernée par le frottis multiple. Les mains sombres se dressent, brandissant des serbis enflammés, et la forêt de Bois Caïman n'est plus qu'un fourmillement de lucioles humaines qui réclament justice. Dans la clairière en son mitan, est dressé le grand tambour, l'Assotor sacré, et le frappeur inspiré en fait jaillir le son qui hèle ! Délaissant leur couche de hardes, ils accourent de toutes les habitations voisines, et les lointaines, saisissant le sens du rhombe retransmis, se mettent, elles aussi, en branle.]

(127–28)

Here Mother Sun is no longer a character in the play but a teller of stories. She keeps these stories in an active tense but refers to only parts of the body: the bare feet making demands, the raised hands holding torches. In a disjunctive pairing, the language here is both mystical and highly juridical: the feet "demanding recognition from the land that tore them away—until it confesses, having been worked over by all their furious stomping." Here the language of recognition, the awarding of the status of citizen or human by the nation-state, becomes transformed into a quite different interaction, between masses of people and the earth beneath their feet. At this moment, the Haitian forest is "a kaleidoscopic gathering of human fireflies suing for justice." In this scenario, humanity is not awarded to the colonial subjects; nor is it a status to be achieved at the end of a wider process. Caught in a trance between two islands, Mother Sun narrates a scene of collective action wherein the people involved are not designated through narratives of humanity but described through their actions in concert—the stomping of feet and the raising of hands. In this case, "suing for justice" takes place outside of the courtroom, through the drum that brings these feet and hands together, with torches that will set the plantations on fire.

At this moment, intimacy does not mark a romance, or even affection, but the closeness of traditionally separated fields. The law creeps into the home, the trial in the kitchen, the stomping feet and the fires on the front porch. This closeness makes visible the brutality of living with violence, sometimes inside or written on the body. But it also points to a version of what could have been or what might still be, investing the past with a potential to unfold into a new present. In many ways, the histories told by Smoke and Mother Sun, weaving the Haitian Revolution into the Middle Passage into the Insurrection of the South, return us to the woman Cyrille's claim, from the transcript of the military trials, that everything was happening again, now. To end at the beginning and to begin at the end suggest a different understanding of historical causality, or, in the words of the woman Cyrille, the possibility that the ruins of the past might be reanimated in a different present.

Fire's Daughters ends there, on the eve of the insurrection. It is a strangely happy ending for a story whose protagonists will soon be sentenced to death, life imprisonment, or exile. Says Mother Sun, amid the beating of the Assotor and the sound of a thousand feet, "The Iron God Ogun will transform your ribbons into bullets! Tomorrow, they'll plunge into the bodies of those who refuse to let us be human beings!" (46). But we know that the ribbons did not become bullets. The pepper-water Molotovs and the rocks thrown from the women's skirts did not stop the French cavalry. The tonics made of rum did not make the skin invulnerable. It was a rout, the former slaves entirely outmatched in terms of military power. *Fire's Daughters* ends just before this defeat.

In some ways, this is the wrong story, or would seem to leave us with the wrong impression of the insurrection as a historical event. However, the military trials that followed the insurrection aren't entirely excluded from the narrative. In the final scene, we can't quite forget the prologue's list of names, as an *after* to the play's present tense. At this moment, some of the names from the prologue become reworked into the play's ongoing narrative. Rosanie, Annarose, the Mother, and Smoke name the people that they will join on the first night of the insurrection. It is an echo of the play's prologue that transforms the civil status of the accused into a more diffuse register of personhood. Here the names become more intimately configured as people caught up in a network of affiliation. They are spoken to and claimed: "They call you 'Papa Turiaf,' for despite your youth you are wise and courageous" (46); "We call her 'Surprise,' because who would believe a little seamstress, as shy as a hummingbird and as thin as a bamboo pole, could set fire to the town jail?" (46). "Tomorrow, at nightfall, the torches of Telgard, the red-haired negro; of Jorite Moutoussamy, the big Indian; of Astérie, the chambermaid; of John Bull Titote, cane cutter by profession; of Roro Privat, the carpenter will illuminate the slow climb towards the Hills" (47).

Consider the beginning and ending of the play as imperfect echoes. In each, the list of names is a kind of memorial, in that it makes public an otherwise little-known history. But this naming also expands our sense of the legal archive, reproduced in whole or reworked into a more intimate network of affiliation—"We call her 'Surprise.'" This is a moment when the archive is not an accumulation of facts about the past but a tactic for the present. The archive, in this sense, is something used, and the particulars of this use are different each time the play is performed, wherever and whenever the play is performed. That is to say, the list of names is a tactic in the present tense of its performance. Like all tactics, it can be reiterated to different effect, on the street, in the square, or at the theater. The list of names makes space for a demand with an uncertain content, one that broadly marks out something else or other than the perpetual accumulation of colonial bodies imprisoned, exiled, and murdered by the state. The content of this demand might look different given the time and place of its articulation, depending on who is there to say and hear it. But the names of the accused are the same, and saying them on stage takes some time. There is Fleurius René-Corail; Léo Magloire, known as Tamarind Tree; Eugène Marius, known as John Bull Titote; Sonson Lacaille, known as Turiaf; Alcide Gruau, known as Flea Face; Augustin Lubin, known as Devil; Massamba; Alcide Bolivar; Dimbo, known as the Good Nigger; Louis Telgard; Jorite Moutoussamy; Roro, known as Private Alexander; Portaly Lacaille, known as Taly; Magdeleine Clem, known as Smoke; Scholastic, wife of Siméon; Lumina Sophie, known as Surprise; and Roseanna Sun. What changes in each performance is the demand this naming animates, the *to whom* and *for what*, or the rough contours of an *against*, in the here and now of its saying.

2

The Long Middle

Militant Suffrage from Britain to South Africa

In 1914, the Criminal Record Office at Scotland Yard began to circulate surveillance photographs of known suffragette militants. The photographs come with a numbered key that lists identifying features, including age, height, eye color, hair color, and crime. The images are not uniform, so the resulting photomontage looks a little haphazard. According to the Central Officer's Special Report, this inconsistency was caused by nonparticipation on the part of the prisoners. For instance, the actress Kitty Marion (age 42, 5 foot 5½ inches, blue eyes, auburn hair, arson) refused to have her photograph taken at Holloway, so police used what looks like a newspaper publicity still.[1] Some of the images have been doctored. Evelyn Manesta (age 26, 5 foot 2 inches, gray eyes, fair hair, damage) also didn't want her picture taken, but a warden held her in place by the neck (figure 2.3). In the photograph circulated for surveillance purposes, the warden's arm has been cut out of the picture, so that it looks like Manesta is all sharp angles, tilting oddly to one side, eyes closed.

The Metropolitan Police began to circulate the surveillance photographs after a number of suffragettes destroyed paintings in public galleries to draw attention to their cause. Though some of the women pictured were convicted of museum damage, most were chosen because they were serial offenders for the destruction of property. After the passage of the 1913 Cat and Mouse Act, hunger-striking prisoners could be released to hospice if their health warranted serious medical concern, then rearrested to finish the sentences after they had recovered. As a result, many women were perpetually in and out of prison over the next two years. In the spring of 1913, for instance, Mary

FIGURE 2.1 "Suffragettes 1–10." Photograph composite, 1914.
Source: Wallace Collection, © The National Archives, London.

Fig.	Name.	Year born	Height Ft. In.	Eyes	Hair.	C.R.O. Number	Crime.
1	Scott Margaret	1888	5. 3	Blue.	D.Brown.	S.168379	Damage.
2	Hookin Olive.	1881	5. 3½	Brown	Brown	S.169280	Conspiry.
3	McFarlane Margaret	1888	5. 1	Hazel	Brown	S.168518	Damage
4	Wyan Mary @ Nellie Taylor.	1864	5. 1	Brown	Brown	S.168705	Damage
5	Bell Annie @ Hannah Booth and Elizabeth Bell.	1874	5.6½	Blue	Lt.Brn.	S.165769	Damage
6	Short Jane @ Rachel Peace.	1882	5. 3	Blue	Brown	S.168517	Arson
7	Ansell Gertrude Mary	–	5. 4	Grey	Tg.Grey	S.169570	Damage
8	Brindley Maud	1866	5. 3	Grey	Grey	S.167057	Damage
9	Oates Verity	..	5. 0	Brown	Brown	S.172313	Damage
10	Manesta Evelyn	1888	5. 2	Grey	Fair	S.166692	Damage

FIGURE 2.2 "Key to suffragette images," 1914.
Source: Wallace Collection, © The National Archives, London.

FIGURE 2.3 "Evelyn Manesta, suffragette, under restraint for a prison photograph."
Source: Prison Commission and Home Office Prison Department, 1913. © The National Archives, London.

Raleigh Richardson (age 31, 5 foot 5½ inches, brown eyes, brown hair, arson) was apprehended for window breaking, sent to Holloway Prison, released through the Cat and Mouse Act, arrested four more times on new charges, sent back to Holloway, released early through the Cat and Mouse Act again, then arrested nine days later. By the end of the month, she had been sentenced and released, then rearrested for obstruction.[2] The 215-page handwritten *Index of Women Suffragettes Arrested* lists the dates and locations for her arrests, which tended toward the same areas: in March on Bow Street, April on the Thames, July on Bow Street and then in North London, August on Bow Street, October on Feltham Street and then, eleven days later, London Sessions; the next year, March, on Bow Street; then London Sessions, two days later (figure 2.4).[3]

I linger on the particulars of these archives because I want to feel out this sense of political action as something that, while sometimes spectacular or militant, also goes on and on, back and forth, day in and day out. Most widely, this chapter is concerned with the ways that these catalogue-heavy

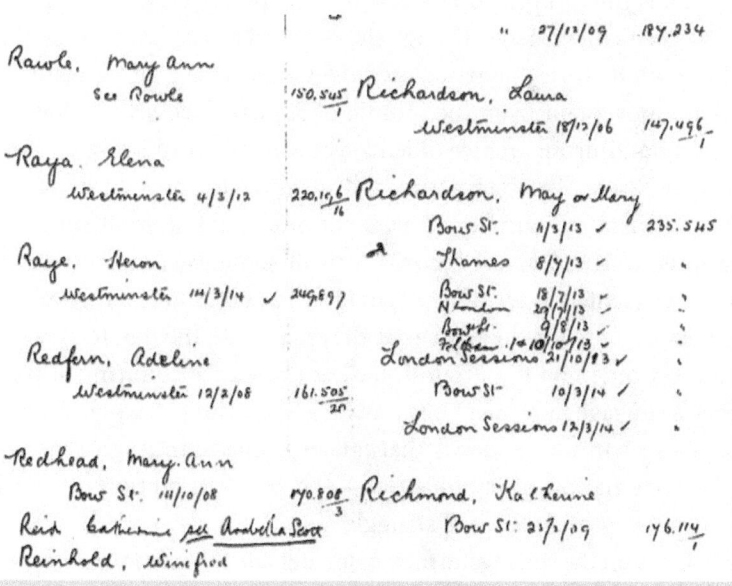

FIGURE 2.4 Arrest record of Mary Raleigh Richardson (detail). *Amnesty of August 1914: Index of Women Suffragists Arrested, 1906–1914 (1914–1935)*.
Source: Government Papers, the National Archives, Kew.

archives reveal what I call the long middle of the militant suffragette movement, severed from the demand for the vote. Histories of the women's movement often position militant tactics as a bargaining chip for suffrage but rarely theorize the day-to-day life of the tactics themselves as a world-making practice. In recovering these archives, this chapter looks to understand the ways that an extended campaign of window breaking, bomb planting, prison hunger strikes, and nocturnal arson might have looked from the ground, from the perspective of the people involved. Though my focus on the daily life of tactics is informed by more contemporary debates in communization theory that emphasize the means of struggle as opposed to the endpoint of demands, what follows will situate the local particulars of first-wave feminist direct action as productive of its own, historically specific theory and praxis of revolution.[4]

In many ways, my reconsideration of early women's movements, through emphasis on the cyclical nature of riot and arson campaigns, hopes to locate a prehistory (certainly one among others) for the occupation of squares, highways, and airports so visible as a form of protest today. To tell this story necessitates the formulation of new reading practices, as a way to reorient early women's movements through the rubric of tactics, rather than the more well-known histories of articulated demands. This chapter resituates the women's movement from the middle of its historical arc, with particular focus on building an archive of female citizenship through attention to the daily experience of women acting and speaking together. To construct this archive, I turn to a number of texts not often held up to literary scrutiny: mugshots, indexes, arrest records, prison sentences, meeting schedules, tables of contents, life writing, plot diagrams, and unfinished novels. I chose these documents for the ways that they illustrate the day-to-day political action of women on the ground. Rather than an accounting of the wider women's suffrage movement or first-wave feminism as a whole, this chapter highlights a feminist tendency that can be glimpsed through a shared focus on the reclamation of public space—and the reformation of social relations—in the present tense of struggle.

My focus on the suffragette movement outside the rubric of the vote builds on the important work of Ewa Płonowska Ziarek, who has studied the ways that the more common division of factions into militant/nonmilitant obscures a more diffuse political inclination focused on what the suffragist Teresa Billington-Grieg called "the right to revolt."[5] While Ziarek's work offers an extended reading of suffragists' political writing, I turn instead to a body of literary texts keyed to the experiential life of day-to-day feminist action. In so doing, I take up Janet Lyon's foundational assertion that suffragette militants be considered an avant-garde formation on their own terms, in that their focus on violence, rupture, and direct action precedes and continues into conversation with both the futurist and vorticist movements.[6] Moving across a wide variety of literary genres often classed as conservative or confessional, I position these texts as part of an avant-garde culture keyed to rethinking the temporality of women's action. In these accounts of the women's movement, a focus on tactics in the present tense necessitates a lengthening of narrative middles. In other words, there is a kind of stretching and flattening of narrative chronology to accommodate the temporality of a struggle focused on means in the present tense rather than ends in the future. What follows will track this long middle across a number of linked terrains, including popular suffrage fiction, suffragette autobiography, Rebecca West's unfinished novel *The Sentinel*, and the vorticist journal *BLAST*.

Finally, a focus on action shifts the ways we understand the temporality of the women's movement in relationship to colonial formations and early human rights discourses. Histories of imperial feminism in a transnational perspective often seize upon the ways that women invoked the language of human rights in a universalizing key that relied on a racial timeline wherein white women are classed as farther along on the civilizing spectrum than colonized persons.[7] However, what remains underexplored in these accounts is the way that the language of transnational human rights was mobilized in the courtroom as a defensive tactic against the state. To consider both of these narratives, the last section of this chapter turns to juridical attempts to categorize the force-feeding of hunger-striking suffragettes as a human rights abuse, with particular attention to the 1909 trial of the suffragette Mary Leigh.

Reading Women's Riots

Popular fictional accounts of the wider suffrage movement are disconcertingly alike. With almost perfect regularity, these novels position the suffragist character as the third point in a love triangle. Concerned with politics rather than love, the suffragist temporarily foils the marriage plot. The novel inevitably ends in a marriage, happy or not, with the suffragist cast aside. In an early instance of this trend, Henry James's *The Bostonians* (1886), the suffragist Olive Chancellor demands that the ingénue Verena Tallart renounce heterosexual married love for the women's cause. After much back and forth, on the last page of the novel, Verena abandons the grand opening of her suffragist speaking tour and becomes engaged to the dashing antisuffragist Basil Ransom. Olive is left alone on stage in a pose of dejected expiation. To the highly impressionable Basil, she looks like "some feminine firebrand of Paris revolutions, erect on a barricade."[8] In Elizabeth Robins's *The Convert* (1907), the unearthed romantic past of the suffragette Vida Levering causes a temporary rift in the engagement between the Tory politician Geoffrey Stonor and Jean Dunbarton, who eventually reconcile. Virginia Woolf's *Night and Day* (1919) is only peripherally a suffrage novel in the midst of a wider Edwardian marriage plot: five characters switch places in various romantic couplings, beginning with a mismatch (Katherine and William), a foiled proposal (Mary and Ralph), another foiled proposal (Ralph and Katherine) and then ending, quite neatly, with two engagements: Katherine and Ralph, William and Cassandra. The character that remains unmarried is the fifth wheel of this foursome, the suffragist Mary Datchet, who renounces romantic love for a life of feminist political activism. Mary makes a Faustian bargain both comic and depressing: "as she shaped her conception of life in this world, only two articulate words escaped her, muttered beneath her breath—'Not happiness—not happiness.' . . . Her post should be in one of those exposed and desolate stations which are shunned naturally by happy people."[9]

H. G. Wells's *Ann Veronica* (1909) offers a twist in this pattern. Here the protagonist Ann is the suffragette in question. Ann leaves home, attends university, joins up with the suffragettes, is arrested, goes to prison, renounces the wider suffrage movement, then declares her love for her older, married professor Capes, who cannot secure a divorce from his estranged wife. This is a marriage plot that does not quite end in a marriage, according to the church. However, Ann does unambiguously renounce the women's movement in order to live in extramarital romantic partnership with Capes. More vexed, but just as autobiographically inclined, is Ford Maddox Ford's *Some Do Not* (1924), which begins with the unhappy marriage of Sylvia and Tietjins, complicated by Tietjins's affair with the suffragette Valentine Wannop. Colmore's *Suffragette Sally* (1911) strays from this model in part—at the end of the novel, the suffragette protagonist dies after being forcibly fed and beaten in prison. Across this disparate set of novels, the suffragist follows two plot arcs: she is the other woman, a spinster cast aside, or she renounces her former life of politics in favor of romantic love.

In this way, popular suffrage fiction follows the classical eighteenth-century bildungsroman. These novels of youthful development traditionally posit a problematic, refractory personality that internalizes social norms in a process of education. Over the course of the novel, the protagonist's eventual harmonization with existing society becomes optimistically painted as an individual choice. In the work of Goethe or Flaubert, the most cited of the genre's progenitors, a young male narrator enters the world rife with hopeful illusions. Over the course of the novel's development, this Wilhelm or Frédéric loses his illusions to become, finally, a mature subject in accordance, however unhappily, with the norms of bourgeois society. Over the course of the novel, the protagonist's eventual harmonization with existing society becomes optimistically painted as an individual choice. Such novels leave us with a protagonist in accord with social norms. "The bourgeoisie," writes Franco Moretti, "are cured of the mental poison of 'prejudice'—the aristocrats manage to curb the humiliating indifference of their 'pride.'"[10] Thus class divisions become resolved, resuturing the social antagonisms that might lead to revolution. The classic eighteenth-century bildungsroman, in Moretti's memorable phrasing, "narrates how the French Revolution could have been avoided."[11]

In Rita Felski's influential account, the presence of a female protagonist offers the nineteenth-century bildungsroman a different kind of politics. For Felski, woman's entrance into the public sphere was no small thing; it was a revision of the very category "woman."[12] For Felski, the heroine's movement out of the private sphere is also a movement into historical time. In these later novels, the heroine's youthful development does not necessarily produce an accordance of self and the given world but rather lays the foundations for the possibility of an antagonistic relation to the norms of bourgeois society. Building on Felski's intervention, I want to reconsider suffrage autobiographies as antibildgungsromans. In this case, the narrative does not serve as a revision of the category "woman" but as a revision of the temporality of the women's *revolution*.

Like the novel of development, these autobiographies begin, in almost every instance, with a youthful subject making her way into the world. The course of the text follows the development of the individual alongside the development of the women's movement. However, this development proceeds according to an unusual formal structure. To understand this difference, it is helpful to turn, momentarily, to Bakhtin's description of the bildungsroman, which documents man's emergence alongside a changing historical landscape. Here the protagonist does not develop against an "immobile background of the world, ready-made":

> He emerges *along with the world* and he reflects the historical emergence of the world itself. He is no longer within an epoch, but on the border between two epochs, at the transition point from one to the other. This transition is accomplished in him and through him. He is forced to become a new, unprecedented type of human being. What is happening here is precisely the emergence of a new man.[13]

What I want to seize on here is this sense of a "new, unprecedented type of human being." When we turn to the firsthand accounts of the women's movement, a corpus that includes a surprising number of texts, this sense of "a new type of human being" follows, but it looks quite different. That is to say, against traditional accounts of the bildungsroman, the suffragette autobiography presents a new sort of human being at the very *beginning* of the story, rather than at its end.

I should be clear: these texts are autobiographies, not novels. Yet though these firsthand accounts often quote from the historical record, repeating speeches verbatim, they also frequently tarry with the conventions of fictionality. Alongside the more famous works by Emmeline Pankhurst and her daughters, Christabel and Sylvia, a partial list of suffrage autobiographies reads as follows: Teresa Billington-Grieg, *Towards Women's Liberty* (1907); Constance Lytton, *Prisons and Prisoners* (1914); Annie Kenney, *Memories of a Militant* (1924); Margaret Wynne Nevinson, *Life's Fitful Fever* (1926); Lady Rhondda, *This Was My World* (1933); Evelyn Sharp, *Unfinished Adventure* (1933); Cicely Hamilton, *Life Errant* (1935); Emmeline Pethick-Lawrence, *My Part in a Changing World* (1938); Elizabeth Robins, *Both Sides of the Curtain* (1940); Clara Codd, *So Rich a Life* (1952); Mary Raleigh Richardson, *Laugh a Defiance* (1953); Mary Gawthorpe, *Uphill to Holloway* (1962); and Hannah Mitchell, *The Hard Way Up* (1968). Though this corpus has not attracted a great amount of critical scrutiny, what secondary literature exists generally approaches these texts according to the conventions of autobiography. Key words include "authenticity," "testimony," "self-representation," and "confession."[14]

However, I want to consider this body of work as an experiment in narrative chronology. Though straightforward at the level of the sentence—and often somewhat cloying in the narration of sentiment—the suffrage narratives are strangely plotted. Here the transformation of the protagonist occurs at the beginning of the narrative, rather than its end. What follows is something like a sine curve, an up and down of discrete, often repeating events that do not lead to a dramatic denouement. An unresolved dialectic of mobilization and repression, this new structure turns against the progressive nature of the bildungsroman.

Though Annie Kenney is neither the most eloquent author (that would be Teresa Billington-Grieg) nor the most steadfastly militant of the suffragettes (Mary "Slasher" Richardson is a strong contender there), Kenney's narrative will become our first test case, in part for the unblushing sincerity of her opening lines: "All through my life, at least all of my thinking life, I have been on a quest. My search has been with one object in view, and that object has been to find myself."[15] In this way, *Memories of a Militant* (1924) begins with the author's youthful ambitions, though the text quickly covers this ground. In two short chapters, Kenney grows up and goes to work in a Lancashire cotton factory. She attends confirmation classes and joins a traveling choir. Then, thirty pages into this three-hundred-plus-page work, Kenney swiftly joins the suffragette movement and is arrested for disrupting a meeting in the Free Trade Hall. Here we find the language of the attainment of self-knowledge not at the end of the narrative but very close to its beginning: "The following week I lived on air; I simply could not eat; I wanted to be quiet and alone. I did not feel elated or excited. A sense of deep stillness took possession of me. It was as though half of me was present; where the other half was I never asked" (*MM* 28). "I knew *the* change had come into life. The old life had gone, a new life had come. Had I found on my return that I had taken on a new body, I should not have been in the least surprised. I felt absolutely changed. The past seemed blotted out. I had started on a new cycle" (*MM* 42).

We might be skeptical of these accounts of metamorphosis or find the prospect of self-realization somewhat saccharine. The avant-gardes, in their perpetual war against the coherent subject of the realist novel, would certainly take this more critical stance. Yet the point I would like to make has nothing to do with skepticism or sentimentality. What is most important here is a somewhat old-fashioned matter of plotting—of one thing happening after another. These moments of transformation, literally imagined through the taking up of a new body alongside the taking up of a new politics, happen at the very beginning of the story. After this, the narrative does not really develop toward some gain, say, for example, the vote: "How we should win, when we should win, I never asked," writes Kenney. "I lived then as I have lived nearly all my life, not in the past or in the future, but in the 'eternal now.' To live in the 'now' makes life far simpler" (*MM* 38).

To imagine this "now," Kenney's narrative follows a wavering arc, not quite an escalation, but a continual wax and wane of political mobilization and police repression. Some enumeration is necessary to understand this sense of rising and falling action on repeat. *Memories of a Militant* progresses as follows: there is the time spent in Strangeways Jail, then London, a small protest, back to Manchester, the General Election, propaganda, London again, organization, a dry spell, frustration, private meetings, public meetings, mobilization in the East End, committee meetings, banner making, arrest, Holloway Prison, boredom, a raid on Parliament, many more arrests, Holloway Prison again, release, a speech, travel, holiday, Germany, propaganda, Switzerland, a raid on Parliament, arrest, a different prison, speeches, the hunger strikes, the Conciliation Bill, a pageant, a march, a riot, mass arrests. At this point, we have arrived, approximately, at the midpoint of Kenney's three-hundred-plus-page narrative. Here she notes, somewhat wryly, "My life in 1911 was spent largely in repeating all I had done in 1910" (*MM* 167).

Continuing to move from event to event, *Memories of a Militant* seems to have too much plot, to be so overpopulated with events that any given chapter appears as a list of things simply happening, one after another. This sense of the list is possible, in part, because there is a strange horizontality to these plotted events, as though no single action were any more important than another. Boredom, prison, speeches, pamphlets, arrest, banner making. Turning points are lacking, as are transitions. Discussions of consequence are generally avoided. The book seems to be one long middle, lacking defining moments and narrative resolution. Against the bildungsroman's arc of development, this account of the suffragette movement turns back and forth, on and on, as a sort of picaresque of revolutionary action: we do this, we do that. Indeed, most of *Memories of a Militant* hews to this very particular sense of the list. These are not lists that detail abundance. We do not hear about every kind of person or the details of any particular landscape. These lists are not Whitman's or Zola's. They do not capture or fill out the multiplicity of a world in realist detail. That is to say, Kenney's use of the list

THE LONG MIDDLE   79

does not occur at the level of the sentence. The contents of the lists are the contents of a plot through which a character moves, quite quickly: London, a protest, arrest, prison, release. Even the most careful reader is bound to lose track, a bit, of these oft repeating events, because there is no easily locatable progression toward a goal.

Lest this experience seem confined to Annie Kenney's account, I want to consider a broader survey of tables of contents, themselves read as texts. Consider, for example, the chapter progression of Mary Raleigh Richardson's *Laugh a Defiance*:

I It All Starts
II "Black Friday"
III I Am a Militant
IV Prison
V Derby Day
VI A Funeral
VII We Were Everywhere
VIII In Parliament
IX Broken Glass
X I Call on the Bishop
XI A Police Raid
XII Hyde Park
XIII The Garden Party
XIV Boating on the Thames
XV A Cancelled Meeting and a Protest
XVI At the London Pavilion
XVII Inside Holloway
XVIII Outside the Old Bailey
XIX Holloway Again
XX "Cat and Mouse"
XXI The "Agent Provocateur"
XXII Tea with a Judge
XIII What We Stood For
XIV Re-Arrest and an Escape
XV An Invitation to Bristol
XVI "A Petition, Your Majesty!"
XVII Débutantes
XVIII Christmas Party

XIX News from the World Outside
XXX An Invitation from Mrs. Pankhurst
XXXI A Mystery
XXXII The Foreign Office Reception
XXXIII Psychiatrists
XXXIV At Mrs. Lyon's
XXXV The Rokeby Venus
XXXVI Convalescence
XXXVII Arson
XXXVIII War
XXXIX Peace[16]

Like Kenney, Richardson writes an overpopulated plot not just because many things happen but because they happen over and over, in different variations ("Holloway Again"). As early as the fifth page, the climactic moment of "self-realization" occurs: "I was a mere novice—yes, an uncertain, faltering one right up to the night when the great gathering of women came together." (There is, here, a paragraph break.) "After that everything was changed" (*L* 5). The chapters that follow move from place to place, from acts of mobilization to the experience of police repression: "We Were Everywhere," "Re-Arrest and an Escape." After a long detailing of actions, Richardson's narrative ends with a petering off. The women's movement is suspended with the onset of war: "Thus, uneventfully, the most eventful women's movement known to history came to an end" (*L* 191). That last chapter, "Peace," is less than a page long. There Richardson recalls, through a stated obligation for historical accuracy, a necessary "mention" of the constitutional suffrage reform achieved after the war.

As the table of contents might suggest, Richardson's writing is rather high-toned; she is a maker of definitive proclamations: "I Am a Militant," "We Were Everywhere." Kenney's chapter titles are more straightforward, often linking a series of actions through the dash phrase. The contents of chapter 12 make a small narrative unto themselves: "I VISIT MR. ASQUITH'S CONSTITUENCY: EAST FIFE—WE STORM PARLIAMENT—MANY ARRESTS—THE BEGINNING OF MILITANCY IN LONDON—HOLLOWAY—THE OLD SUFFRAGE SOCIETIES GIVE THE MILITANTS A DINNER ON THEIR RELEASE." Meanwhile, Sylvia Pankhurst separates her narrative into nine books, each containing a dozen or so chapters with briefer headings and the odd quotation: "IX. BLACK FRIDAY—DEATH OF MARY CLARK—AMERICA X. THE TRUCE RENEWED XI. END OF THE TRUCE—REBELLION SPREADING 'LIKE FOOT AND MOUTH DISEASE.'" Set side by side, this selection of tables from Richardson, Kenney, and Pankhurst resemble variations on the list form, on long middles differently articulated, differently styled, but nevertheless, in each case, beginning with the politicization of the subject and then moving back and forth, from event to event, without a secure narrative conclusion.

In many ways, these tables of contents visually resemble a weekly column appearing in *Votes for Women*, the official newspaper of the WSPU. The title for this column varied across the years. It appears as "The Revolutionaries," "The Revolutionary Movement," and "Actions of The Revolutionary Party." The column details arrests, protests, meeting times, and court dates.

It is worthwhile to spend a moment really working through these particulars, in order, as they appear on the page. Subsequent histories of the suffrage movement almost always cite this archive in the endnotes, as a useful, if dry, enumeration of fact seemingly divorced from subjective experience. See, for example, Antonia Raeburn's early history of the women's

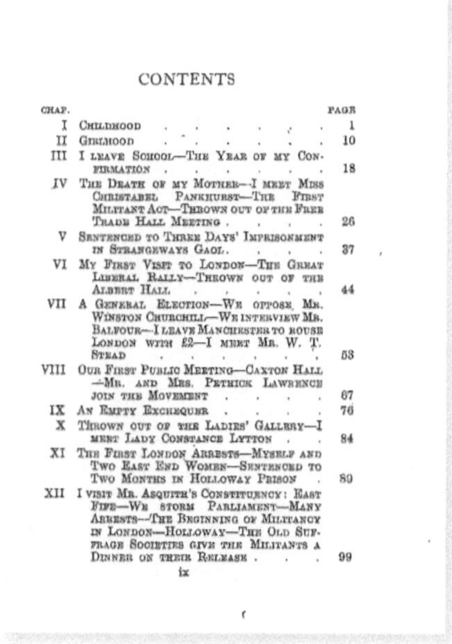

CONTENTS

CHAP.		PAGE
I	Childhood	1
II	Girlhood	10
III	I leave School—The Year of my Confirmation	18
IV	The Death of my Mother—I meet Miss Christabel Pankhurst—The First Militant Act—Thrown out of the Free Trade Hall Meeting	26
V	Sentenced to Three Days' Imprisonment in Strangeways Gaol	37
VI	My First Visit to London—The Great Liberal Rally—Thrown out of the Albert Hall	44
VII	A General Election—We oppose Mr. Winston Churchill—We interview Mr. Balfour—I leave Manchester to rouse London with £2—I meet Mr. W. T. Stead	53
VIII	Our First Public Meeting—Caxton Hall—Mr. and Mrs. Pethick Lawrence join the Movement	67
IX	An Empty Exchequer	76
X	Thrown out of the Ladies' Gallery—I meet Lady Constance Lytton	84
XI	The First London Arrests—Myself and Two East End Women—Sentenced to Two Months in Holloway Prison	89
XII	I visit Mr. Asquith's Constituency: East Fife—We storm Parliament—Many Arrests—The Beginning of Militancy in London—Holloway—The Old Suffrage Societies give the Militants a Dinner on their Release	99

ix

FIGURE 2.5 Annie Kenney, table of contents, *Memories of a Militant* (London: Edward Arnold, 1924), ix.

CONTENTS

		PAGE
	PREFACE	ix
I	It all Starts	1
II	"Black Friday"	7
III	I am a Militant	11
IV	Prison	15
V	Derby Day	19
VI	A Funeral	23
VII	We Were Everywhere	27
VIII	In Parliament	36
IX	Broken Glass	39
X	I Call on the Bishop	44
XI	A Police Raid	49
XII	Hyde Park	53
XIII	The Garden Party	58
XIV	Boating on the Thames	63
XV	A Cancelled Meeting and a Protest	68
XVI	At the London Pavilion	71
XVII	Inside Holloway	74
XVIII	Outside the Old Bailey	79
XIX	Holloway Again	82
XX	"Cat and Mouse"	86
XXI	The "Agent Provocateur"	90

FIGURE 2.6 Mary Raleigh Richardson, table of contents, *Laugh a Defiance* (London: George Weidenfeld & Sons, 1953), vii.

CONTENTS
BOOK V

CHAP.		PAGE
I.	STUDENT DAYS—THE W.S.P.U. APPEARS IN THE LOBBY	171
II.	MILITANT TACTICS BEGIN	189
III.	THE YOUNG LABOUR PARTY	201
IV.	THE PETHICK LAWRENCES—THE STRUGGLE IN THE LADIES' GALLERY—DEPUTATION TO CAMPBELL-BANNERMAN	206
V.	CLEMENTS INN	220
VI.	HOLLOWAY PRISON	228
VII.	THE BREAK WITH THE LABOUR PARTY	241
VIII.	THE LONDON COSSACK, "QUI VEUT LA FIN VEUT LES MOYENS"	252

PART II
BOOK VI

I.	THE WOMEN'S FREEDOM LEAGUE AND THE W.S.P.U. TRIUMVIRATE	261
II.	ASQUITH BECOMES PRIME MINISTER—"PREMIER'S GREAT REFORM BILL!"—VOTES FOR WOMEN	275
III.	"HELP THE SUFFRAGETTES TO RUSH THE HOUSE OF COMMONS!"	288
IV.	THE HUNGER STRIKE—THE FIRST STONE THROWERS	301
V.	FORCIBLE FEEDING	312
VI.	HARRY	320
VII.	"JANE WARTON"	326
VIII.	THE TRUCE AND THE CONCILIATION BILL	334
IX.	BLACK FRIDAY—DEATH OF MARY CLARKE—AMERICA	342
X.	THE TRUCE RENEWED	351
XI.	END OF THE TRUCE—REBELLION SPREADING "LIKE FOOT AND MOUTH DISEASE"	356

BOOK VII

I.	ARREST OF THE PETHICK LAWRENCES—FLIGHT OF CHRISTABEL PANKHURST—DEFEAT OF THE CONCILIATION BILL	370
II.	MRS. PANKHURST AND THE PETHICK LAWRENCES AT THE OLD BAILEY	386
III.	ARSON AND THE POPULAR AGITATION	393

FIGURE 2.7 Sylvia Pankhurst, table of contents, *The Suffragette Movement: An Intimate Account of Persons and Ideals* (London: Longman, 1931).

FIGURE 2.8 "The Revolutionaries," *Votes for Women*, April 10, 1914, 428.

FIGURE 2.9 "Actions of the Revolutionary Party," *Votes for Women*, March 20, 1914, 6.

FIGURE 2.10 "At Bow Street on Wednesday. The Home Secretary's Intervention—Sir Albert de Rutzen's Comments. 109 Prisoners Discharged—34 Awaiting Judgment—19 Cases Adjourned Till Thursday," *Votes for Women*, November 25, 1910, 129.

movement. This table is taken directly from the "Votes for Women" column and reproduced, without comment, in Raeburn's appendix.

I am less interested in this weekly column as a historical record of what really happened, although I believe the events listed to be fairly accurate. Rather, I want to highlight the aesthetic of these timelines as a visualization of the chronology of political practice. That the timeline, as a visualization of history, is no neutral or objective fact is not a new point. In his well-known discussion of *The Annals of St. Gall*, Hayden White argued, some time ago, that the timeline reveals an understanding of history particular to the medieval period. In the annals, there is no indication of cause and effect, no distinction between natural disaster and human action. For White, this record imagines a world "in which things *happen to* people rather than one in which people *do* things."[17] What imagination of history and, with it, of political action can be found in the "Revolutionaries" column? Note, first, among the dates of arrests and releases, that this is the imagination of a world in which women do things to history; as the titles remind us, these are actions. But what, exactly, are the important things? Why is the burning of buildings listed in the same breath as damage to letters and dates of prison release? Why are these rather sensational acts given no more space than upcoming court dates and meeting times? Where is the annotation of what mattered and didn't? My contention is that these timelines visualize a story

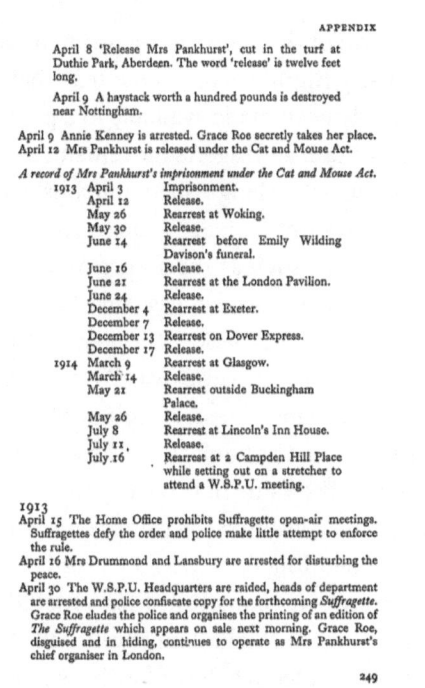

FIGURE 2.11 Antonia Raeburn, *The Militant Suffragette Movement* (London: Michael Joseph, 1973), 249.

about a revolution that is ongoing, one in which we do not yet know, with any certainty, the final consequence of any given political act. That is to say, these timelines do not present a perspective from a later historical moment that views all suffrage action as a cumulative movement toward the parliamentary vote that we know ensued. Rather, these timelines, these tables of contents, and the list-like plots of the suffrage autobiographies create a historical perspective from the middle, what Annie Kenney referred to as the "now." This perspective of the middle involves the estrangement of the means of struggle in the present tense from ends in the future. In many ways, such a perspective muddles the political actions of a group and the way that we make such actions legible, as important or merely incidental, many years later.

Rebecca West's Revolutionary Picaresque

What might a perspective of the "now" of the women's movement look like in a more conventionally literary work? One text that might answer this question has only recently been made available to a popular audience. A fictional account of the militant suffragette movement, the handwritten manuscript of *The Sentinel* (1911–1913) languished unpublished and misfiled in the University of Tulsa's library until 2002.[18] Though *The Sentinel* is not dated, a number of historical details, such as the scenes of force-feeding and direct references to specific suffrage riots, suggest that West was working on the novel circa 1909–1912. During this period, the teenage Cicely Isabel Fairfield, who had not yet settled on a pen name, was living in Edinburgh. She had been involved in the suffrage movement there since the age of fourteen. That said, I don't want to approach the book as a mere apprenticeship effort leading up to grander things. The value in this early work is not what it predicts but the way we can see the author trying things out—the appropriation of a language and then the shedding of it, after a paragraph or two, the dipping into various mannerisms, the sometimes lead-footed prose—before the solidification of something we might definitively call West's style. It would seem that the search for an adequate form for the women's movement was a matter of trial and error. West needed to get it wrong not because she was naïve or untried but because this getting it wrong, so often expressed as a shuttling back and forth between styles, becomes the very form—perverse, illogical, repetitive—in which the novel resides.

The Sentinel has three sections. The first mimes the conventions of a female bildungsroman. A sixteen-year old Adela Furnival becomes infatuated with the conniving aristocrat Neville Ashcroft. She loses her virginity to him in a scene of ambiguous consent and then, devastated by her sin, rejects his proposal of marriage. West uses a series of somewhat purple nature metaphors to convey sexual feeling: "His hand gripped her wrists, and he prepared to open the floodgates and be tossed in the sea of his self-made sentiment" (10); "Her life, before so barren and desert-[like], was flooded now by a terrible menacing ocean" (20). There are allusions to primordial instincts: "At his touch she felt a subtle, anesthetic sense of animal satisfaction stealing over her" (14–15). The rejection of marriage is a conversation laced with exclamations: "'I gave up so easily, so easily!'" "'O God!'" "'My darling!'" "'You make me wish I was dead!'" "'To hear a child wish for death!'" At the end of this first section, Adela rejects her suitor by appealing to her own weakness: "'My sin was that I gave myself to you without the sanction of love.... That night I obeyed an animal craving'" (23).

To think about this first section and the ways that it differs from the rest of the book, we might recall the famous a visualization of chronology in the now-unfashionable work of Gustav Freytag. The first section of *The Sentinel* mimes the dramatic structure of Freytag's pyramid: introduction, rising action, climax, falling action, and closing action, or *denouement* as resolution or catastrophe. Adela leaves school, is seduced, and then evades marriage. But the rest of *The Sentinel*, and thus the bulk of the novel, follows a very different, though extremely symmetrical timeline: Parliament Square riot, arrest, Holloway Prison, recovery; Smithburn Riot, evasion of arrest, recovery; Smithburn Town Hall smash, arrest, Yorkshire Prison, recovery; Haymarket Theater Riot. In many ways, this recursive plot resembles the long middle of the revolutionary picaresque we saw earlier, in the suffragette autobiographies and the "Revolutionaries" newspaper column.

On one hand, Freytag's model is useful because it evaluates the dramatic weight of turning points and what might be called filler. Between riots and prisons, Adela rejects a series of marriage proposals, first from a Labour Party candidate and then (twice) from the dashing young socialist Robert Langland. It is easy enough to see, from this more global perspective, the way that *The Sentinel* plots the women's revolution as a back and forth, gain and loss: the forward momentum of political mobilization and the hardships of state repression. On the other hand, this macroscopic model cannot account for what happens at the level of the sentence. What we cannot see in the graphic representations of chronology is the way that this particular movement, the back and forth, infects the singular perspective of Adela in the midst of any given action. Thus, in the first riot, in London, Adela finds herself tossed in a crowd "so thickly pressed that she could not raise her hands from her sides" (37). Adela wanders, "backwards and forwards"; she is "knocked up and down," tossed "hither and thither" (38). A few pages on, we find Adela "drifting again in the midst of the shifting thousands" (40). There are snatches of dialogue. ("'My dear you look very shaken! This is no place for you girls to wander alone'" [37]). Eventually, mounted police surround Adela for arrest, but this does not quite serve as rising action: "five horses circling round her. They went round and round" (41).

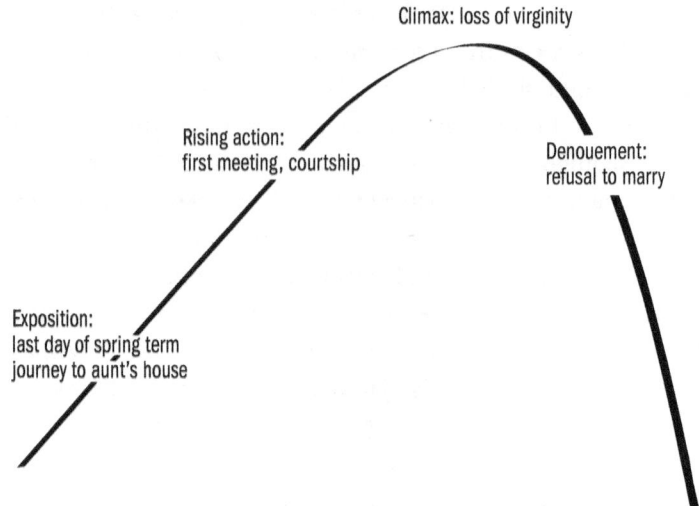

FIGURE 2.12 Rising and falling action in *The Sentinel*, section one.

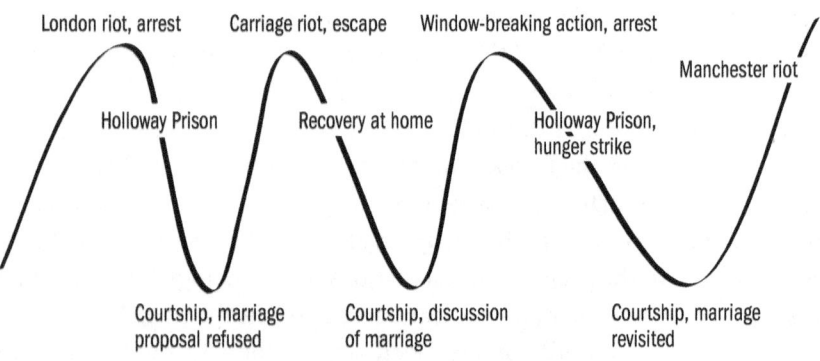

FIGURE 2.13 Rising and falling action in *The Sentinel*, section two.

Back and forth, hither and thither, round and round, side to side, to and fro—*The Sentinel* is shot through with movement that shuttles from one point to the next but not *toward* anything. The crowd scene is all rocking bodies, shrillness, and agitation. Prison, on the other hand, affords a more monotonous sort of back and forth. This is "a life of inaction and fatigue," a kind of regulated madness of one thing after another, in anonymous groups,

THE LONG MIDDLE   89

that destroys the very "faculty of computing any series of actions as a whole" (50). A schedule determines the day in increments that "set [Adela] walking aimlessly around an asphalt yard, now in the dank blue shadow of the wall, now in the fierce yellow heat of the dusty sky . . . round and round the asphalt yard" (50–51). An even more dismal view of this *back and forth* returns, somewhat differently, when Adela temporarily abandons the women's movement. "That sense of orderly purpose was gone. She was adrift" (121). Now in the comfortable parlor of Mary Hereford, repetition becomes a more cyclical thing, as an endless progression of babies, one had after the other. Mary is perpetually pregnant and in the midst of housework; she has "always on her lap new babies and old stockings" (124). When Adela returns to her suffragette work, to yet another riot, she becomes caught in a more desperate sort of to and fro: "In a frenzy she rolled over and over, twisting her wrists" (206). More sardonic is the moment when, waiting to emerge from a closely packed room, Adela fears that she will vomit, then reflects that the "decencies had already been violated over and over again" (218).

Not looping, cyclical, or desperate, the Town Hall window-breaking demonstration offers yet another version of circularity—a back and forth of thrown stones. The suffragettes fling iron bolts strung out on a rope through the glass ceiling of the town hall, "shattering a pane of glass at every blow" (223). On the roof of the building next door, a half a dozen men launch at the suffragettes "a constant fire of stones, slates, small steel blocks with sharp edges, and dried dung" (223). The stones find their mark on both sides. "Adela was repeatedly struck by the flying missiles: a steel block drew blood on her temples" (223). The demonstration results in arrest and Adela's third return to prison, this time the space of a more violent kind of *back and forth*. Guards carry Adela's inert body, swinging her "from side to side" (227). As women are beaten in their cells, the hallways "echoed with the same horrid noises of assault and resistance" (227). During the hunger strikes, Adela moves in and out of solitary confinement for medical evaluation. "She could not count the times on which she had been dragged before the gang of visiting magistrates, faced them defiantly, and at their bidding been flung back into the punishment cell" (237). Meanwhile, the mob outside, likened to an animal, emits a "gentle uproar of cheers and countercheers, as if the wild beast was coughing and choking" (221).

It is typical to link repetition to compulsion, as though one cannot help going through the motions, again and again. Compulsion is irresistible, irrational; it implies that we are made to do something beyond our will. What I have been tracking in *The Sentinel* is the repetition of a particular motion that, in its variations, does not seem, to me, compulsive. Indeed, this motion, this back and forth, is used so thoroughly, in every instance, good and bad, that it becomes difficult to attach a descriptive or even evaluative label. West's back and forth, side to side, hither and thither sometimes happens to people in a manner brutal or boring. Sometimes people *do things*; they move across spaces, back and forth, sneeringly, elated, in love. All of these imaginations of movement, through syntax, through plot, through the swaying of bodies or ejection of food, can't be just one thing or the other, a symptom of this good thing or of that bad one. At the same time, West's use of this back and forth does create a particular chronology of revolution that, I will argue, only looks circular because the end is unknown.

In this way, through all these variations on the back and forth, *The Sentinel* imagines a narrative form to answer the question: How do you tell a story about a revolution that isn't over yet? How do you tell a story of gains and losses, what was a mistake, what should have been done, where the turning points lie, if you don't know the final outcome? Are all these actions the slow rise toward triumph? Do they signal a decline of sanity or discipline? Without the vote as a discrete demand, without success or failure as a conclusion in sight, what does a story of the women's revolution look like?

These questions emerge, in part, from Hannah Arendt's late work *The Human Condition* (1958). A defense of democratic politics during the height of the Red Scare, written in response to what Arendt saw as the failures of democracy in the USSR, *The Human Condition* reconsiders the human subject from the perspective of political action. Though feminist critics have long since rejected Arendt's account of action because it considers the private sphere apolitical, I find her emphasis on action particularly useful for a feminist politics because it allows for models of praxis outside of preexisting parliamentary or party programs. Like Luxemburg, Arendt focuses on the process of political actions, rather than on their demands or programs. This account of practice and process highlights the contingency of any action, as experienced by the people acting and speaking together. Arendt highlights this contingency as productive of a narrative problem. For Arendt, historical narrative conceals the contingency of any political action, making sense of beginnings and endings after the fact. On the other hand, for political actors engaged in any given struggle, events have a kind of opacity, in that final consequences cannot be securely predicted. The later tallying up, of action and consequences in light of a demand achieved or not, casts a new light on these struggles, not for the actors in their midst but for the historian, who, from a different temporal vantage, can see a new kind of story:

> What the storyteller narrates must necessarily be hidden from the actor himself, at least as long as he is in the act or caught in its consequences, because to him the meaningfulness of his act is not in the story that follows. Even though stories are inevitable results of action, it is not the actor but the storyteller who perceives and "makes" the story.[19]

I think here of Marx in *The Civil War in France*, chiding the communards for not seizing the banks. That this was a fatal flaw, contributing to the outcome of failure, could only be visible from a much later purview.

What I have been tracing in this chapter, through the autobiographies, tables of contents, timelines, and, finally, *The Sentinel*, as a movement between seemingly equivalent events, back and forth, at the level of plot and at the level of the sentence, is the attempt to imagine a narrative form apart from the backward gaze of the storyteller and, thus, apart from the demand for the vote as the final endpoint of the women's movement. For West, this round and round the prison yard, the smashing of windows and dodging of stones, the body swung back and forth, the *hither and thither* of the crowd, over and over, takes on various casts. This repetition can be monotonous, insistent, or frantic. It might be a kind of lull, a dull progression, or an exhilarating movement of bodies on the street moving together. But we cannot pinpoint this form—the back and the forth—as definitively good or bad in any one case, as leading to success or failure, because the outcome of these cycles is unknown. Riot, arrest, recovery, on repeat, become isolated as means of struggle that do not lead to a final demand, achieved; instead, this struggle itself, as a means in the present tense, becomes the content of women's revolution.

This focus on means, on actions isolated from a single demand, may seem like a matter of temporality alone. But a focus on means, in effect, changes the space of politics, or where we might imagine political action to reside. As a case in point: *The Sentinel* ends in the midst of yet another riot. Adela is arrested and carried by the police through a hostile crowd. The crowd is the subject of the last sentence: "From side to side of the square, under glittering sky it stretched an inky sea, occasionally churned up by its varying excitements or seamed by the fiery course of the trams. It raged in cheers and countercheers around her and clotted into arguing knots in her wake" (252). There are not individual people here. The *back and forth* of arguments, severed from an end, creates a space between people that, in this instance, is strangely animated. This movement is not just about the temporality of the way we imagine revolution; it also creates a new kind of space between people acting and speaking. This space of political action, what Arendt sometimes calls "the space of appearance," is, in her words, the "organization of the people as it arises out of acting and speaking together, and its true space lies between people living together for this purpose, no matter where they happen to be."[20] Hence, political action is not located in an individual or a courtroom. Rather, "action and speech create a space between the participants which can find its proper location almost any time and anywhere."[21] For West, all that back and forth, to and fro, creates a sense of the *between* as the location of politics. This perspective turns away from the arc of individual action or self-realization, away from the arc of the continental bildungsroman, away from the backward account of political action as a singular success or failure, and toward the creation of new spaces for politics made in between people acting and speaking in the present tense.

Some might find this back and forth, the scratching through the smaller details, dissatisfying. There are no great heroic acts in *The Sentinel*. There is no revolutionary success, predicted in the future or assigned to the present. Instead, in the street, in the home, and in the prison, the back and forth of mass struggle, of mobilization and repression, creates a realm of politics that is between people and not attached to any individual person. These spaces are not havens of communal life. Antagonisms play out on women's bodies, again and again. Against the shining optimism of the utopian socialists of what could be in the future, this is a very particular movement, worked out within the confines of a narrative that inches back and forth within the limits of the given. Yet this inching back and forth, hither and thither, riot and Holloway again, resets the demands of the bildungsroman. In *The Sentinel*, the outcome of the vote is not the final question or the answer to the plot of one's life. Nor is the outcome of a larger revolution that combines socialist and feminist tendencies. Rather than a future of demands, for the women's vote, for the proletarian revolution, the narrative arc of the novel stalls out in a long middle that works with what is available in the present tense: what conversations, what social ties, what limits; what can be done, now, here, and what that doing looks like. This imagination of the present, as opposed to a better future, is not always particularly cheerful. In fact, there is often a withering shoddiness there. This imagination must forgo the projection of newer, better worlds. In the long middle of the narrative present, there are more limits, more realities, more boredom, more bodies that cannot be disappeared and spaces that are not ideal.

What I have been drawing out as a distinction between the utopian future and the spaces of the present, incidentally, occurs as a conversation toward the end of *The Sentinel*. Adela is approached by an artist who asks her, "'How does it feel to be absorbed in the present?'" He explains, "'I'm an artist. An artist's a man who can't concentrate himself on the present—he's diffused through Eternity, through the Universe'" (245). In many ways, this brief conversation prefigures a more famous debate about politicized art and temporality just a year later. In 1914, Ezra Pound and Wyndham Lewis will introduce a new avant-garde, British vorticism, in the journal *BLAST*. Poised against aestheticism and Italian futurism, *BLAST* announces a new temporality for politicized art: "Our new vortex plunges to the heart of the present" (7). Though there is not space here to discuss the often-heated dialogue between vorticists and suffragettes, I should say that Rebecca West's writing appears in *BLAST* as well. Despite this inclusion, West is often written out of the histories of the vorticist avant-garde. It is only more notable, then, that *The Sentinel* prefigures the more famous manifestos of 1914. What if *The Sentinel* were included amid this fray, as an avant-garde antimanifesto or counterprogram for feminist praxis?

Of course, the vorticist manifestos also rework a much earlier program for revolution. *The Communist Manifesto* famously begins with a predictive mode, to account for the general stages of the development of the proletariat: "A spectre is haunting Europe—the spectre of communism."[22] This haunting will end at the proper historical stage: in the future, when industrialization is sufficiently advanced to move from "veiled civil war" to a key moment "where that war breaks out into open revolution."[23] In *The Sentinel*, West imagines a different sort of specter, along with a distinct historical experience:

> With curious childishness she speculated on the excellent opportunities for Suffrage work open to her if she became a ghost. The most determined

> Liberal stewards could not oust a ghost from a public meeting: to a ghost the most obstinate of Prime Ministers could not refuse an audience. A ghost could rush the House of Commons without fear and without check, could perhaps pulverize the British constitution by routing the Legislative Chambers whenever and wherever they met.
>
> (220)

How curious indeed, is this imagination of a freedom from law's punishment. But this ghost would not be seen by the politicians she haunts. She would be invisible in a public meeting, ignored in a prime minister's office. For West, the spectral is not, as it was for Marx, a metaphor for what is to come. Instead, the invisibility of this ghost, a fantastic creature, literalizes a subject position lived in the present tense. Fantastic, too, is the female citizen, as a creature somehow residing within the scope of the law yet outside law's formal recognition. This is a subject strangely human and not-human, alive and not, embodied and invisible, in terms of the law that encompasses living beings. The suffragette-ghost attends public meetings, riots at the House of Commons, and is a perpetual heckler of the Legislative Chambers, "whenever and wherever they met." West literalizes the no one and nowhere of tactics as ghost: here is the subject for a form of action that belongs to no proper person and no proper place. As suffragette ghost or frothing crowd, *The Sentinel* offers an alternative to the stagism of Marxist orthodoxy or a focus on future demands. Alongside the suffragette autobiographies and the "Revolutionaries" columns, *The Sentinel* becomes an antiprogram or countermanifesto focused on action in the present tense. For West, this plotting of revolution reimagines the spaces where political action is possible and the kinds of people who can affect such changes, not by waiting for a perpetually receding future horizon, when the conditions will be ripe, when a revolution will be possible, but by focusing on many smaller beginnings, hither and thither, back and forth, here, now, in the present tense.

Leigh v. Gladstone, or the Right to Refuse

In 1909, the WSPU sued the home secretary, prison governor, and medical officer for damages on behalf of Mary Leigh after she was force-fed in

Winson Green Prison. The story of the trial is not straightforward or confined to a single document. What follows pieces together the wider publicity around this event, moving across newspapers, trial reports, letters, opinion columns, and medical logs. This archive is purposefully diffuse because the ways that these documents do not agree is important. Their divergence reveals the juridical construction of female citizenship as something shot through with contradictions. In the course of the trial, Leigh was considered a woman in need of protection, a wicked personality, a threat to society, an undisciplined prisoner, an exemplary plaintiff, and a primitive savage, all at the same time. What follows examines this archive as one last instance of the narrative temporality of women's action, this time understood through a more juridical language of contract, torture, and human rights.

At that time, the hunger strike was a novel problem for both domestic and international law. The first hunger strike in England, of any political tendency, was only earlier that year. The suffragette Marion Wallace Dunlap began fasting while imprisoned at Holloway in July 1909 to protest her treatment as a common rather than political prisoner. Fearing public backlash if Dunlap were to die in prison, Home Secretary Herbert Gladstone released Dunlap after ninety-one hours. Though Dunlap acted on her own accord, the WSPU quickly embraced the tactic of the prison hunger strike, which was understood to have originated in the Russian prisons of the tsarist regime. In the years leading up to the war, more than five hundred women participated in what they called the "Russian method" of the hunger strike, which was subsequently, perhaps more famously, used by Irish and Indian nationalists in the following decades.[24]

By the time Leigh was arrested, in September 1909, some dozen suffragettes had taken up the prison hunger strike and been released from their sentences early due to ill health. Leigh was arrested during a disruption of the People's Budget Meeting at Bingley Hall, where Lord Asquith was in attendance. She was part of a larger contingent of women who had stationed themselves on a neighboring rooftop, then flung rocks and bottles onto the roof and through the windows of Bingley Hall. Leigh used a hatchet to remove the roof's slates and threw those down as well. Charged with two counts of resisting, Leigh was sentenced to four months' imprisonment with hard labor, alongside her collaborators Charlie Marsh, Mabel Capper, Patricia Woodlock, and Laura Ainsworth, who all received shorter sentences.

Arriving to prison arm in arm, singing the "Marseilles," this group began a hunger strike on the first day of their sentences. When medical officers began force-feeding the prisoners a week later, the status of this response became a source of heated debate in the House of Commons. *Votes for Women* published the conversation concerning the prisoners' treatment at some length, including MP Philip Snowden's inquiry, "May I ask if the hon. Gentleman will convey the suggestion to the Home Secretary that he should make application to Spain or Russia in order to adopt the most brutal and up-to-date methods of barbarism?"[25] As Kevin Grant has noted, this language also invokes a wider historical frame: Henry Campbell-Bannerman famously coined the term "methods of barbarism" in 1901 to describe the British war crimes of the Boer War, including the burning of homes, the destruction of crops and livestock, and the deportation of women and children to concentration camps. In Campbell-Bannerman's usage, methods of barbarism could be keyed to a backward movement on the civilizing spectrum, for victim and perpetrator alike. Over the next decade, this new term, "methods of barbarism," became a signal for human rights violations more widely, particularly in colonial contexts or interstate wars. The phrase was often combined with its opposite, the "principles of humanity."[26]

Whether as a direct reference to the Boer War or not, the suffragette press seized upon the language of colonial barbarism and torture. The 1910 cover of *Votes for Women* featured a suffragette undergoing nasal feeding under the heading "The Government's Methods of Barbarism" (figure 2.14).[27] The victim appears to be in a faint, though we are led to believe that she had been resistant and so necessitated five people to restrain her: one to tie her ankles to a chair, another to lean on her knees, two to brace themselves against her arm, and one to hold back her head. The artist included strange markings, perhaps meant as wrinkles, on the hunger striker's dress, as though the wardens had left handprints. Below the image, there is a notation that the cartoon will be reprinted as a poster, for further distribution. Indeed, over the next four years, cartoons, posters, and reproduced first-person testimony of force-feeding proliferated to increasingly graphic effect. These accounts lingered on bodily restraint, as well as the repetition of specific injuries: lacerations to the nasal passages, mouth, and throat; bitten tongues; broken teeth; fluid accidentally poured down the larynx; persistent vomiting. Despite doctors' claims that the practice was uncomfortable but not dangerous, the suffragette press reported serious complications: Lilian Lenton (age 23, 5 foot 2 3/4 inches, brown eyes, dark brown hair, arson), the youngest of the suffragettes in the surveillance photographs that opened this chapter, developed septic pneumonia after liquid entered her lungs; the actress Kitty Marion, of the publicity-still headshot, was force-fed 232 times, became suicidal, and set her bedsheets on fire; in Perth Prison, Scotland, Frances Gorden had tubes inserted in her bowels; Fanny Parker was force-fed through the rectum and vagina, resulting in pelvic injuries.[28] Drawing on these accounts, suffragettes weaponized suffering as a tactic in itself: "To these 'methods of barbarism' we have opposed the gentler methods of a *militancy of suffering*," wrote Mrs. Saul Solomon in a 1911 letter to *Votes to Women*.[29]

However, in *Leigh v. Gladstone*, the primary matter before the court was contractual, rather than criminal. The attorneys for the defense highlighted the state's responsibility to protect its female citizens. In so doing, they positioned force-feeding as a medical procedure necessary to prevent hunger strikers from dying while under the supervision of the state. On the other hand, Leigh's lawyers concentrated their efforts on defining force-feeding as a violation of bodily autonomy and a form of domestic torture. While Leigh's lawyers noted her suffering and the potential for injury, their primary argument was that she did not consent to a medical procedure.

The trial was not a success for Leigh. Within the course of two minutes, without leaving the box, the jury decided against the plaintiff. However, the novelty of the hunger strike and force-feeding, as new techniques of protest and repression, did spark off a wider, ongoing debate understood through terms largely absent from the trial: "civilization" and "humanity." The point I want to make concerns the ways that these terms hypothesized a temporal schema, this time for the state's practices of repression. In his report, published in *Votes for Women*, F. W. Pethick-Lawrence concluded: "By this decision of the Lord Chief Justice, a person once committed to prison is deprived of one of the essential human rights, the right to forbid an operation upon his body without his consent."[30] In a different article, seven months later, Pethick-Lawrence repeats this formulation word for word and adds the following framework: "When the annals of these times come to be written historians will stand aghast at the extraordinary and inhuman methods by which the Government attempted to put an end to the hunger strike, and they will wonder how in this civilized age such a course of action could be permitted by the people of the country."[31]

It is a common enough practice to imagine how historians will write up the present. In his condemnation, Pethick-Lawrence also suggests his own historical narrative, akin to the juridical humanity I discussed in the

FIGURE 2.14 "The Government's Methods of Barbarism," *Votes for Women*, January 28, 1910, 1.

preceding chapter. In this account humanity is not necessarily a natural state, belonging to all persons, but something that occurs at the end of a more teleological process of humanization or, in this case, civilization. Pethick-Lawrence mourns what he sees as a British turn backward on the civilizing spectrum, allowing for "inhuman methods" of treatment. Many of Pethick-Lawrence's interlocutors make the same point but more explicitly position the freedom of white British women in negative relation to colonial subjects. See, for instance, Emmeline Pethick-Lawrence's "Women or Kaffirs?" or Kathleen Tanner, who also asks a rhetorical question, this time upon witnessing protests for native rights: "I wondered how soon the men demonstrating against the denial of human rights in South Africa, would realize that the women of their own nation are really in not much better case."[32]

These comparisons imagine an internationalist solidarity between British women and South Africans but also obscure quite a bit in the process, creating a form of equivalence, through injury, across two materially different populations. This imagining, therefore, allows for a more critical return to Arendt's action-centered framing of the political, which sets aside the agency of the sovereign subject in favor of the "organization of the people as it arises out of acting and speaking together."[33] Arendt does not qualify a rubric for participation, so her construction of the people does not account for the historical articulation of racialized differences between them or for the ways that the imagination of solidarity is not always truthful or innocent.

At the same time, my focus on the languages of human rights and barbarism in the feminist press obscures the experiential content of the prison hunger strike, as another long middle of resistance, this time expressed through serial acts of refusal. *Leigh v. Gladstone* looks very different if we pay closer attention to Leigh herself, rather than to the reporting that surrounded her trial. In her testimony, Leigh is clear that she did not consent to a medical procedure. But Leigh makes much wider use of a somewhat different language for this action, as an act of refusal. Consider, for instance, Leigh's statement to her solicitor, which was published in full in *Votes for Women* while she was still imprisoned. The statement is relatively straightforward, without frills. Leigh recalls that she began her hunger strike immediately. She was the first prisoner to be force-fed, on the third day of fasting. At this point, Leigh's statement goes into greater detail about the negotiation surrounding this treatment, beginning with the doctor's warning:

> He then said: "You must listen carefully to what I have to say. I have orders from my superior officers" (he had a blue official paper in his hand, to which he referred) "that you are not to be released, even on medical grounds. If you still refrain from food I must take other measures to compel you to take it."
>
> I then said: "I refuse, and if you force food on me I want to know how you are going to do it."

He said: "That is a matter for me to decide."

I said he must prove I was insane, that the Lunacy Commissioners would have to be summoned to prove I was insane, and that he could not perform an operation without the patient's consent. The feeding by the mouth I described as an operation and the feeding by the tube as an outrage. I also said: "I shall hold you responsible and shall take any measure in order to see whether you are justified in doing so."

He merely bowed and said: "Those are my orders."[34]

During her courtroom testimony, Leigh repeated much of this statement verbatim. However, the solicitor's questions revealed a more detailed timeline. After October 7, Leigh began vomiting after each feeding. On October 29, she was examined by two doctors but refused to answer their questions. On October 30, Leigh was released early but refused to leave the prison grounds.

In the trial, the solicitors invoke the language of consent, as do suffragist supporters in the feminist press. However, it is notable that Leigh primarily uses the language of refusal. While consent marks a right, even within a scenario of inequality, refusal is something a little more difficult to define. It seems a misnomer to claim a right to refusal, because in so many cases refusal occurs in a space where rights are partial or lacking, as an action of last resort. Refusal marks the limits of rights, in spaces where recognition as a subject or citizen is not necessarily possible. For this reason, refusal doesn't need to make a demand or have a desire. It can be a response.

To feel out this version of refusal, beyond the space of the courtroom, I want to refract *Leigh v. Gladstone* through one more archival object, the medical logs of the prison force-feedings (figure 2.15).[35] I don't end with these logs because I think they express the truth of what really happened. What the log books show is the texture of repetition in a way that no other documents have. At Winson Green, the medical officer was extremely punctilious. Every day he would account for each woman in turn, as to her manner of resistance: whether a tube was inserted into the mouth or the nose; which nostril was used, so as to alternate; whether vomiting occurred; if she would take food by the mouth or from a cup; her spirits, as lethargic or not; her approximate color and temperature. However, the other logs in the British National Archives, for Jane Short and Rachel Pease, are much less detailed.[36] Here is a doctor's shorthand, with dates and squiggles, meant to notate that a force-feeding occurred. In comparisons to the other kinds of shorthand

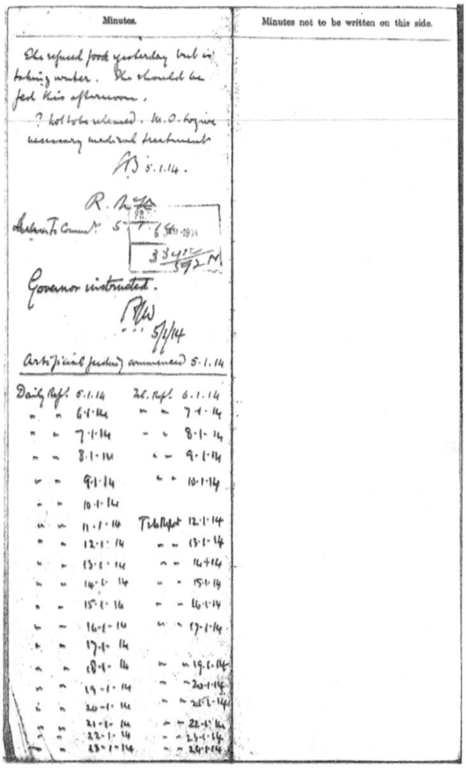
Minutes. | Minutes not to be written on this side.

She refused food yesterday but is taking water. She should be fed this afternoon.

? not to be released. M.O. to give necessary medical treatment

5.1.14.

Governor instructed.

5/1/14

Artificial feeding commenced 5.1.14

Daily Rept. 5.1.14	M.O. Rept. 6.1.14
" " 6.1.14	" " 7.1.14
" " 7.1.14	" " 8.1.14
" " 8.1.14	" " 9.1.14
" " 9.1.14	" " 10.1.14
" " 10.1.14	
" " 11.1.14	Tele Rept 12.1.14
" " 12.1.14	" " 13.1.14
" " 13.1.14	" " 14.1.14
" " 14.1.14	" " 15.1.14
" " 15.1.14	" " 16.1.14
" " 16.1.14	" " 17.1.14
" " 17.1.14	
" " 18.1.14	" " 19.1.14
" " 19.1.14	" " 20.1.14
" " 20.1.14	" " 21.1.14
" " 21.1.14	" " 22.1.14
" " 22.1.14	" " 23.1.14
" " 23.1.14	" " 24.1.14

FIGURE 2.15 "Rachel Peace and Jane Short, suffragettes, forcibly fed."
Source: Government Papers, the National Archives, Kew, 1912–1914.

this chapter has considered, including tables of contents, lists, and indexes, these marks seem the most antinarrative, the least story-like story, I have located.

At this moment, in England, in the years leading up to the war, prison logs are useful for the ways that they allow a visualization of a long middle, apart from a demand. To break off from the matter of the demand also means to give up on a unified political intentionality. In her testimonies, Leigh changed her mind about what the hunger strike meant to achieve. In some cases, she claimed it was the vote; in others, treatment as a political, rather than common, prisoner; at one point, she claimed to be fasting to protest the treatment of her imprisoned comrade, who had been locked in a cell for two days. Here the matter of *why* changes and can be articulated in any number of future-oriented frames, particularly in the retrospective, as connected to Boer War abuses or essential human rights. What does not change is the *against*, or the ways that this sense of *against* offers a particular kind of social world in the present tense of struggle.

For now, it is enough to say that, across this chapter, I have tried to situate what this particular experiment with ongoingness meant, in a local sense, for the suffragettes themselves and across a wider imperial landscape. Did Mary Leigh imagine herself as a part of a vast colonial narrative? I expect the answer is yes and no, but there is no way to be sure. Even with the firsthand testimony, filtered and approved by the WSPU-funded lawyers, there is no way to really get at what Leigh really wanted. As a final turn to the archive, the prison medical logs are useful for the ways they do not answer these questions. It is possible to read these notations as a record of injury to an increasingly frail body, sometimes imagined across continents, in an appropriation and transformation of colonial suffering. This should not be forgotten. But it is also possible to understand each notation as a decision made within a space of extremely limited freedom. Either way, those marks are shorthand for much that is left out of the retrospective histories that position the riots, arson campaigns, and hunger strikes as mere episodes leading to the more important end that was the women's vote. Seen apart from this ending, the marks on the page tell a story about the practice and process of female citizenship, through the creation of social bonds and a limited kind of world making. Each mark signals acts of refusal, but it is difficult to say what is being refused: food and drink, of course, but also protection, respectability, safety, health, futurity. It is possible to try to imagine being in the middle of this daily kind of history and the various desires it invoked. This is the very thing I have set out to do, of course. But I like to turn back to the medical log for the way it renders these narratives so bluntly artificial, as so many hasty marks left on the page, standing in for all the hours and days of saying no.

PART II

THE REPRODUCTIVE ATLANTIC

3

The Art of Not Having Children

Birth Strike, Sabotage, and the Reproductive Atlantic

P ublic lecture, Société de géographie, Paris, 1892: Journalists in attendance estimated that the crowd of antivivisectionists, anarchists, syndicalists, university students, feminists, and neo-Malthusians numbered nearly two thousand people.[1] This is probably an exaggeration, amid a general reportage high on outrage, but nevertheless it is certain that Marie Huot's lecture on population control attracted a large and lively audience. As secretary of the League Against Vivisection, Huot was already notorious as an animal rights activist given over to militant direct actions, including an umbrella attack on the anatomist C. E. Brown-Séquard.[2] She was also a proponent of animal population control. In one of her more controversial anecdotes, Huot described how she would dispose of newborn puppies by tying a heavy stone around their necks and then throwing them in a body of water.[3] According to a different account, Huot advised the audience to control their housecat population by taking kittens directly from their mothers' flanks and drowning them in a pot of water with a heavy lid.[4] Allegedly, Huot claimed that the same might be done for unwanted human infants.[5] Huot went on to argue for the full-scale extinction of the human species through the use of birth control in order to end suffering for both man and animal. She noted, however, that she was primarily concerned with the welfare of animals.

A week later, *La Semaine Vétérinaire* wrote up a disapproving account of Huot's lecture as a call for a "birth strike," or in a more literal translation, a "strike of wombs [*grève des ventres*]."[6] Whether or not Huot used these words remains a subject of scholarly debate.[7] However, it is certain that Huot made famous a conceptual analogy that would migrate into loftier political circles on the international extreme Left over the next four decades. In this analogy, the production of people to fight in wars is likened to the industrial production of commodities. Through the birth strike, women might call the production of people to a halt and therefore occupy a position of bargaining power with the nation-state, potentially stalling the expansion of capitalist enterprise more widely.

Though never dominant in the wider movement for birth control reform, the birth strike was most closely associated with Paul Robin's League for Human Regeneration, which published Huot's lecture as a pamphlet in 1909. Financed in part through the distribution of birth control manuals, the league quickly took off as an international neo-Malthusian organization, with offices in France, Germany, Italy, Argentina, Mexico, and Cuba. In the years before World War II, debates on the birth strike appeared in both the transatlantic worker's newspapers and avant-garde little magazines, developing beyond a single institutional formation into little-known fringe groups and anarchist offshoots. Across these more international domains, adherents of the birth strike dropped the matter of purposeful human extinction. Instead, they argued that the limitation of reproduction would deprive capitalism of workers and soldiers to exploit, eventually resulting in a worldwide revolution.

The birth strike militarizes the language of human population, but it makes proletarian women, and not the state, the agents of political change. This is a eugenic argument, but it is not a part of the more familiar biopolitical narratives of the early twentieth century. Traditionally, scholars interested in the history of population control have tended to focus on the intersection between eugenic science and the modern nation-state. In these histories, eugenic science offers justification for state management of the population, be it through legislation surrounding contraception, the criminalization of homosexuality, the forced sterilization of ethnic groups, or state-sanctioned genocide. In each case, population control operates in the service of the nation-state, to shore up racial homogeneity and the heteronormative family as constitutive of proper citizenship. For adherents of the proletarian birth strike, workers' self-management of reproduction offers a biopolitics *against* the state.

Adherents for the birth strike thus framed nonprocreative sex as a political act, shifting the public/private divide of reproductive labor in ways that bear on the reproductive politics of our present history. Since *Griswold v. Connecticut* (1965) established the legality of birth control, a number of landmark rulings on reproductive rights in the United States have hinged on the privacy doctrine, including the legalization of interracial marriage (*Loving v. Virginia*, 1967), abortion (*Roe v. Wade*, 1973), sodomy (*Lawrence v. Texas*, 2003), and same-sex marriage (*Obergefell v. Hodges*, 2015). In light of this juridical history, legal scholars have long since argued that the right to privacy is a poor foundation for reproductive rights because it upholds a distinction between the private sphere of the home and the public sphere of politics.[8] The right to privacy allows for the state's noninterference in the domestic sphere, or the "right to be left alone," in a way that presupposes the domestic sphere as a realm of freedom for all people. In this way, the privacy doctrine renders matters of sexuality and reproduction somehow outside the boundaries of the political, beyond the interests or responsibility of the state.

I will argue that this more familiar legal narrative of reproductive rights, through the language of personal privacy, obscures a more radical lineage of feminist, queer, and antiracist organizing in the early twentieth century. Rather than viewing reproductive liberty as an individual *right to privacy* to be granted by the state, these groups positioned the birth strike as a direct action, a collective *tactic for equality* in the larger struggle against capitalism. To track this imagination of feminist direct action, the first half of this chapter takes up the proletarian birth strike and sabotage as explicitly conjoined public tactics. In transatlantic print cultures, the proletarian birth strike invokes a class divide between workers and owners. The strike favors one side of this antagonism, so that human regeneration occurs through technoscience that favors the working classes. However, this classed narrative of freedom takes its coordinates from the legacies of the transatlantic slave trade and contemporaneous colonial development policy. Across these documents, full humanity becomes a teleological category set at the end of the proletarian revolution. The full humanity of the postrevolutionary period comes into view in contrast to the zero degrees of freedom assigned to slaves and colonial subjects, thus shifting the geographic terrain of what is commonly called the American birth control movement.

To account for this conjuncture, this chapter turns to a transnational framework, or what I call the "Reproductive Atlantic." On one hand, the Atlantic serves as a literal geography: opening in Paris, this chapter then turns to 1913 Berlin, skirts across middle America, and ends in Harlem at midcentury. However, I will also theorize the Atlantic as an analytic category in its own right, building on the insights of Paul Gilroy, Brent Hayes Edwards, Laura Doyle, and Alys Eve Weinbaum.[9] In so doing, I torque Gilroy's original formulation, focusing more particularly on the Atlantic intersections of white and black women's reproduction. This intersection, what Weinbaum calls the "race-reproduction bind," offers one concrete way to move beyond a progressive historical narrative, instead probing the mutual relation between reproductive rights and racialized injuries. In so doing, I look to resituate reproductive justice as a neglected site in the historical formation of human rights discourses. This turn to the interrelation between domestic and international law begins with a question: Why are some injuries understood in a national framework and others subject to international norms? Or, as a number of feminist scholars of international law have asked in a more speculative framework: What happens when crimes that happen in the private sphere become tactically resituated in terms of international forms of solidarity, such that domestic violence might be reconsidered as torture, police violence as genocide, or access to gender-affirming surgery as a right to life?[10] The end of this chapter takes up these questions of international jurisdiction more directly through the U.S. Civil Rights Congress's 1951 petition to the United Nations *We Charge Genocide*.

For now, by marking this Atlantic geography, I reconsider debates on reproductive futurity beyond the heteronormative white family and the nation-state, moving into a series of entanglements between racialized groups, non-normative sexualities, and diasporic communities. Taking the alignment of women's reproduction and industrial production as a starting point, the chapter surveys new models of reading and action premised on the medical protocol or, in its more literary offshoots, the instruction manual. In this discourse of instruction, theories of action produce subjects that are distinctly experimental, though not necessarily through the rubric traditionally associated with the avant-gardes. Akin to the manifesto, the instruction manual—for birth control, industrial sabotage, or, in some cases, both—focuses on the *what* of actions rather than the *who* of an injured subject. Reading across sex manuals, birth control pamphlets, little magazines, and petitions for their instructive content, I argue that these discourses move beyond our more traditional accounts of birth control as a rights-based demand in order to establish a distinctly internationalist practice of reproductive justice.

Proletarian Birth Strike

Sozialdemokratische Partei Deutschlands (SPD) public meeting, Berlin 1913: The crowd was mostly women. Tables were removed from the hall so that there would be more space for people to stand. After 8:00 PM, the police had to seal the doors as a safety measure, to prevent overcrowding. Klara Zetkin was the first speaker, and she didn't want to be there. Right at the start, Zetkin called the birth strike a "bourgeoisie quackery."[11] To have to treat the subject at all with any serious consideration, at this low point in the history of social democracy, was an embarrassment, she claimed. The logic of the argument that followed was a bit slippery. Zetkin was known for composing her speeches quite carefully in advance, so one wonders if these words, entered in the meeting's minutes, were a bit ad hoc. First, Zetkin argued that the artificial restriction of births as a "weapon in the revolutionary struggle" equated population decline with the more important work of trade unions and social reform. In what might be the speech's most burning insult, Zetkin called this sort of equation a "bourgeois-anarchist viewpoint" centered on the individual family rather than the proletariat as a whole. Zetkin concluded with the SPD party line: the thing to focus on, the real enemy, was the capitalist system. Anything else was a distraction.

A few weeks later, there would be another meeting, with much of the same. Here Zetkin was a bit more conciliatory. She argued that birth control, "like love, religion, literary taste, etc.," was a private matter not under the purview of the SPD.[12] At this second meeting, the Marxist revisionist Alfred Bernstein repeated the anarchist-syndicalist view, more prominent in France: if proletarian women collectively limit their offspring, in what was effectively a birth strike, this would deprive the state of soldiers and factory workers. Without such a "life marrow" to exploit, capitalism would be brought to its knees. From there on out, things got more antagonistic. Zetkin was booed. The women in the crowd favored the birth strike, even if the party leadership did not. One audience member, a Mrs. Schulz, suggested that Comrade Zetkin did not know anything about the conditions of the poor burdened by an abundance of children. Mrs. Schulz to Zetkin: "You strike yourself." At this point, the meeting is called to an end.

Perpetually inconsistent on the matter of birth control, the SPD had been pressured to put a debate on the agenda because Drs. Moses and Bernstein had been raising the issue in public meetings. Articles in *Vörwarts* and *Die Neue Zeit* had taken up the matter at length, most often with reference to the then popular brochure *Blessed with Children: And No End to It?* The brochure was written by the Swiss doctor and anarchist Fritz Brupbacher, who had been to Paris and encountered Marie Huot's work in 1898.[13] Though a little later than anarchist currents elsewhere on the continent, the German socialist debate on the birth strike that came into prominence in 1913 was therefore part of a more expansive intersection between leftist and eugenic groups across Europe.

At this time in France, anarchism and neo-Malthusianism had become nearly synonymous.[14] Under the tutelage of Paul Robin, the use of birth control became framed as "a sign of revolt."[15] Posters for the League de la régénération humaine proclaimed a "revolution in procreation" directed toward the common good. After an international conference at The Hague in 1910, Robin's organization included neo-Malthusian groups across a wide swath of southern Europe and South America. Liga de regeneración humana was represented by Catalonian revolutionaries in eastern Spain and, across the Atlantic, in Argentine labor journals including *La Protesta Humana*.[16] The far-flung groups associated with the league did not use the same language or program but remained distinct for their close association with anarchism and the framing of birth control as a revolutionary weapon against the ruling classes.

These debates can be found across a wide array of anarchosyndicalist periodicals and birth control manuals. In Italy, the most popular book on neo-Malthusian politics was the anarchist Secondo Giorni's *L'art di non fare figli* (The art of not having children), a birth control manual illustrated with woodcuts that demonstrated the use of contraceptives.[17] In New York, *The Masses* regularly covered the proletarian birth strike debates in Germany, along with homegrown editorials on the revolutionary effects of birth control (figure 3.1). Amid consistent coverage of the Margaret Sanger indictment, the anarchist journal *Mother Earth* published a special birth control number in 1916, in which Emma Goldman argued for birth control as both a women's right and an antiwar measure: "Capitalism cannot do without militarism and since the masses of people furnish the material to be destroyed in the trenches and on the battlefield, capitalism must have a large race."[18] In 1920, Margaret Sanger called for "A Birth Strike to End World Famine" with more precise direction, asking all women to refrain from childbirth for a period of five years.[19]

It would be possible to follow the wider debates about birth control across a spate of radical presses and little magazines. In recent years, both Layne

THE ART OF NOT HAVING CHILDREN   111

FIGURE 3.1 Max Eastman, "Revolutionary Birth-Control." Drawing by K. R. Chamberlain: "The Jones Family Group (Mr. Jones believes that Family-Limitation is criminal)." *The Masses* 6, no. 10 (July 1915): 21.

Parrish Craig and Aimee Armande Wilson have written important accounts of interwar modernism through its convergence with the wider birth control movement.[20] However, amid the vast archive of birth control discourses in the early twentieth century, I am interested in the narrower matter of the birth strike, for the ways that it likens industrial production and women's reproduction. To look more closely at this likeness in the leftist press reveals two distinctly narrative modes: the first uses narrative to render a sympathetic engagement with a suffering subject; the second sets aside narrative in favor of instructions, or a series of actions to be accomplished in the future tense, amid many subjects.

As I noted in the introduction to this book, scholars of liberal human and civil rights often rely on this first mode, of sympathetic identification, to account for the emergence of universal rights discourses more generally. In *Inventing Human Rights: A History*, Lynn Hunt identifies the eighteenth-century epistolary novel as a key narrative invention that paved the way for the discourses of universal rights. Through the fictional exchange of letters, these novels allowed readers to empathize with literary characters across the lines of class, gender, or nation. Through this passionate identification with the suffering of strangers, "epistolary novels taught their readers nothing less than a new psychology and in this process laid the foundations for a new social and political order."[21] Hunt thus resituates Jürgen Habermas's account of the rise of the public sphere in the more specific terms of rights discourse. Following Habermas, Hunt argues that the epistolary novel made readers aware of a universal capacity for interiority through the public declaration of private feelings. Though Hunt notes that this sympathetic identification did not always result in social action, that feeling with and acting for might naturally go together is a long-standing expectation of humanitarian narratives. In response, a number of scholars have criticized the expectation that making visible unnoted or unmarked suffering will result in action. In Joseph Slaughter's critical summation, "all sentimental models of humanitarianism valorize a disturbing condescending dynamic by which noble adult male master readers learn, from stories of suffering, to empathize with the common illiterate female child servants."[22]

The IWW pamphlet *Sabotage: The Conscious Withdrawal of the Workers' Efficiency* (1915) begins with some of the more practical problems with this familiar humanitarian ideal. The author and Wobbly activist Elizabeth Gurley Flynn writes on behalf of workers who already understand "that neither appeals for sympathy nor abstract rights will make for better conditions." She explains,

> For instance, take an industrial establishment such as a silk mill, where men and women and little children work ten hours a day for an average wage of between six and seven dollars a week. Could any one of them, or a committee representing the whole, hope to induce the employer to give better conditions by appealing to his sympathy, by telling him of his misery, the hardship and the poverty of their lives; or could they do it by appealing to his sense of justice? Suppose that an individual working man or woman went to an employer and said, "I make, in my capacity as wage worker in this factory, so many dollars' worth of wealth every day and justice demands that you give me at least half." The employer would probably have him removed to the nearest lunatic asylum.[23]

Rather than tell a story about injustice, Flynn's manual offers instructions for industrial sabotage as a tactic for change. Rather than convince or explain, the pamphlet suggests many ways that workers might collectively sabotage their own production as a bargaining tool. Though *Sabotage* contains many stories, it is not itself a narrative and certainly does not attempt to capture the reader's sympathy. Instead, *Sabotage* offers the reader precise instructions. In the event that the more well-known tactics of strike or collective bargaining have failed, Flynn enumerates a number of other, more experimental forms of contestation. For instance, on the docks, longshoremen might frequently drop boxes of fragile materials or let wine kegs fall into the sea. In the factory, a bit of vinegar can be put in the reed of the loom, to ruin the silk. In restaurants, a more casual attitude toward rats and mice might have concrete effects.

Toward the end of the pamphlet, Flynn turns to a different sort of sabotage, through self-directed population control. This section begins with praise of syndicalist propaganda in Europe, voiced as a quotation from a model worker: "Not only will we limit the product in the factory, but we are going to limit the supply of workers on the market."[24] Flynn sees this family planning as way to produce a better quality of offspring through lower quantity. In this case, the limitation of offspring is a collective act "in the spirit that produces sabotage," if not a "strictly scientific definition."

Flynn's consideration of birth control among other tactics of industrial sabotage may seem like an unlikely inclusion, but contemporaneous print cultures frequently coupled family planning and more familiar strategies of direct action. In the birth control issue of *Mother Earth*, Reb Raney's "The Crowbar vs. Words" unambiguously affirms Flynn's argument. Raney begins, "When a person gets ready to Act, the first thing that person does is to Forget THEORIES."[25] The idiosyncratic capitalization reveals a general sense of exasperation on the part of the author, who complains about the uselessness of "Paper teachings," "meaningless treaties," against "half-baked decrees, dust-covered prerogatives and over-clothed Decreers."[26] Raney notes that the readership of *Mother Earth* most likely already supports birth control, so need not be convinced. The article therefore does not argue for the good of birth control and focuses instead on instructions for future actions. Raney informs her readers that Emma Goldman is currently in jail for distributing pamphlets that offer direct information about how to prevent births. This is not a warning. Raney would like to see a general expansion of such illegal actions: "DO the thing that she did only do it Moreso." However, if we consider the issue of *Mother Earth* as a unit, this division between *feeling* with and *doing* for are not so clearly separated. Directly after Raney's article appears "A Human Document," an open letter addressed to Emma Goldman. The letter begins with the autobiographical life narrative of G, a thirty-four-year-old woman. Here is the epistolary mode of a suffering subject: G narrates her own birth to an overworked, frail mother and addict father. She details a series of disabilities owing to these conditions: first partial blindness, then a hip disease that left one limb shorter and caused muscle degeneration. Early on, doctors tell G that she will not live through childhood or that her children will be crippled and blind. For these reasons, G renounces all thoughts of marriage. She has found a beloved of her own advanced age but cannot marry unless she discovers a way to not have children. It is easy enough to note the ways this letter makes its appeals, "in the name of human love," according to a distinct hierarchy. "I have come to you with my 'hurt' just as a little child runs to its mother for comfort and sympathy," writes G.[27] The author calls herself a "delicate-looking, harmless little creature" awaiting rescue. However, the letter is more canny than it might seem at first glance for the ways the humanitarian narrative also serves as a veiled site of instruction. Late in the letter, G explains how a woman might prevent contraception. She puts it as a question: "Will that book by Dr. Robertson, 'Limitation of Offspring' give me the knowledge I crave?"[28] The answer to the question is yes, as we expect G well knows, thus making the letter both a plea for sympathy and an indirect form of birth control instruction.

Indeed, many of the textual effects I have noted thus far are the result of censorship. To avoid the censors, articles might name a book about contraception but not the methods found within it. The letter thus tells and doesn't tell: what appears to be a call for sympathy is also an indirect suggestion for action. In these cases, the reading public is the hypothetical political actor, as a medium for the distribution of medical knowledge. The object distributed, be it Dr. Robertson's *Limitation of Offspring* or any other of the hundreds of manuals available in the early twentieth century, is a form of knowledge gestured toward but not reproduced. Moving from *Mother Earth* to early-twentieth-century birth control manuals more widely, we might ask: How do we read an instruction manual as both a textual form and an illegally circulated medical practice?

By the end of World War I, the transatlantic circulation of birth control materials had become anatomically explicit. These documents tend to offer lists and diagrams, with little to no literary flair. *Why and How the Poor*

Should Not Have Many Children, by Emma Goldman and Ben Reitman, describes to the reader how to use condoms, cervical caps, and diaphragms, alongside a number of home-made douches. Marie Stopes's *Wise Parenthood* (1918) offers a guide to contraceptive techniques much more explicit than her more well-known classic *Married Love*. I cannot begin to catalogue the birth control manuals that proliferated in the interwar period so will restrict my closer consideration to one moment from Sanger's *Family Limitation*, which features an anatomical drawing of a woman's pelvis to show the proper insertion of a diaphragm (figure 3.2).

> Follow the directions given with each box, and learn to adjust it correctly; one can soon learn to feel that it is on right. After the pessary has been placed into the vagina deeply, it can be fitted well over the neck of the womb. One can feel that it is fitted by pressing the finger around the soft part of the pessary, which should completely cover the mouth of the womb. If it is properly adjusted there will be no discomfort, the man will be unconscious that anything is used, and no germ or semen can enter the womb. . . .
>
> I recommend the use of the pessary as the most convenient, the cheapest and the safest. Any nurse or doctor will teach one how to adjust it; then women can teach each other.[29]

If this text is a medical technology, what kind of subjects does this technology make? Sanger is easy enough to locate as a source of authority. She notes matters of preference: the pessary as preferable to the postcoital douche with a solution of boric acid, alum, citric acid, or cider vinegar. More interesting is the hypothesized *you* of the reader, who begins as a singular subject, identified with the anatomical drawing, then expands into a more diffuse network of information: "Any nurse or doctor will teach one how to adjust it; then women can teach each other." This sort of branching occurs more explicitly in the flowchart "How to Establish a Birth Control Clinic," which visualizes networked subjects in a series of interlinked bodies: citizens, physicians, ministers, social agencies, lay committees, and so on (figure 3.3). The how-to poster pictures a series of steps as a visual hierarchy, rendering *then* or *next* as lines and squares. Though arranged chronologically, these steps show a lateral entanglement between persons and institutions necessary for health care outside of legal medical institutions. This picturing

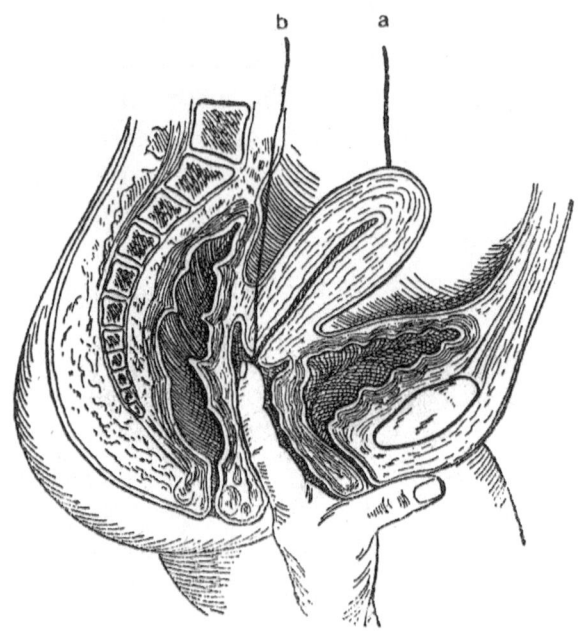

Finger touching mouth of womb.
a—womb ; b—mouth of womb.

SPONGES.

FIGURE 3.2 Margaret Sanger, *Family Limitation*, 6th ed. (1917), 13.

represents the reader to herself, as a hypothetical figure-to-be. By following the steps of the how-to guide, the reader inhabits the role of the skirted icons pictured. In this way, the how-to poster or the birth control instruction manual are not so much narratives as procedures directed at the second person: *you*. These procedural texts enumerate steps toward reproductive autonomy that include the reader as a hypothetical political subject connected to a wider public sphere.

The early birth control manuals and clinics thus offer a clear precursor to better-known second-wave efforts to seize the means of reproduction through what became known as the women's health care movement. In a groundbreaking history on the convergences between feminism and

THE ART OF NOT HAVING CHILDREN   117

technoscience, Michelle Murphy focuses our attention on the ways that this movement emerged through a diverse set of techniques shared outside of legalized medical institutions: health manuals, homemade abortion devices, self-help seminars, consciousness-raising groups, and living room health clinics. Rather than frame these groups through the language of resistance or revolutionary subjectivity, Murphy turns to what she calls "protocol feminism": "a mobile set of practices, a mode for arranging knowledge production and health care, in other words, a *protocol—a procedural*

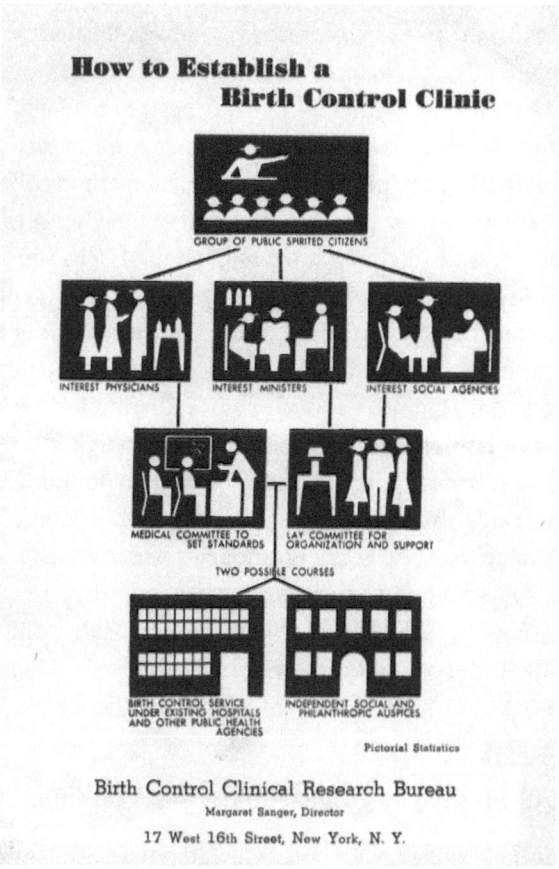

FIGURE 3.3 Pamphlet, "How to Establish a Birth Control Clinic," Birth Control Clinical Research Bureau, undated.
Source: Birth Control Clinical research Bureau, New York, NY. Margaret Sanger Research Bureau Records, Courtesy of the Sophia Smith Collection, Smith College.

script that strategically assembles technologies, exchange, epistemologies, subjects, and so on."[30] In this consideration of protocol, Murphy names a set of formal guidelines as well as the "choreographed arrangement of subject positions and institutional players"; this arrangement then generates historically specific capacities for the subjects involved, "to act, to matter, to care, to be counted, to attach, to emote, to narrate, to ignore, to work, to value, to politicize, and so on."[31] In other words, these protocols make up a field of possibility and vulnerability for different kinds of politicized subjects.

Turning from Murphy's work back to the medical diagrams in *Family Limitation*, the formation of the subject hypothesized by the text, the subject that identifies with the pictured woman, is a subject formed *through* a set of learned techniques. "Any nurse or doctor will teach one how to adjust it; then women can teach each other." The hypothesized readership is a subject that comes after the mobilization of protocol. In a more formal sense, the hypothesized subject, the feminist who uses illegal methods of birth control, moves from the future to the present. That is to say, our sense of this person, as a subject, emerges through the processes detailed in the book.

In the next section, a closer attention to this strange temporality will allow for wider reconsideration of the discourses surrounding birth control as a medical protocol that produces a distinct characterological form. This turn to character does not offer a psychological distinction between flat and round, nor does it point to the distribution of the reader's attention in terms of major or minor. Instead, the humanity of the female character is a teleological process made through a process of collective actions. This characterological form crosses the genre boundaries between history and fiction. It produces a subject as the answer to a question. The question emerges through a consideration of a famous historical personality and a hypothetical future, as in "What would Emma Goldman do?"

The Subject of Tactics, or What Would Emma Goldman Do?

A strategy requires a subject with both will and power. Strategy also depends upon a specific spatial relation. The city, army, or business requires a place of its own, a kind of base, from which potential competitors or enemies might be managed. In the years after the war, the increasingly professionalized American Birth Control League would become such an institution and develop a long-term strategy for the legalization of contraceptives. However, in the early decades of the twentieth century, the considerably less organized anarchist and syndicalist proponents of birth control focused instead on direct action in different terms, as a tactic. For Michel de Certeau, a tactic names a mobile action belonging to no proper person and no proper place. "The space of a tactic is the space of the other. Thus it must play on and with a terrain imposed on it and organized by the law of a foreign power. It does not have the means to *keep to itself*, at a distance, in a position of withdrawal, foresight, and self-collection."[32] If the subject of strategy is a robust agent, a fully developed person or institution, the subject of tactics is something more difficult to name, without a distinct location or premeditated goals.

To locate this subject of tactics, I turn to the short-lived anarchist newsletter *The Woman Rebel: A Monthly Journal of Militant Thought* (1914). In wider histories of the American birth control movement, *The Woman Rebel* is often remarked upon but seldom read with close attention. An early, largely independent production of Margaret Sanger, the magazine took its subtitle taken from an IWW pamphlet, a translation of the French that comes, more distantly, from the French socialist Louis Auguste Blanqui: "No Gods No Masters." The subtitle begins to express the ways that *The Woman Rebel* was not explicitly focused on reproductive rights but associated with a larger problem of class struggle. At this early moment in her career, Sanger connected birth control, a term she coined in the newsletter, with the struggles of the working class, arguing that only when women were sexually emancipated, their energies redirected from their families, could a social revolution take place.

The journal advertised for a particular type of woman reader. A subsection of the April 1914 edition announces, "REBEL WOMEN WANTED":

> WHO deny the right of the State to deprive women of such knowledge as would enable them to take upon themselves voluntary motherhood.
>
> WHO deny the right of the State to prohibit such knowledge which would add to the freedom and happiness of the people.
>
> WHO demand that those desiring to live together in love shall be provided with such knowledge and experience as Science has developed, which would prevent conception.
>
> WHO will assist in the work of increasing the demand for this information.

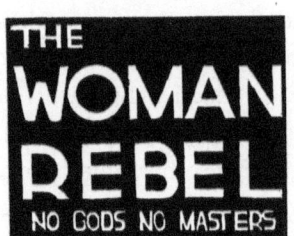

FIGURE 3.4 *The Woman Rebel* 1, no. 6 (August 1914): 1.

WHO have the courage and backbone to fight with "THE WOMAN REBEL."

Against this outrageous suppression, whereby a woman has no control of the function of motherhood.

WHO are willing to enter this fight, and continue to the end.[33]

This might be an advertisement for women already in existence, to bring like minds together. However, the list of wanted women, and much of the content of *The Woman Rebel*, is better understood as a set of instructions geared toward the future. Like Flynn's manual for sabotage, the magazine hypothesizes a female subject who is made through a series of actions. Within the wider arc of *The Woman Rebel*, this advertisement is a bit of an anomaly.

Most often, these instructions for women come in the form of historical lessons. Each issue of *The Woman Rebel* includes a number of short biographies of model rebel women, including Mary Wollstonecraft, Louise Michel, Marie Spiridonova, George Sand, and Theroigne de Mericourt. Elsewhere, poems salute Emmeline Pankhurst and Mother Jones. In some cases, the line between historical subject and fictionalized character becomes a bit blurry. Some articles animate their biographical personages. For instance, "Cleopatra" begins with a monologue that passes between ancient history and the present day. It starts in the first person, as though Cleopatra were directly addressing her readers. She claims, "I have no right to demand rights! I have no feeling to be the master of men! I have no right for rights! For I have all rights! I take all rights!"[34] Is this meant to be a speech that Cleopatra *would* say? It is a critique of rights at a distance from Ptolemaic Egypt, no doubt. But this historical vagueness allows the monologue to do double work, as the imagined speech of an Egyptian queen and a plausible critique for the right to birth control in present-day America.

The conditional, what Cleopatra *would* say, appears as a key mode in other articles. Some speak directly to the reader in the imperative tense: "Feminists—Come out from under the cover of morbid respectability and let's get a look at you! How many could be a Voltairine de Clayre [sic], a Louise Michel, an Emma Goldman or an Elizabeth Flynn?"[35] Here is the interrogative form with which I began, one that frames a hypothetical future: what Cleopatra *would* say, what Emma Goldman *would* do. To answer the question involves an imaginative leap, so that biographical history becomes so much raw matter, to be reworked to suit the present day. This imagination involves a form of sympathy but breaks with the models of identification most common to the humanitarian narratives I discussed earlier. To do as an Emma Goldman would do involves sympathetic identification. But the site of identification is not suffering. It is not even feeling. Rather, the reader identifies with action: a history of political acts and their hypothesized extension in the future.

To focus on the conditional imagination allows for a shift in emphasis, so that *The Woman Rebel* can be understood not as a little magazine but as a compendium of portable tactics. Some articles are more forthright about this effort. "The Militants in England" details the recent work of the suffragette movement abroad as so many tactics to be considered at home: "Acids were poured into letter boxes, telegraph wires cut, plate glass windows smashed, fire engines called out on false alarms and ministers baited wherever they went."[36] The front-page column, "In Defense of Assassination," takes up the recent deaths of three anarchists, accidentally killed by dynamite while constructing a bomb. Noting that the "czars of industry" use the police force and soldiers as weapons, to break strikes or intimidate workers, the article concludes that workers must turn to militant tactics in return, as the weapons of the weak:

> The point I wish to bring out it this—since the great mass of people are by force of circumstances unable to use the same weapons employed by the better educated and privileged class, this does not preclude the working class from using whatever other means of defense may be at its disposal, such as the strikes, boycott, sobatage [sic] or assassination.[37]

In general, *The Woman Rebel* does not have much to say about assassination, but the final issues of the journal become increasingly focused on a single tactic, the hunger strike, which had recently gained prominence through its widespread use by the British suffragettes. According to the *New York Times*, the anarchist Becky Edelsohn was the first woman to stage a hunger strike in the United States. Arrested for inciting a riot, Edelsohn turned to the hunger strike during her imprisonment at Blackwell's Island. Along with the *Times*, *The Woman Rebel* became increasingly focused on Edelsohn's narrative. In the August 1914 issue of *The Woman Rebel* there are five separate articles on Edelsohn: "A History of the Hunger Strike" details Edelsohn's arrests for speaking against the war with Mexico (April 22) and after the Colorado National Guard attacked a tent city of striking miners in what became known as the Ludlow Massacre (July 20). Another article includes Edelsohn's letters, smuggled out of Blackwell's Island, during her second imprisonment. Most strikingly, the cover-page article, "Becky and the Respectables," makes clear a distinction between Edelsohn and an opposite class of persons, including judges and the Catholic church. In a separate article, the "respectables" are personified by the sociologist Katherine B. Davis, the police matron for the Bedford Reformatory for Women and commissioner of corrections of New York. Residing on Blackwell's Island on opposite sides of the law, Davis and Edelsohn supply model types based on localized actions, rather than on inherent characteristics. Readers are asked to think about what they would do if they were in each woman's place. Interestingly, *The Woman Rebel*'s anonymized editorial collective offers its own preemptive response to this sort of inquiry. "The question has been asked: What would THE WOMAN REBEL do with Rebecca Edelsohn if she were in Dr. Katherine B. Davis' position? No woman rebel would ever find herself in such a degraded position. The view of the revolutionary woman is expressed adequately enough in other columns in this number."[38] Here again, readers are urged not to feel with Edelsohn or Davis but more literally to imagine themselves in such a position and then to focus on action, to do what these women would do.

This imagination is a mode of reading premised on action, but the type of action matters too. For this narrative mode to work, the tactic has to be considered as a mobile kind of action, without a proper person or proper place. It can belong to anyone. In *The Woman Rebel*, reading for tactics involves an imaginative leap into the past actions of other people, but this leap is particular for the way it literalizes much of the rhetoric of sympathetic identification, to turn it toward different ends. As Elizabeth Gurley Flynn notes, in *Sabotage*, claims about suffering or justice might have little effect on the owners of a silk mill. However, the readers of *Sabotage* might engage in a different sort of projective imagination, by treating the histories of work slowdown and birth strike as a set of practices to be reproduced. Read as instruction, these histories offer a mobile set of strategies to assemble knowledge, technologies, and—finally—subjects. *The Woman Rebel* is clear on this point. Tactics develop a particular type of personhood. The article on Police Matron Davis and prisoner Edelsohn notes that sociologists of Davis's stripe look upon prisoners "with pity if not sympathy, as long as the victims submit tamely." This dynamic changes with a shift in behavior: "Only when the victims rebel, revolt, inaugurate a hunger-strike, or in any way indicate that they are of human flesh and blood ... is the expert in correction ready to revert to methods of torture."[39] In this narrative of subject formation, the no place and no person of the portable tactic paradoxically indicates that the female political actor has become human. But this becoming-human of the prisoner is what prompts a host of new cruelties that remain unnamed.

The insistence that female victims become human through an act of the will does not consider the ways that, for some, sheer willpower might not be enough. Here and elsewhere, white women offer a standard for women in general, as a universal category. Consider again the question addressed to hypothetical readers: "How many could be a Voltairine de Clayre [sic], a Louise Michel, an Emma Goldman or an Elizabeth Flynn?" Racial difference across the category "women" is not a part of this scenario, nor does it appear in frequent allusions to white workers as wage slaves. To be sure, at this early moment, *The Woman Rebel* argues for human betterment through class uplift, rather than racial purity. However, these discourses are nevertheless marked by the status of the slave as a zero degree of freedom. After Sanger was indicted for obscenity charges for the content of *The Woman Rebel*, she arranged for the following letter to be sent to President Woodrow Wilson. Unpublished in Sanger's lifetime, the letter asks the president: "While men stand proudly and face the sun, boasting that they have quenched the wickedness of slavery, what chains of slavery are, have been or ever could be so intimate a horror as the shackles on every limb—on every thought—on the very soul of an unwilling pregnant woman?"[40] After World War II, Sanger's reliance on the language of slavery becomes even more pronounced, as we shall see in the next section. For now, it is enough to mark this teleological process, from wage slave to human subject, for the way it assumes a somewhat pliable world, ready to be molded, or at least to fracture, with the application of collective force. In turning to Harlem, the vectors of force and threat are different, in the midst of what James Weldon Johnson called the Red Summer of 1919. In this case, the understanding of a pliable world is different too, in terms of how it might yield or scar. This is a story that will lead back to the wider question of reproductive justice and feminist tactics, but for now I begin on a more local scale, with the absent future of the black child.

Queer Futures in Harlem

In October 1919, *The Crisis: A Record of the Darker Races* published a children's number. The table of contents lists "Pictures of Seventy-Four Colored Children" (figures 3.5a–b). There are several pages devoted to yearbook-style portraits, the children alone or in groups. These are interspersed amid the usual articles. Portraiture accompanies the stories and editorials as well. The children look like models, posed in a studio and professionally shot. They adorn the page like an advertisement. Though some of the literary sections of the magazine are on theme, the baby photographs do not always illustrate

THE ART OF NOT HAVING CHILDREN   125

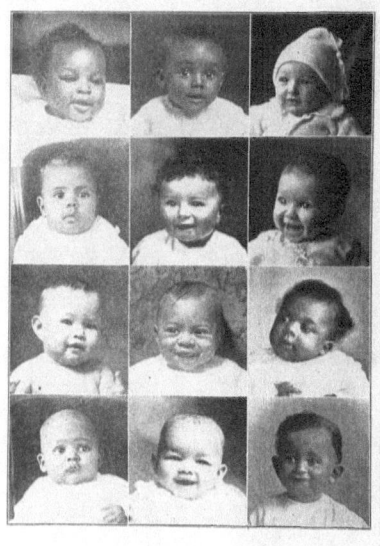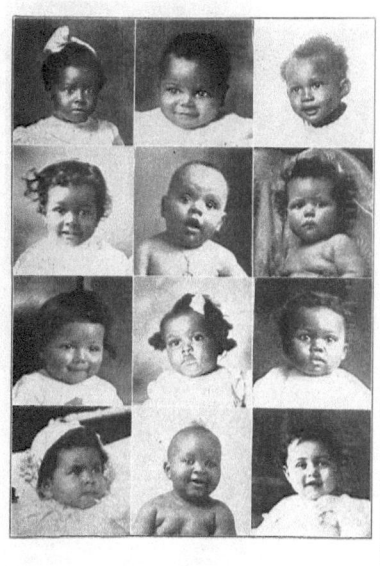

FIGURE 3.5 "The Baby Figure of the Giant Mass of Things to Come," *The Crisis: A Record of the Darker Races*, October 1919, 302–3.

or refer to the written content they are set beside. A diapered baby appears at the top of W. E. B. Du Bois's editorial, which is primarily about the lynching of black men in Texas (figure 3.6).

"Since 1889 Texas has lynched 338 human beings—standing second only to Georgia and Mississippi in this horrible eminence," Du Bois writes.[41] Du Bois goes on to write about Congressman James Francis Byrnes, of South Carolina, who has accused the magazine of inciting the race riots in Washington and Chicago. On the pages that follow, baby photographs illustrate the letters to the editor. They are appended to poems and fairy stories. Nine newborns, bundled in a row, illustrate Walter White's postmortem on the summer's race riots in Chicago (figure 3.7). The photograph was likely appended after the article's writing—White makes no mention of infants. His article ends with a quotation from the *Associated Press* report: "Negros are not planning anything, but will defend themselves if attacked."[42] A number of the following pages are entirely given over to portraits of babies and small children.

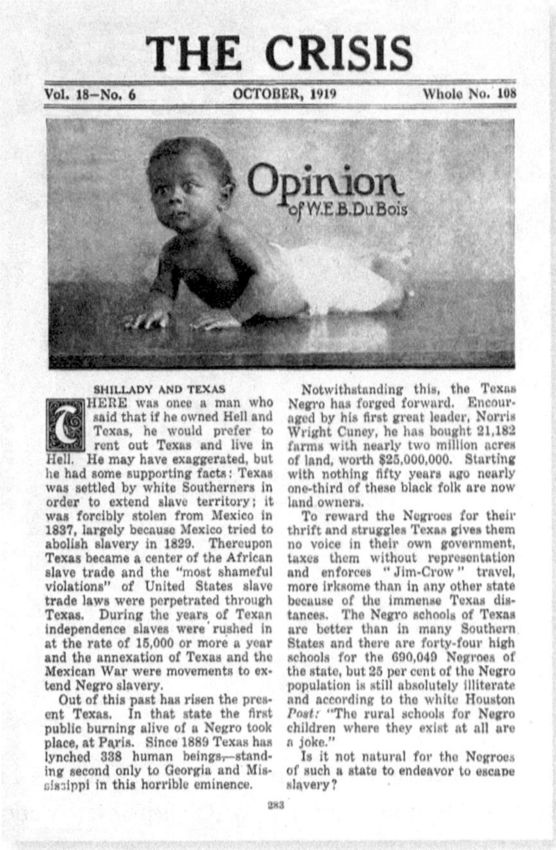

THE CRISIS

Vol. 18—No. 6 OCTOBER, 1919 Whole No. 108

SHILLADY AND TEXAS

THERE was once a man who said that if he owned Hell and Texas, he would prefer to rent out Texas and live in Hell. He may have exaggerated, but he had some supporting facts: Texas was settled by white Southerners in order to extend slave territory; it was forcibly stolen from Mexico in 1837, largely because Mexico tried to abolish slavery in 1829. Thereupon Texas became a center of the African slave trade and the "most shameful violations" of United States slave trade laws were perpetrated through Texas. During the years of Texan independence slaves were rushed in at the rate of 15,000 or more a year and the annexation of Texas and the Mexican War were movements to extend Negro slavery.

Out of this past has risen the present Texas. In that state the first public burning alive of a Negro took place, at Paris. Since 1889 Texas has lynched 338 human beings,—standing second only to Georgia and Mississippi in this horrible eminence.

Notwithstanding this, the Texas Negro has forged forward. Encouraged by his first great leader, Norris Wright Cuney, he has bought 21,182 farms with nearly two million acres of land, worth $25,000,000. Starting with nothing fifty years ago nearly one-third of these black folk are now land owners.

To reward the Negroes for their thrift and struggles Texas gives them no voice in their own government, taxes them without representation and enforces "Jim-Crow" travel, more irksome than in any other state because of the immense Texas distances. The Negro schools of Texas are better than in many Southern States and there are forty-four high schools for the 690,049 Negroes of the state, but 25 per cent of the Negro population is still absolutely illiterate and according to the white Houston *Post:* "The rural schools for Negro children where they exist at all are a joke."

Is it not natural for the Negroes of such a state to endeavor to escape slavery?

283

FIGURE 3.6 W. E. B. Du Bois, "Opinion," *The Crisis: A Record of the Darker Races*, October 1919, 283.

The children's number was an annual affair. Du Bois called it the most popular issue but also noted a disturbing conjuncture. "To the consternation of the Editors of *The Crisis* we have had to record some horror in nearly every Children's Number—in 1915, it was Leo Frank; in 1916, the lynching at Gainesville, Fla; in 1917 and 1918, the riot and court martial at Houston, Tex., etc."[43] The juxtaposition of children's portraits and the reportage on lynching was, then, not entirely unique to 1919. Over the past decade, it had become standard that the issue devoted to children would include jarring adjacencies. Take, for instance, the toddler adorning "The Looking Glass," posed in

FIGURE 3.7 Walter White, "Chicago and Its Eight Reasons," *The Crisis: A Record of the Darker Races*, October 1919, 293.

the photography studio alongside her stuffed horse. Below her *The Crisis* reprints Claude McKay's "If We Must Die" (figure 3.8). Just above McKay's fighting words, adjacent to the lynching reportage, the portraits celebrate black children as a promise for a different sort of life. This is a heterosexual future based on the reproduction of the nuclear family, but it is also a gesture of resistance amid a culture of racial violence. The children's isues are saccharine and a little campy—but they are also brutal. The juxtapositions between baby photographs and lynching reports remind us that the pictured children are always already in a structural relation to premature death.[44]

In *Unnatural Selections: Eugenics in American Modernism and the Harlem Renaissance*, Daylanne K. English considers the children's issues of *The Crisis* alongside a wider survey of the racial-uplift narratives of the 1920s and 1920s. English argues that racial uplift during this period frequently took up the language of eugenic science as a common good. These arguments promoted black motherhood particularly among upper-class families, for the betterment of the race. As a point of contrast, English situates the emergence of a new genre among New Negro women writers working between 1916 and 1930: the antilynching drama. These works situate healthy black motherhood as a historical impossibility amid a culture of lynching, often through representations of women who refuse to become mothers or murder the children they have. Across the work of writers including Alice Dunbar Nelson,

FIGURE 3.8 Claude McKay, "If We Must Die," *The Crisis: A Record of the Darker Races*, October 1919, 300.

Mary Burrill, and Angelina Weld Grimké, lynching offers an inversion of the logic of eugenics, "a most unnatural form of selection, one designed to reinforce white supremacy and sustain black powerlessness, regardless of the quality and education of either whites or blacks."[45] In her reading of antilynching dramas, English primarily focuses on Grimké's best-known work, *Rachel*, which was first performed in 1916 and published in 1920. Though I will not discuss this play at length, I want to highlight one moment that will become important in the pages to come, for the ways that it situates lynching as a form of structural violence, what English calls a form of "unnatural selection," embedded in the possible futures of the black child:

> **Rachel:** If Jimmy went South now—and grew up—he might be—a George?
> **Mrs. Loving:** Yes.
> **Rachel:** Then, the South is full of tens, hundreds, thousands of little boys, who, one day may be—and some of them with certainty—Georges?
> **Mrs. Loving:** Yes, Rachel.
> **Rachel:** And the little babies, the dear, little helpless babies, being born today—now—and those who will be, tomorrow, and all the tomorrows to come—have *that* sooner or later to look forward to? They will laugh and play and sing and be happy and grow up, perhaps, and be ambitious, just for *that*?
> **Mrs. Loving:** Yes, Rachel.[46]

To be a George is to be prematurely dead. Though the above scene is rife with evasion—all those italicized *that's*—enough of the play has passed by this time for the audience to know, as do Rachel and Mrs. Loving, that to be a George means to be pulled from your bed in the middle of the night by a group of white men and hanged by the neck from the trees in your yard, alongside your father. George is a future that might apply to Jimmy and that will with some certainty happen to some of the thousands of black boys living in the American South. As a possible future, George signals a vulnerability to premature death as a basic, nonnegotiable fact. George marks, in effect, the lack of a future for some black boys that here reads as statistical inevitability. Note how the dashes stutter across this otherwise straightforward grammar, as though the train of associations is forcibly broken and then retethered into sentences. This lack of futurity is almost unthinkable, or better not thought. But the answers also suggest that this lack is normal, or at least lived with day in and day out as a kind of common sense. ("Yes." "Yes, Rachel." "Yes, Rachel.")

Unlike the calls in *The Woman Rebel* to imagine oneself as an Emma Goldman or a Louise Michel, this scene of projection is not about sympathy or action. The passage does not ask us to feel as a George might feel or do as a George might do. George's death stands in as one component in a wider structure of violence. George is a destination that some will reach, regardless of how they "laugh and play and sing and be happy and grow up." The way that this future is structural common sense sometimes makes it seem, in this passage, like absolute inevitability. For this reason, Rachel responds with a preemptive conditional: "How horrible! Why—it would be more merciful—to strangle the little things at birth."[47] Rachel does not, in fact, strangle her children. But at the end of the play, she does refuse her suitor's marriage proposal, to avoid having children at all and thus save them from growing up to face the brutality of a white mob.

When *Rachel* was published in 1920, some critics accused Grimké of advocating race suicide.[48] Though the comparison goes unnoted, this critique inserts *Rachel* into the wider arc of birth control materials I have already discussed, in that it positions *Rachel* as an instruction manual for the prevention of conception. Grimké responded to these claims in no uncertain terms. "Since it has been understood that 'Rachel' preaches race suicide, I would emphasize that that was not my intention. To the contrary, the appeal is not primarily to the colored people, but to the whites."[49] Grimké explained that she was looking to reach white women through the shared fact of motherhood. By demonstrating the effects of lynching on black mothers and children, Grimké hoped to sway white women, so that they might "see, feel, and understand just what effect their prejudice and the prejudice of their fathers, brothers, husbands, sons were having on the souls of colored mothers everywhere."[50]

What follows will more firmly connect Grimké's writing to the American birth control movement through attention to her short story "The Closing Door," published in two 1919 issues of *The Birth Control Review*. Through Agnes's dialogue, the story cannily refracts the language of the birth strike as narrated by white feminists. What was then in anarchosyndicalist circles the utopian promise of recognizing women as producers becomes, for Agnes, a nightmare of forced objectification: "'Yes!—Yes!—I!—I!—An instrument of reproduction!—another of the many!—a colored woman—doomed!—cursed!—put here!—willing or unwilling! For what?—to bring children here—men children—for the sport—the lust—of possible orderly mobs—who go about things—in an orderly manner—on Sunday mornings!'"[51]

The monologue describes a relation of persons as part of a wider racialized structure that disallows individual agency. What Agnes cannot do, in this scenario, is protect her children from the mob violence that killed her brother. For Grimké's critics, this stance was often described as pessimism, in contrast to a more heroic notion of resistance or redress. In a review of *Rachel*, the *Washington Star* claimed: "The action progresses by way of episodes calculated to show the futility of individual effort on the part of the colored people, since no amount of effort is able to overcome the arrogance of the white race."[52] The language that Grimké prefers is closer to doom—a marked destiny, as though one were living the life of a character in a book already written. This sense of foreboding permeates the story as always already over, narrated in retrospect.

"The Closing Door" is narrated by a character seemingly peripheral to the action, the teenager Lucy. At the beginning of the story, Lucy has been passed around to a number of relatives, then comes to live with Agnes Milton, who is happily married to her husband, Jim. In the opening stages of the story, Lucy narrates the family's happiness as a thing of the past, foreshadowing an unmarked violence to come. Some of these scenes focus on the relations between Jim and Agnes, but a number of them are erotically charged interactions between Agnes and Lucy, with reference to kissing, touching, and secrecy. At the story's midpoint, Agnes learns of her brother's lynching and descends into numb terror. After she gives birth to a son, she murders the infant so that he will not grow up to be another victim of racial violence.

How do we navigate between depictions of same-sex desire, mob murder, and infanticide? As one answer to this question, what follows situates "The Closing Door" as a meditation on action, though quite different than the narratives of individual rights found in *The Woman Rebel* or the Berlin birth strike debates. Rather than a focus on right—the right to privacy, the right to contraception, the right to stage a birth strike, the right to be left alone—Grimké's work takes up the wider racialized field of reproductive justice. This wider scale allows for a consideration of the body as a terrain of contestation that can encompass same-sex desire and the structural vulnerability to premature death without equating the two, or making one a reparation for the other's brutality.

⸺

Published from 1917–1940, *The Birth Control Review* was a different sort of magazine than its discontinued predecessor, *The Woman Rebel*. The *Review* had an editorial staff and offices outside Sanger's living room. It was more likely to publish the testimony of medical experts and push for the legalization of contraception as a single-issue demand. In the 1920s, the *Review*, alongside the wider birth control movement, became increasingly medicalized, focused on the eugenic science of biological racism. From 1919 to 1920, Grimké's stories ran alongside another serialized book, Warren S. Thompson's *Race Suicide in the United States*. First published in *Scientific Monthly*, Thompson's research relied on statistical methods to forecast the decline of what he called America's "native stock." In a series of elaborate graphs, Thompson supplied figures for the proportion of children to women according to distinctly valued categories: urban white, rural white, urban negro, rural negro. Alongside Warren, both lay writers and scientists increasingly turned to the question of the birth rate more generally, often through the racialized language of human quality over quantity.

This eugenic turn to the quality of human stock was not just a racial argument. As Roderick Ferguson and Siobhan Somerville have argued, scientific racism and the formation of homosexual identity at the turn of the century were discourses that depended on each other, so that racial and sexual deviance can be historically understood as mutually reinforcing.[53] Note, for instance, the frequent appearance of Havelock Ellis in *The Birth Control Review* alongside Warren's serialized text. Better known as the author of *Sexual Inversion*, in the *Review* Ellis offers an extended, largely sympathetic analysis of Lothrop Stoddard's popular text *The Rising Tide of Color*. Though skeptical of some of Stoddard's more extreme positions, particularly the rising threat of Bolshevism, Ellis agrees that unchecked procreation would have a critical effect on the "relation between the primary human races, White and Colored."[54] The article indirectly racializes its audience, the royal *we*, as white: "Since by the prejudice of color, we must mostly be on [Stoddard's] side in this matter, we may profitably meditate on the reasonable considerations he brings forward."[55] Primarily among these considerations is the eugenic destiny of "our civilization," a human stock often enumerated as universal but also, implicitly and explicitly, marked by the exclusion of blackness.

Given the double threat of Ellis and Warren in *The Birth Control Review*, it is more than unexpected to find therein Grimké's short story "The Closing Door."[56] Even more difficult to account for are the scenes of same-sex desire that appear at the beginning of the story, as so many loose threads. Some are glancing claims of affection. "I have cared for people. I care for Jim, but Agnes Milton is the only person I have ever really loved. I love her still."[57] At other moments, Lucy recalls episodic fragments. Lucy is struck with affection when Agnes describes her wrinkles as a positive effect of smiling too much. "For reply I leaned forward and kissed them. I loved them from that time on," Lucy recalls (12). The next section offers what might be the most explicitly homoerotic scene in the story, as a conversation full of unmarked referents and doublespeak. "Here is another memory of her—perhaps the loveliest of them all," Lucy begins. It is a May evening, and Lucy is trying to thread a needle. She finds herself blinded by Agnes: "two soft hands were clapped over my eyes." I quote the entire scene as it is separated from the other text on the page, from beginning to end:

> "Please don't be cross," came the soft voice still close to my ear.
> "I'm not."
> At that she chuckled.
> "Well!" I said.
> "I'm trying to tell you something. Sh! Not so loud."
> "Well!" I said a third time, but in a whisper to humor her. We were alone in the flat, there was no reason I could see for this tremendous secrecy.
> "I'm waiting for you to be sweet to me."
> "I am. But why I should have to lose my needle and my temper and be blinded and sweet just to hear something—is beyond me."
> "Because I don't wish you to see me while I say it."
> Her soft lips were kissing my ear.
> "Well, I'm very sweet now. What is it?"
> There was another little pause and during it her fingers over my eyes trembled a little. She was breathing quicker too.
> "Agnes Milton, what *is* it?"
> "Wait, I'm just trying to think *how* to tell you. Are you sure you're very sweet?"
> "Sure."
> I loved the feel of her hands and sat very still.
> "Lucy!"
> "Yes."
> "What do you think would be the loveliest, loveliest thing for you to know was—was—there—close—just under your heart?"
>
> (12)

This scene is retroactively constructed as secret, even if this occlusion appears unnecessary inside the shuttered doors of the flat. ("We were alone in the flat, there was no reason I could see for this tremendous secrecy.") It is quite literally a scene of blindness as well—for the duration, Agnes's hands cover Lucy's eyes. The knowledge to be shared is perpetually missing, set in the gaps of ellipsis or understood through assumption. Agnes has something to tell Lucy, but the referent—the something—never appears in the passage, at least not overtly. Instead there is telling and not telling, through abbreviated dialogue that might seem like so much filler between the more straightforward actions: "Her soft lips were kissing my ear." "She was breathing quicker too." "I loved the feel of her hands and sat very still." Later it will become clear that the knowledge to be shared is Agnes's pregnancy. But isolated here the scene suggests that the "loveliest, loveliest thing for you to know" might be any number of things not related to heterosexual reproduction.

Much of this passage borrows its language from a letter in the Grimké archive, sent to the author from Mary Burrill, rumored to be her lover. Dated 1896, the letter inquires, "Could I just come to meet thee once more, in the old sweet way, just coming at your calling, and like an angel bending o'er you breathe into your ear, 'I love you.'"[58] In her response to Burrill, Grimké writes, "Oh Mamie if you only knew how my heart beats when I think of you and it yearns and pants to gaze, if only for one second upon your lovely face."[59] Though not word for word, much of the Lucy/Agnes scene picks up on this language: "I took her hands from my eyes and turned to look at her. The beauty of her face made me catch my breath."[60] The similarities between biographical letter and fictionalized story, as though one were a re-creation of the other, become more pressing when we note that Mary Burrill's dialect play *They That Sit in Darkness: A One-Act Play of Negro Life* appears alongside "The Closing Door" in the September 1919 edition of *The Birth Control Review*.

The love scene is a public secret, appearing in print, but it remains illegible to people outside of the Grimké-Burrill epistolary romance. However, these scenes go nowhere. They are not effectively folded into the wider narrative. Indeed, by isolating these fragments I also erase a major effect of their reading, in that these moments appear within a wider atmosphere of foreboding, perpetually marked by Lucy's oblique references of a bad end for Agnes and Jim. "There was just the merest suspicion of a cloud over their happiness, these days, they had been married five years and had no children,"

Lucy recalls (10). This sense of inevitable doom becomes particularly vexed when Agnes connects her own future to a literary character, through a story of star-crossed love already written. Agnes asks Lucy, "Do you remember Kipling's 'Without Benefit of Clergy'?" (12). First published in 1890, the story takes place in British India, where the civil servant John Holden lives with a young Muslim woman, Ameera, secreted away at the edge of the city. The couple are unmarried by necessity because public knowledge of the interracial affair would ruin Holden's career. They exist, therefore, "without the benefit of clergy," despite "every rule and law" that would prevent their courtship. In swift succession, the couple's infant son dies, followed by Ameera. The aspects of the story seized upon by Agnes are the early days of erotic bliss, of potentially unholy or unsanctioned happiness in love, to be followed by swift retribution. Agnes quotes Ameera's warning from the story, as a way to avoid future harm: "We must make no protestations of delight but go softly underneath the stars, lest God find us out" (13).

Thus far I have noted two different intertexts that fold themselves into the story: the love letter, emerging through the scenes of same-sex desire, and Kipling's narrative of Anglo-Indian love, modeled by John Holden and Ameera. Early in Grimké's story, a third, more historical narrative emerges. In a flashback that seems to leap into an alternative time/space altogether, Lucy recalls, "I used to pray that in some way I might change places with her and go into that darkness where though, still living, one forgets sun and moon and stars and flowers and winds—and love itself, and existence means dark, foul smelling cages, hollow clanging doors, hollow monotonous days" (11). This hope refigures the Middle Passage as an impossible memory haunting the narrator's present—a haunting that occurs with such intensity that, by the end of the story, Agnes fully enters this space of death. Like the slave ship, the infanticide belongs to a history out of sync with the wider arc of the story. In the following pages, I want to look more closely at this representation of infanticide, as both a reanimation of slavery's reproductive violence and a reconsideration of black women's agency through a longer, vexed history of slave resistance.

Jennifer L. Morgan begins her history of gender and reproduction in New World slavery with the uneasy relation between infanticide and individual agency. In turning to women's reproduction as a historical frame, Morgan situates the black female body as a terrain of contestation that spoils a strict binary between resistance and accommodation.[61] In this context, the matter of reproduction entails a reconsideration of agency more generally, so that the birth of children that enables the continuation of slavery does not immediately signal accommodation. In the same way, practices of birth control, abortion, or, in some cases, infanticide, cannot immediately be understood as a form of resistance. Lacking autobiographical testimony, it is impossible to speculate upon the intentions behind such practices. There is ample documentation, however, of planter concerns over the low birth rates of slaves. In the mid-nineteenth century, Southern medical journals investigated this population trend somewhat obsessively. Noting entire families of slave women that did not bear children, Dr. E. M. Pendleton explained that "the blacks are possessed of a secret by which they destroy the fetus at an early stage of gestation."[62] In the *Nashville Journal of Medicine and Surgery*, Dr. John H. Morgan documented the use of a number of abortifacients, including tansy, rue, pennyroyal, cedar berries, and camphor.[63] In 1826, the Reverend Henry Beame claimed that in Jamaican slave populations, the "procuration of abortion is very prevalent . . . there being herbs and powders known to them, as given by obeah men and women."[64] Common abortifacients included manioc, yam, papaya, mango, lime, and frangipani.[65] Women might take a "corset leaf" infusion or tie a twig of *Jatophra* (physic nut, or nettlespurge) to a string, placing it in the womb to cause a miscarriage. Midwives were known to administer the emetic cerasee, wild Tansy, the water germander, or the seeds of a sandbox tree.

Most troubling for the planter class were infanticides named as a stillbirth. In a consideration of census reports from 1790 to 1860, Michael P. Johnson estimates that more than sixty thousand slave infants were reported as smothering deaths.[66] However, Johnson and others conclude that this high rate of infant death is more likely attributable to sudden infant death syndrome than purposeful suffocation. Of course, high infant mortality rates could also be attributed to malnutrition, overwork, and insufficient living conditions; these more sensible arguments were also noted during the antebellum era. In Greene County, Alabama, beginning in 1852, the children of George Hays sued William Gould for poor oversight during the administration of their father's will, resulting in a loss of capital. According to the suit, Gould had appointed an overseer who has a "cruel, brutish and inhuman disposition."[67] During the years of his administration, the "breeding women on said Plantations were rendered almost entirely worthless as such" and "subject to continual miscarriages." The plaintiffs estimated a loss of "some forty children through either barrenness of the females or abortions."

Abolitionist texts often focused on the deaths of women and children caused by the inhumane conditions of plantation society. However, slave infanticide proved to be a more difficult topic for the ways it rendered mothers both victim and criminal. Though largely absent from slave narratives, abolitionist texts, and plantation journals, a partial record of slave infanticides can be gleaned from court records. In *Jane (a slave) v. The State* (1831) the defendant was convicted by the Missouri courts of "knowingly, willfully, feloniously and of her malice aforethought" giving "a certain deadly poison" to her infant child Angeline. Several days later, when the poison failed, she allegedly "choked, suffocated, and smothered" the child with her bedclothes.[68] In the wider abolitionist literature, most publicized case of infanticide concerns the runaway slave Margaret Garner. In 1856, trapped by slave catchers in Cincinnati, Ohio, Garner killed her three-year-old daughter, slashing her throat with a butcher knife. In Paul Gilroy's account, the Garner case signals an important turn in abolitionist literature, when the use of violence became sanctioned as a tactic, alongside education reform and legislative change, to oppose the wider institution of slavery.[69]

Grimké's turn to infanticide as a protest against racial violence thus invokes a wider historical legacy. Ultimately, the afterlife of plantation slavery is one of three distinct chronotopes, or spheres of time and space, that appear in the story. There is first the living death of the slave ship, linked to Agnes's desperate murder of her son as a choice between modes of death. There is the doomed interracial coupling of Ameera and John Holden in Kipling's British India. And finally, there is the same-sex romance between Agnes and Lucy, as a reanimation of Grimké's correspondence with Mary Burrill. All of these narratives operate according to registers of secrecy. But these chronotopes are not equivalent or even of a piece. Occurring as discrete sections in the story, they do not map smoothly onto one another. Ameera's death through cholera is unlike Agnes's choice to murder her infant. Agnes's choice operates according to a different frame of possible action than what would be available to the women on the slave ship, where "existence means dark, foul smelling cages, hollow clanging doors, hollow monotonous days."

The way these discrete chronotopes do not fit together thus allows for a meditation on agency in terms of the differential fields of possibility available to African American women at midcentury. In this way, Grimké's story offers an alternative to the rights-based claims of white feminists within the birth control movement, turning away from an individual choice to use contraception to the wider field of what Dorothy Roberts and others have called "reproductive justice."[70] In Roberts's foundational account, the American birth control movement primarily associated the right to bodily privacy with the experience of white feminists. In response, Roberts reframes racial justice as a central component in the wider project of reproductive autonomy, to consider both "the full range of procreative activities" alongside racialized social forces that affect or inhibit these choices, including uneven vulnerability to premature death and sexual violence; access to health care, a living wage, and housing; and state-sponsored medical oversight, sterilization, and children's welfare services.[71] Roberts thus situates reproductive justice beyond the matter of privacy or contraception. Rather than a practice to be followed, this sense of bodily autonomy entails a rethinking of the presumed universality of the subject of tactics, to differentiate between the possible futures available to racialized groups.

In "The Closing Door," Grimké juxtaposes many of these sites as entangled forms of intimacy and violence. It is montage at its most cruel and disturbing: the love scene next to the slave ship, the choleric death in India, the lynching in a nameless city of the American South, the reanimation of infanticide as a vexed form of resistance. In this rendering, there is a lack of absolute causation. One of these scenarios does not prevent the other or even make it more livable. There is no salvation to be had in the love scenes between Lucy and Agnes. Both Agnes and her baby die. What I want to mark is entanglement, rather than instruction. For Grimké, the wider field of reproductive justice encompasses a number of categories that cannot be understood as foils for or solutions to the others: the futures of black children, the threat of mob violence, same-sex desire, reproductive autonomy, childlessness. To hold these together is uncomfortable because they are not of a piece. Against the other materials considered in this chapter, "The Closing Door" refuses to give historical lessons as so many instructions to follow, step by step. It does not say, kiss your female lover, murder your infants, or do not have children at all, though this last case has been the implicit understanding of many readers. History is still there, but not as a lesson. Grimké narrates actions and subjects, but the crux of the story is about making visible the relations between chosen pleasures and unasked-for violence, some families and others, children, no children, and variable futures, caught up in the wider field of reproductive justice.

We Charge Genocide

So far I have said many things that Grimké's writing is not: not a humanitarian narrative, not instructions for race suicide, not a protocol for a birth strike, not a guide to lesbian romance. To understand what the story is requires a different viewpoint, one that moves beyond a national context and into a wider Atlantic history. The following pages take up a question: Why does it matter that Grimké links lynching crimes in the United States with colonial death in India? What does this international geography suggest, not as a mode of comparison, but as an argument about the remedies and entitlements for reproductive justice in a transnational framework?

These questions are already moving toward a different sort of vocabulary, one that shifts away from the birth strike and into the demographic contexts of international law. At midcentury, discourses about the links between birth control began to turn away from the language of race suicide and invoke the relatively recent neologism "genocide," from the Greek word *genos* (race) and Latin suffix *-cide* (killing). Coined by the Jewish Polish jurist Raphael Lemkin in 1943, genocide quickly gained international recognition as new legal category for the mass killing or disabling of a human group.[72] Though Lemkin's work often cited the race laws of the National Socialists, he also argued that the term "genocide" should be understood within a five-hundred-year history of colonial occupation that sought to change human demographics to favor colonial powers. However, Lemkin did not think that genocide should apply to racial conflict in the United States and said so directly, in the *New York Herald Tribune* in 1951.[73]

The occasion for Lemkin's public statement was a 1951 petition to the United Nations from the Civil Rights Congress (CRC), *We Charge Genocide*. This was a media event widely covered by the international press. Paul Robeson presented copies to the UN Secretariat in New York, while William L. Patterson distributed copies at the UN's Paris meetings. There is a performative element to this presentation, but in this last section I want to look more closely at the document itself, to consider *We Charge Genocide* as an archive of international reproductive politics. Most widely, I want to reconsider this document as a tactic, one that seizes upon the postwar public debates about genocide to argue for racial justice. In this way, *We Charge Genocide* uses the language of human rights to make demands that reach beyond the forms of justice that can be remedied by national law.

We Charge Genocide is book length—240 pages. It opens with a lynching photograph, of two black men hanging in such a way that they might be embracing, the bound arm of one tucked under the chin of the other. Their names are Dooley Morton and Bert Moore, and they died in Columbus, Mississippi. But Morton and Moore are not the protagonists of this document. The following pages are about title and copyright, then Articles II and III of the Convention on the Prevention and Punishment of the Crime of Genocide appear in full, with lettered outlines of "acts committed with intent to destroy, in whole or in part, a national, ethnical, racial or religious group."[74] There is a table of contents and a list of petitioners in alphabetical order by last name. The introduction uses the names as components of the *we* that charges the government of the United States with the violation of the Convention on the Prevention and Punishment of the Crime of Genocide. This is a particular *we*: "Many of your petitioners are Negro citizens to whom the charges herein described are not mere words. They are facts felt on our bodies, crimes inflicted on our dignity" (*WC* 7). The *we* of the petition marks two classes of persons: those injured by the U.S. government and those who address this government with a demand for remedy. This demand connects U.S. racial injustice with the wider historical arc of the last war and the threat of a new war to come:

> We, Negro petitioners whose communities have been laid waste, whose homes have been burned and looted, whose children have been killed, whose women have been raped, have noted with particular horror that the genocidal doctrines and actions of the American white supremacists have already been exported to the colored peoples of Asia.... Jellied gasoline in Korea and the lynchers' faggot at home are connected in more ways than that both result in death by fire. The lyncher and the atom bomber are related.
>
> (7)

These sentences create ties across national lines through a shared history of injury. But they also make an argument about jurisdiction. The argument goes like this: Lynching is a crime that occurs in the United States but concerns the world. It is an ongoing crime. See the early addition to this document, of violent deaths that happened between the first printing, in October 1951, and now, December 1951. These deaths can be catalogued and classified. Some are mob murders, and others take place at the hands of the police. Indeed, the police can be considered a structural source of black death: "Once the classic method of lynching was the rope. Now it is the policeman's bullet" (8). All of these claims are buttressed with evidence, which makes up the bulk of the document. The materials come from black newspapers like *The Crisis* and from the labor press, black yearbooks, prison records, and sociological reports. Some crimes have been reported firsthand, by the petitioners. The petition notes that the vast majority of crimes have not been recorded. "Negro men and women leave their homes and are never seen alive again. Sometimes weeks later their bodies, or bodies thought to be theirs and often horribly mutilated, are found in the woods or washed up on the shore of a river or lake" (9). However, the petition is not a new kind of memorial. *We Charge Genocide* is a document that uses these deaths to make its demands.

Most of the time this evidence appears in list form, though the lists are not always the same. Early on, in the opening statements, the lists of names look to convince a white audience. There are the causes célèbres like the Martinsville Seven or the Trenton Six, who have been largely ignored by the white press but well documented elsewhere. Another subtitle enumerates "Other Race Murders," then "Incitement to Genocide," then "Klan Terror." But this is still the introduction. The longest section of the petition is the chapter "The Evidence," at 138 pages.

These pages present documented crimes at the federal, state, and municipal levels, from 1945 to 1951. The lists are subdivided into categories according to the aspects of the Convention they violate, then arranged chronologically. The year 1946 begins, "*February.*—FRANK ALLAN, taxi driver . . . *February.*—JAMES MAGNUM, 17 years old . . . *February 5.*—A policeman of *Freeport, L.I., New York* . . . *February 9.*—PVT. NATHANIEL JACKSON" (61). Most of the victims are men, but there are some women and children. In 1950, January 8: "Ruby Nell Harris, 4, Mary Burside, 8, and Frankie Thurman, 12, of *Kosciusko Mississippi*" (74). That same month, "Mrs. Mattie Debardeleben, of *Birmingham, Alabama,* refused to sell some chickens to three Federal revenue agents and a deputy sheriff. They beat her and she died 'of a heart attack' on the way to jail" (74).

I have tried to imagine a midcentury reader presented with this evidence. To read line by line would take hours. It would tax the attention, in that one death or rape or fire begins to blur with the others that resemble it. But it is not a document that promotes skimming, from month to month, say, or for key words. To continue reading, page after page, the mind makes up certain patterns: these deaths by hanging, those rapes that were survived, the typical lynching, the atypical lynching, the weapons used, the beatings that were fatal. There is the exceptionally monstrous, as a category of its own, and this distinction is part of the work of the evidence. These lists create new categories of violent acts and divisions within them, as in whether or not parts of the body were cut off and taken for souvenirs.

This formation of new categories, from the lists of names, makes the petition nearly unreadable. It is difficult to select a single case from these lists of evidentiary facts, because the work of this list is to represent an aggregate: *and this, and this, and this, again, again, again.* Nor can the connections between parts achieve any coherent pattern: the list is also a collage, taken from different accounts in the black press, and so lacks conjunctions that order: *then, next, so that, therefore.* In aggregate, these pages of evidence chart out the connections between interracial rapes, the accusation of rape, childbirth, child murder, the murder of adult men, and the murder of adult women as all caught up in the reproduction of the race as a human group, or in starker terms, as a matter for black survival.

This structure cannot be inserted into a humanitarian narrative because it does not make space for interiority. The project of sympathy with a single suffering subject is blunted by the unmanageable effect of so many names. Instead, in these pages, the human is a discourse that can be claimed and used as a collective practice. To reframe American racial violence as genocide that threatens the human group, and therefore a matter of reproductive justice, is a tactical interpretation, not an ethical one. It expands the question of jurisdiction, of *who decides*, beyond a purely legal or national framework. To call the U.S. government's policy against African Americans genocide changes the content of the crime "genocide" in this claiming. This expansion is also an experiment, in saying and doing, in that the final boundary of justice is not a legal one or even a matter of national concern. In this framework, justice entails the imagination of something else, something otherwise than the crimes that have been and the ways they have or have not been punished within a national frame. This imagination disarticulates national law from justice but does not require a positive content for what justice would entail.

We Charge Genocide necessitates an internationalist juridical scope, one that connects domestic reproductive politics with war crimes abroad as a threat to the human group. Alongside the birth control manuals, Grimké's writing, and the other materials in this chapter, the petition weaponizes the injured body as a subject of action. The politics of this gesture are contextual. Internationalist humanitarian claims can certainly be used for many different ends. As theorized in this chapter, the tactic is a mobile form, without content, that can be manipulated for any political outcome. My purpose here is not to prescribe a course of political action. It is to understand the ways that the language of the human was appropriated by both the Far Right and a militant, feminist, and antiracist Left. These groups turned to the language of human population to create an arsenal of tactics against the state, rather than focus on the reproductive rights that the state might grant. In so doing, they make up one of the less familiar histories of human rights, a history based on practices of sexual citizenship rather than claims for a shared humanity. These conjunctures make visible a different geography of potential action, not just in the legal terms of who decides, but in terms of who is entitled to make demands.

Though I have primarily focused on these practices as a self-directed biopolitics, I do not mean to suggest that they forestalled the ongoing governmentality of sexuality through an increasingly securitized state. As a counterpoint, the next chapter will turn to a more governmental version of biopolitics, this time in Germany. No doubt, these materials posit a different kind of reader than *The Woman Rebel* or *We Charge Genocide*. Rather than a subject of tactics, hypothesized in the future, this turn to governmental strategy absents individual experience altogether, as so much unreliable testimony, ceded to the authority of fact. For this story about government and the biological futures it might promise, I turn to the primary genre of the humanitarian narrative: the case study.

4

Rhineland Bastards, Queer Species

An Afro-German Case Study

In a 1921 protest rally in Munich, the American journalist and former actress Ray Beveridge presented the crowd with a Rhineland bastard.[1] Newspaper reports estimate that he was about nine months old. There is no record of the baby's name or what happened to him after the rally. Beveridge claimed that the existence of the mixed-race child was proof of interracial sexual violence widespread in the occupied zones of the Rhineland. The child's health also served as a point of comparison. In her autobiography, *Mein Leben für Euch!*, Beveridge includes a portrait of herself, posed between the mixed-race baby and a white German boy about six years old. The photograph presents the children as evidence in a zero-sum game of limited resources, so that the mixed-race child's health comes at the expense of the white boy's frailty. The caption is descriptive: "Left a black bastard, right an undernourished German child."[2]

The photograph displays the children as embodied proof in a criminal landscape where questions of harm and liability were becoming difficult, if not impossible, to establish. Just a year earlier, the U.S. Foreign Affairs Committee had launched an investigation into the Rhineland allegations, resulting in the published report "Colored Troops in the French Army." The twenty-page document unambiguously concludes that the claims of widespread murder, mutilation, and rape between races were fabricated.[3] Nevertheless, the Interallied Rhineland High Commission allowed that "crimes of this nature" were difficult to prove in a court of law and often went unreported. Given this ambiguity, the report made sour note of Beverage's international speaking tours and expressed concern that her popularity might sway American support for the postwar alliance. According to the American commissioner, Beveridge was only one particularly successful example of a much wider effort to revoke the Treaty of Versailles by inciting racial hysteria at home and abroad.

The treaty had called for a fifteen-year occupation of the Rhineland to securitize the western border and ensure the payment of reparations. However, it was not the fact of occupation but a contingent of the occupying army that became the heart of the controversy. In the years after the war, the partial occupation of the Rhineland by French African troops, including Algerians, Tunisians, Moroccans, and Somalis, would provoke an international press sensation, the "Black Shame on the Rhine [*Schwarze Schmach am Rhein*]." At this time, British leftists, imperial feminists, and a number of conservative groups became involved in a massive wave of international propaganda that aligned the sexual threat posed by African soldiers with the metaphorical "rape" of Germany through punitive foreign policy. Using this logic, leftist groups from the International Women's League to the British Labor Party appealed to the newly formed League of Nations to revisit the language of the treaty on behalf of the women of Germany.

On both sides of the Atlantic, these groups wrote and distributed sensational propaganda. However, they also took up a more juridical language, through the rhetoric of the legal case study, explicitly following the model of the congressional report. Widely distributed to a popular audience, these often two-hundred-plus-page pamphlets were divided into chapters and subchapters. They acted as a compendium of evidence, including photographs, witness testimony, pages of facts and figures, and extensive quotations from government officials. Beyond the case of the Rhineland, in the United Kingdom, Belgium, France, Turkey, and colonial Africa, the official inquiry into war crimes became a particularly visible genre during the interwar period. These inquiries acted as evidence to establish the criminal liability of a nation in the eyes of a transnational public sphere. Focused on theaters of war, in which national laws could not apply, these legal case studies invoked the "laws of humanity" found in the Hague and Geneva Conventions as the proper authority to distinguish between just and unjust acts of war.

Across this transatlantic public sphere, the mixed-race body and the specter of interracial rape behind it became central to the formation of "humanity" as a category of right in interwar foreign policy. As an extension of war crimes, "crimes against humanity" entered positive international law as a marker for violations that occurred beyond the framework of war between nations. However, the formation of the legal category "humanity" also contained a racialized marker through the distinction between "civilized" and "uncivilized" forms of cruelty.[4] In the years after the armistice, the propaganda surrounding the Rhineland controversy reworks the category of humanity in a more proleptic mode, signaling a reproductive future threatened by queer life and racial mixture. Across this wider public sphere, the mixed-race body functions as bodily evidence and as a metaphor, to negotiate the ways intention, liability, and harm can be pluralized to apply to identity-based groups like races and nations. In this chapter, I situate the genre of the legal case study alongside the development of the "laws of humanity" in the postwar treaties as a key point where international law and biological racism converge in new taxonomies of the human.

As a site of medical and legal controversy, the Rhineland controversy shifts our more heroic narratives of modernism, particularly through the Weimar-era work of the feminist activist, queer artist, and Dada outlier Hannah Höch. While Höch has most often been considered within an avant-garde tradition, I recast her work amid the rise of biological racism, focusing on what a number of art historians have noted as explicit references to the Rhineland controversy in her Weimar-era photomontages. In Höch's series *From an Ethnographic Museum* (*Aus einem ethnographischen Museum* [1924–1934]), depictions of the mixed-race body appear on pedestals, addressed to a public gaze. However, Höch rejects the more monumental aspects of museum culture, instead turning to a visual grammar of the miniature, ephemeral, disposable, or brittle. In Höch's ethnographic period, the scale of the artwork invokes a more intimate model of looking, one associated with personal photograph albums or scrapbooks. Here texture and scale become important: layered over one another in a series of craft-like images, the cut-out fragments offer a tactile mode of interaction in the here and now.

At this time, the legal case study and ethnographic museum become strangely congruent forms, addressed to the public negotiation of a racialized national polity imagined as both new and eternal at once.[5] To set these genres side by side reveals the vexed histories of collage—and its subset, photomontage—as these techniques cross between administrative and aesthetic sites. Both the case study and museum are then versions of what Janet Lyon has called "public genres" formed in a vexed alliance and opposition to the bourgeois public sphere.⁶ If the bourgeois public sphere hypothesizes a space of rational debate among equals, a shared set of freedoms, and an abstract equality, the manifesto can be understood as a genre taking shape amid and against these currents, "geared to contesting or recalibrating the assumptions underlying a 'universal subject.'"⁷ Drawing on Lyon's foundational work, I want to recast the legal case study and ethnographic museum as more minor public genres that forgo a unified subject of declarations: the *I* or the *We*. Unlike the manifesto or petition, these more minor modes of public address operate through displays of physical evidence that seem to speak for themselves. Often accumulated in massive quantities, the evidentiary display functions as a mountain of seemingly incontrovertible fact, collaged together without order or caption, to address and invoke a transnational public sphere.

Cast in this light, Höch's late work is distinct from the heroic negation or traumatic recovery so associated with a politicized avant-garde. Rather than speaking with or for the proletariat in the service of revolution, Höch uses the magazine cutout to investigate forms of group identity, or the fact of a *We*, as a polity mired in questions of gender, race, and sexual identity. This rethinking of identity-based affiliation involves a number of questions of political mobilization on the ground more pertinent to the formation of Berlin Dada amid the November Revolution and the rise of National Socialism in the later years of the Weimar era. In a field of lived antagonisms, to what extent did having a common enemy mean being on the same side? What if this kind of alliance were a mere tactic, only a poisonous necessity, in order for collective action to have some sort of purchase on the world outside? Were the formations of such groups always already violent, a kind of standardization that could only prioritize the rights of some by ignoring the interests of others? What, exactly, did it mean to take a position, to take a side, when the lived reality of political militancy, of being a part of this group or that one, was so desperately far from the forms of experience that political activism meant to achieve?

So often the language surrounding the avant-garde casually hypothesizes a group identity. Recall the more famous claims of the group that called itself Dada: "We proclaimed our disgust, we made spontaneity our rule of life, we repudiated all distinctions between life and poetry," writes Tzara, that indefatigable promoter of doctrine.⁸ Or here is Georges Hugnet, in an early history that might be considered extremely generous or extremely naïve: "Dada spontaneously offered its services to the proletariat and went down into the streets."⁹ It goes without saying, for Hugnet and others, that the artists in question and the proletariat that they serviced represent a general subject based on the specific body of a heterosexual male citizen. Here is Huelsenbeck, along the same lines: "Dada hurts. Dada does not jest, for the reason that it was experienced by revolutionary men and not philistines."¹⁰ Rather than consider the truth or untruth of such claims and what they might mean for the artworks involved, I want to look more closely at the imagination and praxis of this collectivity, *We Dada*, in and among other identity-based groups. In what follows, I want to reconsider the people who spoke for this *We* and the people it disappeared.

Exhibit A: Black Shame on the Rhine

In the spring of 1920, E. D. Morel flooded the British socialist press with a series of articles on the occupation of the Rhineland. By this time, Morel had made a name for himself as a humanitarian focused on British foreign policy, although his pacifist stance against the war had hurt his reputation considerably.¹¹ Twenty years earlier, Morel had written a series of infamous exposés on forced labor in the Congo Free State. Given the publicity surrounding these articles, he is often credited as instigating the European movement for native rights in central Africa. In one common but overly generous formulation, Morel became known as "the man who put an end to the Congo atrocities."¹² Nevertheless, the public outcry over the exposé on forced labor gave Morel the political momentum to establish the Congo Reform Association. Over the next decade, the association would garner support from the likes of Joseph Conrad, Anatole France, Arthur Conan Doyle, Booker T. Washington, and Mark Twain. If not the most discerning journalist of his time, Morel had to be one of the most prolific: in the first two decades of the century, he wrote a prodigious number of articles, pamphlets, and books on seemingly every major issue in British foreign policy, often published within the week of the events in question.¹³

The first articles on the Rhineland crisis appeared in the *Daily Herald*, a newspaper that began as a worker's strike bulletin, turned to a syndicalist politics, backed the militant suffragette movement, and celebrated the Russian Revolution. This writing touched upon the conditions of the Versailles

Treaty but focused with particular hysteria on the presence of colonial soldiers on the Franco-German border. By this time, Morel had written at length against the war-guilt clause of the Versailles Treaty. But in this much more infamous series, he invoked a racialized threat as yet another reason for Britain to agitate for a new foreign policy. The first article had a narrative title, and the rest continued in this vein: "Black Scourge in Europe, Sexual Horror Let Loose by France on Rhine, Disappearance of Young German Girls" *Daily Herald* (April 10, 1920); "Brutes in French Uniform, Danger to German Women from 30,000 Blacks, Brothels Not Enough," *Daily Herald* (April 12, 1920).[14] From this series, Morel compiled the pamphlet *The Horror on the Rhine*, which ran through eight editions by 1921. Foreign-language translations were published in Germany, France, the Netherlands, and Italy.[15] In the years that followed, the Rhineland occupation would generate an international protest movement in English-speaking socialist circles. In London, the National Conference of Labor Women immediately composed a resolution calling for the withdrawal of the African troops. Within the week, the British section of the Women's International League for Peace and Freedom organized a protest meeting featuring Morel as a speaker. Sponsoring organizations included the luminaries of socialist feminist groups in the United Kingdom: the Association of Women's Clerks and Secretaries, the Fabian Women's Group, the Independent Women's Social and Political Union, the National Federation of Women Teachers, the Standing Committee of Industrial Women's Organizations, the National Federation of Women Workers, and the Women's Co-Operative Guild.[16]

In London, Claude McKay wrote a letter to the editor of the *Daily Herald* as a direct response to the racial bias of Morel's articles. The *Herald* declined publication. However, in what was to become a long partnership, McKay contacted Sylvia Pankhurst, who had recently left the mainstream suffragette movement in favor of socialism. Through Pankhurst, "A Black Man Replies" appeared in *The Worker's Dreadnought*. The article posed a number of critical questions: "Why all this obscene, maniacal outburst about the sex vitality of black men in a proletarian paper?"[17] In his later memoirs, McKay reasons that the Rhineland controversy meant to prop up the procommunist labor unrest in the Rhineland, which had been quickly dampened by the French occupying forces. "Searching for a propaganda issue, the Christian radicals found the colored troops in the Rhineland. Poor black billy goat," McKay concluded.[18]

In Germany, the Rhineland controversy produced a massive literature from the right and left wings, including railway propaganda leaflets, postcards, questionnaires, newssheets, pamphlets, and broadsheets.[19] Cultural responses included pulp novels, novelty coins, and a feature film. Many of these materials were the work of newly enfranchised German feminists, who invoked the Rhineland controversy, and with it the threat of interracial sexual violence, to serve a number of ends.[20] In 1920, the League of Rhenish Women (RFL) was founded to coordinate women's organizations already in action. Over the next several years, the league published its own propaganda materials following the model set by Morel. Most successful was the brochure *Colored Frenchmen on the Rhine: German Women's Desperate Appeal* (*Farbige Franzosen am Rhein. Ein Notschrei deutscher Frauen*). Eventually translated into five languages and internationally distributed, *Colored Frenchmen* consisted of highly graphic reports documenting alleged sexual violence. What follows will consider a cross section of case studies, including *Colored Frenchmen*, as the emergence of a distinct genre of medical-legal evidence tied to the difficulty of proving criminal liability in cases of sexual assault. Amid the wider arc of highly sensational, often pornographic materials that make up the Rhineland controversy, the case study on interracial sex crime emerges here as a distinct, if often overlooked, genre in its own right.

Thomas Laqueur has situated the medical case study, alongside the autopsy and parliamentary inquiry, as a paradigm for humanitarian narrative originating in the mid-eighteenth and nineteenth century.[21] As "children of the empiricist revolution," this cluster of genres amasses a wealth of particular detail as "the sign of truth." Like the realist novel, the case study uses detail to create a sense of the real more authoritative than the subjective testimony of victims or bystanders. This quality of detail, of the body laid out, examined, enumerated, and diagnosed, appears in a strictly medical language shot through with authority and thus pointedly distinct from sensational fictions of monstrosity or miracle. Laqueur notes that the parliamentary report, or "blue book," appeared during the same period and likewise relied on an empiricist collection of fact, though on a much larger scale. The blue books, and the novels that borrowed from them, worked to evoke a reader's sympathy for the suffering of strangers. In this new discourse, readers worked their way through minute particulars, detail by detail, as a way to establish a clear narrative of cause and effect, suffering and its external remedy. Through this readerly method, the parliamentary report situated industrial accidents or mining conditions as a problem to be resolved "in the interests of humanity."

Alongside the more sensational discourses of the Rhineland controversy, the genre of the case study persists as a warped and partial form. Most often, these materials resemble a court docket, in that they enumerate crimes. But this enumeration itself involves an amalgamation of so-called facts and sensationalist prose. Consider, for instance, this leaflet from the German Ficte-Bund, which takes the evidence in Margarete Gärtner's *Farbige Franzosen am Rhein* as its source material:

> It is a fact that a French officer to whom an outraged young wife applied for help, bawled out to her: these fellows have been away from home now for 2 ½ years and must have it. And they are especially keen on fair hair (Police Court Sitting of 10 April 1920).
>
> It is a fact that black soldiers are outraging boys and infect them with venereal diseases;
>
> It is a fact that girls are seized, tied on seats or held by the black soldiers and then violated until they expire;
>
> It is a fact that mothers who run to help their ill-used children have been simply shot down;
>
> It is a fact that white women have been torn from their beds and that their fettered husbands had to look on whilst their wives were being outraged;
>
> It is a fact that up to the beginning of 1921 the following cases have been put on record by the police:
>
> 40 cases of attempted rape
>
> 70 cases of accomplished rape
>
> 20 cases of sexual misdemeanour of various other kinds
>
> 7 cases of unnatural intercourse with boys[22]

In terms of formal packaging, the leaflet is not all that different from *The Treatment of Armenians in the Ottoman Empire* or *The British Case in French Congo*. The lines between state inquiry and its fictive doubles here begin to blur, as each account of history inhabits a similar genre of facticity, all invoking the expertise of doctors, police, and medical experts. These documents raise questions: What amount of detail renders an inquiry authentic? What kind of detail appears true? What facts can be trusted, if all sides are making claims on truth?

The anaphoric quality of "It is a fact" also appears in the speeches of Ray Beveridge, whose portrait opened this chapter. Translated into English and printed as a broadsheet by Ferdinand Hansen's Overseas Publishing Company, fifty thousand copies of Beveridge's speech were distributed in Hamburg and New York:

> It is a fact that 60% of the children, begot by French soldiers, come into the world tainted with syphilis. It is a fact that bastards mostly inherit the bad qualities and vices of both parents. It is a fact that thousands of Black men in spite of the compulsory brothels still walk about with their sexual desire unsatisfied. It is a fact that the Moroccans are worse than the Blacks. It is a fact that the White French Colonial Troops exceed their Black comrades in brutality and bestiality. It is a fact that the number of Colored Bastards is steadily increasing in the occupied territory.[23]

Here again, "It is a fact" floats free from other information, as a justification in its own pronouncement. *It is a fact* answers objections in advance, as a grammar of truthfulness that, if surrounded with enough iterations of detail, mimes certainty through its perpetual restatement.

Compared to Beveridge's speech, E. D. Morel's *The Horror on the Rhine* is more adept in the genre of legal explanation, in that it offers a compendium of different modes of testimony. Police reports sit alongside a number of other genres of professionalized verification. There are epigraphs, directed to a wider public: "to the civilized world," "to the women of the world." There is a preface, a foreword, and an author's note. All of these introductory materials directly respond to criticisms past, as a way to establish the truth content of what follows. These pages note the testimony of Colonel Petersen, a Swedish officer, as a firsthand witness; a reply to critiques from the United States; and the enumerated remarks of Arthur Ponsonby, who assures the reader, in roman numeral one, "I have myself examined copies of the documents relative to the specific cases."[24] Morel's text is also heavily footnoted, with frequent citations: a speech from Foreign Minister Dr. Köster; word from an inhabitant of the Palatinate to an English friend; a timetable from the brothel at Muenchen-Gladbach; extracts from *Zukunft* and *Le Populaire*; a "batch communicated to a well-known British philanthropic society by a

German lady doctor, who received them from Princess Marie zu Erbach, President of the German National Union of Friends of Young Girls." On this matter, Morel notes, "Their accuracy is vouched for."[25] There are depositions of witnesses and civic authorities, letters from French officers, magistrate reports, and medical certificates. Appended letters from Henri Barbusse and Jean Longuet, of the French Socialist Party, appear without introduction or commentary.

All of these documents are framed by the language of fact. There are facts in hiding: "The full facts have been concealed from the French public"; "The facts leaked out," in a footnote on the case of Maria Schnur; people "kept in the dark with regard to the facts." "This fact has been kept out of the press," writes Morel. There are facts still undergoing investigation by a "Swedish Commission." There are facts to be worried over, as to their truth: "I much regret the fact; if fact it be." Some facts, it appears, bear no question: these are the facts to be faced, the "concrete facts," the "Obvious, public admission of *the fact*." In many cases, the facts are italicized, "This again, *is a fact*." There are facts known by "All decent-minded people in France," facts to be grasped, facts acted upon, facts that "had long been known" or "advertised to the world." Facts are transitions ("in fact," "that fact," the "fact itself"), punctual cousin to more extended witness testimonies.

Midway through *The Horror on the Rhine*, in section 5B, "Outrages Upon Women," Morel devotes several pages to verbatim police records surveying alleged assaults, divided by region. Each incident is marked with a time and place, though names have been elided. Unlike the *It is a fact* litany, there is little editorializing:

> *Reported from Urbach.*—March, 1920. Two women and a young man, the son of one of them, fetching wood in a cart; assaulted by four "Coloured" soldiers; girl escapes; son holds his mother in his arms; their cries attract attention and the soldiers make off.
>
> *Reported from Bensberg.*—March, 1920. Watchmaker walking with his wife; attacked by four "Coloured" soldiers, demanding that women should yield herself; both man and woman severely mauled; their cries bring passers-by, and the soldiers move off without accomplishing their purpose.
>
> *Reported from Kaiserlauten.*—A batch of cases ranging from December, 1918, to May, 1920. Cases include two cases of indecent assault upon boys aged seven and eleven respectively, in the latter case a medical

examination reveals that the victim has contracted syphilis; and eight cases of attempted rape by soldiers, variously designated as "Coloured," "Moroccan" and "Black." These attempted cases of rape include two accompanied by housebreaking—one of them the virtual siege of an inn, in which a girl, pursued by a "Coloured" soldier, had taken refuge, by some thirty African soldiers, until relieved by the "French police." In the six remaining cases the assaults took place in the fields.

Reported from Trier.—Several cases, ranging from September, 1919, to June, 1920. The cases include indecent assault upon a boy, accompanied by serious laceration, by the "Moroccan" servant of the French Captain Laurent, billeted in the house (punishment promised); and a particularly horrible case of rape, accompanied by robbery, of a servant girl aged twenty-one, in the neighbourhood of the barracks, by three "Coloured" soldiers. Victim taken to hospital.

Reported from Mainz.—May, 1920. Working girl of nineteen seized on the road to Wiesbaden by a "Moroccan" soldier guarding a waggon-shed. Raped with great violence after being threatened with a bayonet.

Reported from Karlsruhe.—Batch of cases, June, 1920. The cases include the raping of a woman by two "Black" soldiers. A man and woman, on the way to Eueneheim, sprung upon by "five or six Coloured soldiers" hidden in the corn; man threatened with bayonet, woman dragged into the cornfield and raped by three of the soldiers, and robbed. Two cases of attempted rape in the same neighbourhood.[26]

The police reports are full of small details: the errand for wood, the watchmaker walking with his wife, the guardian of the wagon shed, the bayonet. Characteristics of the people involved come piecemeal: a girl and a boy here, a young woman, a woman of thirty-four, a woman of thirty-one, the two boys, a list of girls from Saar, the prostitute. I have quoted at length, but these reports go on for much longer, one after another. The reports weaponize lengthiness, so that the sheer accumulation of detail creates a problem for the reader, who can either skim these pages or inevitably begin to confuse them, as one case blurs into the next.

This weaponization of detail, as a lengthiness that provokes certain readerly modes, is a central feature of the wider cultures of transatlantic war propaganda. The most famous governmental inquiry of this kind is a publication that appeared at the start of the war, the *Report on Alleged*

German Outrages in Belgium, also known as the Bryce report. The Bryce report offered an investigation on "acts of inhumanity" in German-occupied Belgium, in thirty pages of text and an appended three hundred pages of evidence.[27] Compared to the Belgian or French commissions or the extended series in the *New York Tribune*, "The Rape of Belgium," the Bryce report is quite minimalist. The *New York Times* praised the report for its choice to bypass sensation and adornment. "The report is 'lawyer-like,'" the *Times* claimed, "but its authors write as though they were addressing a board of judges, not a jury."[28] Here was reportage that appealed to "judgment, not to the passions." According to the *Times*, the Bryce report had "little more literary merit than does a catalogue or index."

Index, appendix, catalog, report, brochure, case, evidence, deposition: these modes of explanation, all tinged with the prestige of empiricism, appear in official inquiries and their offshoots, which are too numerous to count. What is significant here is not only the sheer number of documents in circulation, from congressional reports to sensational renderings, but the increasingly visible status of evidence as a basis for facticity. These claims for evidence sit alongside narratives overtly sensational and prurient. Tales of bayoneted infants, women with their breasts cut off, and an encyclopedic array of perverse sexual acts among soldiers, women, boys, and animals can be found. But the thing about these lists of names and dates, which appear in Axis and Allied materials alike, is the way they suggest that such facts speak for themselves. These documents make claims on rationality, not the passions. They are fervently anti-art, as a kind of untruth to be avoided.

In this turn to the genre of catalog or index, the audience invoked, a transatlantic public sphere, is tasked with forming an ethical judgment in lieu of a national court. The pamphlet culture of the interwar era could invoke a public, or competing publics, to weigh in on the "laws of humanity" in part because this language of judgment was then in contested emergence as a new category in positive international law. In M. Cherif Bassiouni's history, the 1899 and 1907 Hague Conventions established a basis for "laws of humanity" as an extension of war crimes, to cover unprecedented or unimaginable acts not already enumerated in positive international law.[29] Assembled piecemeal from the mid-nineteenth century to World War II, the "laws of humanity" were most often coupled with ideas of civilization and general conscience. According to the 1907 Convention, these are the "laws of nations as they result from the usages established among civilized peoples, from the laws of humanity and the dictates of the public conscience."[30] The first application of this overarching principle, sometimes referred to as the Martens clause, occurred in 1915, when Britain, France, and Russia issued a joint statement against the Ottoman massacre of Armenian populations as a "crime against civilization and humanity." The 1919 Commission uses this language with some frequency. Indeed, as the B-side to the much more pared-down, diplomatically approved Treaty of Versailles, the 1919 Commission offers some sense of the juridical arguments then ongoing to determine liability in times of war. Famously, the American delegates wrote a dissenting opinion, in which they argued that "humanity" was a moral, not legal, concept.[31]

After World War II, "crimes against humanity" became codified to mark aggression between a government and its own citizens during times of peace or war. However, at this early moment, what might establish liability in a theater of war was still in formation. What is somewhat obscured in the reading of the international conventions and more clear in the wartime booklets is the racialization of humanity as a fundamental part of this process. As A. Dirk Moses has argued, our current international legal norms emerged through a colonial divide between civilized and uncivilized peoples. To understand this legal genealogy, it is more accurate to follow a cluster of associated terms, rather than a single lineage. At this moment, "savage," "barbaric," "uncivilized," and "inhuman" are differentially invoked across a number of international declarations as the natural states of non-Western peoples.[32] This division then justifies the founding paradox of the League of Nations and associated institutions, which invoke a universal humanity but nevertheless maintain the colonial divide through the mandate system, under the rubric of humanizing uncivilized peoples.

The discourses of the Rhineland controversy can thus be situated within a wider history, amid the rise of the parliamentary inquiry and its propagandistic offshoots in the early twentieth century. This massive, often overlooked legal archive reveals an alternative history of early human rights discourses, beyond the more familiar scope of the official doctrine of the League of Nations. As Laqueur has argued, the nineteenth-century blue books established a humanitarian narrative directed at injury of strangers, primarily through attention to industrial accidents. Organized as a legal case study, these booklets assembled huge amounts of factual evidence as a way to identify sources of harm and their governmental remedy. However, as I have argued, the parliamentary inquiry changes function in the early twentieth century as it circulates beyond parliament to address a transatlantic public. In this case, the inquiry and its unofficial doubles look to establish the liability of nations, rather than individuals, according to the judgment of a transatlantic public sphere. In this way, the transatlantic public sphere invoked by the parliamentary inquiry constitutes an alternative theater of justice during the early formation of international positive law. Dissatisfied with the postwar treaties, a wide array of political coalitions, on the right and the left, invoked a transnational public as a replacement source of legal authority. As a compendium of so-called fact, these documents seek out alternative sources of moral judgment to establish victimhood and blame through a repurposed, often racialized, language of humanity. The pamphlets thus refigure "humanity," not as a fact of birth, but as a status to be awarded through the collective judgment of a transatlantic public sphere.

Exhibit B: Hannah Höch, Disturbingly Close

From 1924 to the early 1930s, Höch completed a series she called *From an Ethnographic Museum*. A number of other photomontages from this period also use African or Asian art, but they are not part of the series. This wider tendency could be understood as a turn to primitivism or a rejection of the institutional cultures of art, though neither catch-all tendency quite fits. What I will call, rather loosely, the ethnographic period of Höch's work incorporates racial mixture with the visual rhetoric of a museum display. These images display the human figure as an amalgamation of parts, often posed on some sort of base. The bodies are often topped by African masks. In many cases, at least one eye is pasted on from another head. Höch particularly liked replacing or excluding the torso, setting a stone belly or subject's head as emerging directly from the legs, like a humanoid plant.

There are a number of works in this vein. Consider, for instance, the racially charged *Bride* (1933) and, earlier, *The Sweet One* (1926), *Indian Dancer* (1930), and *Mother* (1930). Or note the many horrible infants: *Our Dear Little Ones* (1924), *Children* (1925), *Equilibre* (1925), *Antique Frieze* (1930), *The Scream* (1930), *The Small P* (1931), and *Peasant Couple* (1931). Across the series, the amalgamated bodies seem corroded or petrified. The junctures look painful. When the cutouts are combined into a single figure, there seems to be a lot of piercing, sometimes what looks like biting or burning. When there are two characters or three, the mode of relationality, one to the other, suggests strangulation or puncture. For these reasons, the series has often been called grotesque, which seems not quite right. There is nothing of the lower body here—no blood, shit, sewage, nothing dirty or slimy. Nor do I see the image as abject, as death asserting its materiality in bodily fluid, defilement, or the open wound. In Höch's series, wounds are closed and bodies are clean.

Unlike the montages from the Dada period, these images distinguish between the figural and what seems like a decorative background, usually cut-out colored paper or a gouache wash. That background is flat, but this is a different kind of flatness than the simultaneous montage of *Cut with the Kitchen Knife*. To see this difference, consider a photograph from the First Dada Fair, of the large photomontage *Cut with the Kitchen Knife*, surrounded by other Dada works, all set rather closely together (figure 4.1). This is 1920, well after the momentum of the revolution has passed. Though they advertised for months, Hausmann called the event the "last Dada hurrah."[33] It was a retrospective that did not quite admit itself as such, because doing so would reveal that the avant-garde impulse was over, inevitably dead. But the pictures do not seem particularly mournful to me. No one appears to mark this as a referendum on the life or death of the avant-garde. There are still all those slogans. Just to the right of Höch's elbow: *Art is dead Long Live the New Machine Art*. The other posters make similar claims: *Down with Art. Dilettantes, Revolt against Art. Down with bourgeois morals*. Of course, this is the poster that I seize upon: *Dada is on the side of the revolutionary proletariat*.

So gaudy, so brash, this early work. It's as though the entire thing were an exclamation point. *Cut with the Kitchen Knife* assembles all these parts into a generalized flatness, so any journey taken by the viewer, from one cut-out to the next, is a choose-your-own-adventure. I like to think of *Cut with the Kitchen Knife* as a particularly loud work, with all those fragments shouting their presence in different voices—Here we are! Here! Over here! Do what you want with us! Then there are the lettered words, amid all those bodies and parts: *Dadaisten, Dada, dada, the Anti-*. If the images suggest a lawlessness of narrative, a flatness that allows the eye to roam and connect the parts as a matter of chance, those words make it clear the group to which such technologies belong: *We, Dada*.

Set *Cut with the Kitchen Knife* against the sculptural infant from the ethnographic period nine years later (figure 4.2). What happened, between 1920

FIGURE 4.1 Raoul Hausmann and Hannah Höch in front of their works at the First International Dada Fair, Berlin, 1920.
Source: Berlinische Gallerie.

FIGURE 4.2 Hannah Höch, *Ohne Titel (Aus einem ethnographischen Museum)* (*Untitled [From the Collection: From an Ethnographic Museum]*). 1929. Collage and gouache on paper. 26 x 17.5 cm.
Source: Scottish National Gallery of Modern Art, Edinburgh. © 2019 Artists Rights Society (ARS), New York / VG Bild-Kunst, Bonn.

and 1928? Most baldly, Höch moves from flatness to the figural. This move creates space for a narrative as a matter of opposed sides. If the early collage was an assemblage of raw materials, set amid the other, to spark off one another willy-nilly, these later pictures are more composed. Most starkly, the turn to the figural combines white, African, female, and male bodies, but not into equivalence or harmony. To look at the photomontage becomes, in the most extreme, narrative case, an exercise in taking sides. Rather than consider these parts as something that comes together to make a new amalgamated human, I want to consider the way the images stage ongoing relations of racial and gendered enmity. In this perspective, the fragments do not come together. They remain in a transitive mode: in the midst of biting or mauling, often piercing, one another.

∞

Let us return to that earlier image, the sculptural infant, from the *Ethnographic Series*. In the baby picture, colors are tasteful and symmetrically arranged. The black bars frame and echo the squares. Flatness foregrounds a single figure, which seems to exist nowhere, in no time. The baby is on display, clearly enough. It has a sense of staged publicness, as if addressed to an audience. Here is what Michael Fried famously called "theatricality," or the "to-be-seenness" of an image that addresses the beholder.[34] In the *Ethnographic Series*, this scene of beholding does not just include one spectator but many: the public that walks through the museum, around the pedestals and display cases.

In these images, the fiction of a sculptural object held up on a pedestal is not itself ethnographic. The beholder does not stand in the role of a participant-observer, regarding the ongoing life of a foreign culture. Rather, these images summon the visual rhetoric of the ethnographic *museum*. Höch claimed that the series was inspired by a 1926 visit to the Rijks Ethnographic Museum in Leiden, though she had been interested in African art since the early Dada period. In one of her few remarks on the series, Höch was careful to distinguish her own work from other artistic currents. At this point, the avant-gardes had been interested in a primitivist aesthetic for some time.[35] Picasso's first encounter with African art was in 1907, at the Musée d'Ethnographie de Trocadéro; Carl Einstein, a member of the Dada circles frequented by Höch and Haussmann, published the first German book on

African sculpture, *Negerplastik*, in 1915. Many of the photographs used in the *Ethnographic Series* come from the art magazine *Der Querschnitt*, which regularly included images and articles about non-Western art. By the late 1920s, *Der Querschnitt* began using montage practices too, most often setting portraits of African and European people side by side, without caption.

"The expansion of ethnographic research at the time only took in the 'primitives,' especially Negro art," recalls Höch. "The German Expressionists manifested this often in their oil paintings. I enjoyed experimenting in a less serious, but always precise way with this material."[36] This is rather polite. At first blush, Höch's series looks like a direct parody of the expressionist turn to non-Western art as a site of primordial energy. However, I am hesitant to set up Höch's work as the heroic, antiracist alternative to modernist primitivism. The lines of influence are much more contaminated. Indeed, the art historian Maud Lavin has urged critics to avoid the "straightjacket of dichotomy" so often prompted by Höch's work, "with Höch being constructed as the savior-artist and the mass media of her time as the duper of women."[37] In her consideration of the *Ethnographic Series*, Lavin sees Höch's work as ambiguous, sometimes partaking of a critical "distanced irony," sometimes verging on a messier attitude toward racial otherness, "disturbingly close and grotesque."[38] In what follows, I want to press on this messier aspect, the "disturbingly close," in part through a reconsideration of the tactile, craft-like quality of Höch's cut-outs.

First scale: the images from Höch's ethnographic period are not monumental, the way one might expect. All of the ethnographic pictures are quite small—the baby montage, one of the bigger ones, measures seven by ten inches. *Monument 1: From an Ethnographic Museum* could be held in one hand. Flimsy, too, are the pasted-on layers. These materials were not meant to last, so the magazine papers bubble. Blobs of glue are visible where they have seeped out from under the paper. The cutting was not done with tremendous care. Note, for instance, the line of the child's back, where the ridges have been snipped off into one too-smooth line. The chest has an obtuse angle where an angle should not be.

This smallness summons up a distinct mode of looking. It is most obvious to begin with the kind of looking prompted by the magazines from which the images were taken. Indeed, in histories of the avant-garde, it has become a commonplace to cite the distracted attention of the magazine or newspaper reader as the modality that avant-garde photomontage recreates. This makes sense in terms of *Cut with the Kitchen Knife*. However, Höch's later turn to the miniature requires peering in, as though we were looking through someone's scrapbook or photo album. This sort of looking is more closely allied with a more intimate sense of touch—the pages turned in the hand, their surface familiar. For this reason, these images require an alternative account of photomontage, distinct from the more familiar theories of the avant-gardes.

I'll start with what might seem obvious, with our knowledge that the photographic cutout had an existence before it entered the artwork. To put this more simply, on any given body in Höch's corpus, the lack of a hand is not a hand that the artist did not finish. In the photomontage, the severed hand was once whole. We know that, in the making of the larger work, the hand was cut off or perhaps torn from a whole body in a larger photograph. This somewhat banal knowledge, that the photographic hand has been severed, does strange things to the viewer. Just try to look at the sculptural infant and not see, at the edge of the severed wrist, where the rest of the hand should fall. The space is infused with that absence. It cannot quite be forgotten that the amalgamated parts on the page were cut out, then put back together. Of course, this process of severing is quite bloodless. My point is syntactical, about the structuring of negative space.

This reading borrows from Rosalind Krauss's work on sculpture as a medium based in both time and space. For Krauss, it is important that the beholder of the sculpture cannot see every angle at once. She must walk around the sculpture, assembling a series of incommensurate viewpoints together, as a kind of looking that happens in time.[39] When Höch's photomontages become figural, the cut-outs necessitate a similar suturing of incommensurate viewpoints. Because this is a photomontage rather than a sculpture, many of these viewpoints can only be imagined. All the same, this is still a looking that happens across time, in that the viewer reconstructs a genealogy of the image that assembles incommensurate viewpoints, including the present cut-outs and the wholes to which they might have originated. This is always a work of partial imagination; we can only know that something used to be there—the hand at the end of the severed wrist. We know that the severed wrist once had a hand attached to it; even if we do not view the original, the fact of this past life still informs the viewing. This knowledge jumbles any reading of the image that presumes the wholeness of the figure depicted. The figure consists of parts put together, but it would be hasty to assume that the amalgamated parts make a new human, a new consolidated subject with which a viewer might sympathize.

Consider the problems of locating a single subject, a doing and saying of the figure represented, in *Love in the Bush* (*Liebe in Busch* [1925]) (figure 4.3). The picture is most often understood as a direct reference to both the Rhineland controversy and the wider history of German colonialism in Africa. It might be a love scene, as a number of critics have suggested. The art historian Maria Makela writes, "the woman's smiling face and coquettish glance suggest not only that she enjoys the embrace she is receiving, but she may have initiated it."[40] I wouldn't entirely discount Makela's reading. However, I would like to suggest, alongside it, a number of alternatives. There is also that white hand that so clearly grips the woman's wrist. If we start with the hand that grasps the wrist and turns the arm, this is a scene of sexual violence. There is that proprietary lean to the arm, as it moves around and behind the woman's head. But then the vectors of race become unclear. Why is the hand white? It might be that the baby is the result of the seduction/rape, in a strange temporal fast-forward. But then where is the father? If we start with the baby's face, then the narrative is something entirely else, perhaps a mother's love for her child, perhaps infanticide. The more I look at the image, the more unsure I am if the woman is laughing. At the same time, the more I look at the image, the more I can't unsee the strange forward tilt of the baby's head, as though the body that should go with it were somehow thrown or tipping.

We could start again. The woman's head sits on top of what look like trousers. A puffy sleeve sprouts from her neck. This body is distorted, jumbled with other bodies of different racial configurations. To reassemble these forms into a single figure and situate them into a narrative—a woman, a rape, a seduction—papers over much of what the process of looking involves. This process happens across an imagined temporal arc that negotiates the cut-outs against the imagined bodies from which they have been severed. This imagining involves a play of presence and absence. There is the baby's head, *there*, then *not-there* the rest of the body, its approximate size and the correct angle that sets the head on the neck. There is that puffy sleeve and its arm *there*, but *not-there* the bodice, as what might be a sweetheart neckline or something more plunging. There are the mannequin legs *there*, but *not-there* the torso that should go with them, which also might be a bit tilted, maybe leaned against a wall. To render these parts into a single story, or

164   THE REPRODUCTIVE ATLANTIC

FIGURE 4.3 Hannah Hoch, *Love in the Bush*, 1925. Photocollage on paper. 9 x 8.5 in. *Source*: The Modern Art Museum of Fort Worth, TX. © 2019 Artists Rights Society (ARS), New York / VG Bild-Kunst, Bonn.

several possible narratives, does not account for the conjectural spaces in the picture, what I have described as negative spaces, the *not-there*, where the viewer can try out different formulations for what used to be a complete image.

Half-Breed (*Mischling* [1924]) is about this negative space (figure 4.4). It is most common to approach this image as the representation of a single, mixed-race woman who is suffering. In an extended reading of *Half-Breed*, Matthew Brio regards the woman's suffering as a key facet of the image's reception, in that this sadness elicits empathy and critique: "the close focus on the woman's sorrowful and distorted face encourages the spectator to

FIGURE 4.4 Hannah Höch, *Mischling (Half-Caste)*. 1924. 11 x 8.2 cm.
Source: Collection of IFA, Stuttgart. © 2019 Artists Rights Society (ARS), New York / VG Bild-Kunst, Bonn.

empathize with her and thus to take a dim view of colonial exploitation."⁴¹ Biro thus situates the portrait along two lines. In the first case, *Half-Breed* offers a critique of German colonial fantasies, in that it aligns miscegenation with the woman's suffering. In the second, the image offers a critique of the Rhineland propaganda, in that it humanizes rather than objectifies the mixed-race woman. In both cases, Höch's decision to represent a single person, rather than a scenario of sexual violence, is a significant and critical gesture. *Half-Breed* therefore "focuses on the uniqueness and particularity of an individual born of ethnically diverse parents, thereby humanizing her and suggesting that she should be treated in a civilized and morally responsible manner."⁴²

Biro's conclusion requires that we regard *Half-Breed* as a depiction of a single, mixed-race woman with whom we, the viewers, might sympathize. I want to look more closely at the ways that Höch's late work complicates the project of sympathy, and with it humanization, as a site of interpretive violence. This begins with a reconsideration of the seemingly commonplace assertion that *Half-Breed* is a representation of a single, suffering woman. What I have been describing as the chronology of photomontage offers a different perspective that might be best framed by two questions: What changes if this is not a depiction of a single woman? What changes if we regard the image instead as a scenario of ongoing sexual and racial violence? That is to say, in the following pages, I want to approach the image in a way that maintains a sense of conflict between the discrete parts, through a chronology of negative space, or what is *there* and *not-there*. Maintaining this sense of conflicting parts requires a longer process of negotiating incommensurate perspectives, one at a time.

To demonstrate this mode, I want to begin with the original photograph used in *Half-Breed*, which can be found in Höch's scrapbook (figure 4.5). Here the woman appears to be content, her mouth slightly open. In the scrapbook, images can have captions that describe the actions therein. On the left, below a child climbing a palm tree, the text reads: "The happiness of the uncivilized: the ten-year-old Pe'a, called the 'flying fox,' climbing a huge palm [Das Glück der Uncivilisierten: Der zehnjährige Pe'a, der Fliegende Fuchs, genannt, beim Erklettern einer riesenhohen Palme]."⁴³ To the right, for the woman leaning against a hut: "The style in the jungle [Die Mode im Urwald]." Below the children: "Future generations of Massaï-Land ["Het Toekomstige Geslacht van Massaï-Land]." On the opposite page, a woman washes a baby in a tub: "Those who are accustomed to even higher heat levels: a Senegalese bath without beach or comfort [Die an noch Höhere Hitzegrade gewöhnt sind: ein Senegalesen-bad ohne Strand und Komfort]." The captions promise a kind of narrative legibility: this child happy, this other one accustomed to the heat. The captions also suggest an authority to define not only types of people but their feelings and futures. At the same time, it is uncertain what Höch meant the scrapbook to be: a source for material, a site of inspiration, a conceptual art piece. I do not turn to these original photographs for the truth content behind the photomontages. That is to say, I am not interested in determining the correct expression or correct projected emotion of *Half-Breed*. Rather, I cite the images in the scrapbook, alongside their captions, as a mode of picturing that assumes the emotional legibility of the subjects rendered.

Half-Breed makes no such promises. It is only possible to caption this image, to narrate what it is about, by consolidating the parts into a single, hybrid figure. To maintain a sense of conflict between the parts involves a narrative too long for a caption, one that attends to the chronology of interpreting suffering and sympathy among persons whose interests are opposed. Each version of this narrative looks different according to its point of origin. If we begin with the white mouth as a gag, then the mouth behind the mouth is a suffering mouth, the mouth of a victim. It is a black mouth gagged by whiteness. But this is an odd thing to do, to imagine the mouth behind the mouth. It is, on its own, merely a hypothesis. Why can't the woman be smiling? Why does she need to be suffering? What clues to suffering are there, besides the mouth that has been set over her mouth? I find myself peering into the textures of the reproduced image, as though a closer inspection of the rest of the face, the laugh lines or the direction of the gaze, might lend some sort of clue to the mouth behind the mouth. The eyes are somewhat glassy, but that might just be the flash. There might be a tear on the cheek, or perhaps the line is a scar; it is impossible to tell. There is that scratching around the chin. What if the black woman is not choked but eating that white mouth, consuming whiteness? Would we then imagine the mouth behind the mouth as victorious? As wrathful?

In each narrative, of suffering or not, there is a tiny emendation, a minor tic or edit, in the imagination of the mouth that we can't see but know to be there, behind the other mouth. This is a narrative revision of what is *not-there*, the mouth behind the mouth, as though we, the viewer, could so

FIGURE 4.5 Hannah Höch, *Album* (Berlin: Hatje Cantz, 2004), n.p.

easily tweak its corners, prodding the lips this way or that way, touching the teeth, and, in the process of looking, change the narrative to accommodate one imagined expression or its alternative. This revision over time is the visual effect I call both intimate and profoundly disturbing. To say what the image is about, what is happening, has to involve a series of hypotheses, all variously linked to saying, touching, swallowing, peeling, and suffocating, as we imagine first this way, then that way, the mouth behind the mouth. To wrest a message from the image involves peeling back a layer of skin and manipulating an unseen mouth, being *in* a mouth to make it speak. The mouth behind the mouth is the key to this image, what the image is about. But to get to this aboutness, to describe what is happening, involves a more tactile grammar of violence and interpretation combined, or the perpetual imagination of a layer of skin peeled off and your hand in someone else's mouth.

My reading of Höch's ethnographic period draws upon another contemporaneous response to the punitive measures of the Treaty of Versailles, this time from the conservative legal theorist Carl Schmitt. Published in 1932, *The Concept of the Political* is perhaps best known for the introduction of the friend-enemy distinction as the content of political life. In Schmitt's formulation, politicized group identity emerges through the public delineation between friend and foe. This distinction produces a *We* through antagonism rather than through compromise or debate. What is less often remembered about these pages is the way Schmitt situates international humanitarian norms as an incoherent alternative to the friend/enemy divide. In Schmitt's account, friend and enemy have no distinct moral content; however, "humanity" serves as a generalizable ethical concept that might be torqued to the advantage of a distinct group. Echoing the claims of an early speech on "The Rhineland as an Issue in International Politics," Schmitt positions the rhetoric of humanity in international treaties as a tool used by American imperialists and the League of Nations alike: "To confiscate the word humanity, to invoke and monopolize such a term probably has certain incalculable effects, such as denying the enemy the quality of being human and declaring him to be an outlaw of humanity; and a war can thereby be driven to the most extreme inhumanity."[44] The passage is followed by a footnote, so what might seem like a critique of the calculated use of universal norms quickly takes on a more concrete referent. The footnote adds that certain populations have been historically considered "'proscribed by natures,' e.g. the Indians, because they eat human flesh."[45] Schmitt continues with a narrative of civilizing violence: "And in fact the Indians of North America were then exterminated. As civilization progresses and morality rises, even less harmful things than devouring human flesh could perhaps qualify as deserving to be outlawed in such a manner. Maybe one day it will be enough if a people were unable to pay its debts."[46] The reference to reparations makes German citizens fellow victims to the exterminated Native Americans, though the purpose of the phrasing is to point out a discrepancy between what Schmitt depicts as the validated genocide of Native Americans and what is framed as an overly punitive reaction to the nonpayment of war debts.

Höch is an unexpected and crucial interlocutor to Schmitt's writing on international law for the ways that her work negotiates the racialization of humanity in the aftermath of the Treaty of Versailles. In the ethnographic series, the process of beholding the images, of looking and saying what they are *about*, in the bluntest sense, is caught up in a more tactile grammar of opposed sides. To render these works as performative would invest them with authority, to catalogue, know, or sympathize with the subjects rendered as friends or enemies, human or not. But *Half-Breed* is about the problem of speech, of speaking for or on behalf of a wider group. It is a latecomer to a Dada tradition invested in slogans and manifestos and for this reason is importantly distinct. Here I think of Martin Puchner's claim, in *Poetry of the Revolution*, that the manifesto art of the avant-gardes involves a contest between the theatrical and the performative: while the theatrical lacks the authority of action, the performative makes worlds and identities.[47] Höch's ethnographic period does not invoke this battle. The pictures are merely theatrical. They do not make worlds or identities. They do not propose a new world or way of doing. They do not imagine an *otherwise*. Here is a form of *against* that does not posit a *We* behind it.

This sounds like nihilism, and in some ways it is. The next section will investigate late modes of Dada nihilism as a commentary on reproductive futures amid the rise of National Socialism. For now, in the wider arc of this chapter, I want to highlight the way that the legal case study and the ethnographic museum begin to resemble each other when set side by side, as competing responses to the postwar era. Each forgoes the unified *I* or *We* of the manifesto. They are less about any given demands or imagination for the future than about the construction of the *We* that might lie behind such claims. These forms invoke an audience and, in many ways, are about the divvying up of this audience into groups whose interests are opposed. Who this audience is and how it engages with the disparate fragments are parts of the genre's theatrical dimension. What these genres test is the way that physical evidence might be put on display, to be felt with in the service of a wider judgment. In different ways, these works dramatize our habits of interpreting the suffering of other people and the ways we might put this injury to use to determine the boundaries of a racialized polity.

Picture Books, Animal Babies, Queer Species

Another essential reason for our racial deterioration is the mixture with alien races. In this regard there remains a residual of the Black shame on the Rhine that must be eliminated. These mulatto children are either the products of violence or their mothers were whores. In both cases, we haven't the slightest moral obligation to this progeny of an alien race [Fremdrassige]. Approximately 14 years have passed; those of the mulattos who remain are now coming of reproductive age; thus, there is little time for long explanations. Let France and other nations deal with their racial problems as they like; for us there is only one possibility: eradication of all aliens, particularly those born of the damage wrought by this brutal violence and immorality. As a Rhinelander I demand the sterilization of all the mulattos left to us by the Black Shame on the Rhine.

—Dr. Hans Macco, *Race Problems in the Third Reich* (1933)

Dr. Macco's demand for sterilization comes before the fact, just as state agencies were beginning to catalogue the racial background of black German children. Though statistical collections and surveys had begun as early as 1924, state agencies began a more concerted effort to track and register black Germans between 1933 and 1937. The passage of the Law to Prevent Hereditarily Sick Offspring provided a legal basis for compulsory sterilization, though originally designed to reduce "heredity feeblemindedness," schizophrenia, manic depression, epilepsy, and other physical handicaps.[48] It is difficult to ascertain the exact number of sterilizations because many were conducted outside the auspices of the law. However, historians estimate that of the six hundred to eight hundred Rhineland children, approximately 285 underwent compulsory sterilization.

In *Other Germans: Black Germans and the Politics of Gender and Memory in the Third Reich*, Tina Campt situates Dr. Macco and the 1933 law as one episode in a wider history spanning colonial fears of racial parity, the threat of racial mixture animated by the Rhineland controversy, and National Socialist racial policy. By the mid-1930s, the sterilization of the Rhineland children marks a historical break. "Unlike in the Kaiserreich and the Weimar Republic," Campt writes, "in the Third Reich the threat of racial endangerment formed a central part of a political regime structured around race as the fundamental basis on which the state was organized and functioned."[49] Drawing on the work of Campt and others, I want to highlight the particular temporality of this administrative purview, through the ways that it positions racialized human populations in terms of a hereditary future.[50] If the laws of humanity invoked by the interwar treaties sought to determine group forms of injury and harm that had already occurred, here is the opposite temporal trajectory. Dr. Macco names a separation between *us Rhinelander* and the "alien race" that looks to avert a future crisis. Dr. Macco never mentions the category "humanity," but nevertheless invokes the category in a proleptic mode, as a population that will be threatened by racial mixture in the future. At this moment, I would argue, Höch was also working through the connection between imagined futures and racialized reproduction. For this reason, it is important that her work from this period turns away from human figuration altogether.

This is 1939, when Höch retreated to the suburbs of Berlin, where she would stay for the duration of the war. During this time, she wrote a children's book, ostensibly for money. *Picture Book* (*Bilderbuch*) includes nineteen photomontages of imaginary animals, alongside small rhyming poems. It was not a commercial success, and the book would not become widely available for another twenty-five years. In the republished edition, in 2010, Gunda Luyken's postscript is oddly sunny. "To counter the grey postwar years," Luyken writes, "Höch developed in 19 collages and accompanying texts a magical world populated by fantastic exotic plants and animals."[51] Indeed, *Picture Book* offers a taxonomy for animal species that do not exist. These are composite forms, chimeras of sorts, often of mother animals and animal babies. Nevertheless, the book does not seem particularly age-appropriate for children. The pictures are not as gruesome as the images from the ethnographic period, mostly because the components of the animals are just colors and shapes, not recognizable as parts of severed bodies. But the poems are cheerily bleak, if not outright desolate. There is very little that could be called whimsical.

This last section turns to the *Picture Book* as a continuation of the *Ethnographic Series* at a distinctly different historical moment. Most of this chapter has focused on the early 1920s, during the Weimar period and the height of the Rhineland controversy. In turning to 1939 and the Third Reich, I also want to situate a different historical horizon for the Dada photomontage. At this moment, Höch continues to use imagery that invokes racial mixture. But the referential status of these images shifts with the rise of National Socialism. A closer look at the poems in *Picture Book* renders this later work as a somewhat covert meditation on the fate of the *Mischlinge*, now entering their teenage years.

Little Baby Gamma

In Patchamatak dwelled his grandmamma
And dined on only fruitgrapes fine.
But this little, gentle Gamma
Was born on the River Rhine
Where he simply eats forget-me-not
and knows nothing of the fruitgrape's lot.

Der kleine Gamma

Im Patschamatak lebte seine Grossmama.
Und sie ass nur Musenpampelein.
Aber dieser kleine, sanfte Gamma
ward geboren an dem Rhein.
Er frisst Vergissmeinnicht da schlicht
und weiss von Musenpampeln nicht.[52]

To be "born on the River Rhine" locates the baby animal in the occupied regions of the Franco-German border, but the tropical scenery in the accompanying image, those palm trees and beaches, summons up a more divided colonial legacy. Somewhat more furtively, Höch connects the family lineage of Baby Gamma to another alien race, the homosexual. "Patchamatak" is the code name for a utopian land of free love imagined by Matilda (Til) Brugman, an artist in her own right and Höch's partner, with whom she lived from 1926 to 1936.[53] The made-up word is mentioned in the women's letters to each other and in Brugman's short story "Warenhaus der Liebe" ("Department Store of Love").

Allow me to take a brief detour through "Department Store of Love" as a hermeneutic, one that allows us to reconsider the rapprochement of homosexuality and racial mixture in Höch's later work. "Department Store of Love" is a direct parody of Magnus Hirschfeld's Institute of Sexual Science, which Brugman visited in 1931.[54] At that time, the exhibition room of the institute was a cross between medical display and anthropological exhibit, meant to offer the Berlin public visual evidence of the biological determination of non-normative sexualities. Diagnostic photographs lined the walls, allowing viewers to read the body as evidence.[55] The captioned photographs of non-normative bodies allowed the public to identify homosexuals and other perversions through their morphology: the bearded lady, the Uranian man with overdeveloped breasts. The museum also displayed objects of anthropological interest, including religious objects, or "fetishes," of so-called primitive cultures.

Brugman's story is a gleefully obscene fever dream of Hirschfeld's Institute as a capitalist enterprise. There is not much in the way of plot or character. Rather the story is over-packed with human types, one after another. When the store opens, it is surrounded by all "enlightened authorities, as well as the fire brigade, medical doctors, specialists, the police, Incessant Society & Co., church representatives, youth associations, gymnastics clubs, nurses, grand hoteliers, fashion shops, travel clubs, societies for combating sexually transmitted diseases, presidents of the realm."[56] Then come a succession of characters: the doctor from the University of Love in Patchamatak, as a thinly veiled Magnus Hirschfeld; the old man who visits in the middle of the night, to obtain the object of his childhood fantasies, a chamber pot that he will wear on his head. There is a sixty-year-old lady who wants to wear only the leather insides of riding breeches, wheeled out on a toilet; a man who desires rubber baby butts, clothed and unclothed; a teenage kleptomaniac who hides all number of objects—light bulb, fountain pen, periscope, rubber truncheon, wooden leg—inside and about her person. As the store becomes wildly successful, the details come faster, in fistfuls. There is urine sold by the liter, sugar feces, baby bottles, and nail clippings. Some request paper-mâché Oedipus complexes; others prefer to live in the store and receive sweat gland extracts. Thankful clientele organize a parade, and the store documents a new brand of types to display: the man who disappears a canary in and out of his mouth, for minutes at a time; the woman who rides a sea lion and requests to live with her hindparts permanently underwater. A tent is set up for sex-change surgeries. At this moment, the easy availability of what the story refers to as "love-objects" creates universal peace and happiness.

> It was a confusion, a roughness, a gloom and a din, a festive mood, an elevated feeling, a peaceful life like never before on earth. Everyone sat with his love where it suited him, and enjoyed his earthly existence. We received telegrams from Yellowstone Park, from the middle of the ocean, from the top of the Himalayas, the North Pole and the Sahara, that others had arranged similar festivities, and humanity was thankful finally to escape the fetters of the most insane prejudice regarding love and for the first time to live in complete happiness. We looked at each other happily . . . all our ideas, which were founded in science, were now applied without inhibition in reality. [Es war ein Durcheinander, ein Radau, ein Getobe und Getöse, eine festliche Stimmung, ein gehobenes Gefühl, eine friedliches Ausleben wie noch nie zuvor auf Erden. Jeder saß mit seiner Liebe, wo es ihn paßte, und genoß seine irdische Existenz. Wir erhielten Telegramme, daß man im Yellow-Stone-Park, mitten im Ozean, auf dem Himalaya, am Nordpol und in der Sahara ähnliche Feste arrangiert habe und daß überall die Menschheit, dankbar, endlich den Fesseln der irrsinnigsten Auffassungen in der Liebe entkommen zu sein zum ersten Male vollständig glücklich lebe. Wir sahen uns beglückt an . . . alles unsere Idee, was die Wissenschaft gefunden, auch ungehemmt in Wirklichkeit umzusetzen.][57]

Even descriptions come in the form of a list, as though miming a kind of breadth through meticulous coverage, in the mode of an evidentiary display. No observation is singular; the plot moves instead through a parade of characters and their fetishes, as though straining to get in every possible variation of person or thing. These variations tend toward the absurd and silly, rather than what is sexy or truly obscene. All the same, it is difficult to convey the story's frantic energy, particularly when the parade turns into a riot. In the midst of the celebration, "military hordes" descend upon the revelers, demanding the surrender of the love-objects: "The army erected bonfires, broke what they could get their hands on, kicked what had just been the object of the most tender love. They strangled the burp from a woman's body and trampled the surrounding glands."[58]

The end of the story is then a strange fizzle, everything suddenly resolved. After paragraphs of description, the denouement is all dialogue. As the Commandant tells it, the Supermarket of Love has created a state crisis in reproduction: enchanted with their love-objects, the population is no longer having babies. One cannot fight wars with happiness, the Commandant lectures. However, the store's proprietors have foreseen this problem and prepared, for the League of Nations, a surprise: "Right now, we are giving birth to 1,000,000 million celluloid children on the five continents." With that, everything is tidily over: "The battle against love was dismissed, as the League of Nations, with a patronizing gesture, accepted the promise of the celluloid children."[59]

Brugman most likely wrote "Supermarket of Love" from 1931 through 1933, before the National Socialists shut down Hirschfeld's institute. However, by the time of *Picture Book*, Höch would be able to note eerie likenesses between Brugman's imagined riot and the real-life closure of the Institute for Sexual Science. By 1933 its archives had been looted and its libraries burned in the street. To read *Picture Book* against "Supermarket of Love" means, in some ways, to reconsider the solution proffered by Brugman's story: not the happiness of thankful humanity, free to choose, but the quick solution of celluloid children to fight the nation's wars. In this historical matrix, one might ask, what reproductive future could possibly be desirable? *Picture Book* is an ambivalent answer to this question, through a turn to the reproduction of species not found on this earth, through humanoid eggs and mutant swan couplings, mixed-blood giraffes and flying bird-squirrels. Most of these characters are silly: Dublet decides to lay a red egg; the Runfast builds a nest to house her "thousand baby fastrunlets"; Madame Marklet, the matronly seagull, dispenses cod liver oil and porridge to her eggs, one of which has incongruously hatched a crying human infant. The nonprocreative creatures are often named as strange or ugly: Shellkeglet is an "odd bird," "not very pretty" but pure in heart. The Brushfurlet will "never be seen as a beauty queen." The sourpuss moth-monster Unsatisfeedle lives in the wrong body: "he wanted the black dress / But God gave him the white."

On one hand, the turn to the creaturely in *Picture Book* can also be understood as an attempt to evade the censors. At this time, Höch could not publicly display any of her photomontages. Nevertheless, Höch's sense of what art should do or be was becoming more militant, even as it turned abstract or fantastical: "These phantasms are not escapist, they are attacks, and no longer about creating moods," she writes in 1946.[60] Certainly, *Picture Book* is a strange kind of attack, with its rhyming couplets and animal babies. In the last poem, "Gentlebread," the scene of reproduction becomes more explicitly queered, in its narration between "she" and the feminized object of her desire, through the German gendering of noun forms and adjectives, "this one."

Gentlebread

She should decide—
and it will not be avoided
longer, that even this Delicate, Fine one
if she herself with This one,
then woe and anguish will follow.
Life is inadequate.

Das Liebkübchen

Sie soll sich entscheide
und es wird sich nicht vermeiden
lassen, dass selbst diese Zarte, Feine
wenn sie sich mit Diesem eine
Jenem Weh und Unheil müsste geben.
Unzulänglich ist das Leben.[61]

Much depends on how we read that last two lines. The speaker might be an omniscient narrator, in the key of the fate, warning that "woe and anguish will follow." Or that last line, "Life is inadequate," could be response to this threat, spoken by the partial animals on the page. In this later version, the object of critique is not an enemy that is a person, but a structure, a distribution of risk, vulnerability, freedom, and constraint. The poem does not give us an alternative to this structure. But it does suggest new social ties, not through what is named "human" or what is felt together, but through the shared sense of rejection: *not this, not anymore.* "Life is inadequate" could be a pronouncement on high, to acclimate to a disappointing present. Or it could be the Gentlebread's response, as an attack on the status of *this life, here, right now* as something that ought to change.

Here again, this sense of attack is importantly distinct from the earlier Dada currents. Indeed, a common story about the avant-garde, and about the short-lived formation named Dada in particular, goes like this: Dada was the rejection of everything, dreamed up by a group of men in Zürich sick of it all. Dada art was always saying *No*, to art itself, of course, but also to war, meaning, life, tradition, nature, progress, god, value, world. This persistent rejection, resulting in a somewhat romantic nihilism, was at the end of the day a response to the horrors of war. Dada was an art against meaning in the wake of a historical course than began to seem not only cruel, but meaningless in its cruelty. In this familiar story, the nihilism of Dada is a direct consequence of men's experience on the battlefields or, for the likes of the New York expatriates, in enforced exile to avoid the draft. The trauma induced by the Dada collage, with its war cripples and fecal humor, is then understood as a kind of repetition that reduplicates the trauma of the Great War.[62]

Höch's early work takes part in these currents. In an interview, Höch narrates the early moment of Dada as a spontaneous coalition of unlike forces, not quite melding into the same thing but somehow with one another all the same:

> We were all as if we had been strapped into a corset and were then released into freedom, automatically. Not just the Dadaists. Why and how things happened in this time is unprecedented. The workers with the Spartacists, the philanthropists with anti-war supporters in all areas, the militarists with the putsch, the anarchists with terror or individual anarchy, the religious converts felt and gave themselves to Christ, Buddhism, or ancient Chinese religions, and the suffragettes made women's rights matter. This

movement was cut off at the beginning of the war. Even with Annie Besant at the head of the English. So I was also not on a side, but saw as my task in all this to attempt to capture this turbulent time visually. The result was *Cut with the Kitchen Knife* . . . and others.[63]

Earlier in the interview, Höch gets frustrated with the attempts to make her own up to former communist sympathies. ("You sound like the Grand Inquisitor!" is one response to this sort of questioning.)[64] Given the anticommunist climate of the Cold War period, the affirmation or denial of a political tendency is vexed. However, what comes afterward, about taking a side, seems to me quite sincere. What is important is the sense of neutrality. "So I was also not on a side, but saw as my task in all this to attempt to capture this turbulent time visually. The result was *Cut with the Kitchen Knife*," says Höch, in retrospect. After the revolutionary period, during the era marked by the Rhineland controversy, the possibility of not being on a side no longer seemed feasible, in part because these factions, though sometimes named "human" or "German," were becoming increasingly determined by biological markers.

Most widely, the matter of being on a side, of party, nation, forms, or species, lies at the center of the two linked narratives that make up the case of the Rhineland controversy. In the first scenario, the experimental practices of the avant-garde, namely collage, emerge in administrative forms of statecraft, including the legal case study and the ethnographic display. These documents, I have argued, assemble a compendium of evidence to access the liability of nations in the eyes of an international public sphere. This reading suggests an alternative site of legal authority to institutions like the League of Nations during the early formation of the "laws of humanity." In the second scenario, the lines of influence are reversed. Höch's ethnographic period addresses a nationalized public sphere in the guise of a museum display. Here the racial determination of intention and harm is a scene of violence in which the beholder is implicated. Rather than floating above sides, in the play of moving parts, these later works require a taking of sides. By the time of *Picture Book*, Höch may have rejected the side of the human, but she had not necessarily found an alternative ground on which to stand.

In *Picture Book*, Höch turns to the alien-animal species to sidestep the biological language of the racialized human and instead make connections between alternative forms of life: the alien, the creaturely, the sexually

180   THE REPRODUCTIVE ATLANTIC

non-normative. These terms are not equivalent, but they might each be sites of enunciation for the text on the page. Better to say that in that last turn to animal-alien species, Höch is working through the ways that shared forms of antagonism, rather than injury or equivalence, might make up a coalitional force. That said, *Picture Book* might just as easily be a sort of zoo or taxonomy, all its animal composites sorted. It could go either way. By this time, the collaged display of evidence, addressed to a public to reassemble and judge for itself, did not necessarily suggest an inherently democratic alternative to the laws of nations or their administrative institutions. What kind of freedom was this, to see the evidence laid out on display, without order, and judge for oneself, if was claimed by *The Horror on the Rhine* and the Dadaists alike?

I read the end of *Picture Book* as an ambivalent response, one not entirely sure of its success or failure. On the page opposite "Gentlebread," the last page of *Picture Book*, there is a sitting swan and two flying squirrels, mid-descent (figure 4.6). It is hard to imagine a form of flying that looks less like

FIGURE 4.6 Hannah Höch, *Picture Book* (Berlin: Green Box Kunst Editionnen, 2010), n.p.

flight. The squirrels are hanging, rather. This stillness is consistent across the book, as though each creature were caught suspended. What is clear enough is the sense of taxonomy, as though the book were some sort of zoo, all alien races, bastards, and lesbian swans. The creatures are organized into a serial display but then left in a freeze-frame. There is the omniscient voice of the categories as natural fact, eternal and given, or the speaking bird-swan-squirrel *she* who voices an objection. I like to think of these figures as hanging on that last line, "Life is inadequate." It might be one of two options: a pronouncement of fate, spoken from the voice of the structure, or a complaint about *this life*, spoken from the creature within it, as a mode of contestation. This suspension, what might go either way, is as hopeful as Höch gets. It is a gamble for the wartime years, the ending not set out in advance. Here are the creatures that will or will not crack into life and look around them. There is a mountain of detail, sorted into categories, to make of what you will: the paper fibers as tufts of hair, the palm trees, the X-ray baby giraffe, Madame Markel primly in her vase, wings folded. A mutant swan tipped slightly forward, squirrel-headed and legless, waits for her eggs to hatch.

PART III

CONVERGENCES IN INSTITUTIONAL HUMAN RIGHTS

5

Surrealism's Inhumanities

Chance Encounter, Lesbian Crime, Queer Resistance

Man Ray's 1922 portrait of the marchesa Casati was a mistake. The session took place at the Hotel du Rhin rather than a studio, so that the marchesa might be surrounded by her things. It was an old building, and Man Ray burned out the fuses with his electric lights. Taking the rest of the photographs with the room's normal lighting meant a longer exposure, so Casati had to hold all of her poses perfectly still. This was tiresome work. When Man Ray developed the negatives later that night, they were all blurred. In his autobiography, Man Ray claims he initially considered the blurred negatives worthless. He made only a couple of prints, selecting the images with "a semblance of a face."[1] However, Casati adored the blurred portraits. She said they were an accurate representation of her soul.

The blurring effect is most striking in the last portrait of the series, where Casati looks directly into the camera (figure 5.1). Though it is a medium close-up, Casati's facial expression is difficult to determine. Most of the face is washed out, receding into a mask-like flatness. The eyes wobble more than anything else, so that the photograph takes on a vibrational quality. The blurriness around the eyes forces the viewer to choose between opposing expressive possibilities: Casati in a moment of amorous contemplation, Casati as frightened, Casati as manically possessed. In its most unworldly guise, the image catches the sitter in a moment of enchantment, as though it was *her* concentrated effort to stare through the lens that has jostled the frame. From another angle, the photographic image does violence to its subject, jouncing the head around until the eyes are unsteady, then raking

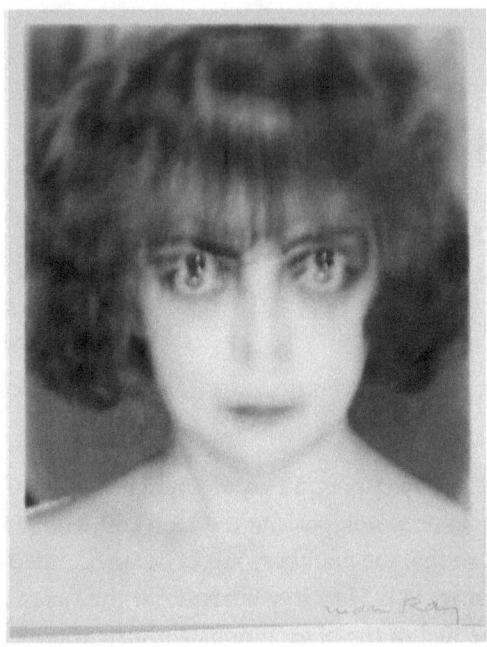

FIGURE 5.1 Man Ray, *Marquise Casati*, 1922. Black and white photograph, 18 x 24 cm. *Source*: © Man Ray Trust 2015 / Artists Rights Society (ARS), NY / ADGAP, Paris.

those strange lines across the neck. Part of the tonal ambiguity arises from the lips, which waver, too, between opposing poles. The upturned corners of the mouth may just be another effect of the blurred negative. They do not quite match Casati's four eyes. We might play this game of either/or indefinitely. The portrait is interesting for the way it so carefully renders all markers of a facial expression but then smudges these markers between opposing modes. Both affectively and spatially, the image produces a slight dizziness.

Analysis of the archival plate proves Man Ray's account of Casati's portrait to be apocryphal.[2] The photograph's famous blurring effect was achieved through a quite purposeful double exposure. Man Ray's narrative of the electrical snafu and the ruined negatives is merely a good story, rendered more interesting by our certainty that he made it all up. However, it is not entirely surprising that Man Ray might attribute one of his most famous photographic inventions to chance rather than premeditation. Having arrived in Paris exasperated with the New York Dada scene, Man Ray quickly took up the helm of a burgeoning surrealist moment in Paris. Though often interpreted as a classic surrealist image, the portrait of Casati sits chronologically between the highpoints of the two avant-gardes.

At this time, Casati was most famously known as the former muse of futurism. This label had been bestowed upon her several years earlier by F. T. Marinetti, in reference to Casati's long-term romantic entanglement with the futurist poet and novelist Gabriele D'Annunzio. Man Ray's portrait of Casati was taken in 1922, the year that the March on Rome ousted Prime Minister Luigi Facta and established Benito Mussolini as the leader of the Italian Fascist Party.[3] The PNF articulated their new program through the language of male virility, a language taken in part from the futurist movement. It was D'Annunzio who, as a military commander, initiated many of the political practices associated with fascism's cult of leadership. During the occupation of Fiume, D'Annunzio popularized the balcony address, the Roman salute, the chant "*Eia, eia, eia! Alala!*," and the black shirt.

The marchesa's notorious promiscuity had rendered her persona non grata amid the sexual politics of Italy's new regime, even before the March on Rome.[4] Just before her arrival in Paris, Casati lived in Capri, an oasis in Italy for the homosexual high society. Hearing rumors of the marchesa's scandalous sexual practices, the owner of the villa the marchesa intended to rent reneged at the last moment. In the years following 1922, Capri began to lose its status as a liberal oasis. The fascist regime considered both homosexuality and nonreproductive sexual practices as detrimental to Italy's future. Nonreproductive sex would not produce a new generation of Italian men as heroes for the empire.[5] While Casati's outrageous costumes and libertinage had rendered her a muse in the early years of futurism, she did not retain this position of prestige during the rise of the fascist regime.

I begin with the story of Casati's portrait to situate the chance procedure as an aesthetic form with a specific material history. In the early decade of the twentieth century, European women's sexual deviance was primarily understood through *heterosexual* acts like prostitution or promiscuity.[6] The interwar period marks the slow accretion of a number of different types of female sex crime: deviant heterosexual acts (promiscuity, prostitution), gender inversion (the masculine woman), and same-sex object choice (female homosexuality). Casati's promiscuity was heterosexual sexual behavior, but in Italy this behavior could be lumped together with homosexually more generally as a form of nonreproductive sex that posed a eugenic threat.

This more accretive sense of female sexual deviance intersects with a history of European racism more generally. In 1903, Otto Weineger's enormously popular book *Sex and Character* provided a pseudoscientific argument for the ways that both feminine and masculine characteristics extend beyond biological sex into racial types. In Weineger's account, people exist somewhere on a spectrum of male and female characteristics. On one end of the spectrum, the ideal type Woman is entirely passive, irrational, immoral, and illogical; on the other end of the spectrum, the ideal type Man is entirely active, rational, moral, and logical. Woman is concerned solely with matters of familial reproduction; Man takes up an interest in culture, politics, arts, and society. Both the homosexual man and the Jew reside on the Woman end of the gender spectrum and thus possess feminine characteristics—lechery, lustfulness, weakness, laziness, and, most importantly, a lack of autonomous self. Though the presumed effeminacy of Jews and homosexuals has a much longer history, Weineger's book provides a touchstone for the brand of European racism that George Mosse has defined as a "scavenger ideology."[7] Rather than focus on one group, this version of racism lumps all outsider groups together under the rubric of a single contagion that threatens the healthy body of the nation. What Mosse calls the "racialization of sexuality" allows for a single dividing line, between insider/outsider, normal/abnormal, that crosses through racial and sexual categories alike. What Mosse does not consider, however, is the way that this racialization also creates a presupposition of what the normative feminine identifies—a white, heterosexual, middle- or upper-class woman who does not work outside the home.

This longer history begins to reveal the ways that surrealism's oft-noted preoccupation with the female form was not just about women per se, but a more complex set of identity categories linked to national citizenship, including race and sexual orientation. Beginning in the 1990s, feminist approaches to the avant-garde most often approached the female form in surrealist work through the language of performativity, particularly in reference to the representation of queer and transgender subjects. In an effort to avoid some of the impasses produced in these readings, this chapter sets aside the language of performativity in favor of a more historical account of the way non-normative sexual identities were produced through the discourses of empire and nation at midcentury. In so doing I focus on the chance procedure as an aesthetic category more suited for the categorical murkiness surrounding non-normative sexual identities at this historical juncture.

Across two world wars, chance becomes a weird and shifty form, one much more difficult to capture than we might have imagined. Part of this difficulty stems from the ways that the imagination of chance is intertwined with the identity categories determining national rights: gender, race, sexuality, and, as we will come to see, a racialized sense of the human. In the early 1920s, surrealist artists hypothesized a rock-solid association between chance and freedom. The incursion of chance into the work of art—as a narrative device, a procedure, a logic of association—was imagined as a countermeasure to means-end rationality. Chance was supposed to open up a space of freedom so that the logic of the dreamworld might bleed into an otherwise mundane daily life. Yet chance shifts registers during the interwar years. What began as an expression of untethered, voluntarist freedom begins to wane. In the 1930s, chance undergoes some alterations, moving from an expression of freedom to a form of lived precarity. In these later works, chance marks an uncertain future tied to the state's purely contingent definition of citizen and noncitizen, human and inhuman. As a form made out of contingency, based on lack of possible control, the chance procedure thus offers a conceptual language to map the uneven distribution of state violence upon raced and non-normative sexual bodies.

The following pages track the shifting boundaries of European citizenship alongside the surrealist imagination of chance, beginning in the early 1920s and moving into the postwar period. During this time, shifts in French family law can be connected to a wider reaction to changing racial demographics across Europe. What follows extends our sense of this historical moment before the outbreak of war and the authoritarian atmosphere of Vichy. The first half of this chapter draws out a history of the interwar period in order to understand the increasingly intimate connections between homosexuality and the rights of citizenship. This consideration situates the criminalization of female sexual deviance not as a sudden wartime measure but as a gradual accumulation of conservative juridical practice during the interwar years, including a landmark case for the criminalization of lesbian identity, *Pemberton Billing v. Maud Allen* (1918).

The second half of the chapter focuses on the multimedia artworks of Claude Cahun, who followed the *Billing* case closely from France. By positioning Cahun alongside the criminalization of homosexual identity, this chapter builds on recent scholarship that looks to contextualize Cahun's work through closer attention to both interwar lesbian cultures and what is today understood as transgender identity.[8] Rather than theorize Cahun's self-representation as either lesbian or transgender, I want to situate the historical ambiguity of her sexual identity as a site of lived vulnerability and administrative violence. To do this, the chapter turns to the archives to follow the resistance campaign waged by Cahun and her partner Marcel Moore in Nazi-occupied Jersey. I read their activism as a continuation of the surrealist chance procedure that moves beyond the artwork into a more worldly domain of constraint. These activist versions of surrealist chance provide an unexpected alternative to liberal human rights discourses in development at the same moment. In a turn from national law to international social policy, the last section of the chapter takes up the centrality of the heteronormative family form as the basis for political consensus at the crossroads of a number of fields, including the *Universal Declaration of Human Rights*, queer/trans theory, and the international avant-gardes.

Laws of the Family

Though demographic decline had been a French concern since 1870, the massive casualties of World War I gave rise to increased anxiety about repopulation. These demographic concerns became the centerpiece of right-wing social thought in the interwar years that associated maternity with greater productivity, national revival, and future success in war. In the interest of national regeneration, natalist-familialist discourses encouraged population growth, but only within the French nuclear family.[9] During a period of increased immigration, inflation, and unemployment, these concerns about repopulation also mobilized a racialized threat. Natalist brochures announced "The White Race in Mortal Danger" and "No More French People, No More France."[10] The publication of declining census results gave these population concerns a quasi-scientific validation and further provoked the fear that Prussian soldiers would outnumber the French in a future war. At this time, the founding of the Counsil supérieur de la natalité (1920) and the Fédération nationale des associations familes de France (1921) created a platform for state control of women's fertility and reproduction. In the interests of repopulating France, the Law of 1920 outlawed abortion and birth control, mandating prison sentences for the publicity and sale of all contraceptive devices. Passed by overwhelming majorities in the Chamber, the Law of 1920 only initiated a longer pattern of conservative family welfare policy that continued into the 1930s. In 1939, the Family Code offered a financial incentive for large families, offering an allowance for mothers that stayed at home, loans for young married couples, and a stipend for the birth of each new child, regardless of income level. Buttressed by a stunning French defeat on the battlefield, often blamed on insufficient numbers of French troops, the Vichy regime intensified this emphasis on the family as the foundation of social order. In a 1940 radio broadcast, Marshal Pétain set out what would become the hallmark of Vichy's moral code: "The right of families is in effect prior to and above that of the individuals. The family is the essential cell; it is the basis of the social structure; it is on it that we must build; if it gives way, all is lost; if it holds, everything can be saved."[11] While the "domestic revolution" of Vichy France is often depicted as a sudden shift from the National Front agenda, this legislation was actually only a continuation of juridical trends begun in the interwar period.[12]

These ongoing concerns about depopulation became attached to the specter of homosexuality as a threat to the nuclear family and thus the health of the nation. In England, Germany, and France alike, any version of sexual permissiveness was also coupled with concerns about the resilience of the nuclear family in a postwar moment, a structure seemingly threatened by homosexuality at large. For the historian Florence Tamagne, the increasing criminalization of homosexuality can be explained through the uneasy political climate of the interwar period: "Sexual decadence, identified with sterility, is thus identified with the national decline and depopulation. The themes of homosexuality and the feminine body are equated to the disintegration of the social body, the symbol of a nation that has become effeminate and infected by foreign elements."[13] Often coupled with the Jew or the foreigner, the homosexual presented a threat of effeminacy and perversion linked to national degeneration.

In the years leading up to the war and after, both Axis and Allied nations began to construct and regulate legal personhood against the specter of depopulation, intertwining women's reproduction, race, and homosexuality as constitutive of citizenship or noncitizenship. Though the 1920s are often regarded as a heyday of sexual liberty in Europe, this sense of increased liberty was not coupled with legal permissiveness. According to the Labouchère Amendment to the Criminal Law Amendment Act, attempted or consummated sexual acts between men were a misdemeanor that could bring a sentence of imprisonment not exceeding two years, with or without forced labor. From 1919 to 1938, case numbers for "unnatural offences" in England increased by a startling 185 percent.[14] Even in Weimar Germany, widely known for its liberal attitudes toward sexuality, homosexual acts were still illegal in the 1920s, and arrest records show a conviction rate comparable to England's. And with the rise of the National Socialist Party, this seemingly permissive atmosphere shifted drastically. After the Röhm Putsch, the revision of section 175 of the Reich Penal Code extended "sex offenses" beyond any sexual acts to include the somewhat vague possibility of "sexual intent." "Serious sex offenses" garnered sentences of up to ten years in prison. Finally, the so-called analogy section stipulated that persons who commit an act against "healthy public feeling" should be punished, even if no definite criminal law was applicable.[15] In 1936, the Reichszentrale zur bekämpfung der Homosexualität und Abortion (Reich Offices for the Combating of Homosexuality and Abortion) was created as a special team within the criminal police assigned to compile records on individuals suspected of being "enemies of the people" or "sex fiends." Under the injunction to preserve and increase the national body, this undertaking involved the registration of suspected homosexuals, transvestites, and abortionists. In 1940, the data bank stored 41,000 names. After Himmler's decree legalizing internment for these populations, Reich records show that fifty thousand were sentenced by Nazi judges and five thousand deported to concentration camps.[16]

In the 1920s in France, homosexuality was not considered a criminal offense. According to the revolutionary laws of 1879 and the penal code of 1810, "sexual perversions" were not subject to prosecution under French criminal law. However, well before the fall of the Third Republic, widespread police surveillance tracked suspected French homosexuals, particularly in the military sector. In a December 1931 report, Toulon's chief of police clarified his mission: "Our role is to monitor, pursue, and indict homosexuals who show up in Toulon and Seyne."[17] Available documents show arrests primarily of noncivilians given sentences ranging from two to six months in prison, sometimes accompanied with fines. In 1942, Pétain amended article 334 of the penal code to increase prison time for "shameless or unnatural acts with a minor of his own sex under the age of twenty-one."[18] However, aside from the Alsace-Lorraine territories, which were turned over to the National Socialists, along with lists of suspected homosexuals, the Vichy regime did not criminalize or repress homosexuality as an identity category, instead focusing on male homosexual acts with minors, particularly among military personnel.[19]

At this moment across Europe, surrealism's rejection of the bourgeois family partially emerges as a rejection of this legal equation between nation, family, and militarism. However, a number of critics have noted the seeming incongruity of surrealism's self-perceived radicalism and the movement's general homophobia. Lawrence R. Schehr states this incongruity in the form of a question: "given the extensive, militant, and continuous cries for liberation that are part and parcel of the Surrealist enterprise, how can Surrealism have been so faithful to a rigid heterosexual model and so critical of homosexuality?"[20] As Schehr notes, this question conflates the aesthetic movement that is called surrealist and the attitudes of surrealism's self-proclaimed *chef*, André Breton. Overt disdain of homosexuality was Breton's line. Because surrealism was often posited as Breton's invention, this stridently antihomosexual stance often becomes associated with the movement entire. However, there was a deep schism on the subject, a tension often fracturing over and across surrealism's alliance with the French Communist Party, which had condemned homosexuality as a bourgeois persuasion.[21]

A number of self-proclaimed surrealists and fellow travelers were either closeted or openly homosexual men, including Louis Aragon, René Crevel, and Jean Cocteau. However, this schism can be seen as more than a matter of lived identity positions, in light of a collective project entitled *Recherches sur la sexualité*, first published in the 1928 edition of *La Révolution Surréaliste*. The *Recherches* were a series of transcribed conversations that looked to achieve scientific clarity on a variety of sexual issues, including man's awareness of the female orgasm, whether there was any objective way to document said orgasm's appearance, the simultaneous orgasm, the morality of onanism, the most enjoyable sexual positions, the desirability of a ménage à trois, impotence, the preferred female body part, the preferred female body part on which to ejaculate, a preference for sexual acts with the lights on or off, whether one prefers a woman young or old, clean or unwashed, with pubic hair or not, and, in one case, with a limp or full mobility. Posed as questions then answered by group members, all of the topics assumed heterosexual partners.

Midway through the first session, Benjamin Péret set the conversation going in a different direction:

Benjamin Péret: What do you think of homosexuality?
Raymond Queneau: From what point of view? Moral?
Benjamin Péret: If you like.
Raymond Queneau: If two men love each other, I have no moral objections to make to their physical relations.
Protests from Breton, Péret, and Unik.
Pierre Unik: From a physical point of view, I find homosexuality as disgusting as excrement, and from a moral point of view I condemn it.
Jacques Prévert: I agree with Queneau.
Raymond Queneau: It is evident to me that there is an extraordinary prejudice against homosexuality among the surrealists.
André Breton: I accuse homosexuals of confronting human tolerance with a mental and moral deficiency which tends to turn itself into a system and to paralyze every enterprise I respect.[22]

Breton's comment is often cited as surrealism's attitude toward homosexuality tout court. Though one is inclined to agree with Queneau's somewhat bland observation that "there is an extraordinary prejudice against homosexuality among the surrealists," attitudes are in fact more complex. When the topic of homosexuality reemerges in the second session, Jacques Baron responds with "visceral antipathy." Man Ray argues that homosexuality is not physically different than heterosexuality. Queneau agrees with Man Ray, finding hetero- and homosexuality "equally acceptable." Aragon sees homosexuality as "a sexual inclination like any other." Jacques Baron agrees with Aragon. Marcel Duhamel admits that homosexual relations might be "not entirely repulsive." This turn of conversation prompts Breton to threaten, twice, to abandon the proceedings: "I am absolutely opposed to continuing the discussion of this subject. If this promotion of homosexuality carries on, I will leave this meeting forthwith."[23] Eventually, Queneau changes the subject, abruptly inquiring, "What does Aragon think of using condoms?"

The interviews that make up the *Recherches* are not surrealism's only—or even definitive—commentary on homosexuality, though these discussions have, in subsequent years, come to occupy a somewhat metonymic position.

But it is notable that, in this case, homosexuality means male homosexual object choice. The rest of this chapter will look toward an alternative view, one not always necessarily optimistic or even utopian, focusing on the historical conjuncture of female homosexuality and what will come to be known later as transgender identity. Moving away from "Woman" as theme and "homosexual" as an abstract moral threat, I read late surrealism's experiments with forms of chance as an attempt to think—and, in some cases, change—the shifting ways gender, sexuality, and race were lived as a position of rights.

Demain Joueur: The Gambling Tomorrow

In its first fits and starts in the 1920s, surrealist chance promised a liberation of the psyche. Mysticism, séances, and dreamscapes were coupled with chance as methods of liberating thought from the strictures of waking life, reason, morality, and aesthetic constraint. See, for example, Tristan Tzara's newspaper-clipping poems. See the games of Exquisite Corpse. See the paint dripping across the canvas, the found urinals and tin cans turned into statues. Perhaps, most famously, see *Nadja* (1928), Breton's most popular effort, achieved in the heroic phrase of surrealism proper. It is here that Breton announces a principle of construction. Breton will narrate his life only insofar as it wanders off a given plan, only

> insofar as it is at the mercy of chance—the merest as well as the greatest—temporarily balking at the commonplace ideas that I have, admitting me to an almost forbidden world of sudden parallels, petrifying coincidences, reflexes surpassing all other flights of fancy, of harmonies struck as though on the piano, flashes of light that would make you see, really *see*, if only they were not so much quicker than all the rest. [soit dans la mesure même où elle est livrée aux hasards, au plus petit comme au plus grand, où regimbant contre l'idée commune que je m'en fais, elle m'introduit dans un monde comme défendu qui est celui des rapprochements soudains, des pétrifiantes coïncidences, des réflexes primant tout autre essor du mental, des accords plaqués comme au piano, des éclairs qui feraient voir, mais alors *voir*, s'ils n'étaient encore plus rapides que les autres.][24]

It is such an earnest beginning, here at the start. Rather formal, Breton puts forth a plan for not having a plan. He renders chance an actor, an animal (one balking or bucking against), and a passageway to mythical sight. I find that repetition, with its insistent italics, to "really *see*" almost heartbreaking. It is so sincere, in a work generally seen as detached, aiming after the objective strains of a case study. How far from the baroquely formal "insofar as" to that injunction to see, to really *see* with its italics, as though we might miss it otherwise. One might consider Breton here stamping his foot. The repetition becomes a kind of injunction, *to see, to really see*, that is immediately taken back, because this sight is then written as too quick for us to grasp. This belated rendering of impossibility, after the list of enticing options, is a little strange. The negation of possibility recalls another kind of taking back that occurs a handful of pages later. After presenting a mystical encounter with chance, Breton notes, in the parenthetical: "(Anyone who laughs at this last sentence is a pig)" (*N* 31).

All of this suggests that Breton was taking a risk—at laughter and disbelief—for the sake of chance as what could deliver the flights of fancy and forbidden worlds. This risk made contingency a narrative principle. Before they were spliced together, these fragments were *found*. They were stumbled across on walks through Paris; they emerged through dream life and mesmerism. In Peter Bürger's formulation, chance events are what "have no place in a society that is organized according to the principle of means-ends rationality."[25] Chance was supposed to be everything that a rationalized world was not. If everything else had been turned into equations, into the pursuit of profits determined in advance, chance was supposed to be the exception to this rule. Chance was mysticism and magic, the primitive, the unforeseeable, what could not be stamped down or made into profits. Chance was supposed to be a kind of wildness in a rationalized world. In its most glorious strains, chance became a means to escape to a different kind of life determined by the magical objects encountered on the street, a sequence of objects that could determine a path and a life. Though Breton sometimes claimed to be petrified by chance, he welcomed it. Chance, it seemed, would only bring about a better, more marvelous future.

For Breton, the chance encounter was not just a structuring principle but a reality effect. In *Nadja*, Breton complains that standard fictional characters, like Julien Sorel, are not realistic enough. As readers, we know that Julien does not really exist. He can be killed off, but there is no Julien Sorel, in anyone's real life, who will die. To make his own novel *more* real, Breton takes the characters in *Nadja* from his own life. These are characters that he, the novelist, cannot entirely control. Their actions, therefore, cannot be determined in advance. Denis Hollier sees, in this indeterminacy, the open-ended future that characterizes surrealism as a whole:

> If [Breton's narratives] transgress the redemptive logic of the novel, this is not only because they permit themselves to invade the space of private life, giving names and printing photos; it's above all because of the surprise that this even constitutes: indexical signs leave doors ajar through which the *demain joueur*, the gambling tomorrow, does or does not make its entry.
>
> Clearly, when during the summer of 1927 Breton goes to the Manoir d'Ango to write the narrative of his encounters with *Nadja*, something in his life is finished which he wants to turn into a book. But he doesn't know how this book will end.[26]

For Hollier, it is essential that Breton began writing *Nadja* "without knowing what its ending was going to be."[27] What is not often questioned, by Breton or Hollier, is the way that this unknown ending could become so uniformly desirable. At this moment, in the 1920s, there was little thought of the ways that chance could have different modes, the way that some of these might always already be a part of means-end rationality, that is, the way that encounters with chance could also be as disastrous as the forms of life they were supposed to oppose. In this later scenario, chance looks less like freedom and more like precarity. This shift emerges through a political modernity that began to make life more precarious for Jewish, female, and homosexual populations in particular. Here I do not mean to descend into biography but to note that these ways of being in the world had material consequences, in terms of income, mobility, and, finally, the rights of man. In the 1930s, Breton's friend and comrade Claude Cahun began to explore the less marvelous sides of the gambling tomorrow. Another way to say this is that Cahun began to explore the ways that the gamble could be lost.

Critical accounts of Cahun sometimes bypass the bleaker aspects of her work, dazzled, perhaps, by the life of the artist as itself a celebratory masterpiece. Claude Cahun—a cross-dressing actress, surrealist poet, essayist, photographer, Jew, French translator of Havelock Ellis, member of Contre-Attaque, fighter in the French resistance, prisoner of the SS, and failed suicide—was largely forgotten after her death, only to be rediscovered in the 1980s.[28] Since then, a number of critics have turned to Cahun as the queer, trans, feminist artist that surrealist historians have forgotten.[29] In these accounts, Cahun is a postmodern feminist avant la lettre. She becomes the overlooked precursor to Cindy Sherman's performative gender identities or the exemplar of femininity as a masquerade, literally played, in the portraits, as what can be put on or taken off as a series of masks. It should be noted that Cahun's own writing often points in this interpretive direction. "Under this mask," writes Cahun, "another mask. I will never finish lifting up all these faces [Sous ce masque un autre masque. Je n'en finirai pas de soulever tous ces visages]."[30]

Following such declarations, Katy Kline sees Cahun's multiple selves as the destabilization of a single subject. This masquerade, in the vein of Joan Rivière, does not conceal an original woman or self. Rather, the "artist and the individual are present within each disguise, any one of which represents an aspect of an extraordinarily complex self."[31] Also citing Rivière's "Womanliness as a Masquerade," Dawn Ades notes that Cahun "constructs a series of masks of either exaggerated or indistinct gender, which bewilderingly proffer feminine or masculine faces or personae."[32] In a more directly poststructuralist mode, Jennifer Shaw reads Cahun's mirrors and masks as "emblems for the partiality of self-knowledge" that sever the cultural link between egoism and a rejection of gender norms.[33] Rosalind Krauss similarly finds in the work of Cahun a "deconstructive stance on the position of the subject" that is perpetually mobile. For Krauss, "subject and object, male and female identifications are continuously changing places."[34]

The bulk of these accounts emerged from the United States in the 1990s. It is therefore not surprising that these critics largely hew to a poststructuralist thesis, where the displacement, mobility, multiplicity, or denaturalization of normative gender roles becomes an enterprise lauded in itself. These critics find, through the use of the mask, the expression of an infinitely mobile performativity that often cites, alongside Rivière's "Womanliness as a Masquerade," Judith Butler's influential theorization of performativity in *Gender Trouble* (1990). Regarding Cahun's work as a symbolic representation of gender as a denaturalized construction, accounts of Cahun's photographs often hew to a narrative of redemption. These accounts suggest that the performance of mobile genders is in itself a kind of victory over a normative society. In an early and influential article, Carolyn Dean responded to critics that valorized gender mobility as a site of inherent freedom, arguing that closer attention to the historical formation of same-sex desire in the interwar period allows us to consider the ways that homosexuality became "the privileged signifier for the erosion of stable (boundaried, coherent, impermeable) heterosexual subjectivity."[35] Building on and extending Dean's work, I want to move beyond a celebration of indeterminate gender identity, to consider instead the distance between aesthetic performance and the lived experience of gender and sexuality during the interwar period. This shift emerges in conversation with Butler's later critique of performativity as an absolute, unconstrained voluntarism, as pure choice or free play severed from material constraints. Urging against a valorization of performativity as mere "theatrical self-presentation," as what might be easily turned on and off, Butler argues for a more complex symbolic structure:

> For sexuality cannot be summarily made or unmade, and it would be a mistake to associate "constructivism" with "the freedom of a subject to form her/his sexuality as s/he pleases." A construction is, after all, not the same as an artifice. On the contrary, constructivism needs to take account of the domain of constraints without which a certain living and desiring being cannot make its way. And every such being is constrained by not only what is difficult to imagine, but what remains radically unthinkable: in the domain of sexuality these constraints include the radical unthinkability of desiring otherwise, the radical unendurability of desiring otherwise, the absence of certain desires, the repetitive compulsion of others, the abiding repudiation of some sexual possibilities, panic, obsessional pull, and the nexus of sexuality and pain.[36]

To imagine Cahun's work as somehow severed from this "domain of constraints," as floating above or around it, does not account for the way that such constructions operate in a restrained field brokered by the unthinkable and unendurable alternatives. However, Butler's sense of constructivism in this passage remains historically abstract, so that constraint exists as a kind of blank limitation. What follows builds on the recent work of a number of scholars, including Rosemary Hennessy, Kevin Floyd, and Cinzia Arruza, who have revisited Butler's vastly influential but largely linguistic theorization in *Gender Trouble* and *Bodies That Matter* to further historicize the temporality of gender performativity.[37] In the case of Claude Cahun, it matters that the performativity in question arises at a moment before the solidification of lesbian or trans identity into a nameable referent. This does not mean that Cahun was working without constraints in a field of open possibility. Rather, it suggests that the historical specificity of sexual freedom and constraint at this moment needs to be further articulated, in this case through a consideration of the criminalization of lesbian identity in interwar Europe. Alongside the increasingly conservative juridical trends that I have already explored, the interwar period witnessed a number of lawsuits concerning female homosexuality, some twenty years after the Oscar Wilde trials. It is not so surprising, then, that the most famous of these lawsuits, *Pemberton Billing v. Maud Allen* (1918), was of particular interest to a young Claude Cahun.

Claude Cahun's *Human Frontier*

In 1918, Cahun wrote an article for *Le Mercure de France* about a defamation trial in London surrounding private productions of Oscar Wilde's *Salomé*. Though Cahun did not describe it then as such, the trial has become a landmark in sexual political history for its sensational efforts to posit lesbianism as a threat to England's success in the ongoing war.[38] The conflict emerged from the right-wing paper *Vigilante*'s suggestion that the private productions of *Salomé* were performed and attended by a secretive lesbian sect referred to as "The Cult of the Clitoris."[39] During the final months of World War I, when the Central Powers were beginning to collapse on the continent, *Salomé*'s lead actress, Maud Allan, sued *Vigilante*'s editor Noel Pemberton Billing for libel. What was most notable about the trial was Billing's defense. Acting as his own lawyer, Billing focused on the speculative existence of a "black book" listing 47,000 British homosexuals identified by the German government. The black book emerged as a rumor—Billing could not produce the actual copy. However, the specter of such a book, and the suggestion that the people who produced *Salomé* and the people who went to the performance were named in the book, caused quite a commotion. The potential existence of this black book, kept by German diplomats, gave Billing's defense a patriotic air. Sexual inversion, pacifism, liberalism, and political treachery became conflated as a singular menace. Billing focused particularly on German Jewish members of the government and the threat of Bolsheviks at large profiting from the war. Somewhat spectacularly, Billing claimed that plays "like *Salomé* are calculated to corrupt and debauch, and to cause more harm for all those that would go see it than the German army itself [telle que *Salomé* était bien faite pour corrompre et débaucher, et causer plus de mal à tous ceux qui la verraient que l'armée allemande elle-même]."⁴⁰ Noting Billing's close connections with Sir William Joynson-Hicks in the House of Commons, subsequent historians have positioned Billing's defense as a publicity stunt meant to prevent the negotiation of peace and topple Lloyd George's government.⁴¹

The British press, for the most part, celebrated Billing's acquittal. Cahun's article condemns this outcome but attributes it to national weakness and, in particular, to British prudery. However, the Billing case comes only a few years before censorship of France's first homosexual revue, *Inversions*. The journal was republished a month later as *L'Amitié*. This second edition included, under a sardonic excuse for scientific objectivity, a poll that asked a number of authors, including Cahun and Havelock Ellis, if and why they found the first issue offensive. *L'Amité* did not last long before it, too, was seized by the police. Editors were sentenced to six months in prison for "propaganda anti-conceptionelle," a somewhat imaginative way to get around the long-standing legality of homosexual speech and praxis in France.⁴²

The Billing trial and the seizure of *Inversions* should not overshadow other aspects of the criminalization of homosexuality, namely, a dramatic rise in the prosecution of "unnatural acts" in France, England, and Germany. This criminalization was not just a matter of infectious representation or perverted acts but something much larger, ultimately aligned with the stability of the nuclear family, overshadowed by fears of population decline, and, finally, foundational as a national prerogative to ensure future success in war. This is not to say that everything was steeped in fear and trembling from beginning to end. In these selected examples we can begin to sketch out an alternative history, one that offers a verso to the celebratory accounts of the interwar era as a kind of sexual utopia, entirely free. Against the imagined abandon of the "women of the left bank," we might recall Colette's warning in 1930 that "two women who have resolved to live alone together are never safe. Everything is permitted them except one kind of quietude."⁴³ In Colette's narrative, the women who dress in men's clothing "never crossed the street or left their carriage without putting on, heart pounding, a long plain cloak which gave them an excessively respectable look and effectively concealed their masculine attire."⁴⁴ Here costume is not necessarily an airy choice but a way of concealing identity in public. Artifice offers a way of surviving in a world that necessitates costumes. Costume offers a mode of becoming more or less invisible in a period when the law did not just proscribe homosexuality but discursively constructed non-normative gender as a threat to national security.

The potential dangers of two women living together offer a particularly felicitous entry into Cahun's photographic work, which, I should say now, appears to have been a collaborative project. As Tirza True Latimer has argued, a wider consideration of photographic negatives, letters, and the unpublished manuscripts unavailable to the earliest Cahun scholars allows us to reclassify these works, shifting from the "self-portrait" to a "joint production" between Cahun and her lifelong partner, Marcel Moore (born Suzanne Malherbe).[45] Latimer notes, for instance, that though almost all of the images depict Cahun alone, they are described in letters to friends as "our photography" or "our amateur efforts." As early as 1929, the *Chicago Tribune*

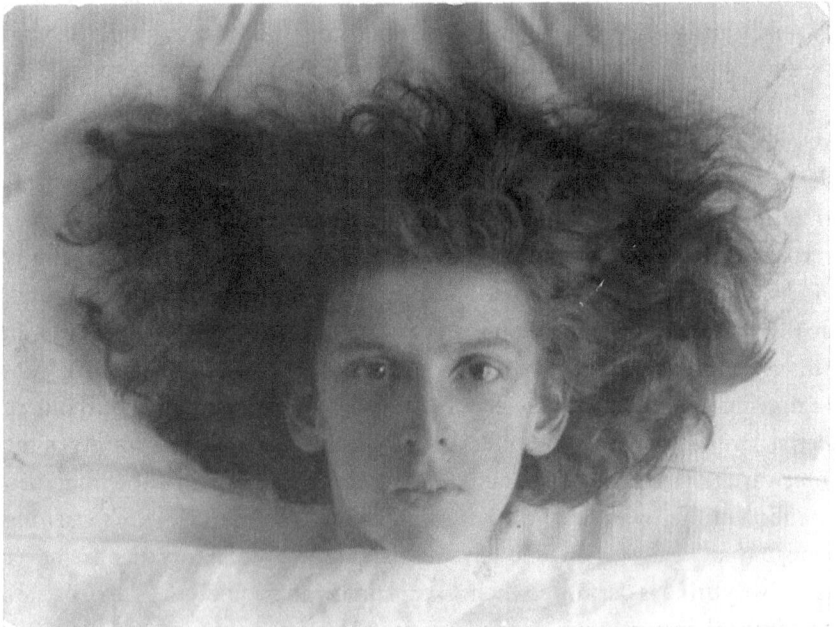

FIGURE 5.2 Claude Cahun, *Self portrait, Claude Cahun as a young girl*, 1914. Photograph.
Source: Courtesy of the Jersey Heritage Collection.

FIGURE 5.3 Claude Cahun, *Self portrait*, 1927. Photograph.
Source: Courtesy of the Jersey Heritage Collection.

"Who's Who Abroad" reports that Moore was "engaged in making a series of distorted photographs of her sister."[46] Most of the photographs would have required a remote switch, attached to a long wire, which we never see in the image. Finally, in a more figural mode, it is significant that Cahun often referred to herself as her lover's masterpiece: "Je suis l'œuvre de ta vie [I am the work of your life]."[47]

Rather than consider the images individually, I want to situate these portraits of Cahun as one long form, or a serial structure that extends over several decades. When they are viewed collectively, the portraits echo one another in small ways. There are, for instance, persistently baroque ornaments off to one side, in an otherwise spare backdrop: the curlicue of the

FIGURE 5.4 Claude Cahun, *I am in training don't kiss me*, 1927. Photograph.
Source: Courtesy of the Jersey Heritage Collection.

drawer handle, the gelled forelock, the wooden spirals of a wardrobe, the seams in a stuffed quilt, thin pieces of seaweed wrapped around the body. Backgrounds tend toward a grid, lacking depth. There are often horizontal gradations in color. Crooked lines sneak into these settings, crossing pillow and hair. There are the innumerable mirrors, gates, and doorways, always making a frame within the frame, usually tilted at some obscure angle. Most famous, perhaps, are the doubles: Cahun and her reflection, Cahun and Moore, Cahun and her shadow. Less noted but visible over the decades are a series of cats: a tabby in the 1920s, a Siamese who tends to dart off, then, after the war, a long-haired breed—the most photogenic, or at least the cat most willing to pose with Cahun in a number of settings and walk on a leash.

FIGURE 5.5 Claude Cahun, *Self portrait (kneeling, naked, with mask)*, 1928. Photograph. *Source*: Courtesy of the Jersey Heritage Collection.

Then there are the costumes. Across thirty years, we see Cahun as a doll, harlequin, sailor, schoolgirl, devil, weightlifter, Buddha. Sometimes these images emerge from Cahun's work as an actress at the Theatre du Plateau. She sprouts what look like aluminum wings, Kabuki makeup, and, in one instance, knee-length blond braids attached to a hat. The self-portraits show Cahun in bed, inside a bureau, wrapped in seaweed, behind windows, and peering through a rubber tire. She stands on walls and hangs from signs. In the 1930s and 1940s, the portraits move outdoors. We find Cahun on the beach, behind a rock, lying in a garden.

What these descriptions accomplish is a sense of narrative—of a series—rather than a collection of single, isolated images. This narrative is an

FIGURE 5.6 Claude Cahun, *Self portrait (double exposure in rock pool)*, 1928. Photograph. *Source*: Courtesy of the Jersey Heritage Collection.

autobiography of sorts—one in costume, as other characters—that begins in the 1920s and continues until Cahun's death in 1954. The photographs transition between categories of identity, moving between masculinity and femininity, between human and alien, between subjects and objects, between people and nature.

Off to the side there are also small moments of humor or delight. Consider, for instance, amid the right angles of the harlequin jacket, that one jaunty pocket, gaping open like a mouth. Or note, in that same photograph, the fragility of the shadow in the crevice of the neck. It looks, almost, like a wound. I find the bracelets on the wrists of the arm encased in rock a quite

FIGURE 5.7 Claude Cahun, *Self portrait (with round frame)*, 1938. Photograph.
Source: Courtesy of the Jersey Heritage Collection.

funny touch. In the collages, amid the stack of severed heads, there is that one waggish skull, imperviously doffing her hat. Cahun's socked foot, pressing against the inside of the wardrobe, offers a droll contrast with her dangling hands. Most beautiful, I find, is the oddly textured, lily-shaped curve of reflected light that snakes around the reflection of the face in the globe.

Yet it becomes difficult to enter a redemptive mode—of triumphant performativity and the freedoms of selfhood entailed—when we turn from the bejeweled wrists and doffing hats to the longer forms that emerge across the series. This shift, from the single photograph to hundreds of photographs, allows certain patterns to emerge. We see Cahun age. She is short-haired and

FIGURE 5.8 Claude Cahun, *Self portrait (lying on leopard skin)*, 1939. Photograph.
Source: Courtesy of the Jersey Heritage Collection.

impossibly thin in the 1920s. In the 1930s her face fills out and the hair darkens. Then her posture changes. She is somewhat hunched in the decades after.

Intriguingly, one word that both Breton and Cahun generally avoid is autobiography. An autobiography most often looks backward, to record the facts of a life already lived. What the surrealists attempt is closer to a fiction taken from life *as* it is lived, dictated by chance, without knowing how the story will end. Because of its ties to the real, this fiction cannot be entirely set under authorial control. Breton reminds us, again and again, how, on the streets of Paris or in the theater house, he is led by the vagaries of chance. Cahun locates a different, visual language for chance, one that looks more like a "domain of constraint." This language emerges, as I have suggested, as a longer form, across a series of images. It almost never hews to the obvious: to ties, ropes, chains, bars. For a more literal rendering of constraint, look to Hans Bellmer's surrealist *Poupées*. In Bellmer's series, the plastic doll body can be easily dismembered and warped. Joints appear to be bound by rope. Limbs are severed. Orifices bulge. In what I consider to be one of Bellmer's most brilliant images, a sleeping doll curves around the staircase like an ornament, mounds protruding where we might expect limbs to go, a roped bow sprouting from her knee. The care with which her hand curves around the top of the staircase, nearly in shadow, as though the post were a lover's shoulder, descends into a number of knobs, nearly tumors, across the chest and where a left arm should be. Next to Bellmer's images, Cahun's portraits seem nearly cheery.

Then again, many of the surrealists had been taking apart bodies for some time. What becomes important, in Cahun's work, is the way this dismemberment signifies a different kind of subject.[48] For Cahun, this dismemberment is nearly invisible. The pattern does not occur in every photograph. It might pop up, say, in one out of ten. Were one looking at a few images, from this year or that year, the tendency would be invisible. However, when the series is considered as a whole, the formally obscure resemblance becomes nearly embarrassing in its obviousness. Here and there, gently, through a trick of light or the play of clothing, Cahun's head or neck appears to be severed from the rest of her body. This beheading is most often a matter of costume. A sheet or scarf sets the skull apart from the body. A black shirt makes the body recede into the background. In the quilt series, a shadow passes under the chin. Later images obscure the head with rocks, masks, or mirrors. The collages make this decapitation explicit, piling heads on top of one another.

In 1930, a variation on dismemberment entitled *Frontière humaine* appeared in *Bifur* (figure 5.9). The title suggests a blurring of boundaries between, as subsequent critics have suggested, male and female, human and inhuman. I see here, too, a kind of agelessness. The strapless top renders Cahun's bust somehow floating in blackness below the clavicle. Most striking is the elongated, shaved head, lengthened, slightly, between two exposures. The trick effects here are quite subtle, almost modest in comparison to Man Ray's overt blur in the image with which I began this chapter—the portrait of the marchesa Casati.

Man Ray claimed that the blurring of the portrait of the marchesa Casati was an accident, though we know this record to be a lie. But the desire to stress the appearance of accident in a photographic image was not limited to Man Ray. Theories of the photographic image are riddled with the language of

210   CONVERGENCES IN INSTITUTIONAL HUMAN RIGHTS

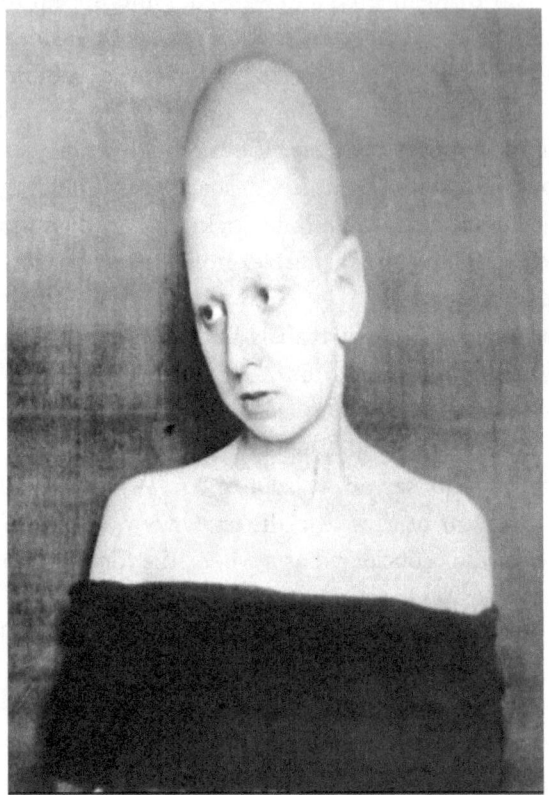

FIGURE 5.9 Claude Cahun, *Frontière humaine*, April 1930. Black and white photograph, *Bifur*, no. 5.

accident. Walter Benjamin describes the role of contingency in photography as the thing that escapes the artist's control or, in an uncanny coincidence, as the very sort of blurring that Man Ray claimed was an unintended effect of a broken light and a fidgety subject in the portrait of Casati:

> No matter how artful the photographer, no matter how carefully posed the subject, the beholder feels an irresistible urge to search such a picture for the tiny spark of contingency, of the here and now [*Jetztzeit*], with which reality has (so to speak) seared the subject, to find the inconspicuous spot where in the immediacy of that long-forgotten moment, the future nests so eloquently that we, looking back, may rediscover it.[49]

Like Man Ray, Benjamin writes contingency as what escapes authorial intention. Quite a few years later, Roland Barthes continues in this vein, renaming the "tiny spark" the *punctum*. Barthes writes, "for *punctum* is also: sting, speck, cut, little hole—and also a cast of the dice. A photograph's *punctum* is that accident which pricks me."[50] In their imagination of a communion between past and present, neither Benjamin nor Barthes fully acknowledges that this sense of escaping intention, as felt by the beholder, could only be a matter of guesswork. Who is to say that that spot or spark was not carefully planned? Benjamin does not give examples, but we might hypothesize some aspects seeming to escape control: a fly on the lens, a splotch of reflected light, the pattern of blowing leaves, the shape of a cloud that looks like a house or bird. That these instances of accident have all become photographic clichés renders the matter of intention even more flimsy. For my purposes, it is useful to make a distinction between two modes: first, the "spark of contingency" as fiction about the past that the spectator imagines and, second, the way that the artist's choice to take up and follow a character from life creates a contingent narrative ending in the *future*. Recall that Breton, in turning away from the purely fictional, began writing *Nadja* by creating uncertainty through narrative, by writing a story "without knowing what its ending was going to be."

Returning, finally, to *Frontière humaine*, what might appear as the free play or voluntaristic freedom of gender performance changes when we look more closely at this embedded pattern that quietly, seemingly nonviolently or nongrotesquely, severs the head from the rest of the body. Cahun's portraits sever the head but do not always throw it away. There is the possibility to read facial expression in a body that, logically, ought to be dead. In *Frontière humaine*, Cahun wavers toward the melancholic—almost tentatively so—but I do not feel confident reading, in the downturned head or upturned eyes, much besides a maybe sincere, maybe farcical kind of expression—a half-felt sense of caution or unease. What are more certain are the photographic trick effects: from a distance, it becomes unclear if we are looking at an animated marble bust or a person turned into stone. Here, too, is an either/or: either this persistent severing of the neck creates a punitive constraint or these shadows become an attempt to shake off the sheer, stubborn material of the body, a body that remains there through costumes and tricks of light, as that which cannot, no matter how much desired, be entirely shed.

Rather than overt bondage, *Frontière humaine* shows constraint as something quieter, almost invisible. Were we to look more closely, the severing or shadow disappears. The weight of the body as sheer material can't quite be cast off, for better or worse. These photographs offer a multiplicity of roles, but this multiplicity, in itself, does not promise freedom. That the series reveals many roles of interchangeable genders and ages, seemingly flexible selves to step into and out of, is not entirely a game played on its own terms. Through these tricks of light, Cahun's portraits feel their ways toward a limited freedom. They suggest a making of new subjects but not the external systems of power and contingency that determine them. The photographs offer a different kind of bet, less spectacularly utopian. Across the series, as a narrative of a subject taken from life, a story begun without knowing how the story would end, contingency—the mystical chance encounter so favored by the surrealists—appears differently. It is not a spark or fleck, not the unforeseen blur, but a sense of time passing beyond the horizon of art. This narrative emerges through a succession of masks and a more bodily "domain of constraint" that renders this visual narrative as a struggle in the present tense, between the freedoms of performance and the fact of a body that cannot, like a hat or a mask, be entirely taken off.

One of the better accounts of such a struggle comes somewhat late in the recognized canon of avant-garde theory, from Renato Poggioli. Rather than the dehumanization claimed by Ortega y Gasset, Poggioli sees in the deforming aspects of abstraction another complementary possibility, one that will take us into the next section:

> In avant-garde figuration there is not only abstractionism and mechanism, but also a new or special way of representing what is human, organic, and living. However, that representation is, as we are wont to say, deformed or deforming. In short, the principle of dehumanization comes to take on much more valid and precise meaning insofar as it is at least partially synonymous with the vaster and less approximate stylistic concept of *deformation*.[51]

Poggioli's argument emerges as one half of a larger debate. The opposing side would argue for an equivalence between dehumanization and aesthetic deformation. It would see in the deforming tendencies of Cahun's work a mere reflection of contemporaneous processes of dehumanization. For

Poggioli, what is deforming in representation is also a way of imagining otherwise or outside of liberal humanism.

It is important to understand that the "new or special way of representing what is human" is not a return to the kind of universalism surrealists initially rejected. That is to say, I do not think that the subjects in Cahun's photographs look to represent a universal, amalgamated human in which we all imagine that we have a part, together. It is more accurate to say that the subjects in these photographs speak from the position of the inhuman, from the gendered, raced, and dehumanized categories that are the exclusion to this norm. This speaking does not mark a heroic freedom; rather, it narrates a struggle between gains and losses, between freedom and a wider set of constraints. Poggioli is primarily concerned with the ways that such practices "represent what is human," leaving aside the ways that the avant-garde made claims beyond the sphere of representation for an art in the service of the revolution. Certainly enough, these claims are often scoffed at or brushed aside as mere theatrics, sometimes beautiful or stunning, but at a distance from the world that they sought to transform. But to understand what I have been writing as a changing attitude toward the chance experiment, from Casati to Cahun, it is not enough to consider the way that a narrative might take its characters from life, not knowing how the story would end. The following section will turn in the other direction, to consider the ways that the surrealist chance experiment was taken as a blueprint to create new forms of action.

Queer Resistance and the Rights of the Human Being

When Trotsky refused to sign the "Manifesto for an Independent Revolutionary Art" (1938), it was, he claimed, because this document was a manifesto on *art*, not revolution.[52] For this reason, Trotsky contended, the manifesto ought to be signed by artists. In a letter to Gérard Rosenthal, Trotsky further explained, with careful and devastating politeness, that Breton's surrealist works pertain to the art world, which is harmless enough. Though these documents use the language of revolution, their primary focus is a response to totalitarian attacks on art. It is a letter without any particular rancor, though we know that Breton, who idolized the exiled leader, was disappointed by Trotsky's refusal as well as by the correspondence following their encounter in Mexico. In a letter to Breton, Trotsky notes, again with crushing politeness: "In all sincerity, your praises seem so exaggerated that I worry a little about the future of our relations."[53] Despite this lukewarm reception of the French avant-garde, the shadow of Trotsky looms large as an influence in the surrealist manifesto, as one sign among many that "Manifesto for an Independent Revolutionary Art" specifically targets fascism in Europe. Eventually signed by Breton and Diego Rivera, the manifesto ends on a now famous chiasmus: *"the independence of art—for the revolution; the revolution—for the liberation of art once and for all."*[54]

Written mere months after D-Day, from Canada, *Arcanum 17* (1944) offers a different account of art and praxis. This revision somewhat unsubtly relocates blame, moving from fascist dictators suppressing art to women's passivity regarding men. Regarding the singular category "Woman," Breton inquires why this population didn't do more to stop the war:

> I've always been stupefied that she didn't make her voice heard, that she didn't think of taking every possible advantage, the immense advantage of the two irresistible and priceless inflections given to her, one for talking to men during love, the other that commands all of a child's trust. What clout, what future would this great cry of warning and refusal from woman have had, this always powerful cry whose potential, because of a dreamlike evil spell, so many beings do not succeed in realizing, if in the course of the last few years it could have sprung up, especially in Germany, and if impossibly it might have been strong enough to resist being stifled! After so many female "saints" and national heroines fanning the combativeness of this or that clan, when will we see a woman simply as a woman perform quite a different *miracle* of extending her arms between those who are about to grapple to say "you are brothers."[55]

There are many things one might say about this passage. It is tempting to dwell for a moment on Breton's characterization of woman's "irresistible powers" and the historical effects these powers might have had. Here again, Breton's earnestness is a bit devastating, not for the desires mentioned but for the ways they are so underexamined, as though the plan for what might have been is self-evident, brokering no possible arguments. More interesting is the articulation of two roles: the imagined absence of women making their supplications for peace between nations heard, compared with the militarism of female heroines in the past, inciting men to war. This either/or, of female passivity or female militarism, was not, of course, an imaginary unique to Breton. It suggests a wider notion of the horizon of possibilities for women as revolutionary—or even wartime—subjects.

Undoubtedly, it was against such notions that Claude Cahun, who had an understandably fractious relationship with Breton, entered into Parisian leftist politics in the 1930s. In the posthumously published work *Confidences au miroir*, Cahun records her frustration with such attempts simultaneously to valorize women and leave them outside of political praxis. Looking across the writing in *Confidences*, coupled with the extant documents detailing Cahun's wartime activism, we find a different imagination of a revolutionary subject, alongside a different imagination of the aims of art in the service of the revolution. Rather than a quelling of tempers or incitement of warring clans, rather than, even, a liberated art, Cahun's efforts begin differently, with a desire to change the way that a historical story might end.

While living in Paris, Cahun was involved in a number of political action groups, including the PCF, Contre-Attaque, and the Association of Revolutionary Artists and Writers. Her 1934 essay *Les paris sont ouverts* (*The Bets Are Open*) criticizes the CFP's demands for revolutionary poetry and committed art. Here Cahun argues that art is distinct from propaganda and protest writing alike, because art is always necessarily ambiguous, capable of being twisted either way. A photograph of hair mixed with straw, Cahun writes, might be seen in two manners: as a portrait of the artist's beloved or as the scene of a riot, the city speckled with a thousand divergent fists and arms (*E* 510). For Cahun, the capability of art not to persuade but to keep these interpretive freedoms open makes it a force for liberation. However, this freedom available in art is not enough. Rather, the essay makes a distinction: direct actions are necessary actions in the world; art does not act but allows for an "indirect action" through the creation of contradictions—riot or hair strewn with straw—that the reader is free to interpret. Cahun's claim that "the bets are open" then has multiple referents. The bet refers to the series of oppositions the essay constructs: between revolutionaries and fascists, between praxis and art, between the riot of fists and the hair of the beloved, between the poetry of the surrealists and the propaganda of the PCF. Choosing sides—the placing of bets—is not a matter of picking one side or the other, art or life. It means understanding the difference between them.

Cahun wrote *The Bets are Open* well before she and Moore initiated a series of direct actions that would get them arrested by the Gestapo and sentenced to death.[56] After the occupation of Jersey, an English Channel island that became the couple's residence in 1937, Moore and Cahun began a four-year campaign of resistance against the occupation. Moore translated BBC news of Axis defeats, which she received via an illegal radio, into German to create her own "news service" as counterpropaganda to the Vichy-controlled Radio Paris.[57] These leaflets were then distributed by the couple in places where German soldiers might come upon them: in coat pockets, pasted onto telegraph poles, on the graves of German soldiers, on German staff cars parked at funerals. On occasion, Moore and Cahun would paint slogans on coins with nail polish (Peggy Sage's Wicked White was a favorite hue) and leave the coins in video arcades. Because tobacco was scarce, the couple found that leaving the leaflets inside empty cigarette packs on the street was a particularly effective method of distribution. During the military tribunal, the Geheime Feldpolizei dossier contained 350 of these leaflets. Cahun estimated that at least 2,500 were distributed during the four-year period (*E* 748). In her letters, Cahun recounts a kind of "scrap-iron fair [*foire à la ferraile*]" of confiscated materials set out on one long table during the trial. From the couple's home, police had stacked, head-high, piles of first editions, hardbacks, paperbacks, folios, journals, anarchist pamphlets, and other printed materials of surrealist, nationalist, or leftist inclinations. There was too, in this pile of illegal materials, surrealist paintings, ribbons of red silk, wooden crosses painted black, the radio, the camera, the Underwood typewriter. ("I noted what they missed," Cahun later wrote in a letter, "the devils, the iron crosses, the panther skull [*Je remarque ce qui manqué: les diables, les croix de fer, le crâne de panthère*].")[58]

Historians speculate that Cahun and Moore were not deported immediately because of the couple's multiple suicide attempts in prison. Believing the propaganda campaign to be part of a larger resistance network, the Geheime Feldpolizei wanted to interrogate the women thoroughly. After six months, a military tribunal sentenced Cahun and Moore to death. As the certain end of the war approached, the German High Command ordered a reprieve of execution. Cahun and Moore remained interned in Gloucester Street Prison in St. Helier until the liberation of Jersey by Allied troops.[59]

Looking to *The Bets Are Open*'s critique of committed art, critics often write Cahun's activism as a sharp break with her earlier convictions.[60]

However, I will contend, Cahun and Moore's participation in the French Resistance was not a break from their earlier surrealist work but a continuation of its aims and procedures. To see this period as a component in a larger series—a work of one's life, as Cahun put it—requires closer focus on the leaflets themselves.

It should be said, then, that the propaganda was not all leaflets and not all BBC news. Initially, Cahun transformed the prewar National Socialist slogan "Schrecken ohne Ende oder Ende mit Schrecken [terror without end or end with terror]."[61] On walks near the military airport, Cahun and Moore would write on walls, cigarette cartons, packing, and bits of wood. "Sieg? Nein: Krieg! ohne Ende [Victory? No: War! without End]." The photomontages have all been destroyed, but Cahun describes one depicting an army regiment that she had "turned in every sense" by covering the men in mud, blocking out their faces, painted red, and inserted in a frame formerly reserved for a portrait of Oscar Wilde. In 1941, the women expanded the operation, posting bulletins, tracts, manifestos, and pseudoconfessions of German soldiers.[62] There was, as well, an object series: black wooden crosses, designed to look like those on the graves of German soldiers, were planted in the ground with the inscription "Für Sie ist der Krieg zu Ende [For them the war is finished]." The aforementioned panther skull was a part of a "plant mixture" painted red to attract attention.

In 1942, Cahun and Moore began signing the leaflets "der Soldat ohne Namen [the soldier without a name]." This fiction—that a German soldier had defected and was looking to persuade other troops to put down their arms—expanded into a wholesale campaign. The women varied languages, style, and type to make it seem like there was an invisible committee of German soldiers looking to end the war. This sense of the mask as yet another pseudonym—the Soldier Without a Name—most closely links the resistance work with the collaborative projects that came before. However, it is not the fact of masking that is important here but the way that the fiction of identity becomes part of a larger process dictated by chance.

Breton shapes the real-life narrative of *Nadja* by recording daily walks around Paris. Passing along the boulevard Bonne-Nouvelle, Breton admits that he doesn't know why it is along this particular street that his feet take him, other than an obscure intuition. People and things encountered offer a narrative dictated by chance, one that he began writing without knowing how the story would end. The boulevard Bonne-Nouvelle leads to the movies and rue Fontaine to the Théâtre des Deux Masques. Each location offers its own set of coincidental persons and things, now stitched together through the chance encounters of the aimless walk.

Though hardly aimless, Cahun and Moore's resistance campaign began as a series of daily promenades in the city. The women would make propaganda each night and then the following day distribute the leaflets around the city.[63] This, too, was a gamble with an uncertain future. Who might find these leaflets, left in cigarette cartons or car windshields, could not be determined. But this gamble, contra Breton, sets "chance" into a different mode. Here the audience is no longer made up of fellow surrealists. Chance does not make art. The purpose of the chance procedure lies with the people who will find it. Here the chance encounter does not lay the groundwork for a narrative with an uncertain future. The chance encounter, achieved through the promenades and the distributed propaganda, attempts to make claims on this future, to change it directly.

I have been arguing that Cahun and Moore's collaborative work—as photographs, as poems as praxis—makes up a series across a life, one that we can read across. The Vichy years, then, are not a break or an end but one moment in a larger process. This process did not end with imprisonment. While interned in Saint-Helier, Cahun used a smuggled pencil to write on sheets of toilet paper. These notes then appear, slightly altered, in the posthumous work *Confidences au miroir*. Composed of dense, Rimbaudian prose poems, the autobiographical work offers an unfinished sequel to the early *Aveux non avenus*. However, rather than a personal testimony, the later work "serves as a signature tune for all the survivors. For laborers, for families and teachers, just as for the survivors of revolutions and wars" (*E* 573).

Not an autobiography and not quite a poem, *Confidences* resembles a more old-fashioned genre, the bildungsroman. Though nonsequential, the text traces a narrative of individual development from youth to maturity. However, in this case, the protagonist is not harmonized with existing society. Nor is she turned into a good, tax-paying citizen. Across the series of works that makes up Cahun's corpus, we can see the formation of yet another kind of antibildungsroman, one that takes up the thematic of individual development antagonistic to social norms and existing society. Or, to flip Franco Moretti's quip about the eighteenth-century bildungsroman, this is the imagination of a novelistic world where revolution *will* take place. As a whole, the surrealist project often tried to agitate for this future, however ineffective these agitations might look in retrospect. Recall that Breton begins *Nadja* with an invocation of Flaubert as one author whom he particularly dislikes. *Nadja*, Breton suggests, will not be a sentimental education but something quite different, in that it follows its protagonist, Breton, not according to a preordained plot but according to the dictates of chance. Rather than shrugging off the specter of *Bildung* from the outset, *Confidences* explicitly takes up the coordinates of this very tradition.

In *Confidences*, Cahun recalls her mistaken impressions of the world as a very young child. There is, first, the mother's hysterical "crises" inexplicitly precipitated by the words "mon petit cochon." The young Cahun hides under the piano to avoid Aunt Marguerite, imagined as an ogress in league with the monsters Hot and Cold. Relocated to her grandmother's house, Cahun plays with marbles and desperately wishes she could read. Here is a process of education: "I get a book. I study it. I know my ABCs [J'en fais un livre. Je l'étudie. Je sais lire écrire]" (*E* 620). This is a narrative of development, but rather than escaping fantasy to face reality, Cahun imagines an even more fantastic end. In a perpetually winding passage, crossing between past and present, a conversation with Socrates and Pygmalion leads to a violent hail of stones. Cahun hides a shard of rock in her palm, which then becomes a sheet of paper. In this dreamscape, at the denouement of maturity, Cahun's personality is not consolidated in accordance with the demands of society. Rather, the subject Cahun becomes a billiard ball rolling in the wrong direction, against gravity. As a bit piece in a game of chance, Cahun undergoes a violent metamorphosis. This is no gentle blossoming. Her body is quite literally taken apart and remade, though not quite correctly:

> You have made multiple errors. The kidneys aren't where they belong. Where in the hell did you get these teeth? They are not mine? And the eyes? You have lost a pair. What have you done? You have divided the other between *that* and me. One could say that you are clever! Look in your medicine bags for the pliers you have left in my throat. [Vous avez commis de multiples erreurs. Les rognons ne sont pas à leur place. Où diable avez-vous pris ces dents ? Ce ne sont pas les miennes ? Et les yeux ? Vous en aviez égaré une paire. Qu'avez vous fait ? Vous avez divisé l'autre entre *ça* et moi. On peut dire que vous êtes calés! Cherchez dans vos trousses les pinces que vous m'avez laissées dans la gorge.]
>
> (*E* 622–23)

Cahun writes this metamorphosis as a Frankensteinian operation, one that peels off the skin, breaks the bones, and removes the entrails so that the body might be reborn. Struggling against the "fatal course" of the billiard ball, Cahun refuses to reconcile these two selves into partners or lovers: "I hate your Patrix and Marioles. Listen, I hate your jazz groups, couples and quintuples. To your singsong choirs, fat duettists, this type of duo that you'd like to inflect on me, I prefer the duel. *Duels are other kinds of songs* [Je hais vos Patrix et Marioles. Entendez-bien, je hais vos unions jazz, couplets et quintuplés. À ces chœurs à chœurs-là, duettistes à la grosse, à ce genre de duo que vous prétendiez m'infliger, je préfère le duel. *Les duels sont des chants alternés*]" (*E* 622).

This happy couple, the harmonic double imagined from without, becomes a social relation of antagonism rather than accordance. Armed with a hat-pin in this fight between the self and that "false double, the mannish-type," Cahun zooms out into a much larger set of social antagonisms. Here, near the end of the text, Cahun turns from the individual battling against herself to the individual battling against society. Citing the internecine conflicts among the surrealists, the dictates of the PCF, and the regime of the National Socialists, Cahun maps out a sphere of constraint and possibility, curiously crossing between past and present tenses: "I think about the fact that I didn't have a choice of weapons. Nor of adversary. Nor of initiative.... I don't have a choice of revolts. What remains is the choice of stones. A dirty little pebble. A clot. [Je réfléchis que je n'avais pas le choix des armes. Ni de l'adversaire. Ni l'initiative.... Je n'ai pas le choix des frondes. Reste le choix des pierres. Un sale petit caillou. Un caillot]" (*E* 622). The present tense writes a continuation between the struggle of the self, *now*, and the larger social groupings that were mentioned earlier. In both cases, "choice" looks like this rock or that one, what can be thrown, but not who or what it can be thrown at. The wordplay in French, *caillou/caillot* (pebble/clot), offers two modes of resistance: the weapon thrown and the stuff of the body. This invocation of the body and the rock, as intertwined weapons, provides a denouement to the Frankensteinian operation a page earlier, leaving us with two dueling selves, unreconciled.

To understand how this passage speaks to both the individual narrative and the situation of French leftist groups in the 1930s and 1940s, it helps to consider Cahun's explanation of her political activism as a choice made under a set of historical constraints. In a letter to Paul Levy, after a drawn-out and often comic settling of scores, Cahun describes her participation in Parisian radical groups as a choice made with her "back up against the wall" because there were no other options that might speak to her situation more closely:

> If I fought alongside comrades of the extreme left, that's because this cause, without being mine, seemed to me just, that it was the only one that effectively opposed Hitler's racism, and the maintenance of certain values, among which the *freedom of expression*—and, by which, not only the maintenance but *the conquest of moral freedom, of the rights of the human being* oppressed by centuries of barbaric superstitions, *were important to me personally*. [Si j'ai lutté avec les camarades d'extrême gauche, c'est que cette cause, sans être la mienne, me paraît juste, qu'elle était la seule qui s'opposât efficacement au racisme hitlérien, et que le maintien de certaines valeurs, parmi lesquelles *la liberté d'expression*—et, par elle, non seulement le maintien mais *la conquête de la liberté des mœurs, des droits de l'être humain* opprimé par des siècles du superstitions féroces, *m'importaient personnellement*.]
>
> (E 716)

The letter was written in 1950. This invocation to the "rights of the human being" emerges just a few years after a more famous claim on freedom, the *Universal Declaration of Human Rights* (1948). However, Cahun's understanding of "human rights"—not just in this letter but throughout her larger corpus—is fundamentally different than that of the *UDHR* and, more widely, the tradition of liberal rights claims that come before it. Based on a number of different national constitutions, the *UDHR* focuses on the rights of the individual within presently existing society. In the *UDHR*, rights are, in most cases, imagined as liberties of the individual personality: to own property, to marry, to speak freely, to be educated. There are a number of negative liberties as well: to be free from torture, slavery, religious persecution. Yet what the declaration calls the "free and full development" of the individual personality in accordance with society does not seek to remake this society, only the individuals living within it. That is to say, these individual rights do not touch the wider system of economic inequalities that bases the prosperity of some on the misery of many.

This distinction between the rights of the individual and the present economic system of inequality that makes the universal implementation of these rights impossible becomes, fittingly, a contradiction upon which *Confidences* ends. Cahun offers a different discourse for the narrative development of the human personality. In *Confidence*, *Bildung* changes directions. The human personality does not grow through its internalization of social norms, coming into peace with society as is. Instead, society changes. The "I" morphs into "we" and then returns to birth:

> In the conditional *everything* is literature: the best organized acts . . . Ah! what mish-mash. "We are not here so that the blood may remain in the veins," they say. "The blood of others" responds another ME. (In the present endless whirlwind . . . here we are products of the chemistry of classes, of races, of species and their mutations, here we are arrested . . . here we are flopping in the nets . . . attacking the mesh . . . here we are corrosive . . . red snippets . . . the writing in the experimental mirror opposes the pragmatic Perpetual. "Watch the double movement in the surface of the water: hair pulled down by its weight and contradictorily in this direction . . ." Leonardo de Vinci . . .)
>
> In the present I shut it down.
>
> Fall back into childhood. . . .
>
> In the past perfect . . . Born-conditioned Cassandra could I therefore think of anything but the future? Daughter of the son of the conditional past. Born-conditioned Cassandra one couldn't have known to have. She has all her claws

> Au conditionnel *tout* est littérature: les actes les mieux organisé. Ah quels mélis-mélos. « Nous ne sommes pas pour que le sang demeure dans les veines », qu'ils disent. « Le sang des autres » . . . répod une autre MOI. (« Au présent tourbillon de la sempiternelle . . . nous voici produits de la chimie des classes, des races, des espèces et de leurs mutations . . . nous voici jugulés . . . nous voici frétillants dans la nasse . . . en attaquant les mailles . . . nous voici corrosifs . . . entrefilets rongés . . . À la Sempiternelle pragmatique s'oppose l'écriture au miroir expérimental « Observer le double mouvement à la surface des eaux : chevelure entraînée par son poids et contradictoirement à cette direction . . . » Léonardo de Vinci . . .)
>
> Au présent je la boucle.
>
> Retomber en enfance . . .

> Au passé antérieur... Née-conditionnée CassAndré pouvais-je donc penser autrement qu'au futur ? Fille du fils du conditionnel antérieur. Née-conditionnée CassAndré on ne saurait avoir. Elle a toutes ses griffes
>
> (E 623)

That first jab, at the proposed equivalence of art and praxis, revisits the distinction made in *The Bets Are Open*: that art can do certain work, and actions can do certain work, but they ought not to be confused. Nevertheless, reading across Cahun's works, "the masterpiece" of a life moving between poetry and praxis, renders this ending as the work of condensation, of the lessons of actions, the stuff of the world, folded back into art. Rather than an individual struggle, the *we* of the passage fights against the structure within which it remains caught—both the endless turn of perpetual sameness and the nets that enforce it. Here again, it is not an expansion of the human but the animation of the inhuman—the fish, the snippets, the myth, the beast with claws, upon which the passage ends. Though the passage plays upon the lures of the future and the conditional, it ends in the present tense, without final punctuation.

This ending is a reconsideration of personal freedom not as a vast emptiness or capability to act but as a set of choices taken within a field of historical constraints. Fish struggle in a net of the perpetual: it is not, perhaps, the revolt that one might have chosen, not the future utopia that is imagined in "For an Independent Revolutionary Art," the manifesto Trotsky would not sign. But here is the writing of a plural subject of history, a historical set of actors, as not quite girl or boy or fish but some grammatical torsion caught between them, as *we*. This "mish-mash" not of art and praxis but of identities both freeing and constrained by nets offers, as well, a different perspective on the relationship between radical women's movements and the avant-gardes. In this chapter, collective praxis, I should note, looks different from the formations that I considered earlier. Rather than action in a solidified movement or party—the WSPU, the American Birth Control Movement, the CFP, and so on—Cahun and Moore's wartime resistance was estranged from a group dynamic because of the isolation of occupied Jersey from the continent.

As Cahun notes, she did not have a choice of revolts. But across these serial works, from photography to leaflets to prison notebooks, we can see a sometimes individual, sometimes doubled, sometimes plural historical actor made and unmade. This process mobilizes identity categories not limited to woman but extending into the complexities of race, sexual orientation, and nation. Originally written out of histories of surrealism, Cahun then sheds new light on more familiar figures. In these works, the inhuman, amalgamated body animates a combinatory axis of racial, sexual, and national categories, not as a part of an abstract universal human declared by law, but as the violent product of law's exceptions.

⁂

Alongside surrealist experiments with chance, this chapter has primarily considered national family law through the intersections of homosexuality and race in the interwar period. However, this perspective is also tied to more famous developments in international law and human rights. During the drafting sessions of the *UDHR*, particular controversy arose over the use and definition of the word "family." The wording for what would become Article 16 went through a number of fraught iterations. During the second session of the commission, Charles Malik of Lebanon made the following proposal: "The family deriving from marriage is the natural and fundamental group unit of society. It is endowed by the Creator with inalienable rights antecedent to all positive law and as such shall be protected by the State and Society."[64] Malik's rationale for this wording emphasized the importance of social life; he argued that "society was not composed of individuals, but of groups, of which the family was the first and most important unit; in the family circle the fundamental human freedoms and rights were originally nurtured."[65] The only objection to this amendment came from the delegate from the USSR, who argued for a wider, nonreligious definition of the word "family."

In the third session of the commission, the delegate from Uruguay argued for the deletion of the phrase "natural" to cover the rights of individuals in possession of "unnatural" or homosexual inclinations.[66] Though the delegates from the USSR succeeded in removing the phrase "by marriage" and "endowed by the Creator" in the definition of the family, the erasure of "natural" did not make it into the final version, which reads as follows:

> ARTICLE 16: (1) Men and women of full age, without any limitation due to race, nationality or religion, have the right to marry and to found a

family. They are entitled to equal rights as to marriage, during marriage, and at its dissolution.

(2) Marriage shall be entered into only with the free and full consent of the intending spouses.

(3) The family is the natural and fundamental group unit of society and is entitled to protection by society and the State.[67]

What is significant here is the way that the purportedly universal subject of rights becomes subsumed under the family and the state. The fact of the state's protection here becomes synonymous with the state's capacity to define and thus regulate what is a "natural" family and what is not. The organizing category of the family, as subject to the state's protection, falls into an implicit heterosexual/homosexual, natural/unnatural binary. The "natural" family is ensured state protection; "unnatural" families thus exist as an exception to this rule.

In a study of the case law of the European Convention of Human Rights over the past three decades, the sociologist Paul Johnson shows how the majority of successful complaints brought to the court concerning sexual orientation refer to violations of Article 8: "Everyone has the right to respect for his private and family life, his home and his correspondence." Thus, the court protects homosexuality in "private family life" but essentially delimits the rights of the homosexual citizen to the private sphere.[68] Such rulings create a split between "sexual rights" in the private sphere and "citizenship rights" in the public sphere, where sexuality is presumably concealed.

A longer view of European legislation, from the natalist policy, to the criminalization of homosexuality, to the definition of the natural family as a universal group, thus allows us to revisit the stakes of the identity categories—race, sexuality, class, gender, nation—with which I began this chapter. A turn away from the thematics of a female muse to this more complex intersection of identity categories as lived is not a matter of checking off all the boxes or even of thinking specifically about the work of the marginalized. Rather, this approach allows us to move from the mysticism in the portrait of Casati to Cahun's fatal billiard ball as more than a purely formal transformation of the chance procedure. Through this legislation, in the long view across two world wars, national economic collapse becomes understood through the lens of identity categories: as a failure of the nuclear family, as the fault of the internal Jew, as the manliness of the state, and the terror of the homosexual. It is not surprising, then, that surrealists of all stripes began to mobilize these very categories not as an essential set of features but as an amalgamation of bodies literally intertwined, with one another and with the uncertain futures of chance, with the gains and losses of not knowing how a story might end. In this longer view, surrealism's imagination of chance becomes many-sided. Chance points to the selection of persecuted identities and the contingency of their death or escape. Cahun's work, as a narrative beginning with the self-portraits, turning to praxis, to prison, and then to *Confidences*, reimagines these categories of identity within a larger field beyond the scope of the individual.

To return to the distance between Man Ray's portrait of Casati, blurred by chance, and Cahun's *Confidences*, we can see the transformation of a formal procedure—the chance encounter—as a shift that attempts to speak for a different historical moment. As I noted earlier, Cahun's work is often considered a precursor to the postmodernism of Cindy Sherman, for the reliance on masks, but this never seemed to me an ideal comparison. With its cinematic overtones, Sherman's work foregrounds performance as a kind of aesthetic magic capable of complete transfiguration. Sherman is all mask, no subject. A more fitting addendum to Cahun's serial works might be Vera Chytilová's *Daisies* (1966), as a referendum on the political claims of the avant-garde. As others have noted, the film's two Maries might be understood as an animation of Hans Bellmer's dolls.[69] Critics use the words *antihumanist* or, more often, *nihilist* to describe their orgies of destruction.[70] See, for instance, that table laden with food to be trampled, the paperwork collages and streamers literally on fire, the two Maries swinging from the chandelier and throwing cake at each other (figure 5.10). Those that claim that the charm of the Maries frees *Daisies* from nihilism forget that the tendency always already had its sparks of pleasure. Who could look at this image of the apples as still life, the bathrobed Maries lighting up streamers, and not see the destruction of the artwork as the last gasp of pleasure left, as ecstatic and nihilist at once?

I point to *Daisies* as one kind of surrealist ending so as to mark out Cahun for another. Of course, it is a different historical moment. Chytilová was working in the midst of state socialist censorship amid the Czech New Wave. From some angles, Cahun's late work incorporates this version of wry negativity. Rather than an art of the marvelous encounter, here surrealism becomes so much detritus, remade and washed up. This detritus might have

FIGURE 5.10 *Daisies*, dir. Vera Chytilová (Czechoslovakia, 1966).

been trash: propaganda leaflets and slogans painted in nail polish. It was written on smuggled toilet paper or, in the case of the collages, lost to the historical record entirely. For Cahun and Moore, those years on the isle of Jersey lay bare the wreckage of a late-stage avant-garde, all scrap iron and panther skulls, the snippets, the beast with claws.

But, contra *Daisies*, these experiments with the chance encounter, exported from the artwork to the war, retain some glimmer of the marvelous. For Cahun, it is important that the chance encounter is not a foregone conclusion—the bets are open. It is a matter of an open future, the taking a character from life, not knowing how the story might end. This version of chance is double-sided. It includes the performance of desired selves and the precarity endemic to a body that cannot be taken on or taken off. But precarity is not the same thing as nihilism.

So here is the second ending: Susanne Malherbe, better known as Marcel Moore, kept notes on the occupation years, for a memoir she never wrote.

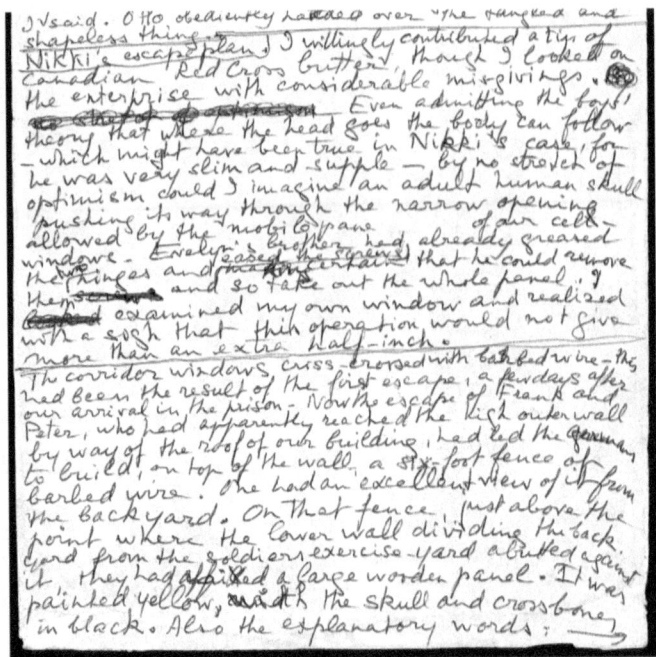

FIGURE 5.11 Suzanne Malherbe manuscript.
Source: Claude Cahun and Suzanne Malherbe Collection, Beinecke Library, Yale University.

Moore is much less grandiose than Cahun, as the latter readily admits. In a letter written from prison, Cahun sometimes refers to Moore when she wants to verify a fact as true. ("I am quoting S. because she is not prone to overstatement.")[71] It is clear enough that Cahun saw Moore as the less iconoclastic of the pair. "What a system, eh?," Cahun writes, in halting English. "Isn't worth dying *against*? But what *for*? That is the question I am writing to answer and have not answered yet. S. can answer it in the human, normal way. In the faithful and patriotic way."[72] This gives us some idea of how Cahun saw herself as neither normal nor human. But it is also a bit of a jab. At that moment, the two women were not seeing eye to eye.

Moore's own account begins to show how whatever we might call the "human, normal way" was not easy to pin down, particularly when telling a story taken from life, without knowing what the ending might be. One manuscript fragment, "Nikki's escape plan," begins:

I willingly contributed a tin of Canadian Red Cross butter, though I looked on the enterprise with considerable misgivings. Even admitting the boy's theory that where the head goes the body can follow—which might have been true in Nikki's case, for he was very slim and supple—by no stretch of optimism could I imagine an adult human skull pushing its way through the narrow opening allowed by the mobile pane of our cell-windows. Evelyn's brother had already greased the two hinges and made certain that he could remove them and ease the screens and so take out the whole panel. I examined my own window and realized with a sigh that this operation would not give more than a half-inch.[73]

On this particular page of scrap paper, Moore goes on to write about other escapes. She is a bare-bones narrator, all short sentences and no adjectives. The fence had a large wooden panel and was painted with a skull and crossbones, Moore tells us. It was right next to the soldier's exercise yard. But we never learn the end of the story, what happened to Nikki, if he made it out or even through the window at all. "Nikki's escape plan" ends with a description of the size and shape of the barbed-wire fence, its colors, and the attached wooden panels. But the manuscript is a fragment. The page breaks off there.

6

The Committee Form

Négritude Women and the United Nations

UN General Assembly, Third Committee
Palais de Chaillot, Paris
14 October 1948

It is Thursday afternoon at the 102nd meeting of the Third Committee.[1] Alexei Pavlov has been speaking for some time. This is not unusual. Even a quick glance across the nearly thousand-page summary record of the Third Committee makes some patterns clear. For instance, it seems that the delegate from the USSR was a talker. During sessions devoted to the International Declaration of Human Rights, Pavlov would frequently hold the floor, sometimes for an hour at a time.[2] When a vote approached, this long-windedness became more tactical. At these moments, Pavlov might bring up more theoretical points, points that, according to the representative from India, did not pertain to the practical case at hand. At other moments, Pavlov would provide a pedagogical interlude for the benefit of the other delegates in the room. Eleanor Roosevelt recalled, "He was a grand orator. The words rolled out of his black beard like a river and stopping him was difficult indeed."[3] John Humphrey's recollection was less polite, more gossipy: "[Pavlov] was the most difficult of all the Russians who worked on the Declaration. Some people said that his bourgeois background—he was the nephew of the great Pavlov—made him vulnerable to criticism back home and that this accounted for the show he never failed to provide."[4]

However, the delegate from the USSR was certainly not the only long-winded diplomat in the room. Sparked into a competitive mindset, France's René Cassin responded in kind. As any veteran of institutional life might imagine, oratorical fever bred competing oratorical fever. America chimed in, as did Greece. The representative from Chile noted that the participation of the USSR was not as constructive as one might expect from a great power. The United Kingdom's representative became somewhat sarcastic about the intentions of the Soviet bloc more generally. The delegate from China quoted Rousseau's theory that man is naturally good, in what appears to be a suggestion for both the decorum of the meeting and the basis of Article 3.

Over the next two months, the committee meetings grew longer and longer, often going late into the night. Vocal formulations of policy became increasingly elaborate, though it seems, from the official record, the Soviet bloc and the Western powers most often talked past one another. Mexico's Pedro De Alba complained that these ongoing debates reduced smaller nations to mere spectators helpless amid the "verbal duels" between competing Cold War powers.[5] In October, after an afternoon debating the legality of such procedures, Charles Malik, the committee's chairman, brought a stopwatch to the committee's night sessions, limiting each speaker to precisely three minutes.[6]

By focusing on who spoke, for how long, and when, I don't mean to suggest that the content of these debates was insignificant. On the afternoon of October 14, the meeting with which I began, Pavlov's speech took on the importance of concrete guarantees for the right to life. To consider an instance where such a right was promised but not enforced, Pavlov drew attention to the continuing practice of lynching in the United States, citing statistics from a recent NAACP report.[7] He went on to describe the discrepancy between average life expectancy in England and India, as recorded by the British press. Pavlov considered death rates from exhaustion, alongside the potential for a worldwide abolition of the death penalty. Certainly, this content is significant, with material ramifications for people who would never see the inside of the Palais de Chaillot. However, as I will argue, the *form* of the committee meeting, as a technology of decision making, is significant too.

In many ways, the dynamic of the Third Committee meetings echoed earlier deliberations in San Francisco in 1945, no doubt because many of the same players had been involved. At this founding meeting of the United Nations, as France, England, the United States, and the USSR came into agreement about the function of the Security Council, the United Kingdom's Alexander Cadogan offered a more candid appraisal off record. In a letter to his wife on the process of establishing the jurisdiction of the Security Council, Cadogan wrote that he expected a final decision soon, but "we shall have all the little fellows yapping at our heels, and it won't be easy. Of course one could crack the whip at them and say that if they don't like our proposals there just damned well won't be any World Organization. But I don't know that that would pay, and it would have to be put tactfully."[8] Given Cadogan's remarks, it is not entirely surprising that Carlos Romulo, the delegate from the Philippines, described himself as "a gadfly, a pest" in the eyes of the great powers. To ensure that the self-determination of all nations appeared in the final charter, Romulo claimed to have haunted the UN corridors, pouncing on unsuspecting delegates in hotel lobbies and men's bathrooms in order to argue his point.[9]

This dynamic, between Great Britain's sense of yapping nations and the Philippines' tactical guile, indicates a wider inequality visible in the establishment of a lasting forum for international diplomacy. Besides the powers of the Security Council, the San Francisco Charter established the United Nations' Trusteeship System, which would obligate the great powers to promote "development towards self-government or independence" in their colonial territories. Critical histories of human rights often point to this charter as a key moment of paradox, when the putatively universal rights of man become split into two kinds, one version for "civilized nations" and another for the "uncivilized territories" still undergoing development.[10] Rather than examine the language of the finished declaration, this chapter considers institutional processes that lie behind the making of such documents. This inquiry means paying attention to who talks, when, and for how long; who experiences themselves as a spectator; how decisions are made; and what kinds of alliances are formed. It includes the misunderstandings, compromises, and infighting. I want to get at the texture of these committee meetings, the boredom involved, the frustration, the micro and macro aggressions, the expertise on display, the strategies of deferral, the horizons of what might be deemed possible, the euphemisms, the ad hominem attacks, the peacemakers, the minor victories, the men holding forth.

This procedural consideration of the committee meeting marks one instance of what Inderpal Grewal has called the governmentality of human rights. Rather than consider human rights as juridical instruments, this perspective instead situates rights as "an ethical regime that put into play a whole range of instrumentalizations of governance."[11] Grewal therefore shifts our sense of governmentality to move beyond the singular nation-state, instead accounting for a transnational arc of nongovernmental institutions that emerged in the last twenty-five years. In taking up the procedural logic of institutional human rights through the committee form at a somewhat earlier, more fungible moment, I hope to expand our historical sense of the ways that human rights discourses situated colonial women as a population and object of knowledge. At this early moment in the codification of international humanitarian norms, the committee meeting becomes a key instrument of colonial governance that produces international norms, but how this governance works is better understood through what Foucault called "a range of multiform tactics."[12] What follows tracks this sense of governmentality as a tactical phenomenon that uses the welfare of women and children as a kind of litmus test: for the relative democratic status of a colony; as a bargaining chip in wider geopolitical treaties; and as a site of sympathetic, protectionist attachment that comes to define the terms of the human and humanity.

More widely, turning to the day-to-day function of the committee meeting, particularly as we move to the middle levels of the UN bureaucracy, is also a turn to the UN Secretariat, then a full-time staff of some four thousand people. Central to this discussion are the stenographers, clerks, secretaries, translators, overseas experts, and other functionaries who do not appear in the official record, including Paulette Nardal, an area expert for the Committee on Non-Self-Governing Territories, Négritude author, founder of the Women's Rally Association, and editor of the black feminist journal *Woman in the City* (*La Femme dans la Cité*).[13] From 1945 to 1951, *Woman in the City* published regular updates on the United Nations, alongside poems, Creole legends, recipes, crosswords, songs, and coverage of grassroots feminist activism in Martinique. More widely, *Woman in the City* documents a somewhat different practice of committee work, initially focused on welfare reform but ultimately foundational to the establishment of a feminist public sphere. These committees have discrete goals, but more important than their stated programs for reform is the politicization of the women who regularly meet and do housework together. The nonsecular cast of the Women's Assembly and its alliance with the institutional forms of the United Nations then allows for a reconsideration of normative or universalizing accounts of women's agency as a resistance to cultural norms. As seen through localized practices, the Martinican case allows for a reconsideration of women's action, unsettling received notions of political desire and self-making behind such actions as generalizable across metropole and colony.

Reading back and forth across the UN archives and *Woman in the City*, I reconsider the committee meeting as a deceptively slippery form of social life, decision making, care work, and governmentality foundational to the development of institutional human rights and a more popular feminist mobilization in Martinique. Ultimately, this more bureaucratic archive will provide a methodology for the close reading of performance and self-making in the Creole tale. Tracking these conversations allows us to map out the fissures in a spoken *We* that perpetually combines and separates populations across national, sexual, and racial lines. In contrast to a more traditional understanding of the public sphere as a space of rational-critical debate among equals, this turn to one of the less celebrated technologies of social organization, the committee, highlights the daily practices of government among markedly unequal persons.

Colonial Hearts at the General Assembly

While the United Nations headquarters were being constructed in Manhattan, the ad hoc committee on information transmitted from the Non-Self-Governing Territories met at Lake Success, New York, in a former airplane factory. Tasked with establishing the procedures of information gathering required under Article 73e, this group created what became known as the Standard Form, an extensive statistical survey on colonial welfare, including labor conditions, housing, education, and public health. In the years after the war, the Standard Form became a flashpoint in the larger Cold War conflict, sparking a series of debates on the quality of life in the colonial territories. While the chairman might remind this committee that it was meant to discuss procedural matters only, according to the official report, "the debates on the analysis prepared by the Secretary General ranged further afield."[14] This ranging took the form of critique, "as some members took the view that, in addition to mentions of procedure, the Committee was competent also to discuss analysis of summaries of the information."[15]

This ranging farther and farther afield created a particular kind of prose. The official record does not record verbatim speech but is a summary in the third person that often turns to the passive voice. In many cases, the speakers blur into "some" or "a number of members." We learn that this or that speaker made a point about X or Y but not what the point was. We read about a vote, but the content of what was voted upon lies in some other record from a different subcommittee. What is consistent here is a stylized flatness, lacking visual detail or adjectives but nevertheless difficult to read for the ornate prepositional phrases: *in respect to which, within the scope of.* Consider, for instance, this moment from the Report of the Special Committee for Non-Self-Governing Territories, from the seven-hundred-plus pages that make up the 1947 *Yearbook* of the United Nations: The USSR has proposed that the data from Indonesia be disregarded because the people of Indonesia have declared themselves an independent state. He does not mention that the Netherlands has not recognized this declaration.

> Various members contended that it was beyond the competence of the Committee, as a result of its terms of reference, to exclude from consideration by the Committee any information which had in fact been transmitted under Article 73e and which was in fact before it in the documents circulated by the Secretary-General. It was further contended by a number of members that in any case the Committee had no power to decide upon the territories in respect of which information should be transmitted. Some members believed that the question of the territories in respect of which information should be transmitted was a matter for the consideration of the General Assembly, and the view was also expressed that it was a matter on which the International Court of Justice might be asked for an opinion.[16]

This goes on for some time. The USSR proposes a draft resolution; the representative from the Netherlands moves that such a resolution is out of order, being "outside the competence of the committee." A vote goes in favor of the Netherlands, though the discussion continues. Who can decide and the scope of these decisions become somewhat lost in the iterative enumeration of possibilities. Though arguments are made in both directions, this point is never settled. Whether or not this committee considers Indonesia's Standard Form, as a symbolic act, the people of Indonesia would certainly remain under the territorial jurisdiction of the Netherlands. Indeed, this debate looks entirely circular; the questions about data collection for the Standard Form become inscribed into a larger debate on sovereignty between the colonial subjects and metropolitan powers. From some angles, it seems that little is accomplished here besides grandstanding. ("The representative of the United Kingdom deplored the lack of a single constructive suggestion in the remarks of the USSR representative.")[17] Interjections broach topics that will never reach a vote; alliances are established through redundancies, such that the same point is made again and again. In many ways, the argument over who can theoretically determine what is a territory and what information might be transmitted from it summons up Hannah Arendt's famous claim, theorized in her coverage of the Eichmann trials, that bureaucracy is a "rule of Nobody" because it turns people into mere functionaries, cogs in a larger administrative machinery, so that no actual person might be held responsible.[18] However, the committee, as a social form, is distinct from this "rule of Nobody." Bureaucracy is a term for the wider structure of the Secretariat, with all the documents included: the memos, the directives, the declarations. The committee meeting is only one part of this wider structure. However, to consider the process of the committee through a record of the minutes allows for a clearer view of discrete persons and the arc of political argumentation, before these debates get anonymized into a clear, univocal directive and then put into functional practice within the wider bureaucratic machinery.

When we consider the verbatim record rather than the official summary, a curious sort of theater emerges, in large part through the seeming circularity of these debates. These off-track conversations are excised from the summary record. But within the limited, administrative form that is the committee meeting, what is off-track or off-topic reveals other conversations, other agendas. In this way, a turn to the verbatim record offers historical speculation about the horizons of the possible, of what might be or what could have been. The off-topic debate opens up a space for performance, one that might be all posturing or redundancy but can also verge on a more utopian imagination, signaling what the human and human rights might *become*, rather than what they legally are.

My understanding of performance as what might allow for a kind of world making, reaching audiences beyond the present bodies, follows recent scholarship on the public sphere but also has a historical legacy specific to UN pedagogy.[19] Beginning in 1949, the *United Nations News* placed advertisements for a "model United Nations" to become a part of high school curriculums, so that students might learn about the democratic process. This pedagogical turn dates back to the 1920s, when the *League of Nations News* placed monthly advertisements for "a working script from which classes may build an accurate reproduction of a session of the League Assembly, together with suggestions for debate." These enactments were a great success. According to the *League of Nations News*, the Intercollegiate Model Assembly of the League of Nations, held for the first time at Syracuse University in 1927, drew an audience of a "thousand or more."[20] The possibility of a wider popular audience applies to major UN deliberations as well, which would be recorded and made available to the public across a variety of venues, including televised news, UN yearbooks, and the *United Nations News*.

With this more theatrical backdrop in mind, I want to turn to one of the more utopian moments of inefficiency, an off-track conversation in which the "little nations" made a lot of noise. It is the fall of 1947, during the ninety-sixth plenary meeting of the General Assembly at Lake Success. It is late in the afternoon, after a series of minor agenda items, including financial reports from the Board of Auditors and the recommendation of the Sixth Committee for the UN to adopt a distinctive flag.

At this moment, delegates are asked to consider a transfer of powers regarding protective anti-sex-trafficking legislation. The committee's chairman, Malik, has provided the assembly with what he politely describes as a "long document" containing the pertinent juridical history, including the 1904 and 1910 conventions on "White Slave Traffic," alongside the League of Nation's "International Convention for the Suppression of the Traffic in Women and Girls" as it was last amended 1933.[21] Though a major sticking point for the League of Nations in the 1920s, what does *not* generate immediate controversy at Lake Success is the abolitionist stance, which renders adult consent irrelevant, in order to foreclose the possibility of state-regulated prostitution: "Whoever, in order to gratify the passions of another person, has procured, enticed or led away *even with her consent*, a woman or girl under age, for immoral purposes, shall be punished, notwithstanding that the various acts constituting the offence may have been committed in different countries."[22]

Later conventions added some emendations to include young boys and specify the age of a minor. But the conflation of woman and child is only made more explicit over the years, through an additional convention on "women of full age" that retains this specification "even with her consent." In his report on this controversial aspect of League of Nations policy, Director Bascom Johnson explained, "it was believed that no woman, even though she be an experienced prostitute, can possibly understand and therefore consent in advance to the sort of exploitation and virtual slavery to which she is often subjected in a foreign country."[23] Here, then, is a very specific abstraction of adult female personhood: the woman in question is not so much erased, excluded, or disciplined, though these might be tertiary effects.[24] According to the language of the convention, the female sex worker possesses a juvenile form of legal personhood, in that the status of her sexual consent is equivalent to a minor's.

Interestingly enough, the debate that immediately follows Malik's introduction concerns territorial jurisdiction, not the legal personhood of adult women, though the two topics quickly become intertwined. The first speaker on the traffic in women and children is the delegate from the United Kingdom, Sir Hartley Shawcross, who talks, with apologies to the audience, at some length. Shawcross explains that England has already applied all the conventions against the traffic in women and children to the colonial territories. That is not the matter up for debate. The point of contention is about the definition of "country." As it stands, if England signs the covenant, all of the colonial territories under England's jurisdiction will be signed on as well. Shawcross would prefer that these territories might each decide for themselves. Implicitly, such decision making would allow the continuation of state-regulated prostitution in the colonial territories, though Shawcross does not spell out this eventuality.

As the representative from Pakistan points out, Shawcross's claim involves a sleight of hand. The colonies in question are under England's jurisdiction, so it is not really them deciding for themselves but England deciding for them. If Shawcross is really so anxious for the colonies to make decisions on their own, the representative from Pakistan notes, then these colonies ought to be granted the right to self-determination immediately, so that they can do so in all cases. In the pages that follow, there appears a lengthy, somewhat circuitous argument for self-declaration, made with some oratorical skill, by the representative from Haiti, recorded only as Mr. Vieux. As a member of a former colony, Vieux appeals to the human principles of the other delegates, on behalf of the women and children in the colonial territories.

"I address myself to your hearts rather than your minds," says Vieux, citing the importance of hope, happiness, and progress.[25] What is most interesting is the end of this very long speech, which comes after one reminder from the committee president to please stay on topic. At this moment, Vieux connects the public address of the committee meeting to the possibility of a world to come:

> Mr. Vieux (Haiti) (*translated from French*): I know very well that nothing will really be changed by the mere ratification of these Conventions. I know that facts are sometimes stronger than principles and that men continue to resist progress; but I also know that if you accept the resolution as it stands, if you utter these words of freedom, greatness and generosity, these words will remain and will bring reality in their train, because words are always the forerunners of reality and shape it.
> *The meeting rose at 1.10 p.m.*[26]

The delegate from Haiti does something quite unusual here, in that he admits that the signing of the convention is a mere formality, unenforceable. It will have little effect on the greater world. But Mr. Vieux asks that the delegates act *as though* this action were real, even though they know it is not. He asks that the audience continue as though there were a connection between words on the page and facts in the world, because this continuing itself is an act of the imagination, and one must imagine a thing, even speak its words, before it can happen. These words are not truth claims or referential fact, but they are not trying to deceive us with lies. Vieux is asking the delegates to enact a known fiction, to say the magic words, as though that saying might enable a kind of doing. In many ways, Vieux asks the delegates to enter a more speculative history, outside or beyond the Cold War conflict or the matter of the delegate's vote. Vieux asks his audience to turn away from the authority of "fact" and consider the more fantastic possibilities of the uttered word.

However, Vieux's argument for racial equality rests upon the subordination of women and children, invoking the hierarchical human family as a model of cross-racial male solidarity. Vieux's rhetorical strategy regroups genres of humanity according to a shared belonging to the conjugal family that requires protection from the extragovernmental body represented in the committee room. Much of the pathos in the speech rests on the male delegates' shared, intimate identification with colonial women and children, who might be left out of the civilizing process afforded to the metropolitan powers. This attachment depends on the rightlessness, indeed the emptiness of these injured subject positions who require protection from the colonial welfare state.

After lunch, Sir Harley Shawcross responds at length to Mr. Vieux. The delegate from the United Kingdom is cutting for the ways that he marks sympathy as the stuff of hearts: a private, feminine quality, one that he too possesses but would not trot out in this particular setting.

> Sir Harley Shawcross (United Kingdom): I am not going to attempt to follow the representative who spoke on behalf of the delegation of Haiti in that exceedingly eloquent, not to say emotional, address which he delivered before we adjourned for lunch. It was, if I may venture to say so, an address which, delivered on some other occasion and about some other matter, would form a very model of that kind of oratory which nowadays unfortunately is all too rare and which I always envy but to which I cannot myself ever attempt to aspire.
>
> With charm and frankness, the Haitian representative said that he had not really studied the question at issue, but he appealed to our hearts. I am all in favor of appealing to hearts. I do not mean feminine hearts but, within reason, to those instincts of humanity and civilization which I hope most of us have within our own hearts. And I ask the Haitian representative to believe, because I am, like him, rather a sentimental person, that, *if there really was anything to touch our hearts in this matter*, I should certainly align myself with him. But we ought, in this assembly, to be careful not to allow our hearts to run away with our heads when, in truth and in fact, there is nothing at all even to excite our hearts. There is nothing to excite our hearts in regard to this matter of constitutional procedure.[27]

At the end of this speech, Shawcross's prose gets a bit strange, even redundant. Shawcross argues that the colonial women and children in question might tug at our heartstrings in another scenario, but in this case they should not. As the speech continues, Shawcross changes from speaking about a subject position, *they, the colonial women/children*, to a description of objects, from *anyone* to *anything*: "if there was really anything to touch our hearts ... there is nothing at all even to excite our hearts." Shawcross is quite adamant on this point. This slippage involves a kind of euphemism, too, in that it would sound not quite as nice to say there was *no one* there to touch our hearts, *no one* to excite our hearts, even though, grammatically, this would be more consistent.

In the space of the committee meeting, claims for referential truth and sympathetic imagination get jumbled as they pass through different speakers, as means for different ends. We might consider this nearly Steinian prose as an experimental language born out of the paradoxical logic of colonial Enlightenment, or we could work through the status of the performative utterance as a legacy that passes in and through the avant-garde manifesto. However, for now, I want to focus on the plasticity that is this subject, the impossible or dispossessed subject, the paradoxical subject, who might flicker between abstraction of Nobody and the materialization of someone, somewhere. This nonperson, the woman-child who is not there and cannot decide, offers a particularly useful model to think through what the younger Marx criticized as the paradoxical quality of liberal rights, which confer formal equality on a theoretical person, an abstract person, but are lived through the modalities of material inequality, including race, nation, gender, and class.[28] The delegates from Haiti and the United Kingdom mobilize this subject in the service of another argument, so that the civilization of the colonies becomes tied to a protectionist stance toward women's paid sexual labor and the concomitant irrelevance of women's consent.

While I want to understand this theatrical digression in the space of the committee meeting as a more utopian moment, a moment when the delegate from Haiti opens up a space of performance, a kind of interruption or irritant against the teleology of the civilizing process, thus allowing for the imagination of other futures, at the end of the day, it should be said, for Mr. Vieux, speaking in the ninety-sixth plenary committee meeting of the General Assembly, these imagined human futures are still the futures of men. In the following section, I will turn to an alternative imagination of human futures as practiced within the committee form, this time in Martinique, beginning with the work of the Négritude writer, feminist activist, and member of the UN Secretariat Paulette Nardal.

Paulette Nardal and the Daily Life of *Woman in the City*

On November 14, 1946, Paulette Nardal boarded the *Sarah R. Bell* from Fort-de-France, Martinique, sailing for Saint-Lucie and then on to New York

City. She would spend much of the winter in Lake Success, serving as an overseas expert for the Division on Non-Self-Governing Territories. In the official record of these meetings, Nardal's presence is not noted. Indeed, there is no mention of specific members of the Secretariat in the official record of the Division of Non-Governing Territories. However, in January, the *New York Age* enthusiastically refers to Nardal as a "U.N. Personality" alongside Eleanor Roosevelt and Lakshmi Pandit.[29] Alongside a headshot of Nardal, the *New York Age* notes that Nardal is the first woman of color serving the Committee of Non-Self Governing Territories, though the paper's column, "Know Your United Nations," does not specify what this service might entail.

However, the best documentation of Nardal's Lake Success period comes from the author herself, though she tends to focus on the political philosophy of the United Nations, not its day-to-day activities. In a published letter addressed to Martinican women, Nardal describes the UN assembly as "the living reality of human solidarity."[30] For Nardal, the pageant of the UN summons up the passion of Christ:

> In contemplating this impressive Assembly, which represents indisputable progress over the former League of Nations, I am convinced that it is through suffering that a universal conscience develops. In considering this coalition of Nations that do not yet all recognize it, but that, in their Charter, set out great principles that are Christian principles, I see the symbol of the mystical Body of Christ actualized.[31]

Nardal's focus on the suffering subject recalls what Henry Shawcross called feminine "appeals to the heart." But Nardal would not brush off this sympathetic gaze toward suffering as a weakly feminine purview. Instead, Nardal translates the secular suffering of war into the Catholic suffering of Christ. This turn revalues humanitarian charity, moving from a feminized sympathy to the "great principles" of Catholicism.

This letter appeared in the January 1947 issue of Nardal's monthly journal, *Woman in the City*, itself the organ for a larger organizing body, the Women's Assembly (Rassemblement feminin). As a loose consortium of Martinican women, the Women's Assembly was primarily devoted to social services, particularly for women and children. However, this organization did not stop at welfare reform. As I will go on to argue, the organization's services would go on to provide an opportunity for Martinican women to become politicized subjects in the wake of their legal enfranchisement. Women gained the vote in Martinique in 1944, an episode that Nardal saw as a pivotal moment of definition for the female citizen newly entering the public sphere. "The Martinican woman has entered the City of Men," she writes, in the journal's first issue in 1945.

Over the next six years, *Woman in the City* published editorials, meeting records, short stories, recipes, crossword puzzles, poems, and regular updates on the United Nations. In a series of editorials, Nardal extends the language of the newly formed United Nations, recasting a charitable impulse toward the abstract human in the no less hierarchical terms of a maternalist feminism. In this way, Nardal argues for cross-racial solidarity in a manner parallel to the Haitian delegate, but working toward a different end. Here again, racialized and gendered bodies are set against one another in a zero-sum game of rights. For Nardal, however, the erasure of racial difference, in the invocation of a human family, offers a way to advocate for the female citizen as a political actor. Martinican women are particularly well suited to fulfill the duties of female citizenship, Nardal argues. These women extend the labor of the home—the care work, the cleaning, the education of children—into the public sphere, becoming mothers to the urban poor. At one point, the journal refers to this civilizing process as a kind of pregnancy, one that will eventually birth a newly educated, civilized working class.[32]

It is clear that Nardal and the state programs of the Women's Assembly promote a universalist, Catholic perspective. This group enthusiastically promoted the mission of the United Nations and hoped to work within, rather than against, its institutional framework. As a political tendency, the Women's Assembly does not easily fit into the topographies of women's action already outlined in this book. The first part of this book outlines what liberal theorists often call positive liberty, or the ability of persons to act, through the actions of the *pétroleuses* and the suffragettes; meanwhile, the second part takes up negative liberties, or the prohibitions against action, through the consideration of actions surrounding birth control and miscegenation. This third part, on the institutional formation of human rights discourses, requires a different analytic, in part to account for the cultural specificity of colonial Martinique.

The tension between universalizing accounts of rights discourses and the cultural specificity of women's experience has been a source of long-standing debate in postcolonial studies. This work highlights the ways that feminist scholars have often relied on a normative, Western model of agency as a form of resistance, valorizing secular action in opposition to religious and cultural tradition. In Saba Mahmood's account, this normative understanding of feminist agency assumes "the capacity to realize one's own interests against the weight of custom, tradition, transcendental will, or other obstacles."[33] As Mahmood argues, this articulation of a clear binary between agency and subordination cannot account for a wide range of actions, particularly among nonsecular or conservative tendencies. *Woman in the City* provides one instance of a Catholic feminist public that requires a different model of resistance, one that will allow for positions that are not nearly as agonistic as those commonly associated with the avant-garde.

A turn to the committee meeting as a form of governmentality and social life allows us to separate the stated intentions appearing in *Woman in the City*, moving to a more embodied understanding of collective self-fashioning in everyday life. Rather than hew to a model of agency as resistance to norms, this turn allows for a distinctive analysis of feminist practices within an institutional setting. In this more tactical imagination of the management of the self, the import of these daily practices does not lie in the stated intentions of the editorial pages, but in the way these practices constitute an individual subject and a feminist public sphere.

For this wider account, I want to read across *Woman in the City* not to track a political position but to access this public more widely. Aside from the editorial pages, recipes, and crossword puzzles, *Woman in the City* is largely chronicle of grassroots mobilization, primarily through the organization of local committees. The first issue devotes a full page to the descriptions of these groups and their internal organization. There is an Aid Committee with monthly dues, a reading group, and a Housewives Association, pledged to "fight against the always too-expensive life." There is a project to create a Sewing Center, to make and distribute linens to new mothers. Members meet twice a week to prepare packages containing infant clothing, diaper linens, towels, and blankets. The broadsheet suggests the formation of a treasury within the Sewing Committee, to organize and distribute funds. The group will eventually split up into neighborhood committees, delivering packages of linens to Gros-Morne, Vert-Pré, Ravine-Vilaine, and Trinité. The Work Commission is similarly subdivided into groups, each overseen by one or two committee directors. The subdivisions are listed alongside the director's names: married and single women, infants, school and the young student, young workers, hygiene and prevention, housework, peasantry, social education, artistic education, propaganda and press, treasury and bookkeeping, neighborhoods.

There are no records of what these smaller committee meetings looked like. It is impossible to say whether the women met on time, what the agenda might entail, if there was arguing, what was boring or frustrating, which people stuck around afterward to chat about other things. There are not many chronicles of the committee meetings of the Women's Rally either, but the few summarized sessions offer some indication of what this social world might look like and what sorts of futures could be imagined inside it. Consider the record from March 1945, as published in *Woman in the City*. The group meets as usual in the cavernous Salle de Mutualité, in downtown Fort-de-France.[34] Madame Joseph-Henri begins the meeting with some notes on the organization of local neighborhoods, then ends this discussion with a complaint voiced as a suggestion, that the choice of a committee director ought to be subject to a vote. Mademoiselle Amelie Yotte's remarks are not noted, because her program has been extensively covered in that issue's editorial. The same goes for Mme Etifier, who is widely applauded. Mlle Emilie Laval talks about social services for tuberculosis and leprosy. Mme Charlotte Lineal is charged with updates on the housekeeping courses and the Housewives Association. Mme Vaucoret offers an update on the Sewing Committee. Mme Saint-Clare and Mme C. Marie-Madeleine suggest a mother's cooperative. Mme Carré is applauded for her recent conference on community involvement.

The reports are brief. The record makes clear that the monthly meeting consists of a report back from the disparate committees tasked with humanitarian aid. On one hand, we might say that the gist of this politics allows Martinique's newly enfranchised female citizens to provide social welfare for one another, outside of or beyond the nation-state. But what I want to say is more pointed than this. The goals of the committees are social services, but this organization also created a public space for political praxis, for unwaged women, mostly housewives, who had no access to union membership or a wider social network. The committees have a stated goal of humanitarian charity but also serve as a means toward the transformation of the subjects involved so that they might articulate wider demands. These demands might be practical (reduced bus fare for children) or much more far-reaching, moving into a more speculative form of world making.

Some of these public addresses from the monthly meetings are included as editorials in *Woman in the City*. For instance, two pages before the March 1945 minutes, in a one-page column signed "Y," Amelie Yotte wonders what will happen to newly enfranchised Martinican women after the war. What Yotte calls the "dawn of new times for French women called to political life" involves more questions than answers. Yotte asks, "What will be her domain? Where will she act?"[35] Other columns are more prescriptive. In the same issue, Mme Danel proposes a program of action in an enumerated list:

1. Encourage marriage and the regularization of free unions
2. Expand the creation of nurseries, orphanages, and kindergartens
3. Institute night guards
4. Find support and aid for disinherited mothers
5. Refine the education of mothers in certain milieus
6. Demand the creation of a residential school for young girls
7. Create a female police force
8. Create asylums and retreat homes
9. Organize conferences in the worker centers and in the neighborhoods
10. Seek the assistance of the government for the realization of the various points of this program

1. Encourager le mariage et à la régularisation des unions libres;
2. Etendre la création des crèches, pouponnières, et jardins d'enfants;
3. Instituer le gardiennage de nuit;
4. Procurer soutien et aide aux mères déshéritées;
5. Parfaire l'éducation des mères dans certains milieux;
6. Solliciter la création d'un internat de jeannes filles;
7. Créer une police féminine;
8. Créer des asiles et maisons de retraite;
9. Organiser conférences dans les centres ouvriers et dans les communes;
10. Réclamer le concours des pouvoirs publics pour la réalisation des différents points de ce programme.[36]

Mme Danel is so direct; we can only wonder about her reaction to the much more elaborate address of Mme Etifier, which begins with Joan of Arc and moves on, in a somewhat circuitous fashion, to what she sees as the major goal of the Women's Rally, to do civilizing work ("faire œuvre civilisatrice") focused on young women and children. Alongside Mme. C and Mme. R on the work commission for students, Mme Edifier asks a rhetorical question that becomes a statement: Why not reach out to women workers, to store clerks, mothers, postal employees, and the like, inviting everyone to neighborhood meetings, where the women might meet, so that they do their knitting, mending, or other sorts of work together?[37] Like Mlle Yotte, Mlle Etifier ends with a nod to the future, after the war: "Our program is vast, we do not have the intention to realize it completely and instantly, we do not have fairy wands."[38]

In this way, Mlle Etifier disavows magic in favor of building long-term infrastructure. However, this infrastructure, in the form of successive committees, often exceeds or subverts the projected program of civilizing work. On one hand, these committees shift our understanding of what might be political labor and who might be a political subject. Calling housewives, mothers, single women, windows, and the elderly, the committees documented in *Woman in the City* create a social world for future actions, not only for social service, but against the power of the colonial state. They do this, in part, by bringing the private labor of housework into the public sphere, so that women might to do this labor together. After some time, the sewing circle also begins to make demands that have nothing to do with sewing, to lay out a program of its own, specifically in conversation with ongoing developments at the United Nations.

Over the years, the imagination of where women's political action might take place and what it would look like takes different forms. There are more enumerated lists and editorial columns. But on facing pages, poems and stories play into this conversation. In the later years of the journal's run, Creole tales appear, often without attribution. This turn to folklore had long been a current in Négritude print cultures. In *Tropiques*, Aimé Césaire and René Ménil write an introduction to Martinican folklore that positions the tale as a history of the transatlantic slave trade: "When we have stripped all the archives, examined all the records, searched all the papers of the abolitionists, it is these stories to which whosoever will return, to grasp, eloquent and pathetic, the great misery of our slave fathers."[39] The tales that appear in *Woman in the City* offer a different sort of archive, one caught, somewhat anachronistically, between the histories of slave trade and the legal paradoxes of black female citizenship. While the committee reports one sort of feminist practice, these stories suggest another, this time in explicit opposition to French colonial law and the civilizing work of the United Nations. To see both of these threads and the way they talk to each other, it becomes important to read more widely across the journal, moving from the meeting minutes to Creole tales.

Testimony and Truth in the Creole Tale

At this point, consider the July 1948 issue of *Woman in the City*. There is news on student participation in a model United Nations; there is an editorial on Social Security; and on the last page, there is the Creole tale "Nélissa and the Three Monsters," attributed only to "Maguy." The story is a page long and moves quickly, with few frills. The storyteller anticipates questions ("What happened? [*Que se passait-il?*]"), then bosses the reader, ("Listen then! [*Ecoutez donc!*]"). This narration allows for frequent interjections, amid the forward momentum of rapidly unfolding events. The young black woman Nélissa, mother of four, wakes up one morning and faints. ("What happened?") Nélissa discovers a monster in her belly. It speaks in Creole. ("*I ka palé!*")

The story moves in spurts and jumps, with no transitions. The Creole monster is suddenly three monsters, whose pink tongues peek out from Nélissa's throat. Despite the agitation of the monster tongues, a doctor refuses to believe that Nélissa could be so cursed and concludes that she is a ventriloquist. Nélissa then goes to the queen of the sorceresses, Valentina, who gives her a prescription for the extermination of the "diabolical progeny [*diabolique progéniture*]." Nélissa pays Valentina three thousand francs to satisfy the angry spirits. According to a crowd of witnesses in the village, Nélissa is cured. ("Bravo! Bravo!")

At this moment, the story stutters and starts again. There are two more endings. Each entails an elaborate staging of truth claims and disbelief. Now the directress of "School B." is telling the story to our narrator, as she has witnessed it. The directress questions Nélissa in front of a class of students to dispel any lingering superstitions about monsters. But Nélissa refuses to deny that the monster existed.

—It's true, Madame, I had a monster, it's Valentina who cured me!

—You were mistaken; my dear Nélissa, you were without doubt a ventriloquist?

—Ventri how, Madame? She said offended.—**Believe what you want. It's me who has suffered! It's me who knows! Believe what you want! Don't believe what you don't want!**

(Ventri what? Madame. Call that what it seems to you.
It's me who has suffered! It's me who knows!
Believe what you want! Don't believe what you don't want).

—C'est vrai, Madame, j'avais un monstre, c'est Valentina qui m'a guérie!

—Vous avez été trompée ; ma pauvre Nélissa, vous étiez sans doute ventriloque?

—Ventri comment, Madame ? dit-elle piquée—Creïe con ou lé. Cé moin qui souffè ! Cé moin qui save.

Crouè ça qui lé. Pas crouè ça qui pas lé!

(Ventri quoi ? Madame. Appelez cela comme bon vous semble.
C'est moi qui ai souffert ! C'est moi qui sais!
Y Croient ceux qui veulent ! N'y croient pas ceux qui ne veulent pas).[40]

"Believe what you want" is not really French or Creole but a combination of the two. The phonetic transcription of the Creole verb allows for a pun in French. The line reads as "*Crieie con ou le* [Say what you want]" and "*criez connu le* [shout what's known]." After the Creole/French pun, Nélissa says, this time in Creole, "Believe what you want. It's me who has suffered. It's me who knows." Here the continued existence of Creole in the story suggests that Nélissa is lying. If Creole is the language of the monster, the speaking voice must be the monster declaring its own extinction from Nélissa's mouth. In this way, the Creole/French wordplay allows Nélissa to make two mutually exclusive claims at once: that the monster existed but is gone and that the monster continues to exist, speaking Creole through Nélissa's mouth. Which version the students understand depends on their knowledge of both French and Creole.

This is a knotty moment. Added on to the testimony's wordplay is another joke, through the French wordplay on belly/womb/ventriloquist (*ventre/ventriloquist*). To be possessed by a Creole monster is also to be pregnant is also to be a ventriloquist, attributing your own voice to another. A second ending offers a variation on this bodily vulnerability, but this time the testimony takes place in court. The sorceress Valentina is summoned by the law for practicing forbidden medicine. Valentina gives testimony, claiming that she only offers aid to the poor and does not accept payment for her services. Then the others assembled in court, the poor that Valentina claims to aid, testify in her favor. Valentina is acquitted, and the tale abruptly ends. But here again, the reader knows that Valentina's testimony in court was a lie: Nélissa paid her five thousand francs. Then the poor assembled in court are liars too, testifying on behalf of Valentina.

It seems clear enough that suffering, knowledge, and truth are not, in this story, equivalent. Here public testimony is tactical, offering a strategy for survival against the law rather than truth before it. What makes bodies vulnerable to the reach of the law becomes labeled as monstrous, and this monstrosity must be hidden through cunning and deception. In the courtroom, this hiding is the work of a community of persons, sorceresses, students, teachers, storytellers, and the poor. Here too is a public culture, assembled as a matter of tactics, to act out the human form that French colonial law based on the material body of a white male citizen. That is to say, in these scenes of testimony, what is human can only be a matter of performance, not nature. Nélissa's claim animates another sort of magic, in which the material body of the French citizen somehow forms the basis of a more universal human right.

Part of this magic might be attributed to the particularly fraught significance of the Creole language in the context of Martinique's class hierarchies after the war. Recall Frantz Fanon, writing seven years later, in *Black Skin, White Masks*: "In the French Antilles the bourgeoisie does not use Creole, except when speaking to servants. At school the young Martinican is taught to treat the dialect with contempt. Avoid Creolisms." Fanon connects ways of speaking to an imagined transformation from black to white and back. "Among a group of young Antilleans, he who can express himself, who masters the language, is the one to look out for: be wary of him; he's almost white. In France they say 'To speak like a book.' In Martinique they say 'to speak like a white man.'"[41]

In "Nélissa and the Three Monsters," ways of speaking before an audience, in French and in Creole, determine the legal personhood of the speaker. At the school and in the court, Nélissa participates in a theater of the human, in that she performs her newly reclaimed humanity even as the continued existence of the monster's speech suggests otherwise. However, this story is canny, in that the monster's existence animates a real legal paradox between abstract rights and material bodies. In many ways, the Creole stories, of this inhuman woman or that one, literalize the legal paradox of the female citizen as folklore, in order to offer more communal tactics for survival, for she-devils or sorceresses, whose livelihood might lie on the other side of the "rights of man." Through cunning, Valentina and her community endow themselves with legal personalities, with the rights of the human and citizen, in the course of telling capital-J Justice a story that cannot be true.

To end with this tale, in this larger discussion of UN bureaucracy and black feminist organizing, allows for a different sort of conversation around the discourses of the human family that emerge in rights declarations. In the tale, the human family is a slippery subject of bilingual wordplay, always saying one thing while suggesting the other. As I have suggested, the tale is less important for the identitarian mobility it might formally project than for the tactical imagination it directly represents.[42]

To end with the tale is also to end with the sort of practices that are not recorded in the UN archives. "Nélissa and the Three Monsters" reveals a social practice of courtroom solidarity set against colonial law. The multilingual wordplay allows for an ending shot through with speculation rather than truth or untruth. However, "Nélissa and the Three Monsters" cannot represent the political tendency of *Woman in the City* as a whole. The women who write the tales, the women who support one another at the court, and the women who attend the committee meetings might be the same women, or not. As a technology of social life, the committee form produces social bonds that are difficult to track outside the recorded profiles available in *Woman in the City*. The Creole tale suggests what some of these connections might look like and how they might form an alternative to the colonial policy regarding women and children in development at Lake Success. These connections, forged between practices of committee work and beyond it, are not the sort of thing preserved in the bureaucratic archives of the United Nations.[43]

Setting the Creole tale next to the model UN report, alongside the reports of committee work and Nardal's service at Lake Success, offers a quite partial, somewhat inconsistent archive for the committee form as a technology of social and governmental life. Focusing on the practices of governmental and social life rather than the juridical documents that legislate it allows for a different purview on the development of institutional human rights, particularly in the decade after the war and before the anticolonial momentum of the Bandung conference in 1955. This is a moment that turns between public dialogue and a more theatrical imagination, in the invocation of other worlds to come.

My turn to the period before Bandung partakes in a wider critical conversation looking to challenge conventional lineages of liberal humanism and human rights that go back to the Enlightenment. Toward this end, Samuel Moyn begins late, in the 1970s, with the Carter administration; Stephen Hopgood starts with the origins of humanitarian institutions in the early nineteenth century; Lydia Liu focuses on the years around 1948.[44] Working in and against these currents, my methodology turns away from the Enlightenment genealogy of universal reason and the self-possessed individual to make visible the particularities of governmental process and local organizing. This chapter offers one version of such a turn, away from Enlightenment political philosophy and into the technologies of government that can be gleaned from a more promiscuous understanding of what constitutes an archive for human rights critique.[45] As methodology, I mean to suggest that our inherited ideas of the human and human rights are not only a matter of juridical history or even Creole tales but linked to more tactical forms of feminist experience, here seen through the daily practices of committee work.

Attention to the localized practices surrounding Nardal, through the formation of weekly committee meetings, turns away from a universal, purely voluntarist or normatively secular notion of feminist agency to consider the specificity of everyday localized practice. In this case, the meaning of the social practice is not its stated aim, nor the juridical documents that might emerge from it, but the ways these practices constitute the individual subject. In attending to these practices, I take up an unorthodox archive: the back and forth of who talks, for how long, and when at Lake Success; Mme Danel's list of demands for social welfare, read aloud in the monthly meetings of the Women's Rally; the circulation of fantastic tales, passed down from the slave ships to Antilles plantations, then translated into print. There are plenty of versions of *against* here, but also other kinds of feminist practices more difficult to categorize.

Theorists of the historical avant-gardes often narrate experiments with art, in service of the revolution or against the prevailing social order, through a set of commonly used forms: montage, collage, chance procedure, fragmentation, dismemberment, abstraction. The committee form, as a tactic or agonistic method, does not generally make these lists. However, tipped through the archive of the United Nations and the Women's Assembly, the committee form can be seen as just that—a form that might allow for experiment, for self-making and other theaters, to invoke worlds and create new publics. In a purely formalist sense, the committee meeting has no politics, good or bad. Like the tactics already discussed, this form belongs to no proper person or place; it can be endlessly appropriated and set toward any end. That said, by turning to this particular conjuncture at midcentury, in the perhaps unexpected coalition between the United Nations and Paulette Nardal, the Négritude avant-gardist and Catholic feminist, the committee form offers a practice of self-making set apart from a declared program of intention. In the first case, the procedural nature of the committee opens space for experiments with the boundaries of the colonial human; in the second, it allows for new forms of social life through the creation of a black feminist public.

In the wider arc of the avant-garde, it helps to recall Marx's claim for the Paris Commune, as a social experiment that required the creation of entirely new kinds of government, to create modes of representation, safety, and public life unlike any that had occurred before. It maybe that Marx's claim for novelty was overstated, but this could also be said for almost any of the more prominent manifestos of the avant-gardes. Less romantic, certainly less resistant or novel, the experiments with the committee form tracked through this chapter nevertheless allowed for the animation of certain paradoxical desires: for the protection of colonial women; for the emancipation of colonial men; for a universal humanity; for a Catholic morality; for a new, liberated female citizen. How these desires could coexist with one another, and the forms of action and self-making they allowed, will be the subject of my epilogue, which turns to the political horizons of human rights discourses in the Cold War period.

Epilogue

Social Reproduction and the Midcentury Witch

Leonora Carrington in Mexico

In the preface to *Caliban and the Witch*, Silvia Federici recounts the ways that her thought shifted after she moved from the United Sates to Nigeria in the 1980s, during the country's adoption of a Structural Adjustment Program with the IMF and World Bank. In Nigeria, Federici was struck by a historical congruency. Though beginning in the 1980s, Nigeria's structural adjustment resembled what Marx had called primitive accumulation. Much like this earlier form of dispossession, structural adjustment destroyed communal property, forcing men to take on waged factory jobs when they could no longer subsist through farming or ranching. At the same time, this shift also changed the nature of social reproduction, that is, the labor of cooking, cleaning, childbearing, childrearing, and other unwaged acts of care necessary to reproduce the population. By proletarianizing the male labor force, structural adjustment created a new sexual division of labor between men's waged labor in the factory and women's unwaged labor in the home.

Drawing these phenomena together in her later book *Caliban and the Witch*, Federici revises Foucault's theorization of biopower to better account for the intersections between colonial dispossession and the sexual division of labor. In this book, Federici situates the state management of the population, particularly along racial lines, alongside territorial dispossession and the subsequent reorganization of the household that created a division between men's waged labor in the factory and women's unwaged labor in the home. In an important revision to both Marx and Foucault, Federici argued that these foundational accounts did not adequately consider sexual difference and so fail to locate the prominence of the witch hunt as a gendered form of discipline that helped establish what she understands as the historical content of patriarchy, the division of labor that renders women's work unvalued and invisible, understood as a naturally occurring resource, a replacement for lands dispossessed during primitive accumulation.

Though most of Federici's study pertains to the sixteenth and seventeenth centuries, her work shows primitive accumulation, or the processes of dispossession, to be ongoing and geographically diffuse, "re-launched in the face of every major capitalist crisis, serving to cheapen the cost of labor and to hide the exploitation of women and colonial subjects."[1] Here Federici turns to a key historical constellation, "when the responses to the rise of socialism, the Paris Commune, and the accumulation crisis of 1873 were the 'Scramble for Africa' and the simultaneous creation in Europe of the nuclear family, centered on the economic dependence of women to men—following the expulsion of women from the waged work-place."[2] In this more modern case, for Federici, the "specter of the witches continued to haunt the imagination of the ruling class" but also served as a technique of power, to allow for the destruction of common resources and a sexual division of labor between men and women that rendered women's labor as a common, even natural resource, like land or water.

In this epilogue, I want to underline the centrality of Federici and the wider body of feminist work surrounding social reproduction as a spur to my own thinking about women's rights movements, beginning with the Paris Commune and ending in the Cold War era. More specifically, I want to situate the Cold War as a kind of ending, seen from an internationalist perspective. Historical accounts of human rights discourses have a certain proclivity for the language of endings—see Coustas Douzinas's *The End of Human Rights*, A. W. Brian Simpson's *Human Rights and the End of Empire*, Stephen Hopgood's *The Endtimes of Human Rights*, or Samuel Moyn's *The Last Utopia*. In Moyn's account, the current institutional regime of human rights serves as a substitute for the socialist utopias of earlier decades. On or around 1977, for Moyn, the decline of actually existing socialism, the failures of anticolonial struggles, and a global economic downturn resulted in a growing sense of mistrust for maximalist schemes of social transformation. In contrast to the maximalist, Moyn argues, "Human rights were a realism that demanded the possible. If so, they were only intelligible in the broad aftermath of other, more grandiose dreams that they both drew on and displaced."[3]

What follows does not pitch itself against this sense of historical rupture but looks to situate the ways that a transatlantic feminist perspective tempers it a bit, adding texture and complexity to what might seem like a closed matter, cut and dried. In so doing, I draw on Steven S. Lee's dissatisfaction with what often seems like, in the accounting for the collapse of state socialism, "an inevitable arc from illusion to disillusion."[4] In *The Ethnic Avant-Garde*, Lee draws out the ties between Soviet and American minority avant-gardes as a tendency that parallels this arc but does not map perfectly onto what has been widely perceived as three endings that intersect—the end of socialism, the historical avant-garde, and history as a whole. In what follows, I also look to sidestep the forms of left melancholy that so often accompany declarations of the end of revolutionary possibility as an end of history.[5] Fittingly, perhaps improbably, I approach these narratives of rupture through a meditation on a late surrealist work written in midcentury Mexico, Leonora Carrington's *The Hearing Trumpet*. This work emerges at a moment of more partial structural adjustment, when postrevolutionary Mexico did not quite fit into our more common Cold War binary schema. A socialist supporter of the Republican forces in the Spanish Civil War and then of the Cuban Revolution, Mexico also took on large structural adjustment programs with the United States. What follows reconsiders Carrington's work in Mexico as a kind of pivot: between a surrealist tradition based in Europe and a newly postcolonial literature; between an increasingly obsolete sense of what continental surrealists called the *marvelous* and a revived *magical realism* most closely associated with Latin America.

Carrington wrote *The Hearing Trumpet*, her only novel, in the early 1950s, though the book was not published until 1974. In one of her few interviews, she notes that it was somewhat odd for her to write a novel by herself. Most often, Carrington wrote novels alongside her closest friend, the Spanish artist Remedios Varo. "I would write a chapter, but I wouldn't tell her what it was. She would write the next chapter, and when we'd written about five chapters, we'd put them together, and it was very fun," Carrington recalls. This is a classic instance of what the surrealists called the Exquisite Corpse—the procedure of letting a narrative come together by chance as a collage of different plots. As an afterthought, Carrington notes that her and Varos's collaboratively written novels have all disappeared, "probably into somebody's garbage can many years since."⁶ The point was the act of writing the novels together, not posterity.

In those years, Carrington and Varo were neighbors, and they spent nearly every day together. They were part of a wider group of European artists in exile who arrived in Mexico during and after World War II, when the Cárdenas government was granting asylum and citizenship to Republican refugees of the Spanish Civil War, persons with Spanish ancestry, and left-wing artists and intellectuals. During these years, Carrington participated in the Posía en Voz Alta theater group and contributed to a number of Spanish-language journals, including the short-lived *S.NOB* and the *Revista Mexicana de Literatura*. These collaborations put her in touch with Mexico's midcentury intelligentsia, an increasingly cosmopolitan set of artists and exiles that included Luis Buñuel, Carlos Fuentes, Octavio Paz, Benjamin Péret, Kathi Horne, Diego Rivera, and Frida Kahlo. However, Carrington recalls this period as somewhat solitary. She describes the particular paradox of being inside a group but not quite of it. "I saw a lot of Remedios, but otherwise I was pretty isolated."⁷

A number of critics have noted the friendship between Varo and Carrington, alongside the similarity of their painted works.⁸ Octavio Paz approached the women as a pair: "There are in Mexico two admirable artists, two bewitching witches."⁹ In this instance, Paz was not being entirely metaphorical. Both Varo and Carrington make up a strain of surrealism particularly interested in alchemy, the occult, the marvelous, the mystical, and the esoteric. Carrington's work includes references to Celtic mythology, Jungian psychology, Egyptian Gnostics, Zen Buddhism, Cabala, Tarot cards, and the Zodiac. Rather than regard these materials as an explanatory apparatus, I follow Jonathan Eburne's suggestion to consider what he calls the "esoteric avant-garde" as a social practice built out of "the modern social and virtual networks of intellectual exchange through which esoteric knowledge is communicated, discussed, resisted, abandoned and appropriated as artistic material."¹⁰

In Mexico City, both Carrington and Varo were familiar with the followers of the Russian mystic George Gurdjieff, who appears in *The Hearing Trumpet* as the self-serious Dr. Gambit, head of an institution devoted to the care of elderly women. Varo, in particular, studied Gurdjieff's teachings and then talked them over with Carrington. Biographers of the two painters often depict Varo as the true believer and Carrington as a somewhat suspicious dabbler, intrigued by occult practices but maintaining a skeptical distance. What interests me is not so much this matter of belief or the doctrines behind it, but the kinds of social life and extrafamilial affinities that emerged around mystical knowledge. As Paz noted, Carrington and Varo were known for their long, meandering walks across Mexico City to attend the open-air markets selling herbs, insects, candles, and potions for *curanderas*. These materials found their way into the women's experiments with cooking, which often appear in Carrington's paintings. The art historian Susan Aberth usefully positions Carrington's domestic imagery as a scene of transformation, one that turns the kitchen into a laboratory for magic and a site of mystical power.[11] In the paintings from the Mexican period, figures often bend over cauldrons or surround tables laden with food. Sylphs recline around picnic blankets; faerie women convene around altar-like stones, sharing broth, yams, and pomegranates. Sometimes the room is empty, the table laden with food and wine for no one, or no one human. In *Grandmother Moorhead's Aromatic Kitchen* (1975), an oversized white goose and a horned goat approach the table, where veiled figures roll the dough and stir the broth. As Aberth notes, this turn toward the domestic sphere as a mystical laboratory occurs just at the moment when Carrington was raising two small children and keeping house for her husband. Carrington's recollection of these years injects a strain of bitterness into what might otherwise be perceived as an all-out glorification of magical domesticity: "I always continued to paint, even when the children were very small. Only when they were ill I dropped everything and my children became my priority. But often I said to my friend Remedios: 'We need a wife, like men have, so we can work all the time and somebody else would take care of the cooking and the children.'"[12]

Part counterfactual history, part apocalyptic fantasia, *The Hearing Trumpet* is an extension of this offhand desire for someone else to do the cooking and mind the children. It is a fairy tale about kinship and reproductive labor that ends in the formation of a feminist commons where no one is a wife and everyone takes part in a shared ethic of care. But overreaching summaries don't do well here. Those propositional claims appear entirely sincere, and Carrington is not. Any summary of feminist aims overshadows the zanier, irreverent wit of the book, which is narrated by a ninety-two-year-old woman, Marian Leatherby. Marian is hunched from rheumatism, functionally deaf, toothless, but generally unfazed by these conditions. "I don't have to bite anybody and there are all sorts of soft edible foods easy to procure and digestible to the stomach," she tells us, before noting that it is better to be a vegetarian anyway, because animals are hard to chew (1). These days Marian is growing a short beard, which might be off-putting to some, but she disagrees: "Personally I find it rather gallant" (3). Her dearest wish is to travel to Lapland, in northern Finland, and be pulled in a sled by a pack of dogs. Alongside her best friend, Carmella, Marian is invested in a long-term project of saving the cat hair from her grooming combs to knit into a jumper. However, the knitting plot is cut off before completion. Using the hearing trumpet of the title, a gift from Carmella, Marian learns that her son is planning to send her to an institution for the elderly. The retirement community turns out to be a magical commune inhabited by an international set of women ages seventy to one hundred, including a former drug dealer and transwoman, Maude; a French marquise, Claude la Chécherelle; the highly mystical Natacha Gonzalez, who lives in an Eskimo igloo; the Jamaican witch Christabel Burns; and the ninety-eight-year-old blind artist Veronica Adams, who nevertheless paints prodigious watercolor cycles on toilet paper. In this topsy-turvy world, Marian embarks on a series of quests, locating ancient Catholic texts, a phoenix, and finally her own likeness stirring a cauldron. She leaps into the pot and becomes the stew that her double eats. There are riddles that must be answered and the emergence of a witch coven. A sudden atomic apocalypse kills off the earth's population and reverses the poles. By the end of the book, only Marian, the witches, and a pack of human-wolf hybrids survive. This is not a tragic finale. "Ice ages pass, and although the world is frozen over we suppose someday grass and flowers will grow again," Marian reflects. Eventually the planet will be repopulated, "peopled with cats, werewolves, bees and goats" (158).

Though the presence of these figures might seem to predict a posthuman impulse before the fact, Janet Lyon aptly contextualizes the status of the animal-human within Carrington's wider canon: "What we might think of as the species-hybridity of the creatures who populate her work—the tusked horses and three-eyed bipeds and so forth—is so robustly ordinary a condition that the term 'hybrid' has no purchase; it can only register as an aberration from the standpoint of humanism, and not within Carrington's non-humanist milieu."[13] Following Lyon, I want to consider this mode of surrealism, where "tusked horses and three-eyed bipeds and so forth" become the norm, as a marvelous world building with a limited timeframe of viability. Carrington was well aware that surrealist experiments could not remain new in perpetuity. *The Hearing Trumpet* takes place in this apocalyptic future, after surrealism has lost its edge. Early in the book, Marian notes, without any particular rancor, that the heyday of the avant-gardes has long since passed. Surrealist experiments are no longer shocking, nor are the more obscene found objects of Dada sculpture. The avant-gardes are now embraced by the cultural institutions that they set out to challenge. Hung in schools and churches, surrealist art is commonplace, even decorative.

> Surrealism is no longer considered modern today and almost every village rectory and girl's school have surrealist pictures hanging on their walls. Even Buckingham Palace has a large reproduction of Magritte's famous slice of ham with an eye peering out. It hangs, I believe, in the throne room. Times do change indeed. The Royal Academy recently gave a retrospective exhibition of Dada art and they decorated the gallery like a public lavatory. Today the Lord Major opened the exhibition with a long speech about twentieth century masters and the Queen Mother hung a wreath of gladiola on a piece of sculpture called "Navel" by Hans Arp.[14]

The narration is unblinking and neutral, as though the enthronement of Arp's underwhelming doodle were a well-worn fact. In what seems like divine justice, Marian, the speaker of this passage, herself exists as a personification of obsolescence as well as a big middle finger to the surrealist cannon. In the years before the war, in the work of Breton and company, surrealists idealized what they called the woman-child, or *femme-enfant*. The woman-child might be an actual person and mistress, as Leonora Carrington was when, at nineteen, she first met Max Ernst, then in his mid-forties. However, this figure was also ever-present in surrealist texts, as a fictionalized liminal body with unprecedented access to irrationality, insanity, and other dreamlike logics.

A number of critics have noted that Carrington's elderly narrator reverses the tradition of the surrealist woman-child, but fewer have connected this reversal to a more global refashioning of the surrealist experiments with the marvelous. In an essay from 1949, the Cuban novelist Alejandro Carpentier famously distinguished between what he called *lo real maravilloso americano* (the marvelous American real) and "the tiresome pretension of creating the marvelous that has characterized certain European literatures over the past thirty years."¹⁵ Carpentier's formulation emerges out of a casually devastating assessment.

> The marvelous, sought in the old clichés of the Brocelianda jungle, the Knights of the Round Table, Merlin the sorcerer and the Arthurian legend. The marvelous, inadequately evoked by the roles and deformities of festival characters—won't young French poets ever get tired of the *fête foraine* with its wonders and clowns, which Rimbaud dismissed long ago in his *Alchimie du verbe*? The marvelous, manufactured by tricks of prestidigitation, by juxtaposing objects unlikely ever to be found together: that old deceitful story of the fortuitous encounter of the umbrella and the sewing machine on the dissecting table that led to ermine spoons, the snail in a rainy taxi, the lion's head on the pelvis of a widow, the Surrealist exhibitions.... By invoking traditional formulas, certain paintings are made into a monotonous junkyard of sugar-coated watches, seamstresses' mannequins, or vague phallic monuments: the marvelous is stuck in umbrellas or lobsters or sewing machines or whatever on a dissecting table, in a sad room, on a rocky desert.
>
> (84–85)

It gets monotonous here, *lo maravilloso*, tacked on at the beginnings of sentences that all start the same way. In these pages, the avant-garde marvelous is yesterday's news. The fact of being named, as a trend rather than a unique marvel, makes each claim sting a little more. What is biting about Carpentier's diagnosis is not just the way it declares these works obsolete but the way it notes how European artists and audiences remain oblivious to this fact. All this time, they are still rattling through the same formulas, that last "or whatever" thrown in to show the particular object in the mashup as irrelevant, no specification needed. That Carpentier is also a brilliant writer, catching the precise timbre of all those tired wonders in a beautiful sendup, is both casual and devastating. Casual as if to say, *See, anyone can do it. Like this.*

In response to the obsolescence of the avant-garde collage of unlike objects, Carpentier formulates his sense of *lo real maravilloso americano* as a historical atmosphere. The idea first struck him, he claims, in 1943, when he was visiting the ruins of the Haitian Revolution: Sans-Souci, the former residence of the revolutionary leader Henri Christophe and the still-standing palace of Pauline Bonaparte. Amid these ruins, Carpentier encountered the living presence of these figures as an eruption of the historical past into the present tense: "I saw the possibility of establishing certain synchronisms, American, recurrent, timeless, relating this to that, yesterday to today" (84). Carpentier goes on to reconsider this synchronism in different terms, to include the persistence of premodern folk traditions and mythologies into the present tense of Latin American life. For Carpentier it is essential that the traditions and mythologies are not a thing of the past but still inspire belief. This version of the marvelous, as an amplification of reality or intensity of the spirit, "presupposes faith" (86). "Those who do not believe in saints cannot cure themselves with the miracles of saints," Carpentier concludes.

"The Marvelous American Real" has since become a canonical site for the theorization of the magical realism characterizing the Latin American novels of the 1960s and 1970s.[16] However, rather than including Carrington's late work in the boom period of the Latin American novel, I want to position her somewhere between the European avant-garde's sense of the marvelous and Carpentier's marvelous real. This is partly a distinction about periodization but most fully a matter of ethnic and national belonging. For Carrington, Latin America was a site of exile, not a homeland. In a late interview, she gets a little testy at the attempts to render her work within a strictly Latin American lineage: "The Mexican traditions of magic and witchcraft are fascinating, but they are not the same as mine, do you understand?"[17]

Given this response, I don't want to pinpoint the assemblages of esoteric materials appearing in Carrington's work as originating from this or that tradition. It is a mashup of sources, Western and non-Western. Instead, what follows takes up how this late work changes the tenor of the marvelous by taking the obsolescence attributed to the European avant-gardes and enfolding it into the artwork as a principle of composition. To borrow Carpentier's language, Carrington's late work lacks faith. It is casual and devastating, as if to say, *See, anyone can do it now. Like this.* However, for Carrington, that is not quite a snarl. The thing I am trying to capture is a kind of knowingness, not quite peaking at irony, about obsolescence and the end of the singular marvel.

I should admit here that this incorporation of the obsolete makes *The Hearing Trumpet* a book I don't particularly like. At first read, this was puzzling. In terms of content, *The Hearing Trumpet* would seem to contain everything my queer Marxist-feminist heart could desire: witches, hunger strikes, communized domestic labor, queer kinship, transgender criminals, animal-people hybrids. But somehow reading the novel feels like walking through a natural history exhibit, the rooms echoing and half-empty. All those enumerated things, the witches, the animal-people, appear outside of time, as though fossilized.

This freezing effect is most directly a result of Carrington's style, which veers toward the dry and detached, almost scientific. The narration remains matter-of-fact in the middle of a strange or threatening monstrosity. There is a calm, unruffled certainty about this narration. It is not quite deadpan, which would entail a strain of knowingness about the humor of the disjunction between the miraculous event and a nonresponse. But it is not just this character or that character who is unruffled. The whole world of *The Hearing Trumpet* is one in which everything has turned into dead specimens—curious but lifeless. It is as though Carrington were still using all the tools of the marvelous but only as artifacts. This artifactual style renders the novel and the characters inside of it like a display about a past world frozen in amber. Consider, for instance, the moment after Maude's accidental murder, when Marian and Anna Wertz climb onto the roof and see the dead woman through a skylight. In a book that has a surplus of unconnected events, Maude's murder is not a key narrative development. The plot is overfull and overpeopled, so things move quickly. In this scene, a woman prepares to wash Maude's corpse and remove her clothing.

After the clothing is removed, we are back to the women on the roof, all reaction: "A moment later Anna Wertz was clutching my arm convulsively, and we both almost fell through the skylight onto the incredible sight below. Maude's stark naked corpse was that of a venerable old gentleman" (104). The illustration that accompanies this passage was drawn by Carrington's son Pablo Weisz-Carrington. It does not quite match the text but reveals its brittleness, as a perspective that turns people into an "incredible sight," like so many marvelous beetles pinned under glass. In the novel, the women peer into the room from the roof. In the illustration, Marian stands near the corpse, hearing trumpet in hand.

This treatment extends into other arenas, from persons to collective actions. At one point, the elderly women stage a hunger strike against the management of the Institution, though they will continue to eat Marian's biscuits in secret. All the same, this collective action marks a break from their earlier comportment. "'Many of us have passed our lives with domineering and peevish husbands. When we were finally delivered of these we were chivvied around by our sons and daughters who not only no longer

FIGURE 7.1 Pablo Weisz-Carrington illustration, in Leonora Carrington, *The Hearing Trumpet* (New York: St. Martin's, 1974), 105.

loved us, but considered us a burden and objects of ridicule and shame,'" says Georgina to the Institution's authorities. "'Do you imagine in your wildest dreams that now we have tasted freedom we are going to let ourselves be pushed around once more by you and your leering mate?'" (122). This would seem like a triumphant moment. But Dr. Gambit is not convinced.

There are not many transitional moments in *The Hearing Trumpet*, which makes recounting its plot something like narrating a dream you have almost forgotten—first this, then this, then that, then a monster. At this point, with no transition, Carmella arrives to save the day. She threatens Dr. Gambit that her niece would be interested in writing a newspaper article about the striking women. But Carmella also offers Dr. Gambit a large payment to accede to the strikers' demands. This is the first time that we, the readers, learn of this sudden windfall, which Carmella claims to have found under the servant's lavatory in the backyard. "It was quite impossible to tell if she was serious or joking," Marian muses in response. "Buried treasure in a servant's lavatory was not impossible but rare, very rare indeed" (123). As Marian notes, it is difficult to tell what is a joke and what is serious. Ultimately, there is a family likeness between Maude's naked body and the hunger strike, in that both are inert, the first quite literally, the second as a tactic that might achieve a demand. The womens' hunger strike might seem a turn toward collective feminist action, but this effort is naïve at best, so that only the highly improbable windfall of buried treasure will save the day.

Through such sleights of hand, Carrington reanimates the forms of the marvelous as a serendipitous kind of spiritualism, without really believing in it. Even so, I think she *wanted* to believe. I say this for the ways that, behind the thoroughgoing parody, hitting upon everyone and everything, the novel also exists as a social form of affinity. As other critics have noted, the novel is a roman à clef, with many of Carrington's friends appearing as characters.[18] Most prominent among these is the Spanish best friend Carmella, as a stand-in for Remedios Varo. In this way, *The Hearing Trumpet* plays upon Varo and Carrington's past efforts in collaborative novel writing through habitual games of Exquisite Corpse. This is a version of surrealism less about the unique artist and more about a collective practice of sociality. It is something that anyone could do.

From this angle, it is possible to reconsider *The Hearing Trumpet* as a memoir of Carrington's surrealist years in Mexico. However, her paintings from this period make me want to turn from the language of memoir to a slightly different idiom, to suggest that this writing of life as it was happening was not so much memory work, but an archive. This thinking emerges in part through a painting from the same period, *Sanctuary for Furies* (1974) (figure 7.2). It looks like a museum display of the ancient past: the bird-women stand petrified, as though they were dipped in amber. There are actual fossils and hieroglyphs arrayed for viewing in a space without any depth. It is not so much that the painting is scary but that a kind of threat hangs about it. There is a sense of intrusion, of having stepped into the wrong room and everyone going quiet.

Sanctuary for Furies looks like a tomb for the remains of an avant-garde imagination. It could also be a space of preservation. From the beginning, Carrington's mysticism relied on the possibility of a recoverable past. I take this more messianic perspective from Carrington's own writing in an

FIGURE 7.2 Leonora Carrington, *Sanctuary for Furies*, 1974. Oil on canvas. 69 x 99 cm.
Source: © Estate of Leonora Carrington / Artists Rights Society (ARS), New York.

exhibition catalogue from 1976. This one of Carrington's few political statements, likely a reference to ongoing struggles for women's suffrage in Mexico:

> The furies, who have a sanctuary buried many fathoms under education and brain washing, have told females that they will return, return from under the fear, shame, and finally through the crack in the prison door, Fury. I do not know of any religion that does not declare women to be feeble-minded, unclean, generally inferior creations to males, although most Humans assume that we are the cream of all species. Women, alas; but thank God, Homo Sapiens!
>
> Most of us, I hope, are now aware that a woman should not have to demand Rights. The Rights were there from the beginning; they must be Taken Back Again, including the mysteries which were ours and which were violated, stolen or destroyed, leaving us with the thankless hope of pleasing a male animal, probably of one's own species.[19]

Historians note that Carrington was marginally involved in the women's rights movements in New York and Mexico in the early 1970s. However, Carrington's art was usually not connected to these activities. What this art animated was the closed circle of intimates in Mexico City. Between the two of them, Carrington and Varo developed a conceptual vocabulary for a scene of domestic care, or what are often referred to as second-generation human rights, focused on economic and social liberties. These are not a claim on the right to freedom but for entitlements like housing, education, standard of living, and elder care. For this reason, the institution of care for elderly women becomes a utopian commons that includes wolf-people and buried treasure. It is also a world with different laws for kinship, shared labor, and sexual norms. In *The Hearing Trumpet*, Carrington and Varos's fictional stand-ins don't need wives to cook and clean for them. But this isn't really utopia, or even a feminist commons, because its existence entails the atomic destruction of the rest of the world's population. Here again, "It was quite impossible to tell if she was serious or joking," says Marian/Carrington, as Carmella/Varo reveals the buried treasure that will solve all of their problems.

At this Cold War moment, the formally socialist Mexican government was becoming increasingly authoritarian, and Mexico was undergoing structural adjustment. Carrington never romanticized communism or even revolution, even when she was living with Max Ernst. However, by 1976, a maximalist program would have appeared increasingly unfeasible. For this reason, I categorize *The Hearing Trumpet* as a late modernist work of surrealist leanings, not for the ways it believes in a recoverable past or a maximalist revolutionary future, but for the ways that it keeps churning through the forms nevertheless, as fossils. It is like knowing a box is empty and shaking it anyway—and shaking and shaking and shaking. Carrington's world building is unarguably abundant, overplotted, and overpeopled—even if the components of the marvelous remain fossils, brittle and worn out. The marvelous is still there, as an archive of social practices, part specimen display, part sanctuary. In this continued, vexed existence, Carrington locates a tension keyed to a moment of historical rupture. The marvelous becomes a dead form, used up, its agonistic force gone. But the marvelous remains in other registers: as an index of social life created through and beyond artworks, as a world-making practice that takes place in the domestic sphere, as an experiment in kinship, and, finally, as the ongoing practices of care these lived relations allowed.

In the United States at this same time, in the 1960s and 1970s, the Wages for Housework Movement marked one coordinate amid a wider feminist turn to social and economic rights, particularly regarding housework and childcare. One of the critiques most often leveled at Wages for Housework was that their concerns about housework were reformist, not revolutionary. These critiques came from more orthodox left-wing movements but also from other socialist and radical feminists. In 1968, in *Revolutionary Letters*, Diane di Prima writes directly to the reader bent on the partial demand: "if what you want is jobs / for everyone, you are still the enemy."[20] The poem, an overlooked masterwork of what some see as the latter-day sequel to the historical avant-gardes, the Beat generation, goes on to include schools, cars, refrigerators, houses, and universities as what is insufficient. The poem ends as a form of instruction to the reader: "you are selling / yourself short, remember / you can have what you ask for, ask for / everything."[21] The poem pivots on the surprise of this ending, which turns enemies into potential allies. There is a grammatical acrobatics in the modifier: the problem with social rights, with the schools and education, is not the desire for such things but the *only* that so often goes along with them—to ask for *only* jobs, or *only* homes, as the limits of what is possible.

This sense of *only* is interesting in part for the ways that it can be weaponized, to belittle demands linked to gender and sexuality as *only* that, set apart from any maximalist imagination of a different social world. Across this book I have tried to understand early women's movements on their own terms, apart from the *only* of suffrage reform, through the kinds of affiliation and belonging created in the day-to-day life of collective action. In so doing, I hoped to reconsider the status of gender and the avant-garde, moving away from female identity—sexualized, insane, muse-like, or manifest into a kind of feminine writing untethered from rationality. Instead, this book has focused on what Hannah Arendt called the subject of action—the lived experience of female citizenship as a practice and process. These experiences and the arts around them suggest alternative models of rights claims, of making demands, of thinking through different modes of obligation and entitlement, of creating forms of affiliation, before these extranational rights were fully institutionalized under the rubric of the United Nations.

As an archive of action rather than identity, this book does not mean to serve as an instruction manual. But I'd be lying if I didn't admit that the questions that drove the project are animated by a history of the present. To locate earlier versions of tactics now familiar, from the naming of names to the occupation of public space, might be considered a bulwark against political loneliness, in that this assemblage allows for glimpses of recognition between the experiences of action now and then, across a historical rupture that so often marks the end of an era of possibility. Revolutionary outcomes can be tragic or farcical, surely. But what I have called the long middle of feminist action is harder to pin down in part because it does not benefit from the kinds of affective closure an ending might provide.

In assembling this archive, I have often been critical of the language of women's rights and human rights, for the limited gains that could be demanded under such a rubric and for the ways these demands might cause injury for populations not deemed women or human. But I have remained interested, nevertheless, in understanding the force of desire that made tactical use of these terms. It makes a better ending, this long middle, as a set of collective needs not given up on. This even when the belief has gone and the work continues, as so many different ways of acting and speaking together.

In retrospect, Carrington's *Sanctuary for Furies* works as another long middle, for the ways that it can pivot between tomb and archive. The painting is not angry or sullen, but it is inhospitable. There is no air in that space. Everything seems to be holding its breath, as though feeling had run out, along with the colors. It is 1974, and I'm not sure that Carrington was a believer in the avant-gardes or the revolutions they heralded, but she was still using marvelous forms, if only in a limited way. So it might be that the creatures pictured are fossils, a prop for the desires of an era now over. Or it could be that this is just a kind of warehousing, to be repurposed later. Nevertheless, the painting holds something open, as a scene of expanding and expansive desires, of marvelous worlds with different rules for what might be demanded or taken back. There's a pipe-smoking Fury, the rhinoceros skull, human-headed birds, a sphinx under the window, and hieroglyphs laid out for the viewer. I see this rendering as a kind of pivot, between a tomb for avant-garde revolutionary marvels long past and an archive for maximalist desires not yet given up on, where you can have what you ask for and you ask for everything.

Notes

Introduction

1. For this distinction between the archive as a neutral fact and process of creating facticity, see Michel-Rolph Trouillout, *Silencing the Past: Power and the Production of History* (Boston: Beacon, 2015). See also Michel Foucault, *The Archeology of Knowledge: And the Discourse on Language* (New York: Vintage, 1982).
2. Wendy Brown, *States of Injury: Power and Freedom in Late Modernity* (Princeton, NJ: Princeton University Press, 1995).
3. Lauren Berlant, "Poor Eliza" *American Literature* 17, no. 3 (1998): 636. See also Lauren Berlant, *The Female Complaint: The Unfinished Business of Sentimentality in American Culture* (Durham, NC: Duke University Press, 2008). For ties between affect and transnational forms of belonging, see Leela Gandhi, *Affective Communities: Anticolonial Thought, Fin-de-Siècle Radicalism, and the Politics of Friendship* (Durham, NC: Duke University Press, 2006).
4. A turn from identity to practice and process has often been cited as one of the central features of Women of Color feminisms active in the 1960s. For an overview of this tendency, see Grace Hong, *The Ruptures of American Capital: Women of Color Feminism and the Cultures of Immigrant Labor* (Minneapolis: University of Minnesota Press, 2006). In the more delimited case of citizenship studies, a shift in emphasis from juridically defined rights to practice-oriented frameworks as a basis for shared identity most widely emerged in the late 1980s and early 1990s. See especially Margaret Somers, "Citizenship Troubles: Genealogies of Struggle for the Soul of the Social," in *Rethinking Modernity*, ed. Julia Adams, Elisabeth Clemens, and Ann Orloff (Durham, NC: Duke University Press, 2005), 438–69. In terms of literary studies, I am greatly indebted to a number of more recent books on the intersections of literary texts and a more capacious, practice-based, embodied, or experimental understanding of citizenship. See especially Jane Garrity, *Step-Daughters of England: British Women Modernists and the National Imaginary* (Manchester: Manchester University Press, 2003);

Mimi Sheller, *Citizenship from Below: Erotic Agency and Caribbean Freedom* (Durham, NC: Duke University Press, 2012); Nadine Attewell, *Better Britons: Reproduction, National Identity, and the Afterlife of Empire* (Toronto: University of Toronto Press, 2014); and Janice Ho, *Nation and Citizenship in the Twentieth-Century British Novel* (Cambridge: Cambridge University Press, 2015).

5. For more on witness and realist genres of human rights, see James Dawes, *That the World May Know: Declaring Witness to Atrocity* (Cambridge, MA: Harvard University Press, 2007); and James Dawes, *The Novel of Human Rights* (Cambridge, MA: Harvard University Press, 2018).

6. Kay Schaffer and Sidonie Smith, *Human Rights and Narrated Lives: The Ethics of Recognition* (New York: Palgrave, 2004), 3.

7. Lynn Hunt, *Inventing Human Rights: A History* (New York: Norton, 2008); Joseph Slaughter, *Human Rights Inc.: The World Novel, Narrative Form, and International Law* (New York: Fordham University Press, 2007); Elizabeth Anker, *Fictions of Dignity: Embodying Human Rights in World Literature* (Ithaca, NY: Cornell University Press, 2012).

8. "Elle était plus enragée qu'une vipère, c'était une furie, elle était courbée en deux sous le faix des fairas qu'elle portait pour alimenter le feu." *Insurrection du Sud*, Counseil de Guerre, second series (September 22, 1870): 80; my translation.

9. For the Greek narrative, see Martha Nussbaum, *The Monarchy of Fear: A Philosopher Looks at Our Political Crisis* (New York: Simon & Schuster, 2018). For considerations of anger as an affect and political practice, see Audre Lorde, "The Uses of Anger: Women Responding to Racism," in *Sister/Outsider: Essays and Speeches* (Toronto: Crossing Press Feminist Series, 2007), 124–133; and Sara Ahmed, *The Promise of Happiness* (Durham, NC: Duke University Press, 2010).

10. Karel Vasak, "Human Rights: A Thirty-Year Struggle: The Sustained Efforts to Give Force of Law to the Universal Declaration of Human Rights," *UNESCO Courier* 30, no. 11 (1977).

11. See Michel Foucault, "Governmentality," in *The Foucault Effect: Studies in Governmentality*, ed. Graham Burchell, Colin Gordon, and Peter Miller (Chicago: University of Chicago Press, 1991).

12. Micheline R. Ishay, *The History of Human Rights: From Ancient Times to the Globalization Era* (Berkeley: University of California Press, 2008), 177.

13. Samuel Moyn, *The Last Utopia: Human Rights in History* (Cambridge, MA: Harvard University Press, 2012), 8.

14. For an overview, see Cinzia Arruzza, *Dangerous Liaisons: The Marriages and Divorces of Marxism and Feminism* (London: Merlin, 2013).

15. Letter from Clara Zetkin to Karl Kautsky, quoted in Jean H. Quataert, *Reluctant Feminists in German Social Democracy, 1885–1917* (Princeton, NJ: Princeton University Press, 1979), 122.

16. V. I. Lenin, *What Is to Be Done?*, vol. 1 of *Selected Works* (Moscow: Progress Publishers, 1967), 115.

INTRODUCTION 273

17. Rosa Luxemburg, "The Mass Strike, the Political Party, and the Trade Unions," in *The Rosa Luxemburg Reader*, ed. Peter Hudis and Kevin B. Anderson (New York: Monthly Review Press, 2004), 182.
18. Anton Pannekoek, "Marxist Theory and Revolutionary Tactics," *Die Neue Zeit* 31, no. 1 (1912), https://www.marxists.org/archive/pannekoe/1912/tactics.htm, italics in the original.
19. Edward Said, "Third World Intellectuals/Metropolitan Culture," *Raritan* 9, no. 3 (1990): 31; Brent Hayes Edwards, *The Practice of Diaspora: Literature, Translation, and the Rise of Black Internationalism* (Cambridge, MA: Harvard University Press, 2003); Cheryl Higashida, *Black Internationalist Feminism: Women Writers on the Black Left, 1945–1995* (Champaign: University of Illinois Press, 2013); Aarthi Vadde, *Chimeras of Form: Modernist Internationalism Beyond Europe, 1914–2016* (New York: Columbia University Press, 2016). For an excellent account of transnational rather than internationalist tendencies, see Samantha Pinto, *Difficult Diasporas: The Transnational Feminist Aesthetic of the Black Atlantic* (New York: New York University Press, 2013).
20. See Charlotte Bunch, "Women's Rights as Human Rights: Toward a Re-Vision of Human Rights," *Human Rights Quarterly* (1990): 486–98; Hilary Charlesworth, Christine Chinkin, and Shelley Wright, "Feminist Approaches to International Law," *American Journal of International Law* 85, no. 4 (1991): 613–45.
21. Antoinette Burton, "'States of Injury': Josephine Butler on Slavery, Citizenship, and the Boer War," in *Women's Suffrage in the British Empire: Citizenship, Nation, and Race*, ed. Ian Christopher Fletcher, Laura E. Nym Mayhall, and Philippa Levine (London: Routledge, 2000), 18–32; Antoinette Burton, *Burdens of History: Feminists, Indian Women, and Imperial Culture* (Chapel Hill: University of North Carolina Press, 1994). Also see Chandra Mohanty, *Feminism Without Borders: Decolonizing Theory, Practicing Solidarity* (Durham, NC: Duke University Press, 2003).
22. For a more extended consideration of the motherhood endowment across the transatlantic feminist press, see Lucy Delap, *The Feminist Avant-Garde: Transatlantic Encounters of the Early Twentieth Century* (Cambridge: Cambridge University Press, 2007).
23. [Dora Marsden, unsigned editorial], "The Drudge," *The Freewoman: A Weekly Feminist Review* 1, no. 12 (February 8, 1912): 222.
24. H. G. Wells, "Mr. Wells to the Attack: Freewoman and Endowment," *The Freewoman: A Weekly Feminist Review* 16, no. 1 (March 7, 1912): 1.
25. "Correspondence," *The Freewoman: A Weekly Feminist Review* 1, no. 20 (April 4, 1912): 396.
26. See "A Constitution for British Soviets: Points for a Communist Programme," *Worker's Dreadnought* 7, no. 13 (June 19, 1920): 1.
27. See Roberto Ludovico, "Renato Poggioli: Between History and Literature," *Studi Slavistici* 10 (2013): 301–10.
28. Renato Poggioli, *The Theory of the Avant-Garde*, trans. Gerald Fitzgerald (Cambridge, MA: Harvard University Press, 1968), 25.

29. See Luiz Madureira, *Cannibal Modernities: Postcoloniality and the Avant-Garde in Caribbean and Brazilian Literature* (Charlottesville: University of Virginia Press, 2005); Cathy Park Hong, "Delusions of Whiteness in the Avant-Garde," *Lana Turner* 7 (2014); Steven Lee, *The Ethnic Avant-Garde: Minority Cultures and World Revolution* (New York: Columbia University Press, 2015); and Ben Conisbee Baer, *Indigenous Vanguards: Education, National Liberation, and the Limits of Modernism* (New York: Columbia University Press, 2019).
30. See especially Laura Wexler, *Tender Violence: Domestic Visions in an Age of U.S. Imperialism* (Chapel Hill: University of North Carolina Press, 2000); Ann Laura Stoler, *Carnal Knowledge and Imperial Power: Race and the Intimate in Colonial Rule* (Durham, NC: Duke University Press, 2002); Ann Cvetkovich, *An Archive of Feelings: Trauma, Sexuality, and Lesbian Public Cultures* (Durham, NC: Duke University Press, 2003); Nayan Shah, *Stranger Intimacy: Contesting Race, Sexuality, and Law in the North American West* (Berkeley: University of California Press, 2012); and Lisa Lowe, *Intimacies of Four Continents* (Durham, NC: Duke University Press, 2015).
31. Jürgen Habermas, *The Structural Transformation of the Public Sphere: An Inquiry Into a Category of Bourgeois Society*, trans. Thomas Burger (Cambridge, MA: MIT Press, 1991), 48.
32. Maria Mies, *Patriarchy and Accumulation on a World Scale: Women in the International Division of Labor* (New York: Zed, 1999).
33. Silvia Federici, *Revolution at Point Zero: Housework, Reproduction, and Feminist Struggle* (New York: PM, 2012); Leopolda Fortunati, *The Arcane of Reproduction: Housework, Prostitution, Labor, and Capital* (New York: Autonomedia, 1996); Tithi Bhattacharya, ed., *Social Reproduction Theory* (London: Pluto, 2017).
34. Silvia Federici, "Introduction: Wages for Housework in Historical Perspective," in *Wages for Housework: The New York Committee, 1972–1977: History Theory Documents*, ed. Silvia Federici and Arlen Austin (Brooklyn: Autonomedia, 2017), 12–28.
35. For an early, influential argument for approaching the Latin American avant-gardes in terms of social practice and community, see Vicky Unruh, *Latin American Vanguards: The Art of Contentious Encounters* (Berkeley: University of California Press, 1994).
36. Fredric Jameson, *The Political Unconscious: Narrative as a Socially Symbolic Act* (Ithaca, NY: Cornell University Press, 1982), 102.
37. See Judith Butler, *Notes Towards a Performative Theory of Assembly* (Cambridge, MA: Harvard University Press, 2018), 75.
38. See Denise Riley, *Am I That Name? Feminism and the Category of "Women" in History* (London: Palgrave, 1988).
39. Magnus Hirschfeld, *Homosexuality in Men and Women*, trans. Michael Lombardi-Nash (New York: Prometheus, 2000), 157–58, 220, 471, 191.
40. Emma Goldman to Magnus Hirschfeld (Berlin, 1923). A draft of the article by Goldman was published in *Yearbook for Sexual Intermediate Types*, issued by the Scientific-Humanitarian Committee IISH/EGP, inventory no. 208, http://hdl.handle.net/10622/ARCH00520.

41. Robert Beachy, *Gay Berlin: Birthplace of a Modern Identity* (New York: Vintage, 2014), 220–40.
42. Beachy, *Gay Berlin*, 222.

1. The Fury Archives: Afterlives of the Female Incendiary

1. "Elles ne sont ni assez hideuses, ni assez vieilles, ni assez criminelles pour inspirer de l'horreur." Léonce Dupont, *La Commune et ses auxiliaires devant la justice* (Paris: Didier, 1871), 233. All translations mine unless otherwise noted.
2. Dupont, *La Commune et ses auxiliaires*, 236.
3. "Gazette des Tribunaux," *Le Figaro*, September 6, 1871, 3.
4. "Gazette des Tribunaux," 3.
5. Gay L. Gullickson, *Unruly Women of Paris: Images of the Commune* (Ithaca, NY: Cornell University Press, 1996), 192.
6. Qtd. in Gullickson, *Unruly Women*, 180.
7. Alice Bullard, *Exile to Paradise: Savagery and Civilization in Paris and the South Pacific, 1790–1900* (Stanford, CA: Stanford University Press, 2000).
8. Alexis de Tocqueville, "First Report on Algeria (1847)," in *Writings on Empire and Slavery*, trans. Jennifer Pitts (Baltimore, MD: John Hopkins University Press, 2003), 135.
9. Tocqueville, "First Report on Algeria," 135.
10. Tocqueville, "Essay on Algeria (October 1841)," in *Writings on Empire and Slavery*, trans. Jennifer Pitts (Baltimore, MD: John Hopkins University Press, 2003), 71.
11. Lieutenant-Colonel de Montagnac, *Lettres d'un soldat: Neuf années de campagnes en Afrique* (Paris: Plon, 1885); trans. Christian Destremeau (1998), 299.
12. Gullickson, *Unruly Women of Paris*, 202.
13. "'Elle était vêtue, dit ce temoin, d'une camisole blanche et portrait une écharpe rouge et un fusil en bandoulière.'" *Le dossier de la Commune devant les Counseils de Guerre* (Paris: Librairie des Bibliophiles, 1871), 157. Translations mine unless otherwise noted.
14. Francis Magnard, "La Femme Libre," *Le Figaro*, June 3, 1871, 1.
15. Magnard, "La Femme Libre," 1: "Le tête qui avait dû être jolie, presque distinguée, gardait dans la mort une expression de haine farouche."
16. Karl Marx, *The Civil War in France*, in *Later Political Writings*, trans. Terrell Carver (Cambridge: Cambridge University Press, 1996), 181.
17. Marx, *The Civil War in France*, 188.
18. Marx, *The Civil War in France*, 187.
19. Marx, *The Civil War in France*, 192.
20. Kristin Ross, *The Emergence of Social Space: Rimbaud and the Paris Commune* (New York: Verso, 2008), 33.
21. Kristin Ross, *Communal Luxury: The Political Imaginary of the Paris Commune* (New York: Verso, 2015), 17.
22. Carolyn J. Eichner, *Surmounting the Barricades: Women in the Paris Commune* (Bloomington: Indiana University Press, 2004), 103.

23. Eichner, *Surmounting the Barricades*, 103.
24. Eichner, *Surmounting the Barricades*, 12–13.
25. Arthur Rimbaud, *Rimbaud Complete*, vol. 1, trans. Wyatt Mason (New York: Modern Library, 2003), 93 (English), 432 (French).
26. "Par une circonstance restée inexpliquée, et à coup sûr fortuite, une sorte de drapeau blanc fur assez longtemps arboré sur l'habitation de M. Codé." Ch. Menche de Loisne, *Insurrection de la Martinique* (Paris: E. Dentu, 1871), 4.
27. Qtd. in Armand Nicolas, *Histoire de la Martinique, 1848–1939* (Paris: L'Harmattan, 1996), 80.
28. Gilbert Pago, *L'insurrection de Martinique, 1870–1871* (Paris: Syllepse, 2011), 32; Nicolas, *Histoire de la Martinique*, 78–81. See also Stephen H. Roberts, *The History of French Colonial Policy, 1870–1925* (London: Frank Cass, 1963), 500–3.
29. "Dans un pays comme la Martinique, où les passions sont ardentes, où l'antagonisme, qui divise si malheureusement les races, est toujours si violent, un propos léger est bientôt tenu par les uns, envenimé par les autres." Loisne, *Insurrection*, 4.
30. Loisne, *Insurrection*, 25.
31. "C'était le droit de tout faire, de se venger, de tuer, de piller, d'incendier et de se partager les propriétés." Loisne, *Insurrection*, 16.
32. Loisne, *Insurrection*, 33–34.
33. Pago, *L'insurrection de Martinique*, 105.
34. "C'est ce que disent aujourd'hui les gens de la Commune en France" (17). Counseil de Guerre, *Insurrection du Sud*, Deuxième Série (September 22, 1870): 71. Translation mine. Cited afterwards in text as *CG*.
35. Odile Krakovitch, *Les femmes bagnardes* (Paris: Olivier Orban, 1990), 94.
36. "La Reine de la Compagnie" (55). For a more extensive biography, see Gilbert Pago, *Lumina Sophie dit "Surprise" 1848–1879 insurgée et bagnarde* (Matoury, Guyana: Ibis Rouge Editions, 2008).
37. "C'est une mauvaise femme, elle est très méchante. Tout son voisinage s'en plaignait" (60).
38. "J'ai suivi la bande, parce que Surprise est une mauvaise femme et qu'elle était capable de m'incendier" (53).
39. The original transcript uses the abbreviations D(question) and R(response) to signal the speech of a prosecution/defense and the speech of the person giving testimony. In my English translation, I added what speaker tags I could to aid the reader. I have preserved the erratic punctuation of the original document but silently corrected any spelling errors.
40. "Quel horrible blasphème dans la bouche d'une femme aussi jeune!" (91).
41. "La nommée Surprise et la femme Cyrille se sont fait remarquer par leur exaltation au milieu de l'incendie" (5).
42. "Elle était plus enragée qu'une vipère, c'était une furie, elle était courbée en deux sous le faix des fairas qu'elle portait pour alimenter le feu" (80).
43. "Quel beau feu ? où est donc St. Pée que je lui coupe un morceau de la gueule pour le griller et le manger" (79).

44. "La loi vous armé d'un pouvoir qui vous permet de rejeter au loin ces incendiaires, fléau de notre Société, faites le si vous voulez éviter à notre colonie de nouvelles horreurs!" (93).
45. Costas Douzinas, *The End of Human Rights* (Portland, OR: Hart, 2000); Anthony Anghie, *Imperialism, Sovereignty, and the Making of International Law* (Cambridge: Cambridge University Press, 2005).
46. Talal Asad, *Formations of the Secular: Christianity, Islam, Modernity* (Stanford, CA: Stanford University Press, 2003), 110.
47. Samira Esmeir, *Juridical Humanity: A Colonial History* (Stanford, CA: Stanford University Press, 2012), 4.
48. Ina Césaire, *Rosanie Soleil et autres textes dramatiques* (Paris: Editions Karthala, 2011). Unless otherwise noted, I will cite the text of the English-language edition, *Fire's Daughters*, trans. Judith Miller, in *New French Language Plays* (New York: Ubu Repertory Theater Publications, 1994), 5. However, I retain the French spelling of the characters' names.
49. Krakovitch, *Femmes Bagnardes*, 94.
50. See Emily Sahakian, "Beyond the Marilisse and the Chestnut: Shattering Slavery's Sexual Stereotypes in the Drama of Ina Césaire and Maryse Condé," *Modern Drama* 3 (2014): 385–408; and Christian P. Makward, "Haiti on Stage: Franco-Caribbean Women Remind (On Three Plays by Ina Césaire, Maryse Condé, and Simone Schwarz-Bart)," *Sites: The Journal of Twentieth-Century/Contemporary French Studies* 4, no. 1 (2000): 129–37; for a critique of the masculinist orientation of creolité, see A. James Arnold, "The Gendering of Créolité: The Erotics of Colonialism," in *Penser la creolité*, ed. Maryse Condé and Madeleine Cottenet-Hage (Paris: Karthala, 1995): 21–40.
51. Ina Césaire, qtd. in Christiane Makward, "'Ensouché fond': Le petit théâtre d'Ina Césaire," in *Rosanie Soleil et autres textes dramatiques*, 6. Translation mine.
52. See Ina Césaire, *La faim, la ruse, la révolte: Essai d'analyse anthropologique du Conte Antillais* (Fort de France, Martinique: Service des Musées Régionaux, n.d.).
53. Césaire, *Fire's Daughters*, 6–7.
54. For a wider discussion of the ways that archival scholarship might endlessly repeat scenarios of violence, see Saidiya Hartman, *Scenes of Subjection: Terror, Slavery, and Self-Making in Nineteenth-Century America* (New York: Oxford University Press, 1997).
55. Diana Taylor, *The Archive and the Repertoire: Performing Cultural Memory in the Americas* (Durham, NC: Duke University Press, 2003).

2. The Long Middle: Militant Suffrage from Britain to South Africa

1. A Central Officer's Special Report form 1914 reads: "I beg to report attending Holloway Prison this morning 16 inst., to take a photograph of Kitty Marion (suffragette) but was unsuccessful, owning to her head being completely covered with a dark green motor veil." *Images from the National Archives Exhibition*, Government Papers,

National Archives, Kew, 1904–1914, http://www.archivesdirect.amdigital.co.uk/Documents/Details/ADDITIONAL-TNA. For further consideration of suffragette mugshots in the wider history of police surveillance, see Linda Mulcahy, "Docile Suffragettes? Resistance to Police Photography and the Possibility of Subject Transformation," *Feminist Legal Studies* 23, no. 1 (2015): 79–99.

2. Diane Atkinson, *Rise Up Women!: The Remarkable Lives of the Suffragettes* (London: Bloomsbury, 2018), 407–8. There is a wealth of historical materials on the British suffragette movement, to which I am very much indebted. Lisa Tickner, *The Spectacle of Women: Imagery of the Suffrage Campaign, 1907-14* (London: Chatto & Windus, 1987), deserves special mention for its penetrating analysis and encyclopedic consideration of suffrage posters, cartoons, and archival photographs. Antonia Raeburn, *The Militant Suffragettes* (London: Michael Joseph, 1973); and Andrew Rosen, *Rise Up Women: The Militant Campaign of the Women's Social and Political Union, 1903-1914* (London: Routledge, 1974), both provide essential accounts of suffragette direct action. See also Caroline Morrell, *"Black Friday" and Violence Against Women in the Suffragette Movement* (London: Women's Research and Resources Center, 1981); Susan Kingsley Kent, *Sex and Suffrage in Britain, 1860-1914* (Princeton, NJ: Princeton University Press, 1987); Sophia van Wingerden, *The Women's Suffrage Movement in Britain, 1866-1928* (London: Macmillan, 1999); and Jill Liddington and Jill Norris, *One Hand Tied Behind Us: The Rise of the Women's Suffrage Movement* (London: Virago, 1978). More recently, Laura E. Nym Mayhall, *The Militant Suffrage Movement: Citizenship and Resistance in Britain, 1860-1930* (Oxford: Oxford University Press, 2003), offers an important revisionist account, focusing on the dialogues between suffragists and their contemporaries. Similarly, Martin Pugh, *The March of Women: A Revisionist Analysis of the Campaign for Women's Suffrage, 1866-1914* (Oxford: Oxford University Press, 2000), looks to revive key debates within a more international context. A collection of archival materials, *Suffrage and the Pankhursts*, is especially helpful for editor Jane Marcus's introduction, "Rereading the Pankhursts and Women's Suffrage," in *Suffrage and the Pankhursts* (London: Routledge, 1987), 1–17.

3. *Amnesty of August 1914: Index of Women Suffragists Arrested 1906-1914*, Government Papers, National Archives, Kew, 1914–1935, http://www.archivesdirect.amdigital.co.uk/Documents/Details/HO45-25665-253239.

4. My understanding of this distinction between the means and ends of revolutionary struggle, or more widely the temporality of revolution, is indebted to communization theory, though my archival materials remain at a distance from the specifics of ongoing debates. See *Endnotes I: Preliminary Materials for a Balance Sheet of the 20th Century* for an introduction and key texts by Gilles Dauvé, Karl Nesic, and *Théorie Communiste*: https://endnotes.org.uk/issues/1.

5. Ewa Płonowska Ziarek, *Feminist Aesthetics and the Politics of Modernism* (New York: Columbia University Press, 2012), 19–50.

6. Janet Lyon, *Manifestoes: Provocations of the Modern* (Ithaca, NY: Cornell University Press, 1999), 92–123. Also see my more extended reading of *BLAST* and the invocation

2. THE LONG MIDDLE 279

to the suffragettes, "Model Citizens and Millenarian Subjects: Vorticism, Suffrage, and London's Great Unrest," *Journal of Modern Literature* 37, no. 3 (2014): 1–17.

7. See Antoinette Burton, *Burdens of History: Feminists, Indian Women, and Imperial Culture* (Chapel Hill: University of North Carolina Press, 1994).
8. Henry James, *The Bostonians*, ed. R. D. Gooder (Oxford: Oxford University Press, 1984), 433.
9. Virginia Woolf, *Night and Day* (New York: Penguin, 1992), 218.
10. Franco Moretti, *The Way of the World: The Bildungsroman in European Culture*, trans. Albert Sbragia (London: Verso, 1987), 64.
11. Moretti, *The Way of the World*, 64.
12. Rita Felski, *Beyond Feminist Aesthetics: Feminist Literature and Social Change* (Cambridge, MA: Harvard University Press, 1989), 136.
13. Mikhail M. Bakhtin, "The *Bildungsroman* and Its Significance in the History of Realism (Toward a Historical Typology of the Novel)," in *Speech Genres and Other Late Essays* (Austin: University of Texas Press, 1986), 51.
14. See Barbara Green, *Spectacular Confessions: Autobiography, Performative Activism, and the Sites of Suffrage, 1905–1938* (New York: St. Martin's, 1997). I discuss how Green's account of suffragist writings complicates this narrative in the last section of this chapter.
15. Annie Kenney, *Memories of a Militant* (London: Edward Arnold, 1924), 91. Hereafter cited in text as *MM*.
16. Mary R. Richardson, *Laugh a Defiance* (London: George Weidenfeld & Sons, 1953), vii–viii. Hereafter cited in text as *L*.
17. Hayden White, *The Content of the Form: Narrative Discourse and Historical Representation* (Baltimore, MD: John Hopkins University Press, 1990), 10.
18. Kathryn Laing, introduction to Rebecca West, *The Sentinel: An Incomplete Early Novel*, ed. Kathryn Laing (Oxford: Oxford University Press, 2002): xiii–liii. Hereafter cited parenthetically by page number.
19. Hannah Arendt, *The Human Condition* (Chicago: University of Chicago Press, 1958), 192.
20. Arendt, *The Human Condition*, 198.
21. Arendt, *The Human Condition*, 198.
22. Karl Marx and Friedrich Engels, "Manifesto of the Communist Party," https://www.marxists.org/archive/marx/works/1848/communist-manifesto/.
23. Marx and Engels, "Manifesto of the Communist Party."
24. Kevin Grant, "British Suffragettes and the Russian Method of Hunger Strike," *Comparative Studies in Society and History* 53, no. 1 (2011): 113–43. See also Joseph Lennon, "Fasting for the Public: Irish and Indian Sources of Marion Wallace Dunlap's 1909 Hunger Strike," in *Enemies of Empire*, ed. Eóin Flannery and Angus Mitchell (Dublin: Four Courts, 2007), 19–39.
25. "Government's Assault on Suffragettes," *Votes for Women*, October 1, 1909, 4.
26. "The Tempest in the Liberal Teacup," *St. James Gazette*, August 29, 1901, 12.

280   2. THE LONG MIDDLE

27. *Votes for Women*, January 1910, 1.
28. June Purvis, "'Deeds Not Words': The Daily Lives of the Militant Suffragettes in Edwardian Britain," *Women's Studies International Forum* (1995): 97–98.
29. "From Mrs. Saul Solomon," *Votes for Women*, November 17, 1911, 105.
30. F. W. Pethick-Lawrence, "Mrs. Leigh's Action Against the Home Secretary," *Votes for Women*, December 17, 1909, 185.
31. F. W. Pethick-Lawrence, "Women's Fight for the Vote," *Votes for Women*, June 3, 1910, 575.
32. Emmeline Pethick-Lawrence, "Women or Kaffirs?" *Votes for Women*, July 9, 1909, 112. Kathleen Tanner, "The Driving Force Behind the Women's Movement," *The Vote*, March 27, 1914, 370.
33. Arendt, *The Human Condition*, 198.
34. "Forcible Feeding. Statement by Mrs. Mary Leigh to Her Solicitor," *Votes for Women*, October 15, 1909, 84.
35. "Imprisonment of eight suffragettes in Winson Green Prison in Birmingham following violent protests and incidents linked to a visit by the Prime Minister, Herbert Henry Asquith, to Birmingham on 17 September 1909. Those imprisoned, with sentences ranging from one to three months, were Patricia Woodlock, Ellen Barwell, Hilda Evelyn Burkett, Leslie Hall, Mabel Capper, Mary Edwards, Mary Leigh and Charlotte Marsh. The file contains a number of medical reports on the health of the prisoners, several of whom went on hunger strike and were forcibly fed. It also contains medical opinions on force-feeding and letters from the prisoners' relatives enquiring about their welfare. A recommendation for the release of Mary Leigh on health grounds was approved and took place on 30 October 1909. There are also details of Charlotte Marsh's early release on 9 December 1909 on account of her father's illness, and of attempts by solicitors representing Mary Leigh to take legal action against the Home Secretary. The file records the official appreciation of the Home Secretary to the Governor and prison staff for their handling of the prisoners." Government Papers, National Archives, Kew, http://www.archivesdirect.amdigital.co.uk/Documents/Details/HO_45_10418.
36. *Rachel Peace and Jane Short, suffragettes, forcibly fed*, Government Papers, National Archives, Kew, 1912–1914, http://www.archivesdirect.amdigital.co.uk/Documents/Details/HO144-1232-229179.

3. The Art of Not Having Children: Birth Strike, Sabotage, and the Reproductive Atlantic

1. For firsthand accounts of the lecture, see *L'Encyclopédie Contemporaine Illustrée*, October 9, 1892; and "Une conférence extravagante," *Le Temps*, October 10, 1892, 3.
2. Angus McLaren, *Sexuality and Social Order: The Debate Over the Fertility of Women and Workers in France, 1770–1920* (Holmes & Meier, 1983), 162.
3. Gaston Percheron, "Causerie," *La Semaine Vétérinaire*, October 9, 1892, 645–46.

3. THE ART OF NOT HAVING CHILDREN   281

4. Marie Huot, *Mal de vivre* (Paris: Generation Consciente, 1909), 13–14.
5. Percheron, "Causerie," 645–46. This assertion does not appear in *Mal de vivre*, which is decidedly more sardonic than the original accounts of the lecture.
6. Percheron, "Causerie," 645.
7. Historians have often attributed the phrase *"grève des ventres"* to Huot's lecture, but more recent scholarship puts this origin in dispute. Ann Cova first refutes Huot as the originator of the phrase in *Maternité et droits des femmes en France: XIXe–XXe siècles* (Paris: Economica, 1997), 114–15. Also see Karen Offen, *Debating the Woman Question in the Third Republic, 1870–1920* (Cambridge: Cambridge University Press, 2018), 255. Whether voiced by Huot or not, the phrase gains traction in the popular press in the years after her lecture. A sample of articles includes Severine, "Retour de Tonkin," *Le Journal*, January 14, 1893, 1; and E. Humbert, "La Grève des Ventres," *L'Ouvirier Syndiqué*, April 1, 1903, 2. Also see Fernand Kolney, *La grève des ventres* (Paris: Genération Consciente, 1908).
8. Catherine MacKinnon, "Privacy vs. Equity: Beyond *Roe v. Wade*" (1983), in *Feminism Unmodified: Discourses on Life and Law* (Cambridge, MA: Harvard University Press, 1987), 93–102; Jean Bethke Elshtain, *Public Man, Private Woman: Women in Social and Political Thought* (Princeton, NJ: Princeton University Press, 1981); Anita Allen, *Uneasy Access: Privacy for Women in a Free Society* (Totowa, NJ: Rowman and Littlefield, 1988); Carole Pateman, "Feminist Critiques of the Public/Private Dichotomy," in *The Disorder of Women: Democracy, Feminism, and Political Theory* (Stanford, CA: Stanford University Press, 1989).
9. This term is most indebted to Paul Gilroy, *The Black Atlantic: Modernity and Double Consciousness* (Cambridge, MA: Harvard University Press, 1995). See also Brent Hayes Edwards, *The Practice of Diaspora: Literature, Translation, and the Rise of Black Internationalism* (Cambridge, MA: Harvard University Press, 2003); Laura Doyle, *Freedom's Empire: Race and the Rise of the Novel in Atlantic Modernity* (Durham, NC: Duke University Press, 2007); and Alys Eve Weinbaum's consideration of the "race-reproduction bind" in *Wayward Reproduction: Genealogies of Race and Reproduction in Transatlantic Modern Thought* (Durham, NC: Duke University Press, 2004).
10. For an overview, see Dianne Otto, "Feminist Approaches to International Law," in *The Oxford Handbook of the Theory of International Law*, ed. Anne Ordord, Florian Hoffmann, and Martin Clark (Oxford: Oxford University Press, 2016), 488–504.
11. "Gegen den Gebärkstreik: Berichte über zwei Volksversammlungen in Berlin," in *Frauenemanzipation und Sozialdemokratie*, ed. Meinz Niggemann (Frankfurt am Main: Fischer Taschenbuch Verlag, 1981), 271; translation mine. See also Robert Jütte, *Contraception: A History*, trans. Vicky Russell (Cambridge: Polity, 2008), 167–71; and Cornelia Usborne, *The Politics of the Body in Weimar Germany: Women's Reproductive Rights and Duties* (Ann Arbor: University of Michigan Press, 1992), 8–10.
12. "Gegen den Gebärkstreik" 275.
13. Jütte, *Contraception*, 169.
14. Francis Ronsin, *Grève des ventres: Néo-malthusienne et baisse de la natalité* (Paris: Aubier Montaigne, 1980), 93–115.

3. THE ART OF NOT HAVING CHILDREN

15. Cited in Christine Dienel, *Kinderzahl und Staatsräson. Empfängnisverhütung und Bevölkerungspolitik in Deutschland und Frankreich bis 1918* (Munster, 1995), 178.
16. Joan Martinez-Alier and Eduard Masjuan, "Neo-Malthusianism in the Early 20th Century," International Society of Ecological Economics, n.d., 13.
17. Linda Gordon, *The Moral Property of Women: A History of Birth Control Politics in America* (Champaign: University of Illinois Press, 2007), 157.
18. Emma Goldman, "The Social Aspects of Birth Control," *Mother Earth*, April 1916, 468.
19. Margaret Sanger, "A Birth Strike to Avert World Famine," *Birth Control Review* 4 (January 1920): 1.
20. Layne Parish Craig, *When Sex Changed: Birth Control Politics and Literature Between the World Wars* (New Brunswick, NJ: Rutgers University Press, 2013); Aimee Armande Wilson, *Conceived in Modernism: The Aesthetics of Birth Control* (New York: Bloomsbury, 2016).
21. Lynn Hunt, *Inventing Human Rights: A History* (New York: Norton, 2008), 39.
22. Joseph Slaughter, "The Enchantment of Human Rights, or What Difference Does Humanitarian Indifference Make?" *Critical Quarterly* 56, no. 4 (2014): 50.
23. Elizabeth Gurley Flynn, *Sabotage: The Conscious Withdrawal of the Workers' Efficiency* (Cleveland, Ohio: IWW Publishing Bureau, 1925), 3.
24. Flynn, *Sabotage*, 28.
25. Reb Raney, *Mother Earth*, April 1916, 479.
26. Raney, *Mother Earth*, 480.
27. G., "A Human Document," *Mother Earth*, April 1916, 481.
28. G., "A Human Document," 482.
29. Margaret Sanger, *Family Limitation* (1917; Margaret Sanger Papers Project, New York University, 2018), 12–13.
30. Michelle Murphy, *Seizing the Means of Reproduction: Entanglements of Feminism, Health, and Technoscience* (Durham, NC: Duke University Press, 2012), 25.
31. Murphy, *Seizing the Means of Reproduction*, 29–30.
32. Michel de Certeau, *The Practice of Everyday Life*, trans. Steven Rendall (Berkeley: University of California Press, 1984), 37.
33. "Rebel Women Wanted," *Woman Rebel* 1, no. 2 (April 1914): 16.
34. "Cleopatra," *Woman Rebel* 1, no. 1 (March 1914): 7.
35. "The New Feminists," *Woman Rebel* 1, no. 1 (March 1914): 2.
36. "The Militants in England," *Woman Rebel* 1, no. 4 (June 1914): 25, continued 31.
37. Herbert A. Thorpe, "A Defense of Assassination," *Woman Rebel* 1, no. 5 (July 1914): 33.
38. *Woman Rebel* 1 no. 6 (August 1914), 45.
39. *Woman Rebel* 1, no. 6 (August 1914), 42.
40. Qtd. in Ellen Chesler, *Woman of Valor: Margaret Sanger and the Birth Control Movement in America* (New York: Simon & Schuster, 1992), 139.
41. W. E. B. Du Bois, "Opinion," *The Crisis*, October 1919, 283.
42. Walter White, "Chicago and Its Eight Reasons," *The Crisis*, October 1919, 298.
43. White, "Chicago and Its Eight Reasons," 285.

3. THE ART OF NOT HAVING CHILDREN   283

44. For a wider backdrop to these questions, see contemporary debates about what Lee Edelson had called "reproductive futurity." Lee Edelson, *No Future: Queer Theory and the Death Drive* (Durham, NC: Duke University Press, 2004); and José Esteban Muñoz, *Cruising Utopia: The Then and There of Queer Futurity* (New York: New York University Press, 2009). My understanding of structural vulnerability to premature death is indebted to Ruthie Wilson Gilmore, *Golden Gulag: Prisons, Surplus, Crisis, and Opposition in Globalizing California* (Berkeley: University of California Press, 2007).
45. Daylanne English, *Unnatural Selections: Eugenics in American Modernism and the Harlem Renaissance* (Chapel Hill: University of North Carolina Press, 2004), 125.
46. Angelina Weld Grimké, *Rachel: A Play in Three Acts*, in *Selected Works*, ed. Carolivia Herron (Oxford: Oxford University Press, 1991), 149.
47. Grimké, *Rachel*, 149.
48. See Gloria T. Hull, *Color, Sex, and Poetry: Three Women Writers of the Harlem Renaissance* (Bloomington: Indiana University Press, 1987), 120-21.
49. Angelina Weld Grimké, "'Rachel': The Play of the Month, the Reason and Synopsis by the Author," in *Selected Works*, ed. Carolivia Herron (Oxford: Oxford University Press, 1991), 413.
50. Grimké, "'Rachel,'" 414.
51. Angelina Weld Grimké, "The Closing Door," *Birth Control Review*, October 1919, 10.
52. Qtd. in Claudia Tate, *Domestic Allegories of Political Desire: The Black Heroine's Text* (Oxford: Oxford University Press, 1992), 210.
53. Roderick Ferguson, *Aberrations in Black: Towards a Queer of Color Critique* (Minneapolis: University of Minnesota Press, 2003); Siobhan Somerville, *Queering the Color Line: Race and the Invention of Homosexuality in American Culture* (Durham, NC: Duke University Press, 2000).
54. Havelock Ellis, "The World's Racial Problem," *Birth Control Review*, October 1920, 15.
55. Ellis, "The World's Racial Problem," 16.
56. For considerations of Grimké and *The Birth Control Review*, see Tate, *Domestic Allegories of Political Desire*, 209-30; Erika Miller, *The Other Reconstruction: Where Violence and Womanhood Meet in the Writings of Wells-Barnett, Grimké, and Larson* (New York: Garland, 2000), 57-100; and Lorna Raven Wheeler, "The Queer Collaboration: Angelina Weld Grimké and the Birth Control Movement," in *Critical Insights: LGBTQ Literature*, ed. Robert C. Evans (Ipswich, MA: Salem Press, 2015), 179-92.
57. Grimké, "The Closing Door," 12. Hereafter quoted in text.
58. Qtd. in Hull, *Color, Sex, and Poetry*, 139.
59. Hull, *Color, Sex, and Poetry*, 139.
60. Grimké, "The Closing Door," 12.
61. Jennifer L. Morgan, *Laboring Women: Reproduction and Gender in New World Slavery* (Philadelphia: University of Pennsylvania Press, 2004), 166-67. See also Deborah Gray White, *Ain't I a Woman? Female Slaves in the Plantation South* (New York: Norton, 1985); Elizabeth Fox-Genovese, "Strategies of Resistance: Focus on Slave Women in the United States," in *In Resistance: Studies in African, Caribbean, and*

Afro-American History, ed. Gary Y. Okihiro (Amherst: University of Massachusetts Press, 1986), 143–65; Marietta Morrissey, *Slave Women in the New World: Gender Stratification in the Caribbean* (Lawrence: University Press of Kansas, 1989); Barbara Bush, *Slave Women in Caribbean Society, 1650–1838* (Bloomington: Indiana University Press, 1990).

62. E. M. Pendleton, "On the Susceptibility of the Caucasian and African Races to the Different Classes of Disease," *Southern Medical Reports* (1949 [1856]): 2:336–42.
63. John H. Morgan, "An Essay on the Production of Abortion Among Our Negro Population," *Nashville Journal of Medicine and Surgery*, August 1860, 117–18.
64. Qtd. in Bush, *Slave Women*, 139.
65. Bush, *Slave Women*, 140.
66. Michael P. Johnson, "Smothered Slave Infants: Were Slave Mothers at Fault?" *Journal of Southern History* 47 (November 1981): 493–520. See also Kelli M. Black, "Creating Infanticide: A Comparative Study of Early Modern British Servant and Antebellum American Slave Women," MA thesis, San Diego State University, 2003.
67. Petition Analysis Record, "To the Honorable Joshua L. Martin Chancellor of the Middle Chancery Division of the State of Alabama," in *Race, Slavery, and Free Blacks*, series 2: *Petitions to Southern County Courts, Part A*. (January 1852–February 1953), folder 009061-011-0265.
68. Jane (a slave) v. the State, Supreme Court of Missouri, Bowling Green District, April 1831, Mo. LEXIS 22. This case is discussed at more length in A. Leon Higginbotham Jr., "Race, Sex, Education, and Missouri Jurisprudence: Shelley v. Kraemer in a Historical Perspective," *Washington University Law Review* 67 (1989): 694–96.
69. Paul Gilroy, *The Black Atlantic: Modernity and Double Consciousness* (Cambridge, MA: Harvard University Press, 1993), 64–68.
70. The lineage of this term can also be located in black feminist organizing of the 1990s, through the SisterSong Women of Color Reproductive Collective. See Loretta J. Ross and Rickie Solinger, *Reproductive Justice: An Introduction* (Berkeley: University of California Press, 2017); Loretta J. Ross et al., eds., *Radical Reproductive Justice: Foundations, Practice, Theory, Critique* (New York: Feminist Press, 2017); and Loretta J. Ross, "The Color of Choice: White Supremacy and Reproductive Justice," in *Color of Violence: The "Incite!" Anthology* (Cambridge, MA: South End Press, 2006), 53–65. See also Dean Spade, "Intersectional Resistance and Law Reform," *Signs: A Journal of Women in Culture and Society* 38, no. 4 (2013): 1–25.
71. Dorothy E. Roberts, *Killing the Black Body: Race, Reproduction, and the Meaning of Liberty* (New York: Vintage, 1997), 6.
72. Raphael Lemkin, "Genocide as a Crime Under International Law," *American Journal of International Law* 41, no. 1 (1947): 147. See also A. Dirk Moses, "Raphael Lemkin, Culture, and the Concept of Genocide," in *The Oxford Handbook of Genocide Studies*, ed. Donald Bloxham and A. Dirk Moses (Oxford: Oxford University Press, 2010), 20–41.
73. Peter Kihss, "Lemkin Decries Accusation of U.S. Genocide," *New York Herald Tribune*, December 16, 1951, 26.

74. Qtd. in *We Charge Genocide: The Historic Petition to the United Nations for Relief from a Crime of the United States Government Against the Negro People*, ed. William L. Patterson, Civil Rights Congress (New York: International Publishers, 1951), n.p. Hereafter quoted in text as *WC*.

4. Rhineland Bastards, Queer Species: An Afro-German Case Study

1. See Peter Collar, *Propaganda War in the Rhineland: Weimar Germany, Race, and Occupation After World War I* (London: I. B. Tauris, 2013), 125–29.
2. Ray Beveridge, *Mein Leben für Euch! Erinnerungen an Glanzvolle und Bewegte Jahre* (Berlin: Deutschen Verlag, 1948), 257.
3. *Colored Troops in the French Army: A Report from the Department of State Relating to the Colored Troops in the French Army and the Number of French Colonial Troops in the Occupied Territory*, 66th Congress (Washington, DC: Government Printing Office, 1921), 12.
4. See M. Cherif Bassiouni, *Crimes Against Humanity in International Criminal Law* (London: Kluwer Law International, 1999).
5. For the paradoxical newness and eternity of the nation's imagined community, see Benedict Anderson, *Imagined Communities: Reflections on the Origin and Spread of Nationalism* (London: Verso, 2016), 11.
6. Janet Lyon, *Manifestoes: Provocations of the Modern* (Ithaca, NY: Cornell University Press, 1999), 32.
7. Lyon, *Manifestoes*, 32.
8. Tristan Tzara, "An Introduction to Dada," in *Dada Painters and Poets: An Anthology*, ed. Robert Motherwell (Cambridge, MA: Harvard University Press, 1979), 403.
9. Georges Hugnet, "The Dada Spirit in Painting," in *Dada Painters and Poets: An Anthology*, ed. Robert Motherwell (Cambridge, MA: Harvard University Press, 1979), 141–42.
10. Richard Huelsenbeck, "Dada Lives!," in *Dada Painters and Poets: An Anthology*, ed. Robert Motherwell (Cambridge, MA: Harvard University Press, 1979), 281.
11. Catherine Ann Cline, *E. D. Morel: The Strategies of Protest* (Belfast: Blackstaff, 1980), 98–115.
12. F. Seymour Cocks, *E. D. Morel: The Man and His Work* (London: George Allen, 1920), 39.
13. Cline, *E. D. Morel*, ix.
14. Foundational accounts of the English-language press can be found in Robert C. Reinders, "Racialism on the Left: E. D. Morel and the 'Black Horror on the Rhine,'" *International Review of Social History* 13 (1968): 1–28; Sally Marks, "Black Watch on the Rhine: A Study in Propaganda, Prejudice, and Prurience," *European Studies Review* 13, no. 3 (1983): 297–333. More recently, see Keith L. Nelson, "The 'Black Horror on the Rhine': Race as a Factor in Post–World War Diplomacy," *Journal of Modern History* 42, no. 4 (1970), 610–11; Christian Koller, *Von Wilden aller Rassen*

niedergemetzelt: Die Diskussion um die Verwendung von Kolonialtruppen in Europa zwischen Rassissmus, Kolonial- und Militärpolitik (1914–1930) (Stuttgart, 2001).
15. E. D. Morel, "Foreword to the Seventh Edition," in *The Horror on the Rhine* (London: St. Clements, 1921).
16. Reinders, "Racialism on the Left," 7.
17. Claude McKay, "A Black Man Replies," *Worker's Dreadnought*, April 24, 1920.
18. Claude McKay, *A Long Way from Home* (London: Pluto, 1985), 62.
19. Sandra Maß, *Weiße Helden, schwarze Krieger: Zur Geschichte kolonialer Männlichkeit in Deutschland, 1918–1964* (Cologne: Böhlau, 2006); Iris Wigger, *Die "Schwarze Schmach am Rhein": Rassistische Diskriminierung zwischen Geschlecht, Klasse, Nation und Rasse* (Munster: Westfälisches Dampfboot, 2006).
20. See Julia Roos, "Nationalism, Racism, and Propaganda in Early Weimar Germany: Contradictions in the Campaign Against the 'Black Horror on the Rhine,'" *German History* 30, no. 1 (2012): 45–74.
21. Thomas Laqueur, "Bodies, Details, and the Humanitarian Narrative," in *The New Cultural History*, ed. Lynn Hunt (Berkeley: University of California Press, 1989).
22. "Outcry Against the 'Black Horror' and an Urgent Appeal to Americans," *Chicago Defender*, September 23, 1922, 15. For the origins of this broadsheet in German, see Collar, *Propaganda War in the Rhineland*, 157.
23. R1603/2566 Allgemeines Schriftwechsel 1921–1922. Jared Poley discusses the entire broadsheet at length in *Decolonization in Germany: Weimar Narratives of Colonial Loss and Foreign Occupation* (New York: Peter Lang, 2007), 188–205.
24. Morel, *The Horror on the Rhine*, n.p.
25. Morel, *The Horror on the Rhine*, 20.
26. Morel, *The Horror on the Rhine*, 20.
27. Nicoletta F. Gullace, *The Blood of Our Sons: Men, Women, and the Renegotiation of British Citizenship During the Great War* (New York: Palgrave, 2002), 26.
28. "Truly a Tale Unadorned," *New York Times*, May 14, 1915.
29. Bassiouni, *Crimes Against Humanity in International Criminal Law*, 61.
30. Hague Convention IV (October 18, 1907), "Convention Respecting the Laws and Customs of War on Land," http://avalon.law.yale.edu/20th_century/hague04.asp.
31. *Violations of the Laws and Customs of War: Reports of Majority and Dissenting Reports of American and Japanese Members of the Commission of Responsibilities, Conference of Paris, 1919* (London: Carnegie, 1919), 1–2.
32. A. Dirk Moses, "Raphael Lemkin, Culture, and the Concept of Genocide," in *The Oxford Handbook of Genocide Studies*, ed. Donald Bloxham and A. Dirk Moses (Oxford: Oxford University Press, 2010), 25–26.
33. Georges Hugnet, *Dictionnaire du Dadaïsme, 1916–1922* (Paris: Jean-Claude Simoën, 1976), 124–25.
34. Michael Fried, *Why Photography Matters as Art as Never Before* (New Haven, CT: Yale University Press, 2008), 35. The scene of beholding is a question that structures much of Fried's earlier work and marks a wider conversation with Hal Foster and Rosalind Krauss, to whom I will refer later in this chapter.

4. RHINELAND BASTARDS, QUEER SPECIES   287

35. See James Clifford, *The Predicament of Culture: Twentieth-Century Ethnography, Literature, and Art* (London: Harvard University Press, 1988); Sieglinde Lemke, *Primitivist Modernism: Black Culture and the Origins of Transatlantic Modernism* (New York: Oxford University Press, 1998); Ann Anlin Cheng, *Second Skin: Josephine Baker and the Modern Surface* (Oxford: Oxford University Press, 2011).
36. Hannah Höch, qtd. in Maud Lavin, *Cut with the Kitchen Knife: The Weimar Photomontages of Hannah Höch* (New Haven, CT: Yale University Press, 1993), 163.
37. Maud Lavin, "The Mess of History, or the Unclean Hannah Höch," in *Hannah Höch* (Munich: Prestel, 2014), 89.
38. Lavin, *Cut with the Kitchen Knife*, 167.
39. Rosalind Krauss, *Passages in Modern Sculpture* (New York: Viking, 1977), 7–38. Also see Hal Foster, "The Crux of Minimalism," which situates Krauss in relationship to critiques of theatricality, in *The Return of the Real: The Avant-Garde at the End of the Century* (Cambridge, MA: MIT Press, 1996), 35–70.
40. Maria Makela and Peter Boswell, eds., *The Photomontages of Hannah Höch* (Minneapolis: Walker Art Center, 1996), 86, image caption.
41. Matthew Biro, *The Dada Cyborg: Visions of the New Human in Weimar Berlin* (Minneapolis: University of Minnesota Press, 2009), 225.
42. Biro, *The Dada Cyborg*, 227–28.
43. Hannah Höch, *Album* (Berlin: Hatje Cantz, 2004), n.p.
44. Carl Schmitt, *The Concept of the Political*, trans. George Schwab (Chicago: University of Chicago Press, 2007), 55. See also William Rasch, "Anger Management: Carl Schmitt in 1925 and the Occupation of the Rhineland," *New Centennial Review* 8, no. 1 (2008): 57–79.
45. Schmitt, *The Concept of the Political*, 54.
46. Schmitt, *The Concept of the Political*, 54.
47. Martin Puchner, *Poetry of the Revolution: Marx, Manifestos, and the Avant-Gardes* (Princeton, NJ: Princeton University Press, 2006), 4–5.
48. Tina Campt, *Other Germans: Black Germans and the Politics of Race, Gender, and Memory in the Third Reich* (Ann Arbor: University of Michigan Press, 2005), 63–80.
49. Campt, *Other Germans*, 64.
50. Also see Jeremy Noakes, "Nazism and Eugenics: The Background to the Nazi Sterilization Law of 14 July 1933," in *Ideas Into Politics: Aspects of European History, 1880–1950*, ed. R. J. Bullen, H. Pogge von Strandmann, and A. B. Polonsky (Totowa, NJ: Barnes and Noble, 1984), 75–94.
51. Gunda Luyken, "In the Magical Realm of Fantasy: Hannah Höch's *Picture Book*," in Hannah Höch, *Picture Book*, trans. Brian Currid (Berlin: Green Box Kunst Editionnen, 2010), n.p.
52. Höch, *Picture Book*, n.p. I use Brian Currid's translation, though I have changed some phrases that syntactically depart from the German-language version.
53. Marion Brandt, "Editorische Erläuterungen und Worterklärungen," in Til Brugman, *Das vertippte Zebra: Lyrik und Prosa*, ed. Marion Brandt (Berlin: Hoffmann, 1995), 207.

54. Julie Nero, "Hannah Höch, Til Brugman, Lesbianism, and Weimar Sexual Subculture," PhD diss., Case Western Reserve University, 2013, 260.
55. Thomas O. Haakensen, "Grotesque Visions: Art, Science, and Visual Culture in Early-Twentieth-Century Germany," PhD diss., University of Minnesota, 2006, 180–213.
56. Til Brugman, "Warenhaus der Liebe," in *Das vertippte Zebra: Lyrik und Prosa*, ed. Marion Brandt (Berlin: Hoffmann, 1995), 73; translation mine.
57. Brugman, "Warenhaus der Liebe," 79.
58. Brugman, "Warenhaus der Liebe," 79–80.
59. Brugman, "Warenhaus der Liebe," 81.
60. Hannah Hoch, "Fantastische Kunst," in *Fantasten-Ausstellung* (Berlin: Galerie Rosen, 1946).
61. Höch, *Picture Book*, n.p.
62. The best version of this literature—written with significantly more nuance than my paraphrase—is Brigid Doherty, "'See: We Are All Neurasthenics!' or, the Trauma of Dada Montage," *Critical Inquiry* 24, no. 1 (1997): 82–132. For a more standard, all-male account of Dada in the context of war, see Robert Motherwell, ed., *The Dada Painters and Poets: An Anthology* (Cambridge, MA: Harvard University Press, 1951).
63. Hannah Höch, "Interview," in *Hannah Höch: Collages, Peintures, Aquarelles, Gouaches, Dessins*, ed. Suzanne Pagé et al. (Paris: Musée d'Art Moderne de la Ville de Paris; Berlin: Nationalgalerie Berlin Staatlich Musseen Preussischer Kulturbesitz, 1976), 25; translation mine.
64. Interview between Eduard Roditi and Hannah Höch, in *Hannah Höch: Collages, Peintures, Aquarelles, Gouaches, Dessins*, ed. Suzanne Pagé et al. (Paris: Musée d'Art Moderne de la Ville de Paris; Berlin: Nationalgalerie Berlin Staatlich Musseen Preussischer Kulturbesitz, 1976), 184.

5. Surrealism's Inhumanities: Chance Encounter, Lesbian Crime, Queer Resistance

1. Man Ray, *Self-Portrait* (Boston: Little, Brown, 1963), 161.
2. Scot D. Ryersson and Michael Orlando Yaccarino, *Infinite Variety: The Life and Legend of the Marchesa Casati* (Minneapolis: University of Minnesota Press, 2004), 125–26.
3. See Stanley G. Payne, *A History of Fascism, 1914–1945* (New York: Routledge, 1996), 92.
4. Ryersson and Yaccarino, *Infinite Variety*, 100–1.
5. See Lorenzo Benadusi, *The Enemy of the New Man: Homosexuality in Fascist Italy*, trans. Suzanne Dingee and Jennifer Pudney (Madison: University of Wisconsin Press, 2012).
6. See Deborah Cohler, *Citizen, Invert, Queer: Lesbianism and War in Early Twentieth-Century Britain* (Minneapolis: University of Minnesota Press, 2010). For further accounts of lesbian identity in the interwar period, see Shari Benstock, *Women of the Left Bank: Paris, 1900–1940* (Austin: University of Texas Press, 1986); Lillian Faderman, *Odd Girls and Twilight Lovers: A History of Lesbian Life in Twentieth-Century*

America (New York: Columbia University Press, 2012); and Laura Doan, *Fashioning Sapphism: The Origins of a Modern English Lesbian Culture* (New York: Columbia University Press, 2001).
7. George L. Mosse, *Nationalism and Sexuality: Respectability and Abnormal Sexuality in Modern Europe* (New York: Howard Vertig, 1997), 134.
8. For accounts of Cahun that turn to the historical context of lesbian Paris, see Carolyn J. Dean, "Claude Cahun's Double," *Yale French Studies* 90 (1996): 71–92; Abigail Solomon-Godeau, "The Equivocal 'I': Claude Cahun as Lesbian Subject," in *Inverted Odysseys: Claude Cahun, Maya Deren, Cindy Sherman*, ed. Shelley Rice (Cambridge, MA: MIT Press, 1999): 111–126; Tirza True Latimer, "Looking Like a Lesbian: Portraiture and Sexual Identity in 1920s Paris," in *Modern Woman Revisited: Paris Between the Wars*, ed. Whitney Chadwick and Tirza True Latimer (New Brunswick, NJ: Rutgers University Press, 2003): 127–144; and Tirza True Latimer, *Women Together, Women Apart: Portraits of Lesbian Paris* (New Brunswick, NJ: Rutgers University Press, 2005). For a consideration of Cahun and transgender theory, see Dickran Tashjian, "Vous pour moi? Marcel Duchamp and Transgender Coupling," in *Mirror Images: Women, Surrealism, and Self-Representation*, ed. Whitney Chadwick (Cambridge, MA: MIT Press, 1998): 36–65; Danielle Knafo, "Claude Cahun: The Third Sex," *Studies in Gender and Sexuality* 2, no. 1 (2001): 29–61; and Christy Wampole, "The Impudence of Claude Cahun," *L'Esprit Créator* 53, no. 1 (2013): 101–13.
9. Miranda Pollard, *Reign of Virtue: Mobilizing Gender in Vichy France* (Chicago: University of Chicago Press, 1998), 9–10, 18; Helmut Gruber, "French Women in the Crossfire of Class, Sex, Maternity, and Citizenship," in *Women and Socialism, Socialism and Women: Europe Between the Two World Wars*, trans. Helmut Gruber and Pamela Graves (New York: Berghahn, 1998), 279–320.
10. Pollard, *Reign of Virtue*, 18.
11. Qtd. in Pollard, *Reign of Virtue*, 33.
12. Francine Muel-Dreyfus, *Vichy and the Eternal Feminine: A Contribution to a Political Sociology of Gender*, trans. Kathleen A. Johnson (Durham, NC: Duke University Press, 2001).
13. Florence Tamagne, *A History of Homosexuality in Europe*, vol. 2: *Berlin, London, Paris, 1919–1939* (New York: Algora, 2004), 252.
14. Tamagne, *A History of Homosexuality in Europe*, 2:253, 2:134, 2:136.
15. Qtd. in Günter Grau, *Hidden Holocaust? Gay and Lesbian Persecution in Germany, 1933–45*, trans. Claudia Schoppmann (Chicago: Fitzroy Dearborn, 1995), 65.
16. Grau, *Hidden Holocaust*, 6. See also William J. Spurlin, *Lost Intimacies: Rethinking Homosexuality Under National Socialism* (New York: Peter Lang, 2009).
17. Qtd. in Tamagne, *A History of Homosexuality in Europe*, 2:194.
18. Tamagne, *A History of Homosexuality in Europe*, 2:302.
19. Michael D. Sibalis, "Homophobia, Vichy France, and the 'Crime of Homosexuality': The Origins of the Ordinance of 6 August 1942," *GLQ* 8, no. 3 (2002): 301–18.
20. Lawrence R. Schehr, *Alcibiades at the Door: Gay Discourses in French Literature* (Stanford, CA: Stanford University Press, 1995), 24.

5. SURREALISM'S INHUMANITIES

21. Christine Bard and Jean-Louis Robert, "The French Communist Party and Women, 1920–1939," trans. Nicole Dombrowski, in *Women and Socialism, Socialism and Women: Europe Between the Two World Wars*, ed. Helmut Gruber and Pamela Graves (New York: Berghahn, 1998), 342.
22. José Pierre, ed., *Investigating Sex: Surrealist Research, 1928–1932*, trans. Malcolm Imrie (London: Verso, 1992), 5.
23. Pierre, ed., *Investigating Sex*, 5.
24. André Breton, *Nadja*, trans. Richard Howard (New York: Grove, 1960), altered slightly for more literal translation; André Breton, *Nadja* (Paris: Gallimard, 2007), 15.
25. Peter Bürger, *Theory of the Avant-Garde*, trans. Michael Shaw (Minneapolis: University of Minnesota Press, 1984), 65.
26. Denis Hollier, "Surrealist Precipitates: Shadows Don't Cast Shadows," trans. Rosalind Krauss, *October* 69 (1994): 128.
27. Hollier, "Surrealist Precipitates," 128.
28. Two photographs of Cahun's work were included in the 1985 exhibition "L'Amour Fou: Photography and Surrealism," Corcoran Gallery of Art, Washington, DC. See Dawn Ades, Rosalind Krauss, and Jane Livingston, *L'Amour Fou: Photography and Surrealism* (New York: Abbeville, 1985). Cahun gained transatlantic prominence with the publication of François Leperlier's *Claude Cahun: L'écart et la metamorphose* (Paris: Jean-Michel Place, 1992).
29. See Gen Doy's "Masks, Masquerades, and Mirrors," in *Claude Cahun: A Sensual Politics of Photography* (London: I. B. Tauris, 2007), for a more through account of this reception history. In reference to Rivière's work, Doy argues, "While the idea of womanliness as masquerade has proved fruitful for cultural and feminist analysis, scholars who have utilized this text have frequently failed to take enough account of its historical context" (53).
30. Claude Cahun, *Disavowals*, trans. Susan de Muth (Cambridge: MA: MIT University Press, 2007), fifth plate.
31. Katy Kline, "Claude Cahun and Cindy Sherman," in *Mirror Images: Women, Surrealism, and Self-Representation* (Cambridge, MA: MIT Press, 1998), 68.
32. Dawn Ades, "Surrealism and the Representation of the Female Subject in Mexico and Postwar Paris," in *Mirror Images: Women, Surrealism, and Self-Representation* (Cambridge, MA: MIT Press, 1998), 115.
33. Jennifer Shaw, "Narcissus and the Magic Mirror," in *Don't Kiss Me: The Art of Claude Cahun and Marcel Moore* (London: Aperture, 2006), 44.
34. Rosalind Krauss, *Bachelors* (Cambridge, MA: MIT University Press, 2000), 37, 50.
35. Dean, "Claude Cahun's Double," 74.
36. Judith Butler, *Bodies That Matter: On the Discursive Limits of "Sex"* (New York: Routledge, 1993), 94.
37. Rosemary Hennessy, *Profit and Pleasure: Sexual Identities in Late Capitalism* (London: Routledge, 2000); Kevin Floyd, *The Reification of Desire: Towards a Queer Marxism* (Minneapolis: University of Minnesota Press, 2009); Cinzia Arruza, "Gender as Social Temporality: Butler and Marx," *Historical Materialism* 23, no. 1 (2015): 28–52.

38. See Gay Wachman, *Lesbian Empire: Radical Crosswriting in the Twenties* (New Brunswick, NJ: Rutgers University Press, 2001), 13–18; and Jennifer Travis, "Clits in Court: *Salome*, Sodomy, and the Lesbian 'Sadist,'" in *Lesbian Erotics*, trans. Karla Jay (New York: New York University Press, 1995), 147–63.
39. Qtd. in Travis, "Clits in Court," 148.
40. Claude Cahun, "La 'Salome' d'Oscar Wilde, le Procès Billing et les 47.000 Pervertis du 'Livre Noire,'" *Mercure de France* (1918): 80.
41. Cahun, "La 'Salome' d'Oscar Wilde," 148. See also Michael Kettle, *Salome's Last Veil: The Libel Case of the Century* (London: Granada, 1977).
42. Carolyn J. Dean, "Claude Cahun's Double," *Yale French Studies* 90 (1996): 75.
43. Collette, *The Pure and the Impure*, trans. Herma Briffault (New York: Farrar, Straus & Giroux, 2000), 135.
44. Collette, *The Pure and the Impure*, 71.
45. Tirza True Latimer, "Entre Nous: Between Claude Cahun and Marcel Moore," *GLQ* 12, no. 2 (2006): 197–216.
46. "Who's Who Abroad," *Chicago Tribune*, European ed. (1929), Jersey Heritage Trust Archives JHT/2003/00001/27.
47. Claude Cahun, "Les Jeux uraniens," unpublished ms., c. 1914, Jersey Heritage Trust (JHT) Archives., St. Helier, Channel Island of Jersey, 34.
48. See Katherine Conley, *Surrealist Ghostliness* (Lincoln: University of Nebraska Press, 2013), for a consideration of the photographs of Cahun's dismembered head in the bell jar and of *Human Frontier* as a reference to the beheaded victims of the French Revolution. In contrast to my own reading, focused on the status of inhumanity in Cahun's work, Conley's extended and insightful reading of *Human Frontier* situates the distorted head in these images as a version of surrealist ghostliness based on the destabilized identity categories of man/woman/human/ghost that can "come close to capturing the human experience in its full complexity, in its fully three dimensional, tactile mortality" (67).
49. Walter Benjamin, "Little History of Photography," *Selected Writings*, vol. 2: *1931–1934*, trans. Rodney Livingstone (Cambridge, MA: Harvard University Press, 1999), 510.
50. Roland Barthes, *Camera Lucida: Reflections on Photography*, trans. Richard Howard (New York: Farrar, Straus & Giroux, 2000), 27.
51. Renato Poggioli, *The Theory of the Avant-Garde*, trans. Gerald Fitzgerald (Cambridge, MA: Harvard University Press, 1968), 176.
52. Mark Polizzotti, *Revolution of the Mind: The Life of Andre Breton* (Boston: Black Widow, 2009), 418–19.
53. Qtd. in Polizzotti, *Revolution of the Mind*, 418.
54. André Breton and Diego Rivera [Léon Trotsky], "Manifesto for an Independent Revolutionary Art, 1938," in *Manifesto: A Century of Isms*, trans. Mary Ann Caws (Lincoln: University of Nebraska Press, 2001), 477.
55. André Breton, *Arcanum 17*, trans. Zack Rogow (Los Angeles: Sun & Moon, 1994), 60–61.
56. For further accounts of the resistance campaign in English, see Claire Follain, "Lucy Schwob and Suzanne Malherbe-*Résistantes*," in *Don't Kiss Me: The Art of Claude*

Cahun and Marcel Moore, ed. Louise Downie (London: Jersey Heritage Trust, 2006), 83–95; Whitney Chadwick, *Farewell to the Muse: Love, War, and the Women of Surrealism* (London: Thames & Hudson, 2017), 165–97; and Jennifer Laurie Shaw, *Exist Otherwise: The Life and Works of Claude Cahun* (London: Reaktion, 2017). Among Cahun's many autobiographical works, the "Lettre à Gaston Ferdière" and the "Lettre au Paul Levy" are the most detailed source of the couple's resistance and arrest. Claude Cahun, *Écrits*, ed. François Leperlier (Paris: Jean-Michel Place, 1992), 709–57.
57. *Jersey Evening Post*, June 30, 1945, 4.
58. Cahun, *Écrits*, 610. All translations are mine unless otherwise noted. Hereafter cited in the text as *E*.
59. See Follain, "Lucy Schwob and Suzanne Malherbe-*Résistantes*," 90.
60. For instance, Leperlier explains Cahun's move to Jersey as a retreat from both surrealism and André Breton. François Leperlier, *Claude Cahun: L'écart et la metamorphose* (Paris: Jean-Michel Place, 1992), 263.
61. Leperlier, *Claude Cahun*, 273–74.
62. Leperlier, *Claude Cahun*, 275.
63. Leperlier, *Claude Cahun*, 227.
64. Qtd. in Johannes Morsink, *The Universal Declaration of Human Rights* (Philadelphia: University of Pennsylvania Press, 1999), 254.
65. Morsink, *The Universal Declaration of Human Rights*, 225.
66. Morsink, *The Universal Declaration of Human Rights*, 256.
67. *Universal Declaration of Human Rights* (1948), United Nations, http://www.un.org/en/documents/udhr/.
68. Paul Johnson, *Homosexuality and the European Court of Human Rights* (New York: Routledge, 2012). Also see Robert Wintermute, *Sexual Orientation and Human Rights: The United States Constitution, the European Convention, and the Canadian Charter* (Oxford: Clarendon, 1995).
69. Bliss Cua Lim, "Dolls in Fragments: *Daisies* as Feminist Allegory," *Camera Obscura* 47 (2001): 37–77.
70. Jonathan L. Owen, "Spoiled Aesthetics: Realism and Anti-Humanism in Vera Chytilová's *Daisies* (1966)," in *Avant-Garde to New Wave: Czechoslovak Cinema, Surrealism, and the Sixties* (New York: Berghahn, 2011), 99–128.
71. Cahun, Correspondence, 1943–45, Claude Cahun and Suzanne Malherbe Papers, 1913–1952, GEN MSS 721, Beinecke Rare Book and Manuscript Library, Yale University.
72. Cahun, Correspondence.
73. Malherbe memoir notes, undated. Claude Cahun and Suzanne Malherbe Papers, 1913–1952, GEN MSS 721, Beinecke Rare Book and Manuscript Library, Yale University.

6. The Committee Form: Négritude Women and the United Nations

1. UN General Assembly, 3rd Session, Third Committee, "Draft International Declaration of Human Rights (E/800), October 14, 1948 (A/C.3/SR.102). Summary record.

6. THE COMMITTEE FORM 293

2. John P. Humphrey, *Human Rights and the United Nations: A Great Adventure* (Dobbs Ferry, NY: Transnational Publishers, 1984), 56.
3. Eleanor Roosevelt, *On My Own* (New York: Harper & Brothers, 1958), 83.
4. Humphrey, *Human Rights and the United Nations*, 56.
5. Qtd. in Mary Ann Glendon, *A World Made New: Eleanor Roosevelt and the Universal Declaration of Human Rights* (New York: Random House, 2001), 151.
6. Glendon, *A World Made New*, 152.
7. UN General Assembly, A/C.3/SR.102, 142.
8. Qtd. in Glendon, *A World Made New*, 12.
9. Glendon, *A World Made New*, 12.
10. See Costas Douzinas, *Human Rights and Empire: The Political Philosophy of Cosmopolitanism* (New York: Routledge, 2007); Samuel Moyn, *The Last Utopia: Human Rights in History* (Cambridge, MA: Harvard University Press, 2010); Brian Simpson, *Human Rights and the End of Empire: Britain and the Genesis of the European Convention* (Oxford: Oxford University Press, 2004); Lydia H. Liu, "Shadows of Universalism: The Untold Story of Human Rights Around 1948," *Critical Inquiry* 40 (2014): 385–417.
11. Inderpal Grewal, *Transnational America: Feminisms, Diasporas, Neoliberalisms* (Durham, NC: Duke University Press, 2005), 122. See also James Ferguson and Akhil Gupta, "Spatializing States: Toward an Ethnography of Neoliberal Governmentality," *American Ethnologist* 29, no. 4 (2002): 981–1002.
12. Michel Foucault, "Governmentality," in *The Foucault Effect: Studies in Governmentality*, ed. Graham Burchell, Colin Gordo, and Peter Miller (Chicago: University of Chicago Press, 1991), 95.
13. For more on Nardal, see T. Denean Sharpley-Whiting, *Negritude Women* (Minneapolis: University of Minnesota Press, 2002); T. Denean Sharpley-Whiting, "On Race, Rights, and Women," in *Beyond Negritude: Essays from Woman in the City*, trans. T. Denean Sharpley-Whiting (Albany: SUNY Press, 2009): 1–17; Brent Hayes Edwards, *The Practice of Diaspora* (Cambridge, MA: Harvard University Press, 2003); Jennifer Wilks, *Race, Gender, and Comparative Black Modernism: Suzanne Lascascade, Marita Bonner, Suzanne Césaire, Dorothy West* (Baton Rouge: Louisiana State University Press, 2008).
14. UN General Assembly, 2nd Session, "Information from Non-Self-Governing Territories, Information Transmitted Under Article 73 (e) of the Charter: Report of the Ad Hoc Committee," September 18, 1947 (A/385), 1.
15. UN General Assembly, "Information from Non-Self-Governing Territories," 5.
16. Report of the Special Committee for Non-Self-Governing Territories, *Yearbook of the United Nations* (1947), 710–11.
17. Report of the Special Committee for Non-Self-Governing Territories, *Yearbook*, 716.
18. Hannah Arendt, *Eichmann in Jerusalem: A Report on the Banality of Evil* (New York: Penguin, 1963), 289.
19. See Lauren Berlant and Michael Warner, who have situated queer culture as a "world-making project, where world, like public, differs from community or group because it necessarily includes more people than can be identified, more spaces than can be

mapped beyond a few reference points, modes of feeling that can be learned rather than experienced by birthright." Lauren Berlant and Michael Warner, "Sex in Public," in *Publics and Counterpublics* (New York: Zone, 2005), 198. For a more extended discussion of world making as poesis in this same volume, see Michael Warner, "Publics and Counterpublics," 114–24. For world making as performance, see José Esteban Muñoz, *Disidentifications: Queers of Color and the Performance of Politics* (Durham, NC: Duke University Press, 2013).

20. "Eleven American Colleges Stage Model League Assembly at Syracuse," *League of Nations News*, June 1927, 22.
21. See Stephanie A. Limoncelli, *The Politics of Trafficking: The First International Movement to Combat the Sexual Exploitation of Women* (Stanford, CA: Stanford University Press, 2010); Nitza Berkovitch, *From Motherhood to Citizenship: Women's Rights and International Organizations* (Baltimore, MD: John Hopkins University Press, 1999).
22. "1910 International Convention for the Suppression of the 'White Slave Traffic,'" League of Nations, *Treaty Series*, 8:278, italics mine. The text of the 1947 protocol cites the 1904 and 1910 Conventions. Full text and status of subsequent antitrafficking legislation can be found in chapter 7 of *Multilateral Treaties Deposited with the Secretary General*, https://treaties.un.org/pages/CTCTreaties.aspx?id=7&subid=A&clang=_en.
23. Bascom Johnson, "International Traffic in Women and Children," *Journal of Social Hygiene* 14 (February 1928): 68–69.
24. For the ways antiprostitution legislation has been used to criminalize sexual relations across the color line, see Jessica R. Pliley, *Policing Sexuality: The Mann Act and the Making of the FBI* (Cambridge, MA: Harvard University Press, 2014).
25. UN General Assembly, 2nd Session, 96th Plenary Meeting, October 20, 1947 (A/PV.96), 349, verbatim record.
26. UN General Assembly, A/PV.96, 350.
27. UN General Assembly, 2nd Session, 97th Plenary Meeting, October 20, 1947 (A/PV.97), 350–51, verbatim record.
28. Karl Marx, "On the Jewish Question," in *Early Political Writings* (Cambridge: Cambridge University Press, 1994), 28–56.
29. Gladys P. Graham, "Know Your United Nations," *New York Age*, January 11, 1947, 7.
30. Paulette Nardal, "United Nations," *La Femme dans la Cité*, January 1947, 2. Translation Sharpley-Whiting.
31. Nardal, "United Nations," 2.
32. *La Femme dans la Cité*, July 1951, 7. All translations mine unless otherwise noted.
33. Saba Mahmood, *Politics of Piety: The Islamic Revival and the Feminist Subject* (Princeton, NJ: Princeton University Press, 2005), 8.
34. "Notre Congrès," *La Femme dans la Cité*, March 1945, 5.
35. "Mais voilà qu'à l'aube des temps nouveaux la femme française est appelée à la vie politique. Quel sera son domaine? Où s'exercera son activité?" Y., "Les Femmes et la Paix," *La Femme dans la Cité*, March 1945, 3.
36. "Causerie de Mme Danel," *La Femme dans la Cité*, March 1945, 2.

37. "Notre programme est vaste, nous n'avons pas l'intention de le réaliser intégralement et rapidement, nous ne possédons pas de baguettes de fée" "Causerie de Mlle Etifier," *La Femme dans la Cité*, March 1945, 5.
38. "Causerie de Mlle Etifier," 5.
39. Aimé Césaire and René Ménil, "Introduction au Folklore Martiniquais," *Tropiques*, January 1942, 8.
40. Maguy, "Nélissa et les trois monstres," *La Femme dans la Cité*, July 1948, 4; Creole in bold; French rendering of Creole phrase in italics.
41. Frantz Fanon, *Black Skin, White Masks*, trans. Richard Philox (New York: Grove, 2008), 4, 5.
42. Here is one version of what Sylvia Wynter has called "being human as praxis," or what I understand as an embodied revision of the inherited legal categories of colonial Enlightenment. However, Wynter positions humanism as a prior ground that might be reanimated: Sylvia Wynter, "Unsettling the Coloniality of Being/Power/Truth/Freedom: Towards the Human, After Man, Its Overrepresentation—an Argument," *CR: The New Centennial Review* 3, no. 3 (2003): 257–337. Also see Alexander G. Weheliye, *Habeas Viscus: Racializing Assemblages, Biopolitics, and Black Feminist Theories of the Human* (Durham, NC: Duke University Press, 2014); Katherine McKittridge, *Demonic Grounds: Black Women and the Cartographies of Struggle* (Minneapolis: University of Minnesota Press, 2006).
43. For a wider discussion of this point, see Achilles Mbembe, "The Power of the Archive and its Limits," trans. Judith Inggs, in *Refiguring the Archive*, ed. Carolyn Hamilton (London: Kluwer, 2002): 19–26.
44. Moyn, *The Last Utopia*; Stephen Hopgood, *The Endtimes of Human Rights* (Ithaca, NY: Cornell University Press, 2013); Liu, "Shadows of Universalism," 385–86.
45. See Gary Wilder, *Freedom Time: Négritude, Decolonialization, and the Future of the World* (Durham, NC: Duke University Press, 2014), for an excellent reconsideration of anticolonial politics beyond the question of national self-determination.

Epilogue. Social Reproduction and the Midcentury Witch: Leonora Carrington in Mexico

1. Silvia Federici, *Caliban and the Witch: Women, the Body, and Primitive Accumulation* (New York: Autonomedia, 2004), 17.
2. Federici, *Caliban and the Witch*, 17.
3. Samuel Moyn, *The Last Utopia: Human Rights in History* (Cambridge, MA: Belknap, 2010), 121.
4. Stephen Lee, *The Ethnic Avant-Garde: Minority Cultures and World Revolution* (New York: Columbia University Press, 2015), 185.
5. Lee, *The Ethnic Avant-Garde*, 198.
6. Paul De Angelis, "Interview with Leonora Carrington," in *Leonora Carrington: The Mexican Years* (San Francisco, CA: The Mexican Museum, 1991), 40.

7. Angelis, "Interview with Leonora Carrington," 42.
8. See especially Teresa Arq, "Mirrors of the Marvellous: Leonora Carrington and Remedios Varo," in *Surreal Friends: Leonora Carrington, Remedios Varo, and Kati Horna* (Surrey: Lund Humphries, 2010), 98–115.
9. Octavio Paz, "Dos Transeúntes: Leonora y Remedios," in *Octavio Paz: Los privilegios de la vista* (Mexico: Centro Cultural Arte Contemporaneo, 1990), 338.
10. Jonathan Eburne, "Leonora Carrington and the Esoteric Avant-Garde," in *Leonora Carrington and the International Avant-Garde*, ed. Jonathan P. Eburne and Catriona McAra (Manchester: Manchester University Press, 2017), 142.
11. Susan L. Aberth, *Leonora Carrington: Surrealism, Alchemy, and Art* (Burlington, VT: Lund Humphries, 2004), 57–96. See also Susan Rubin Suleiman's discussion of narrative frames within frames as a version of the carnivalesque in *Subversive Intent: Gender, Politics, and the Avant-Garde* (Cambridge, MA: Harvard University Press, 1990), 169–79.
12. Nan Mulder, "Leonora Carrington in Mexico," *Alba* 1, no. 6 (1991–1992): 6.
13. Janet Lyon, "Carrington's Sensorium," in *Leonora Carrington and the International Avant-Garde*, ed. Jonathan P. Eburne and Catriona McAra (Manchester: Manchester University Press, 2017), 163.
14. Leonora Carrington, *The Hearing Trumpet* (London: Penguin, 2005), 66. Hereafter quoted in text.
15. Alejo Carpentier, "On the Marvelous Real in America" (1949), trans. Tanya Huntington and Lois Parkinson Zamora, in *Magical Realism: Theory, History, Community*, ed. Lois Parkinson Zamora and Wendy B. Faris (Durham, NC: Duke University Press, 1995), 84. Alejo Carpentier, "De lo real maravilloso americano," in *Tientos y diferencias* (Montevideo: Arca, 1967), 96–112. Hereafter quoted in text.
16. See J. Michael Dash, "Marvelous Realism—The Way Out of Négritude," *Caribbean Studies* 12, no. 4 (1974): 57–70; and Stephen Slemon, "Magic Realism as Postcolonial Discourse," in *Magical Realism: Theory, History, Community*, ed. Lois Parkinson Zamora and Wendy B. Faris (Durham, NC: Duke University Press, 1995), 407–26.
17. Leonora Carrington, in Marie-Pierre Colle, *Latin American Artists in Their Studios* (New York: Vendome, 1994), 84.
18. Eburne, "Leonora Carrington and the Esoteric Avant-Garde," 152.
19. Leonora Carrington, *Leonora Carrington: A Retrospective Exhibition*, exhibition catalogue (New York: Center for Inter-American Relations, 1976).
20. Diane di Prima, *Revolutionary Letters* (San Francisco: City Lights, 1968), 32.
21. Di Prima, *Revolutionary Letters*.

Bibliography

Manuscript Sources and Archives

Beinecke Rare Book and Manuscript Library (New Haven)
Claude Cahun and Suzanne Malherbe Papers
Carl Van Vechten Papers
Mabel Dodge Luhan Papers

Bibliothèque nationale de France (Paris)
Le dossier de la Commune Devant les Counseils de Guerre (Paris: Librairie des Bibliophiles, 1871).
Enquête parlementaire sur l'insurrection du 18 Mars 1871 (Paris: Librairie Législative, 1872).
Insurrection du Sud, Counseil de guerre, Martinique, second series.
de Loisne, Ch. Menche. Insurrection de la Martinique (Paris: E. Dentu, 1871).

Bundesarchiv (Lichterfelde-West, Berlin)
Allgemeines Schriftwechsel 1921–1922

International Institute of Social History (Amsterdam)
Emma Goldman Papers

Jersey Heritage Trust Archives
Claude Cahun Collection

Musée Carnavalet (Paris)
Collection Liesville
Histoire de Paris

The National Archives (London)
Government Papers (1912–1914)
Images from the National Archives Exhibition, 1904–1914
Wallace Collection
Women in the National Archives Collection

Race and Slavery Petitions Project (UNC Greensboro)
Race, Slavery, and Free Blacks, Series II: Petitions to Southern County Courts Part A

United Nations Archives (New York)
Meeting Records
Treaty Collection

Victoria and Albert Museum (London)
Department of Prints and Drawings

Newspapers, Journals, and Little Magazines

Birth Control Review (New York)
Blätter für Menschenrect (Berlin)
Chicago Defender
The Crisis: A Record of the Darker Races (New York)
L'Encyclopédie Contemporaine Illustrée (Paris)
La Femme dans la Cité (Fort-de-France, Martinique)
Le Figaro (Paris)
The Freewoman: A Weekly Feminist Review (London)
Jersey Evening Post (Jersey Island)
Le Journal (Paris)
League of Nations News (New York)
Lucifer the Lightbearer (Chicago)
The Masses (New York)
Mother Earth (New York)
Die Neue Zeit (Stuttgart)
New York Age
New York Herald Tribune
New York Times
L'Ouvirier Syndiqué (Paris)
Jahrbuch für sexuelle Zwischenstufen (Leipzig)
St. James Gazette (London)
La Semaine Vétérinaire (Paris)
The Suffragette (London)

Le Temps (Paris)
Tropiques (Fort-de-France, Martinique)
The Vote (London)
Votes for Women (London)
Woman Rebel (New York)
Worker's Dreadnought (London)
Yearbook of the United Nations

Books and Journals

Aberth, Susan L. *Leonora Carrington: Surrealism, Alchemy, and Art*. Burlington, VT: Lund Humphries, 2004.

Adamson, Walter L. *Avant-Garde Florence: From Modernism to Fascism*. Cambridge, MA: Harvard University Press, 1993.

Ades, Dawn. "Surrealism and the Representation of the Female Subject in Mexico and Postwar Paris." In *Mirror Images: Women, Surrealism, and Self-Representation*, 106–27. Cambridge, MA: MIT Press, 1998.

Ades, Dawn, Rosalind Krauss, and Jane Livingston, eds. *L'Amour Fou: Photography and Surrealism*. New York: Abbeville, 1985.

Ahmed, Sara. *The Promise of Happiness*. Durham, NC: Duke University Press, 2010.

Anderson, Benedict. *Imagined Communities: Reflections on the Origin and Spread of Nationalism*. London: Verso, 2016.

Anderson, Perry. *Origins of Postmodernity*. Verso: London, 1998.

Angelis, Paul. "Interview with Leonora Carrington." In *Leonora Carrington: The Mexican Years*. San Francisco, CA: The Mexican Museum, 1991.

Anghie, Anthony. *Imperialism, Sovereignty, and the Making of International Law*. Cambridge: Cambridge University Press, 2005.

Anker, Elizabeth. *Fictions of Dignity: Embodying Human Rights in World Literature*. Ithaca, NY: Cornell University Press, 2012.

Arendt, Hannah. *Eichmann in Jerusalem: A Report on the Banality of Evil*. New York: Penguin, 1963.

——. *The Human Condition*. Chicago: University of Chicago Press, 1958.

Arnold, A. James. "The Gendering of Créolité: The Erotics of Colonialism." In *Penser la creolité*, ed. Maryse Condé and Madeleine Cottenet-Hage, 21–40. Paris: Karthala, 1995.

Arq, Teresa. "Mirrors of the Marvellous: Leonora Carrington and Remedios Varo." In *Surreal Friends: Leonora Carrington, Remedios Varo, and Kati Horna*, 98–115. Surrey: Lund Humphries, 2010.

Arruzza, Cinzia. *Dangerous Liaisons: The Marriages and Divorces of Marxism and Feminism*. London: Merlin, 2013.

Asad, Talal. *Formations of the Secular: Christianity, Islam, Modernity*. Stanford, CA: Stanford University Press, 2003.

Atkinson, Diane. *Rise Up Women! The Remarkable Lives of the Suffragettes*. London: Bloomsbury, 2018.

Attewell, Nadine. *Better Britons: Reproduction, National Identity, and the Afterlife of Empire.* Toronto: University of Toronto Press, 2014.

Baer, Ben Conisbee. *Indigenous Vanguards: Education, National Liberation, and the Limits of Modernism.* New York: Columbia University Press, 2019.

Bakhtin, Mikhail M. *Speech Genres and Other Late Essays.* Austin: University of Texas Press, 1986.

Bard, Christine, and Jean-Louis Robert, "The French Communist Party and Women, 1920–1939." Trans. Nicole Dombrowski. In *Women and Socialism, Socialism and Women: Europe Between the Two World Wars*, ed. Helmut Gruber and Pamela Graves. New York: Berghahn, 1998.

Barthes, Roland. *Camera Lucida: Reflections on Photography.* Trans. Richard Howard. New York: Farrar, Straus & Giroux, 2000.

Bassiouni, M. Cherif. *Crimes Against Humanity in International Criminal Law.* London: Kluwer Law International, 1999.

Beachy, Robert. *Gay Berlin: Birthplace of a Modern Identity.* New York: Vintage, 2014.

Benadusi, Lorenzo. *The Enemy of the New Man: Homosexuality in Fascist Italy.* Trans. Suzanne Dingee and Jennifer Pudney. Madison: University of Wisconsin Press, 2012.

Benjamin, Walter. *Selected Writings*, vol. 2: *1931–1934*. Trans. Rodney Livingstone. Cambridge, MA: Harvard University Press, 1999.

Benstock, Shari. *Women of the Left Bank: Paris, 1900–1940.* Austin: University of Texas Press, 1986.

Berkovitch, Nina. *From Motherhood to Citizenship: Women's Rights and International Organizations.* Baltimore, MD: John Hopkins University Press, 1999.

Berlant, Lauren. *The Female Complaint: The Unfinished Business of Sentimentality in American Culture.* Durham, NC: Duke University Press, 2008.

———. *The Queen of America Goes to Washington City: Essays on Sex and Citizenship.* Durham, NC: Duke University Press, 1997.

Berlant, Lauren, and Michael Warner. "Sex in Public." In Michael Warner, *Publics and Counterpublics*, 187–208. New York: Zone, 2005.

Beveridge, Ray. *Mein Leben für Euch! Erinnerungen an Glanzvolle und Bewegte Jahre.* Berlin: Deutschen Verlag, 1948.

Bhattacharya, Tithi, ed. *Social Reproduction Theory.* London: Pluto, 2017.

Biro, Matthew. *The Dada Cyborg: Visions of the New Human in Weimar Berlin.* Minneapolis: University of Minnesota Press, 2009.

Black, Kelli M. "Creating Infanticide: A Comparative Study of Early Modern British Servant and Antebellum American Slave Women." MA thesis, San Diego State University, 2003.

Brandt, Marion. "Editorische Erläuterungen und Worterklärungen." In Til Brugman, *Das vertippte Zebra: Lyrik und Prosa*, ed. Marion Brandt. Berlin: Hoffmann, 1995.

Breton, André. *Arcanum 17.* Trans. Zack Rogow. Los Angeles: Sun & Moon, 1994.

———. *Nadja.* Paris: Gallimard, 2007.

———. *Nadja.* Trans. Richard Howard. New York: Grove, 1960.

Breton, André, and Diego Rivera [Léon Trotsky]. "Manifesto for an Independent Revolutionary Art, 1938." In *Manifesto: A Century of Isms*, ed. Mary Ann Caws, 472–76. Lincoln: University of Nebraska Press, 2001.
Brown, Wendy. *States of Injury: Power and Freedom in Late Modernity*. Princeton, NJ: Princeton University Press, 1995.
Brugman, Til. *Das vertippte Zebra: Lyrik und Prosa*. Ed. Marion Brandt. Berlin: Hoffmann, 1995.
Bunch, Charlotte. "Women's Rights as Human Rights: Toward a Re-Vision of Human Rights." *Human Rights Quarterly* (1990): 486–98.
Bürger, Peter. *Theory of the Avant-Garde*. Trans. Michael Shaw. Minneapolis: University of Minnesota Press, 1984.
Burstein, Jessica. *Cold Modernism: Literature, Fashion, Art*. University Park: Pennsylvania State University Press, 2012.
Burton, Antoinette. *Burdens of History: Feminists, Indian Women, and Imperial Culture*. Chapel Hill: University of North Carolina Press, 1994.
———. "'States of Injury': Josephine Butler on Slavery, Citizenship, and the Boer War." In *Women's Suffrage in the British Empire: Citizenship, Nation, and Race*, ed. Christopher Fletcher, Laura E. Nym Mayhall, and Philippa Levine, 18–32. London: Routledge, 2000.
Bush, Barbara. *Slave Women in Caribbean Society, 1650–1838*. Bloomington: Indiana University Press, 1990.
Butler, Judith. "Against Proper Objects." *Differences* 6, no. 2–3 (1994): 1–26.
———. *Bodies That Matter: On the Discursive Limits of "Sex."* New York: Routledge, 1993.
———. *Notes Towards a Performative Theory of Assembly*. Cambridge, MA: Harvard University Press, 2018.
Bullard, Alice. *Exile to Paradise: Savagery and Civilization in Paris and the South Pacific, 1790–1900*. Stanford, CA: Stanford University Press, 2000.
Cahun, Claude. *Disavowals*. Trans. Susan de Muth. Cambridge: MA: MIT University Press, 2007.
———. *Écrits*. Ed. François Leperlier. Paris: Jean-Michel Place, 1992.
———. "La 'Salome' d'Oscar Wilde, le Procès Billing et les 47.000 Pervertis du 'Livre Noire.'" *Mercure de France* 481 (July 1, 1918).
———. "Les Jeux uraniens." Unpublished ms., c. 1914. Jersey Heritage Trust. JHT Archives., St. Helier, Channel Island of Jersey, 34.
Campt, Tina. *Image Matters: Archive, Photography, and the African Diaspora in Europe*. Durham, NC: Duke University Press, 2012.
———. *Other Germans: Black Germans and the Politics of Race, Gender, and Memory in the Third Reich*. Ann Arbor: University of Michigan Press, 2005.
Carpentier, Alejo. "de lo real maravilloso americano." In *Tientos y diferencias*, 96–112. Montevideo: Arca, 1967.
———. "On the Marvelous Real in America (1949)." Trans. Tanya Huntington and Lois Parkinson Zamora. In *Magical Realism: Theory, History, Community*, ed. Lois Parkinson Zamora and Wendy B. Faris, 75–88. Durham, NC: Duke University Press, 1995.

Carrington, Leonora. *The Hearing Trumpet*. London: Penguin, 2005.
———. *Leonora Carrington: A Retrospective Exhibition*. Exhibition catalogue. New York: Center for Inter-American Relations, 1976.
de Certeau, Michel. *The Practice of Everyday Life*. Trans. Steven Rendall. Berkeley: University of California Press, 1984.
Césaire, Aimé, and René Ménil. "Introduction au Folklore Martiniquais." *Tropiques*, January 1942, 8.
Césaire, Ina. "Fire's Daughters." Trans. Judith Miller. In *New French Language Plays*. New York: Ubu Repertory Theater Publications, 1994.
———. *La faim, la ruse, la révolte: Essai d'analyse anthropologique du conte antillais*. Fort de France, Martinique: Service des Musées Régionaux, n.d.
———. *Rosanie Soleil et autres textes dramatiques*. Paris: Editions Karthala, 2011.
Chadwick, Whitney. *Farewell to the Muse: Love, War, and the Women of Surrealism*. London: Thames & Hudson, 2017.
Charlesworth, Hilary, Christine Chinkin, and Shelley Wright. "Feminist Approaches to International Law." *American Journal of International Law* 85, no. 4 (1991): 613–45.
Cheng, Ann Anlin. *Second Skin: Josephine Baker and the Modern Surface*. Oxford: Oxford University Press, 2011.
Chesler, Ellen. *Woman of Valor: Margaret Sanger and the Birth Control Movement in America*. New York: Simon & Schuster, 1992.
Clark, T. J. *Farewell to an Idea: Episodes in a History of Modernism*. Berkeley: University of California Press, 1999.
Clifford, James. *The Predicament of Culture: Twentieth-Century Ethnography, Literature, and Art*. London: Harvard University Press, 1988.
Cline, Catherine Ann. *E. D. Morel: The Strategies of Protest*. Belfast: Blackstaff, 1980.
Collar, Peter. *Propaganda War in the Rhineland: Weimar Germany, Race, and Occupation After World War I*. London: I. B. Tauris, 2013.
Colle, Marie-Pierre. *Latin American Artists in their Studios*. Intro. Carlos Fuentes. New York: Vendome, 1994.
Collette. *The Pure and the Impure*. Trans. Herma Briffault. New York: Farrar, Straus & Giroux, 2000.
Colored Troops in the French Army: A Report from the Department of State Relating to the Colored Troops in the French Army and the Number of French Colonial Troops in the Occupied Territory. 66th Congress. Washington: Government Printing Office, 1921.
Cocks, F. Seymour. *E. D. Morel: The Man and His Work*. London: George Allen, 1920.
Cohler, Deborah. *Citizen, Invert, Queer: Lesbianism and War in Early Twentieth-Century Britain*. Minneapolis: University of Minnesota Press, 2010.
Conley, Katherine. *Surrealist Ghostliness*. Lincoln: University of Nebraska Press, 2013.
Cova, Ann. *Maternité et droits des femmes en France: XIXe–XXe siècles*. Paris: Economica, 1997.
Craig, Layne Parish. *When Sex Changed: Birth Control Politics and Literature Between the World Wars*. New Brunswick, NJ: Rutgers University Press, 2013.

Cvetkovich, Ann. *An Archive of Feelings: Trauma, Sexuality, and Lesbian Public Cultures.* Durham, NC: Duke University Press, 2003.
Dash, J. Michael. "Marvelous Realism—The Way Out of Négritude." *Caribbean Studies* 12, no. 4 (1974): 57–70.
Dawes, James. *The Novel of Human Rights.* Cambridge, MA: Harvard University Press, 2018.
———. *That the World May Know: Declaring Witness to Atrocity.* Cambridge, MA: Harvard University Press, 2007.
Dean, Carolyn. "Claude Cahun's Double." *Yale French Studies* 90 (1996): 71–92.
Delap, Lucy. *The Feminist Avant-Garde: Transatlantic Encounters of the Early Twentieth Century.* Cambridge: Cambridge University Press, 2007.
Dienel, Christine. *Kinderzahl und Staatsräson. Empfängnisverhütung und Bevölkerungspolitik in Deutschland und Frankreich bis 1918.* Münster, 1995.
Doan, Laura. *Fashioning Sapphism: The Origins of a Modern English Lesbian Culture.* New York: Columbia University Press, 2001.
Doherty, Brigid. "'See: We Are All Neurasthenics!' or, the Trauma of Dada Montage." *Critical Inquiry* 24, no. 1 (1997): 82–132.
Douzinas, Costas. *The End of Human Rights.* Portland, OR: Hart, 2000.
———. *Human Rights and Empire: The Political Philosophy of Cosmopolitanism.* New York: Routledge, 2007.
Doy, Gen. *Claude Cahun: A Sensual Politics of Photography.* London: I. B. Tauris, 2007.
Doyle, Laura. *Freedom's Empire: Race and the Rise of the Novel in Atlantic Modernity.* Durham, NC: Duke University Press, 2007.
Dupont, Léonce. *La Commune et ses auxiliaires devant la justice.* Paris: Didier, 1871.
Eburne, Jonathan. "Leonora Carrington and the Esoteric Avant-Garde." In *Leonora Carrington and the International Avant-Garde,* ed. Jonathan P. Eburne and Catriona McAra. Manchester: Manchester University Press, 2017.
Edelson, Lee. *No Future: Queer Theory and the Death Drive.* Durham, NC: Duke University Press, 2004.
Edwards, Brent Hayes. *The Practice of Diaspora: Literature, Translation, and the Rise of Black Internationalism.* Cambridge, MA: Harvard University Press, 2003.
Eichner, Carolyn J. *Surmounting the Barricades: Women in the Paris Commune.* Bloomington: Indiana University Press, 2004.
English, Daylanne. *Unnatural Selections: Eugenics in American Modernism and the Harlem Renaissance.* Chapel Hill: University of North Carolina Press, 2004.
Endnotes I: Preliminary Materials for a Balance Sheet of the Twentieth Century. 2008. https://endnotes.org.uk/issues/1.
Esmeir, Samira. *Juridical Humanity: A Colonial History.* Stanford, CA: Stanford University Press, 2012.
Faderman, Lillian. *Odd Girls and Twilight Lovers: A History of Lesbian Life in Twentieth-Century America.* New York: Columbia University Press, 2012.
Fanon, Frantz. *Black Skin, White Masks.* Trans. Richard Philox. New York: Grove, 2008.
Federici, Silvia. *Caliban and the Witch: Women, the Body, and Primitive Accumulation.* New York: Autonomedia, 2004.

———. "Introduction: Wages for Housework in Historical Perspective." In *Wages for Housework: The New York Committee, 1972–1977: History Theory Documents*, ed. Silvia Federici and Arlen Austin, 12–28. Brooklyn: Autonomedia, 2017.

———. *Revolution at Point Zero: Housework, Reproduction, and Feminist Struggle*. Oakland: PM, 2012.

Felski, Rita. *Beyond Feminist Aesthetics: Feminist Literature and Social Change*. Cambridge, MA: Harvard University Press, 1989.

Ferguson, Roderick. *Aberrations in Black: Towards a Queer of Color Critique*. Minneapolis: University of Minnesota Press, 2003.

Fernández, Joaquín Alcaide. "*Hostes humani generis*: Pirates, Slavers, and Other Criminals." In *Oxford Handbook of the History of International Law*, ed. Bardo Fassbender and Ann Peters. Oxford: Oxford University Press, 2012.

Flynn, Elizabeth Gurley. *Sabotage: The Conscious Withdrawal of the Workers' Efficiency*. Cleveland, OH: IWW Publishing Bureau, 1925.

Follain, Claire. "Lucy Schwob and Suzanne Malherbe-*Résistantes*." In *Don't Kiss Me: The Art of Claude Cahun and Marcel Moore*, ed. Louise Downie, 83–95. London: Jersey Heritage Trust, 2006.

Fortunati, Leopolda. *The Arcane of Reproduction: Housework, Prostitution, Labor, and Capital*. New York: Autonomedia, 1996.

Foster, Hal. *The Return of the Real: The Avant-Garde at the End of the Century*. Cambridge, MA: MIT Press, 1996.

Foucault, Michel. *The Archeology of Knowledge: And the Discourse on Language*. New York: Vintage, 1982.

———. "Governmentality." In *The Foucault Effect: Studies in Governmentality*, ed. Graham Burchell, Colin Gordo, and Peter Miller. Chicago: University of Chicago Press, 1991.

Fox-Genovese, Elizabeth. "Strategies of Resistance: Focus on Slave Women in the United States." In *In Resistance: Studies in African, Caribbean, and Afro-American History*, ed. Gary Y. Okihiro. Amherst: University of Massachusetts Press, 1986.

Fried, Michael. *Why Photography Matters as Art as Never Before*. New Haven, CT: Yale University Press, 2008.

Gandhi, Leela. *Affective Communities: Anticolonial Thought, Fin-de-Siècle Radicalism, and the Politics of Friendship*. Durham, NC: Duke University Press, 2006.

Garrity, Jane. *Step-Daughters of England: British Women Modernists and the National Imaginary*. Manchester: Manchester University Press, 2003.

"Gegen Den Gebärkstreik: Berichte über zwei Volksversammlungen in Berlin." In *Frauenemanzipation und Sozialdemokratie*, ed. Meinz Niggemann. Frankfurt am Main: Fischer Taschenbuch Verlag, 1981.

Gilmore, Ruthie Wilson. *Golden Gulag: Prisons, Surplus, Crisis, and Opposition in Globalizing California*. Berkeley: University of California Press, 2007.

Gilroy, Paul. *The Black Atlantic: Modernity and Double Consciousness*. Cambridge, MA: Harvard University Press, 1995.

Glendon, Mary Ann. *A World Made New: Eleanor Roosevelt and the Universal Declaration of Human Rights*. New York: Random House, 2001.

Gordon, Linda. *The Moral Property of Women: A History of Birth Control Politics in America*. Champaign: University of Illinois Press, 2007.

Graham, Gladys P. "Know Your United Nations." *New York Age*, January 11, 1947, 7.

Grant, Kevin. "British Suffragettes and the Russian Method of Hunger Strike." *Comparative Studies in Society and History* 53, no. 1 (2011): 113–43.

Grau, Günter. *Hidden Holocaust? Gay and Lesbian Persecution in Germany, 1933–45*. Trans. Claudia Schoppmann. Chicago: Fitzroy Dearborn, 1995.

Green, Barbara. *Spectacular Confessions: Autobiography, Performative Activism, and the Sites of Suffrage, 1905–1938*. New York: St. Martin's, 1997.

Grewal, Inderpal. *Transnational America: Feminisms, Diasporas, Neoliberalisms*. Durham, NC: Duke University Press, 2005.

Grimké, Angelina Weld. *Selected Works*. Ed. Carolivia Herron. Oxford: Oxford University Press, 1991.

Gruber, Helmut. "French Women in the Crossfire of Class, Sex, Maternity, and Citizenship." In *Women and Socialism, Socialism and Women: Europe Between the Two World Wars*, ed. Helmut Gruber and Pamela Graves, 279–320. New York: Berghahn, 1998.

Gullace, Nicoletta F. *The Blood of Our Sons: Men, Women, and the Renegotiation of British Citizenship During the Great War*. New York: Palgrave, 2002.

Gullickson, Gay L. *Unruly Women of Paris: Images of the Commune*. Ithaca, NY: Cornell University Press, 1996.

Haakensen, Thomas O. "Grotesque Visions: Art, Science, and Visual Culture in Early-Twentieth-Century Germany." PhD diss., University of Minnesota, 2006.

Habermas, Jürgen. *The Structural Transformation of the Public Sphere: An Inquiry Into a Category of Bourgeois Society*. Trans. Thomas Burger. Cambridge, MA: MIT Press, 1991.

Hacking, Ian. "Making Up People." *London Review of Books* 28, no. 16 (2006): 23–26.

Hague Convention IV (October 18, 1907), "Convention Respecting the Laws and Customs of War on Land." http://avalon.law.yale.edu/20th_century/hague04.asp.

Hartman, Saidiya. *Scenes of Subjection: Terror, Slavery, and Self-Making in Nineteenth-Century America*. New York: Oxford University Press, 1997.

Higashida, Cheryl. *Black Internationalist Feminism: Women Writers on the Black Left, 1945–1995*. Champaign: University of Illinois Press, 2013.

Higginbotham Jr., A. Leon. "Race, Sex, Education, and Missouri Jurisprudence: *Shelley v. Kraemer* in a Historical Perspective." *Washington University Law Review* 67 (1989): 694–96.

Hirschfeld, Magnus. *Homosexuality in Men and Women*. Trans. Michael Lombardi-Nash. New York: Prometheus, 2000.

Ho, Janice. *Nation and Citizenship in the Twentieth-Century British Novel*. Cambridge: Cambridge University Press, 2015.

Höch, Hannah. *Album*. Berlin: Hatje Cantz, 2004.

———. "Fantastische Kunst." In *Fantasten-Ausstellung*. Berlin: Galerie Rosen, 1946.

———. "Interview." In *Hannah Höch: Collages, peintures, aquarelles, gouaches, dessins*, ed. Suzanne Pagé et al. Paris: Musée d'Art Moderne de la Ville de Paris; Berlin: Nationalgalerie Berlin Staatlich Musseen Preussischer Kulturbesitz, 1976.

———. *Picture Book*. Trans. Brian Currid. Berlin: Green Box Kunst Editionnen, 2010.
Hollier, Denis. "Surrealist Precipitates: Shadows Don't Cast Shadows." Trans. Rosalind Krauss. *October* 69 (1994): 110–32.
Hong, Cathy Park. "Delusions of Whiteness in the Avant-Garde." *Lana Turner* 7 (2014).
Hong, Grace. *The Ruptures of American Capital: Women of Color Feminism and the Cultures of Immigrant Labor*. Minneapolis: University of Minnesota Press, 2006.
Hopgood, Stephen. *The Endtimes of Human Rights*. Ithaca, NY: Cornell University Press, 2013.
Huelsenbeck, Richard. "Dada Lives!" In *Dada Painters and Poets: An Anthology*, ed. Robert Motherwell, 277–82. Cambridge, MA: Harvard University Press, 1979.
Hugnet, Georges. "The Dada Spirit in Painting." In *Dada Painters and Poets: An Anthology*, ed. Robert Motherwell, 123–196. Cambridge, MA: Harvard University Press, 1979.
———. *Dictionnaire du dadaïsme, 1916–1922*. Paris: Jean-Claude Simoën, 1976.
Hull, Gloria T. *Color, Sex, and Poetry: Three Women Writers of the Harlem Renaissance*. Bloomington: Indiana University Press, 1987.
Humphrey, John P. *Human Rights and the United Nations: A Great Adventure*. Dobbs Ferry, NY: Transnational Publishers, 1984.
Hunt, Lynn. *Inventing Human Rights: A History*. New York: Norton, 2008.
Huot, Marie. *Mal de Vivre*. Paris: Generation Consciente, 1909.
Ishay, Micheline R. *The History of Human Rights: From Ancient Times to the Globalization Era*. Berkeley: University of California Press, 2008.
James, Henry. *The Bostonians*. Ed. R. D. Gooder. Oxford: Oxford University Press, 1984.
Jameson, Fredric. *The Political Unconscious: Narrative as a Socially Symbolic Act*. Ithaca, NY: Cornell University Press, 1982.
Johnson, Bascom. "International Traffic in Women and Children." *Journal of Social Hygiene* 14 (February 1928): 68–69.
Johnson, Michael P. "Smothered Slave Infants: Were Slave Mothers at Fault?" *Journal of Southern History* 47 (November 1981): 493–520.
Johnson, Paul. *Homosexuality and the European Court of Human Rights*. New York: Routledge, 2012.
Jütte, Robert. *Contraception: A History*. Trans. Vicky Russell. Cambridge: Polity, 2008.
Kenney, Annie. *Memories of a Militant*. London: Edward Arnold, 1924.
Kent, Susan Kingsley. *Sex and Suffrage in Britain, 1860–1914*. Princeton, NJ: Princeton University Press, 1987.
Kettle, Michael. *Salome's Last Veil: The Libel Case of the Century*. London: Granada, 1977.
Kline, Katy. "Claude Cahun and Cindy Sherman." In *Mirror Images: Women, Surrealism, and Self-Representation*, 66–81. Cambridge, MA: MIT University Press, 1998.
Knafo, Danielle. "Claude Cahun: The Third Sex." *Studies in Gender and Sexuality* 2, no. 1 (2001): 29–61.
Koller, Christian. *Von Wilden aller Rassen niedergemetzelt: Die Diskussion um die Verwendung von Kolonialtruppen in Europa zwischen Rassissmus, Kolonial- und Militärpolitik (1914–1930)*. Stuttgart, 2001.
Kolney, Fernand. *La grève des ventres*. Paris: Genération Consciente, 1908.

Krakovitch, Odile. *Les femmes bagnardes*. Paris: Olivier Orban, 1990.
Krauss, Rosalind. *Bachelors*. Cambridge, MA: MIT University Press, 2000.
———. *Passages in Modern Sculpture*. New York: Viking, 1977.
Laing, Kathryn. "Introduction." In Rebecca West, *The Sentinel: An Incomplete Early Novel by Rebecca West*, ed. Kathryn Laing, xiii–liii. Oxford: University of Oxford Press, 2002.
Laqueur, Thomas. "Bodies, Details, and the Humanitarian Narrative." In *The New Cultural History*, ed. Lynn Hunt. Berkeley: University of California Press, 1989.
Latimer, Tirza True. "Entre Nous: Between Claude Cahun and Marcel Moore." *GLQ* 12, no. 2 (2006): 197–216.
———. "Looking Like a Lesbian: Portraiture and Sexual Identity in 1920s Paris." In *Modern Woman Revisited: Paris Between the Wars*, ed. Whitney Chadwick and Tirza True Latimer. New Brunswick, NJ: Rutgers University Press, 2003.
———. *Women Together, Women Apart: Portraits of Lesbian Paris*. New Brunswick, NJ: Rutgers University Press, 2005.
Lavin, Maud. *Cut with the Kitchen Knife: The Weimar Photomontages of Hannah Höch*. New Haven, CT: Yale University Press, 1993.
———. "The Mess of History, or the Unclean Hannah Höch." In *Hannah Höch*, 117–23. Munich: Prestel, 2014.
Lee, Stephen. *The Ethnic Avant-Garde: Minority Cultures and World Revolution*. New York: Columbia University Press, 2015.
Lemke, Sieglinde. *Primitivist Modernism: Black Culture and the Origins of Transatlantic Modernism*. New York: Oxford University Press, 1998.
Lemkin, Raphael. "Genocide as a Crime Under International Law." *American Journal of International Law* 41, no. 1 (1947): 145–51.
Lenin, V. I. *What Is to Be Done?*. Vol. 1 of *Selected Works*. Moscow: Progress Publishers, 1967.
Lennon, Joseph. "Fasting for the Public: Irish and Indian Sources of Marion Wallace Dunlap's 1909 Hunger Strike." In *Enemies of Empire*, ed. Eóin Flannery and Angus Mitchell, 19–39. Dublin: Four Courts Press, 2007.
Leperlier, François. *Claude Cahun: L'écart et la metamorphose*. Paris: Jean-Michel Place, 1992.
Liddington, Jill, and Jill Norris. *One Hand Tied Behind Us: The Rise of the Women's Suffrage Movement*. London: Virago, 1978.
Lim, Bliss Cua. "Dolls in Fragments: *Daisies* as Feminist Allegory." *Camera Obscura* 47 (2001): 37–77.
Limoncelli, Stephanie A. *The Politics of Trafficking: The First International Movement to Combat the Sexual Exploitation of Women*. Stanford, CA: Stanford University Press, 2010.
Liu, Lydia H. "Shadows of Universalism: The Untold Story of Human Rights Around 1948." *Critical Inquiry* 40 (2014): 385–417.
Lorde, Audre. "The Uses of Anger: Women Responding to Racism." In *Sister/Outsider: Essays and Speeches*, 124–33. Toronto: Crossing Press Feminist Series, 2007.
Lowe, Lisa. *Intimacies of Four Continents*. Durham, NC: Duke University Press, 2015.
Ludovico, Roberto. "Renato Poggioli: Between History and Literature." *Studi Slavistici* 10 (2013): 301–10.

Luxemburg, Rosa. "The Mass Strike, the Political Party, and the Trade Unions." In *The Rosa Luxemburg Reader*, ed. Peter Hudis and Kevin B. Anderson. New York: Monthly Review Press, 2004.

Luyken, Gunda. "In the Magical Realm of Fantasy: Hannah Höch's *Picture Book*." In Hannah Höch, *Picture Book*, trans. Brian Currid. Berlin: Green Box Kunst Editionnen, 2010.

Lyon, Janet. "Carrington's Sensorium." In *Leonora Carrington and the International Avant-Garde*, ed. Jonathan P. Eburne and Catriona McAra. Manchester: Manchester University Press, 2017.

———. *Manifestoes: Provocations of the Modern*. Ithaca, NY: Cornell University Press, 1999.

Madureira, Luiz. *Cannibal Modernities: Postcoloniality and the Avant-Garde in Caribbean and Brazilian Literature*. Charlottesville: University of Virginia Press, 2005.

Maguy. "Nélissa et les trois monstres." *La Femme dans la Cité*, July 1948, 4.

Mahmood, Saba. *Politics of Piety: The Islamic Revival and the Feminist Subject*. Princeton, NJ: Princeton University Press, 2005.

Makela, Maria, and Peter Boswell, eds. *The Photomontages of Hannah Höch*. Minneapolis, MN: Walker Art Center, 1996.

Makward, Christian P. "'Ensouché fond': Le petit théâtre d'Ina Césaire." In Ina Césaire, *Rosanie Soleil et autres textes dramatiques*. Paris: Editions Karthala, 2011.

———. "Haiti on Stage: Franco-Caribbean Women Remind. On Three Plays by Ina Césaire, Maryse Condé, and Simone Schwarz-Bart." *Sites: The Journal of Twentieth-Century/Contemporary French Studies* 4, no. 1 (2000): 129–37.

Marcus, Jane. "Re-reading the Pankhursts and Women's Suffrage." In *Suffrage and the Pankhursts*, ed. Jane Marcus, 1–17. London: Routledge, 1987.

Marcus, Sharon. "Queer Theory for Everyone: A Review Essay." *Signs* 31, no. 1 (2005): 191–218.

Marks, Sally. "Black Watch on the Rhine: A Study in Propaganda, Prejudice, and Prurience." *European Studies Review* 13, no. 3 (1983): 297–333.

Martinez, Jenny S. *The Slave Trade and the Origins of International Human Rights Law*. Oxford: Oxford University Press, 2012.

Marx, Karl. *Early Political Writings*. Cambridge: Cambridge University Press, 1994.

———. *Later Political Writings*. Trans. Terrell Carver. Cambridge: Cambridge University Press, 1996.

Marx, Karl, and Friedrich Engels. "Manifesto of the Communist Party." https://www.marxists.org/archive/marx/works/download/pdf/Manifesto.pdf.

Maß, Sandra. *Weiße Helden, schwarze Krieger: Zur Geschichte kolonialer Männlichkeit in Deutschland, 1918–1964*. Cologne: Böhlau, 2006.

Mayhall, Laura E. Nym. *The Militant Suffrage Movement: Citizenship and Resistance in Britain, 1860–1930*. Oxford: Oxford University Press, 2003.

Mbembe, Achilles. "The Power of the Archive and Its Limits." Trans. Judith Inggs. In *Refiguring the Archive*, ed. Carolyn Hamilton, 19–26. London: Kluwer, 2002.

McKay, Claude. *A Long Way from Home*. London: Pluto, 1985.

McKittridge, Katherine. *Demonic Grounds: Black Women and the Cartographies of Struggle*. Minneapolis: University of Minnesota Press, 2006.

McLaren, Angus. *Sexuality and Social Order: The Debate Over the Fertility of Women and Workers in France, 1770–1920*. Holmes & Meier, 1983.
Mies, Maria. *Patriarchy and Accumulation on a World Scale: Women in the International Division of Labor*. New York: Zed, 1999.
Miller, Erika. *The Other Reconstruction: Where Violence and Womanhood Meet in the Writings of Wells-Barnett, Grimké, and Larson*. New York: Garland, 2000.
Mitchell, Juliet. *Women's Estate*. New York: Vintage, 1973.
Mohanty, Chandra Talpade. *Feminism Without Borders: Decolonizing Theory, Practicing Solidarity*. Durham, NC: Duke University Press, 2003.
Montagnac, Lieutenant-Colonel de. *Lettres d'un soldat: Neuf années de campagnes en Afrique*. Paris: Plon, 1885. Trans. Christian Destremeau, 1998.
Morel, E. D. *The Horror on the Rhine*. London: St. Clements, 1921.
Moretti, Franco. *The Way of the World: The Bildungsroman in European Culture*. Trans. Albert Sbragia. London: Verso, 1987.
Morgan, Jennifer L. *Laboring Women: Reproduction and Gender in New World Slavery*. Philadelphia: University of Pennsylvania Press, 2004.
Morgan, John H. "An Essay on the Production of Abortion Among Our Negro Population." *Nashville Journal of Medicine and Surgery*, August 1860, 117–18.
Morrell, Caroline. *"Black Friday" and Violence Against Women in the Suffragette Movement*. London: Women's Research and Resources Center, 1981.
Morrissey, Marietta. *Slave Women in the New World: Gender Stratification in the Caribbean*. Lawrence: University of Kansas Press, 1989.
Morsink, Johannes. *The Universal Declaration of Human Rights*. Philadelphia: University of Pennsylvania Press, 1999.
Moses, A. Dirk. "Raphael Lemkin, Culture, and the Concept of Genocide." In *The Oxford Handbook of Genocide Studies*, ed. Donald Bloxham and A. Dirk Moses, 20–41. Oxford: Oxford University Press, 2010.
Mosse, George L. *Nationalism and Sexuality: Respectability and Abnormal Sexuality in Modern Europe*. New York: Howard Vertig, 1997.
Moyn, Samuel. *The Last Utopia: Human Rights in History*. Cambridge, MA: Harvard University Press, 2010.
Muel-Dreyfus, Francine. *Vichy and the Eternal Feminine: A Contribution to a Political Sociology of Gender*. Trans. Kathleen A. Johnson. Durham, NC: Duke University Press, 2001.
Mulcahy, Linda. "Docile Suffragettes? Resistance to Police Photography and the Possibility of Subject Transformation." *Feminist Legal Studies* 23, no. 1 (2015): 79–99.
Mulder, Nan. "Leonora Carrington in Mexico." *Alba* 1, no. 6 (1991–1992): 6.
Muñoz, José Esteban. *Cruising Utopia: The Then and There of Queer Futurity*. New York: New York University Press, 2009.
———. *Disidentifications: Queers of Color and the Performance of Politics*. Durham, NC: Duke University Press, 2013.
Murphy, Michelle. *Seizing the Means of Reproduction: Entanglements of Feminism, Health, and Technoscience*. Durham, NC: Duke University Press, 2012.

Nairn, Tom. *The Break-Up of Britain: Crisis and Neo-Nationalism*. London: NLR, 1997.
Nardal, Paulette. "United Nations." *La Femme dans la Cité*, January 1947, 2.
Nelson, Keith L. "The 'Black Horror on the Rhine': Race as a Factor in Post–World War Diplomacy." *Journal of Modern History* 42, no. 4 (1970): 606–27.
Nero, Julie. "Hannah Höch, Til Brugman, Lesbianism, and Weimar Sexual Subculture." PhD diss., Case Western Reserve University, 2013.
Nicolas, Armand. *Histoire de la Martinique, 1848–1939*. Paris: L'Harmattan, 1996.
Noakes, Jeremy. "Nazism and Eugenics: The Background to the Nazi Sterilization Law of 14 July 1933." In *Ideas Into Politics: Aspects of European History, 1880–1950*, ed. R. J. Bullen, H. Pogge von Strandmann, and A. B. Polonsky, 75–94. Totowa, NJ: Barnes and Noble, 1984.
Nussbaum, Martha. *The Monarchy of Fear: A Philosopher Looks at Our Political Crisis*. New York: Simon & Schuster, 2018.
Offen, Karen. *Debating the Woman Question in the Third Republic, 1870–1920*. Cambridge: Cambridge University Press, 2018.
Otto, Dianne. "Feminist Approaches to International Law." In *The Oxford Handbook of the Theory of International Law*, ed. Anne Ordord, Florian Hoffmann, and Martin Clark, 488–504. Oxford: Oxford University Press, 2016.
Owen, Jonathan L. "Spoiled Aesthetics: Realism and Anti-Humanism in Vera Chytilová's *Daisies* (1966)." In *Avant-Garde to New Wave: Czechoslovak Cinema, Surrealism, and the Sixties*, 99–128. New York: Berghahn, 2011.
Pago, Gilbert. *L'insurrection de Martinique, 1870–1871*. Paris: Syllepse, 2011.
——. *Lumina Sophie dit "Surprise" 1848–1879 insurgée et bagnarde*. Matoury, Guyana: Ibis Rouge Editions, 2008.
Pannekoek, Anton. "Marxist Theory and Revolutionary Tactics." *Die Neue Zeit* 31, no. 1 (1912). https://www.marxists.org/archive/pannekoe/1912/tactics.htm.
Patterson, William L., ed. *We Charge Genocide: The Historic Petition to the United Nations for Relief from a Crime of the United States Government Against the Negro People*. Civil Rights Congress. New York: International Publishers, 1951.
Payne, Stanley G. *A History of Fascism, 1914–1945*. New York: Routledge, 1996.
Paz, Octavio. "Dos Transeúntes: Leonora y Remedios." In *Octavio Paz: Los privilegios de la vista*. Mexico: Centro Cultural Arte Contemporaneo, 1990.
Pendleton, E. M. "On the Susceptibility of the Caucasian and African Races to the Different Classes of Disease." *Southern Medical Reports* 2 (1949 [1856]): 336–42.
Pierre, José, ed. *Investigating Sex: Surrealist Research, 1928–1932*. Trans. Malcolm Imrie. London: Verso, 1992.
Pliley, Jessica R. *Policing Sexuality: The Mann Act and the Making of the FBI*. Cambridge, MA: Harvard University Press, 2014.
Pinto, Samantha. *Difficult Diasporas: The Transnational Feminist Aesthetic of the Black Atlantic*. New York: New York University Press, 2013.
Poggioli, Renato. *The Theory of the Avant-Garde*. Trans. Gerald Fitzgerald. Cambridge, MA: Harvard University Press, 1968.
Polizzotti, Mark. *Revolution of the Mind: The Life of Andre Breton*. Boston: Black Widow, 2009.

Pollard, Miranda. *Reign of Virtue: Mobilizing Gender in Vichy France.* Chicago: University of Chicago Press, 1998.
Prima, Diane di. *Revolutionary Letters.* San Francisco: City Lights, 1968.
Puchner, Martin. *Poetry of the Revolution: Marx, Manifestos, and the Avant-Gardes.* Princeton, NJ: Princeton University Press, 2006.
Pugh, Martin. *The March of Women: A Revisionist Analysis of the Campaign for Women's Suffrage, 1866–1914.* Oxford: Oxford University Press, 2000.
Purvis, June. "'Deeds Not Words': The Daily Lives of the Militant Suffragettes in Edwardian Britain." *Women's Studies International Forum* (1995): 97–98.
Quataert, Jean H. *Reluctant Feminists in German Social Democracy, 1885–1917.* Princeton, NJ: Princeton University Press, 1979.
Raeburn, Antonia. *The Militant Suffragettes.* London: Michael Joseph, 1973.
Ray, Man. *Self-Portrait.* Boston: Little, Brown, 1963.
Reagon, Bernice Johnson. "Coalition Politics: Turning the Century." In *Homegirls: A Black Feminist Anthology,* ed. Barbara Smith, 343–56. New York: Kitchen Table: Women of Color Press, 1983.
Reinders, Robert C. "Racialism on the Left: E. D. Morel and the 'Black Horror on the Rhine.'" *International Review of Social History* 13 (1968): 1–28.
Richards, Jill. "Model Citizens and Millenarian Subjects: Vorticism, Suffrage, and London's Great Unrest." *Journal of Modern Literature* 37, no. 3 (2014): 1–17.
Richardson, Mary R. *Laugh a Defiance.* London: George Weidenfeld & Sons, 1953.
Riley, Denise. *Am I That Name? Feminism and the Category of "Women" in History.* London: Palgrave, 1988.
Rimbaud, Arthur. *Rimbaud Complete.* Vol. 1. Trans. Wyatt Mason. New York: Modern Library, 2003.
Roberts, David D. *The Syndicalist Tradition and Italian Fascism.* Chapel Hill: University of North Carolina Press, 1979.
Roberts, Dorothy E. *Killing the Black Body: Race, Reproduction, and the Meaning of Liberty.* New York: Vintage, 1997.
Roberts, Stephen H. *The History of French Colonial Policy, 1870–1925.* London: Frank Cass, 1963.
Ronsin, Francis. *Grève des ventres: Néo-Malthusienne et baisse de la natalité.* Paris: Aubier Montaigne, 1980.
Roos, Julia. "Nationalism, Racism, and Propaganda in Early Weimar Germany: Contradictions in the Campaign Against the 'Black Horror on the Rhine.'" *German History* 30, no. 1 (2012): 45–74.
Roosevelt, Eleanor. *On My Own.* New York: Harper & Brothers, 1958.
Rosen, Andrew. *The Militant Campaign of the Women's Social and Political Union, 1903–1914.* London: Routledge, 1974.
Ross, Kristin. *Communal Luxury: The Political Imaginary of the Paris Commune.* New York: Verso, 2015.
———. *The Emergence of Social Space: Rimbaud and the Paris Commune.* New York: Verso, 2008.

Ross, Loretta J. "The Color of Choice: White Supremacy and Reproductive Justice." In *Color of Violence: The Incite! Anthology*, 53–65. Cambridge, MA: South End Press, 2006.

Ross, Loretta J., Lynn Roberts, Erika Derkas, Whitney Peoples, and Pamela Bridgewater, eds. *Radical Reproductive Justice: Foundations, Practice, Theory, Critique*. New York: Feminist Press, 2017.

Ross, Loretta J., and Rickie Solinger. *Reproductive Justice: An Introduction*. Berkeley: University of California Press, 2017.

Rowbotham, Sheila. *Women, Resistance, and Revolution: A History of Women and Revolution in the Modern World*. New York: Random House, 1973.

Ryersson, Scot D., and Michael Orlando Yaccarino. *Infinite Variety: The Life and Legend of the Marchesa Casati*. Minneapolis: University of Minnesota Press, 2004.

Sahakian, Emily. "Beyond the Marilisse and the Chestnut: Shattering Slavery's Sexual Stereotypes in the Drama of Ina Césaire and Maryse Condé." *Modern Drama* 3 (2014): 385–408.

Said, Edward. "Third World Intellectuals/Metropolitan Culture." *Raritan* 9, no. 3 (1990).

Sanger, Margaret. *Family Limitation* [1917]. Margaret Sanger Papers Project, New York University, 2018.

Schaffer, Kay, and Sidonie Smith. *Human Rights and Narrated Lives: The Ethics of Recognition*. New York: Palgrave, 2004.

Schehr, Lawrence R. *Alcibiades at the Door: Gay Discourses in French Literature*. Stanford, CA: Stanford University Press, 1995.

Schmitt, Carl. *The Concept of the Political*. Trans. George Schwab. Chicago: University of Chicago Press, 2007.

Scott, Joan Wallach. *Only Paradoxes to Offer: French Feminism and the Rights of Man*. Cambridge, MA: Harvard University Press, 1996.

Shah, Nayan. *Stranger Intimacy: Contesting Race, Sexuality, and Law in the North American West*. Berkeley: University of California Press, 2012.

Sharpley-Whiting, T. Denean. *Negritude Women*. Minneapolis: University of Minnesota Press, 2002.

———. "On Race, Rights and Women." In *Beyond Negritude: Essays from Woman in the City*, trans. T. Denean Sharpley-Whiting, 1–17. Albany: SUNY Press, 2009.

Shaw, Jennifer Laurie. *Exist Otherwise: The Life and Works of Claude Cahun*. London: Reaktion, 2017.

———. "Narcissus and the Magic Mirror." In *Don't Kiss Me: The Art of Claude Cahun and Marcel Moore*. London: Aperture, 2006.

Sheller, Mimi. *Citizenship from Below: Erotic Agency and Caribbean Freedom*. Durham, NC: Duke University Press, 2012.

Sibalis, Michael D. "Homophobia, Vichy France, and the Crime of Homosexuality: The Origins of the Ordinance of 6 August 1942." *GLQ* 8, no. 3 (2002): 301–18.

Simpson, Brian. *Human Rights and the End of Empire: Britain and the Genesis of the European Convention*. Oxford: Oxford University Press, 2004.

Slaughter, Joseph. "The Enchantment of Human Rights, or What Difference Does Humanitarian Indifference Make?" *Critical Quarterly* 56, no. 4 (2014): 46–66.

———. *Human Rights Inc.: The World Novel, Narrative Form, and International Law.* New York: Fordham University Press, 2007.

Slemon, Stephen. "Magic Realism as Postcolonial Discourse." In *Magical Realism: Theory, History, Community*, ed. Lois Parkinson Zamora and Wendy B. Faris, 406–26. Durham, NC: Duke University Press, 1995.

Solomon-Godeau, Abigail. "The Equivocal 'I': Claude Cahun as Lesbian Subject." In *Inverted Odysseys: Claude Cahun, Maya Deren, Cindy Sherman*, ed. Shelley Rice. Cambridge, MA: MIT Press, 1999.

Somers, Margaret. "Citizenship Troubles: Genealogies of Struggle for the Soul of the Social." In *Rethinking Modernity*, ed. Julia Adams, Elisabeth Clemens, and Ann Orloff, 438–69. Durham, NC: Duke University Press, 2005.

Somerville, Siobhan. *Queering the Color Line: Race and the Invention of Homosexuality in American Culture.* Durham, NC: Duke University Press, 2000.

Spade, Dean. "Intersectional Resistance and Law Reform." *Signs: A Journal of Women in Culture and Society* 38, no. 4 (2013): 1–25.

Spurlin, William J. *Lost Intimacies: Rethinking Homosexuality Under National Socialism.* New York: Peter Lang, 2009.

Stoler, Ann Laura. *Carnal Knowledge and Imperial Power: Race and the Intimate in Colonial Rule.* Durham, NC: Duke University Press, 2002.

Suleiman, Susan Rubin. *Subversive Intent: Gender, Politics, and the Avant-Garde.* Cambridge, MA: Harvard University Press, 1990.

Tamagne, Florence. *A History of Homosexuality in Europe*, vol. 2: *Berlin, London, Paris, 1919–1939.* New York: Algora, 2004.

Tashjian, Dickran. "Vous pour moi?: Marcel Duchamp and Transgender Coupling." In *Mirror Images: Women, Surrealism, and Self-Representation*, ed. Whitney Chadwick. Cambridge, MA: MIT Press, 1998.

Tate, Claudia. *Domestic Allegories of Political Desire: The Black Heroine's Text.* Oxford: Oxford University Press, 1992.

Taylor, Diana. *The Archive and the Repertoire: Performing Cultural Memory in the Americas.* Durham, NC: Duke University Press, 2003.

Tickner, Lisa. *The Spectacle of Women: Imagery of the Suffrage Campaign, 1907–14.* London: Chatto & Windus, 1987.

Tocqueville, Alexis de. *Writings on Empire and Slavery.* Trans. Jennifer Pitts. Baltimore, MD: John Hopkins University Press, 2003.

Travis, Jennifer. "Clits in Court: *Salome*, Sodomy, and the Lesbian 'Sadist.'" In *Lesbian Erotics*, ed. Karla Jay, 147–63. New York: New York University Press, 1995.

Trouillout, Michel-Rolp. *Silencing the Past: Power and the Production of History.* Boston: Beacon, 2015.

Tzara, Tristan. "An Introduction to Dada." In *Dada Painters and Poets: An Anthology*, ed. Robert Motherwell. Cambridge, MA: Harvard University Press, 1979.

Vasak, Karel. "Human Rights: A Thirty-Year Struggle: The Sustained Efforts to Give Force of Law to the Universal Declaration of Human Rights." *UNESCO Courier* 30, no. 11 (1977).

Universal Declaration of Human Rights. 1948. United Nations. http://www.un.org/en/documents/udhr/.

Unruh, Vicky. *Latin American Vanguards: The Art of Contentious Encounters*. Berkeley: University of California Press, 1994.

Usborne, Cornelia. *The Politics of the Body in Weimar Germany: Women's Reproductive Rights and Duties*. Ann Arbor: University of Michigan Press, 1992.

Vadde, Aarthi. *Chimeras of Form: Modernist Internationalism Beyond Europe, 1914–2016*. New York: Columbia University Press, 2016.

Violations of the Laws and Customs of War: Reports of Majority and Dissenting Reports of American and Japanese Members of the Commission of Responsibilities, Conference of Paris, 1919. London: Carnegie, 1919.

Wachman, Gay. *Lesbian Empire: Radical Crosswriting in the Twenties*. New Brunswick, NJ: Rutgers University Press, 2001.

Wampole, Christy. "The Impudence of Claude Cahun." *L'Esprit Créator* 53, no. 1 (2013): 101–13.

Warner, Michael. *Publics and Counterpublics*. New York: Zone, 2005.

Weheliye, Alexander G. *Habeas Viscus: Racializing Assemblages, Biopolitics, and Black Feminist Theories of the Human*. Durham, NC: Duke University Press, 2014.

Weinbaum, Alys Eve. *Wayward Reproduction: Genealogies of Race and Reproduction in Transatlantic Modern Thought*. Durham, NC: Duke University Press, 2004.

West, Rebecca. *The Sentinel: An Incomplete Early Novel*. Ed. Kathryn Laing. Oxford: Oxford University Press, 2002.

Wexler, Laura. *Tender Violence: Domestic Visions in an Age of U.S. Imperialism*. Chapel Hill: University of North Carolina Press, 2000.

Wheeler, Lorna Raven. "The Queer Collaboration: Angelina Weld Grimké and the Birth Control Movement." *Critical Insights: LGBTQ Literature*, ed. Robert C. Evans, 179–92. Ipswich, MA: Salem Press, 2015.

White, Deborah Gray. *Ain't I a Woman? Female Slaves in the Plantation South*. New York: Norton, 1985.

White, Hayden. *The Content of the Form: Narrative Discourse and Historical Representation*. Baltimore, MD: John Hopkins University Press, 1990.

Wigger, Iris. *Die "Schwarze Schmach am Rhein": Rassistische Diskriminierung zwischen Geschlecht, Klasse, Nation und Rasse*. Munster: Westfälisches Dampfboot, 2006.

Wilder, Gary. *Freedom Time: Négritude, Decolonization, and the Future of the World*. Durham, NC: Duke University Press, 2014.

Wilks, Jennifer. *Race, Gender, and Comparative Black Modernism: Suzanne Lascascade, Marita Bonner, Suzanne Césaire, Dorothy West*. Baton Rouge: Louisiana State University Press, 2008.

Wilson, Aimee Armande. *Conceived in Modernism: The Aesthetics of Birth Control*. New York: Bloomsbury University Press, 2016.

Wingerden, Sophia van. *The Women's Suffrage Movement in Britain, 1866–1928*. London: Macmillan, 1999.

Wintermute, Robert. *Sexual Orientation and Human Rights: The United States Constitution, the European Convention, and the Canadian Charter.* Oxford: Clarendon, 1995.

Wollen, Peter. *Raiding the Icebox: Reflections on Twentieth-Century Culture.* Bloomington: Indiana University Press, 1993.

Woolf, Virginia. *Night and Day.* New York: Penguin, 1992.

Wynter, Sylvia. "Unsettling the Coloniality of Being/Power/Truth/Freedom: Towards the Human, After Man, Its Overrepresentation—An Argument." *CR: The New Centennial Review* 3: no. 3 (2003): 257–337.

Ziarek, Ewa Płonowska. *Feminist Aesthetics and the Politics of Modernism.* New York: Columbia University Press, 2012.

Index

abortifacients, 136
"Actions of the Revolutionary Party" (*Votes for Women*), 83
Ades, Dawn, 198
Afro-German case study. *See* Rhineland
Ainsworth, Laura, 95
Alba, Pedro De, 231
Allan, Maud, 200
anarchism, First International and, 7
Anker, Elizabeth, 3
Ann Veronica (Wells), 74
anti-sex-trafficking legislation, 237–239
Appert, Eugène, 40–42, *41*, *43*
Appert, General, 35
Arcanum 17 (Breton), 214–215
Arendt, Hannah: agency and, 99; on bureaucracy, 236; *The Human Condition* by, 90–91; space of appearance and, 92
Arp, Hans, 260
Asad, Talal, 56–57
"At Bow Street on Wednesday" (*Votes for Women*), 84
autobiography: as antibildungsromans, 75–76; event lists in, 78–81, *81–82*; list, 76; narrative chronology and, 77; suffrage movement and, 75–81; surrealism and, 208; transformation timing in, 77–78, 80
avant-garde: as commonplace, 259–260; cultural and political, 17–18; *Daisies* and, 226–227, *227*; deformation, 212–213; distracted attention and, 161–162; esoteric, 257–258; *The Ethnic Avant-Garde*, 256; feminist approaches to, 188; found objects and, 21; group identity and, 147–148; Hugnet and, 147–148; intimate theory of, 16–21; Latin America and, 274n35; marvelous and, 260–262; modernist tradition and, 16; Paris Commune and, 18; Poggioli and, 16–18, 212–213; Pound and, 20; primitivist aesthetic of, 160–161; revolution and, 20–21; suffrage formation of, 73; theatricality and, 170; Trotsky and, 213–214; Tzara and, 147; vorticism and, 93; women's rights and, 3–4. *See also* Dada; futurism; surrealism

"Baby Figure of the Giant Mass of Things to Come, The" (*Crisis*), 124–125, *125*
Bakhtin, Mikhail, 76
Beame, Henry, 136
"Becky and the Respectables" (*Woman Rebel*), 122
Bellmer, Hans, 208–209
Berlant, Lauren, 293n19
Bernstein, Alfred, 109
Bets are Open, The (Cahun), 215, 223
Beveridge, Ray: fact and, 152; Rhineland bastard and, 144–145

bildungsroman: *Confidences au miroir* and, 218–219; *The Sentinel* and, 86–87, *88*; suffrage and, 75, 76
Billing, Pemberton, 200–201
Billington-Grieg, Teresa, 72
birth control movement: abortifacients and, 136; Bernstein and, 109; birth control manuals and, 114–118; *Blessed with Children* and, 110; "The Closing Door" and, 130–131; *Crisis* and, 124–127; epistolary novel and, 111–112; as equality tactic, 107; *Family Limitation* and, 115, *116*, 118; genocide and, 139–143; Goldman and, 110, 114–115; "How to Establish a Birth Control Clinic" and, 115–116, *117*; "A Human Document" and, 114; Huot and, 105–106, 281n7; infanticide and, 135–137; League for Human Regeneration and, 106; *The Masses* and, *111*; Jennifer Morgan and, 135–136; Murphy and, 117–118; nation-state and, 106; overview, 25–26, 107–108; privacy rights and, 107; proletarian birth strike and, 109–118; proletarian women and, 106; queer futures in Harlem and, 124–138; race-reproduction bind and, 108; *Rachel* and, 130; racial justice and, 138; Raney and, 113; reproductive justice and, 138, 284n70; reproductive rights rulings, 106–107; Roberts and, 138; Robin and, 110; *Sabotage* and, 112–113; Sanger and, 119; slave language and, 124; sympathy and, 111–112; tactics, subject of, and, 118–124; *Woman Rebel* and, 119–124, *120*; Zetkin and, 109
Birth Control Review (magazine): Ellis and, 132; issues addressed in, 131–132; *Race Suicide in the United States* in, 132; *They That Sit in Darkness* and, 134
birth strike: Bernstein and, 109; birth control manuals and, 114–118; birth control movement and, 109–118; *Blessed with Children* and, 110; epistolary novel and, 111–112; *Family Limitation* and, 115, *116*, 118; Goldman and, 110; "How to Establish a Birth Control Clinic" and, 115–116, *117*;

"A Human Document" and, 114; *The Masses* and, *111*; Murphy and, 117–118; Raney and, 113; Robin and, 110; *Sabotage* and, 112–113; sympathy and, 111–112; Zetkin and, 109
"Black Man Replies, A" (McKay), 149
Black Skin, White Masks (Fanon), 250
Blanqui, Louis Auguste, 119
BLAST (journal), 93
Blessed with Children (Brupbacher), 110
Bocquin, Lucie Marris, 31
Bodies That Matter (Butler), 199
Bonnefoy, Louise Frédérique, *41*
Bostonians, The (James), 74
Braun, Lily, 8
Breton, André: *Arcanum 17* by, 214–215; autobiography and, 208; homosexuality and, 193–194; *Nadja* by, 195–197, 217–218; Paris walks of, 217–218; Trotsky and, 213–214; woman, characterization of, by, 214–215
Brio, Matthew, 164, 166
Brugman, Matilda: "Department Store of Love" by, 174–177; Institute of Sexual Science and, 174
Brupbacher, Fritz, 110
Bryce report, 154–155
Bürger, Peter, 196
Burrill, Mary, 134
Burton, Antoinette, 11
Butler, Judith, 198, 199
Byrnes, James Francis, 125

Cadogan, Alexander, 232
Cahun, Claude (née Lucy Renee Mathilde Schwob): anti-Nazi propaganda leaflets of, 216–218, 291n56; arrest of, 216; art for liberation and, 215; autobiography and, 208; *The Bets are Open* by, 215, 223; Billings case and, 200–201; celebratory life of, 197–198; chance encounter and, 227; as child, 219; *Confidences au miroir* by, 215, 218–223; *Daisies* by, 226–227, *227*; deformation and, 212–213; dismemberment and, 209, 291n48; dueling selves of, 220; Ferdière letter

INDEX   319

and, 291n56; *Frontière humaine* by, 209, 210, 211–212, 291n48; gambling tomorrow and, 197–200; human rights and, 221; humor and, 206–207; identity categories and, 226; *L'Amité* by, 201; Levy letter and, 220–221; mask and, 198; metamorphosis of, 219–220; Moore and, 201–202, 228; overview about, 26–27; political activism explained, 220–221; posthumous opinions about, 198; poststructuralist thesis about, 198; self portraits, 202–208, 203–208, 212–213; Sherman and, 226; social antagonisms and, 220; societal change and, 222–223; soldier without name and, 217; UDHR by, 221

Caliban and the Witch (Federici): primitive accumulation and, 255; structural adjustment and, 254–255; witch hunt and, 255

Campbell-Bannerman, Henry, 96
Campt, Tina, 172
Capper, Mabel, 15, 95
Carpentier, Alejandro, 260–262
Carrington, Leonora, 27–28; domestic imagery of, 258; esoteric avant-garde and, 257–258; Exquisite Corpse and, 256–257; freezing effect of, 262–263; *Grandmother Moorhead's Aromatic Kitchen* by, 258; Gurdjieff and, 257; Lyon on, 259; marvelous and, 262; in Mexico, 257; Paz and, 257; *Sanctuary for Furies* by, 265, 266, 267, 270; second-generation human rights and, 267; style of, 263; surrealism as commonplace and, 259–260; Varo and, 256–257; woman-child and, 260; women's rights movements and, 267. *See also Hearing Trumpet, The*

Casati, Luisa, 185–187, *186*
case study: Laqueur and, 150; as warped and partial form, 151. *See also* Rhineland
Cassin, Rene, 231
Cat and Mouse Act, 68, 71
Certeau, Michel de, 119
Césaire, Aimé, 247
Césaire, Ina, 35

Chamberlain, K. R., *111*
chance: freedom and, 189; *Nadja* and, 195–197
"Chicago and Its Eight Reasons" (White, Walter), 125, *127*
chronotropes, 137
Chytilová, Vera, 226–227, *227*
citizenship, female: abstract compared to real and, 2–3; coalitional entanglement and, 1–2; as contested terrain, 38; gender of, 35–45; methodological shift related to, 2–3; as subject of action, 1–3, 271n4; transatlantic archive of, 1
citizenship, homosexuality and, 191
"Citizenship Troubles" (Somers), 271n4
Civil Rights Congress (CRC), 139
Civil War in France, The (Marx), 38–39, 91
Cleopatra, 121
"Closing Door, The" (Grimké): agency and, 130–131, 137–138; chronotropes in, 137; doom, sense of, in, 134–135; historical narrative in, 135; individual agency and, 130–131; international geography and, 139; many themes of, 131; reproductive justice and, 138; same-sex desire in, 131, 132–134; secret in, 133–134; *They That Sit in Darkness* and, 134
Codé, Mr., 46, 47
Cold War, 255
Colette, 201
collage: "Marie Jeanne's Hands," 44–45; "Prison des Chantiers à Versailles" and, 40, 42, *43*
colonial law, humanization and, 56–57
Colored Frenchmen (brochure), 150
"Colored Troops in the French Army" (report), 144
committee meeting, of UN: anti-sex-trafficking legislation and, 237–239; bureaucracy and, 236; Cassin and, 231; colonial hearts at General Assembly and, 234–241; conclusions, 251–253; Creole folktales and, 247–252; experimentation and, 253; governmentality and, 232–233; grassroots mobilization and, 244–245; long-winded participants in, 230–231; "Nélissa and the Three Monsters" and,

committee meeting, of UN (*continued*) 251–252; off-topic debate and, 236; overview, 27, 234; Pavlov and, 230; performance and, 236–237; procedural consideration of, 231–234; Salle de Mutualité, 245; self-making and, 253; Shawcross and, 238, 240; Special Committee for Non-Self-Governing Territories, 234–236; theoretical person and, 241; verbatim record and, 236; Vieux and, 238–240; *Woman in the City* and, 233–234, 244–245; world making and, 236–237, 293n19
Communist Manifesto, The (Marx and Engels), 93
Concept of the Political, The (Schmitt), 169–170
Confidences au miroir (Cahun), 215; bildungsroman related to, 218–219; dueling selves and, 220; metamorphosis and, 219–220; as Rimbaudian prose poems, 218; social antagonisms and, 220; societal change and, 222–223
Congo Reform Association, 148
Conley, Katherine, 209, 291n48
Convention on the Prevention and Punishment of the Crime of Genocide, 140
Convert, The (Robins), 74
Craig, Layne Parrish, 110–111
CRC. *See* Civil Rights Congress
Creole folktales: *Black Skin, White Masks* related to, 250; *Fire's Daughters*, 60; testimony and truth in, 248–251; *Tropiques* and, 247; *Woman in the City* and, 247–252
Criminal Law Amendment Act, 191–192
Crisis (magazine): "The Baby Figure of the Giant Mass of Things to Come" in, 124–125, *125*; birth control movement and, 124–127; "Chicago and Its Eight Reasons" in, 125, *127*; "If We Must Die" in, 127, *128*; "The Looking Glass" in, 126–127, *128*; "Opinion" in, 125, *126*; *Unnatural Selections* and, 127–128
"Crowbar *vs.* Words, The" (Raney), 113

Cut with the Kitchen Knife (Höch): Dada period and, 158, *159*; distracted attention and, 161–162; neutrality and, 179
Cyrille, Camille Jean Lois, 50, 52–56

Dada: as commonplace, 259–260; *Cut with the Kitchen Knife* and, 158, *159*; Höch on, 178–179; Man and, 186–187
Daily Herald (newspaper), 148–149
Daisies (Chytilová), 226–227, *227*
Danel, Mme, 246
D'Annunzio, Gabriele, 187
Davis, Katherine B., 122–123
Dean, Carolyn, 198–199
deformation, 212–213
"Department Store of Love" (Brugman): human types in, 174–175; Institute of Sexual Science and, 174; love-objects and, 175; parade of characters and, 175–176; *Picture Book* and, 176–177
Der Querschnitt (art magazine), 161
"Discussion Circle" (*Freewoman*), 14, 15
Division on Non-Self-Governing Territories, 241–242
Doherty, Brigid, 288n62
Douzinas, Coustas, 255
Doy, Gen, 290n28
"Drudge, The" (Marsden), 12
Duhamel, Marcel, 194
Dunlap, Marion Wallace, 95
Dupont, Léonce, 31

Eburne, Jonathan, 257
Edelsohn, Becky, 122–123
Egoist, The (journal), 15–16
Einstein, Carl, 160–161
Ellis, Havelock, 132
End of Human Rights, The (Douzinas), 255
Endtimes of Human Rights, The (Hopgood), 255
Engels, Friedrich, 93
English, Daylanne K., 127–128
epistolary novel, 111–112
Esmeir, Samira, 57
"Essay on Algeria" (Tocqueville), 34
Ethnic Avant-Garde, The (Lee), 256

Etifier, Mme, 246–247
Exquisite Corpse, 256–257

Facta, Luigi, 187
Fairfield, Cicely Isabel. *See* West, Rebecca
family law: Family Code and, 191; identity categories and, 225–226; Law of 1920 and, 190–191; overview, 26–27, 189; racialization and, 190; repopulation and, 190–191; *UDHR* and, 224–225
Family Limitation (Sanger), 115, *116*, 118
Fanon, Frantz, 248
Farbige Franzosen am Rhein (Gärtner), 151
Federici, Silvia, 19, 254
Felski, Rita, 75
female arsonists. *See pétroleuse*
feminism: avant-garde and, 188; first-wave, 24–25; human rights and, 6–16; identity and injury related to, 2, 271n4; political action and, 4–5; socialism related to, 8–10
Femme dans la Cité, La (periodical), 27, 233
Ferdière, Gaston, 291n56
Fire's Daughters (Césaire): beginning and ending of, 66–67; Creole folktale and, 60; endings, 64; housework stage directions in, 59–60; insurrectionary archive and, 58–67; as intimate theater, 58–67; Martinique Insurrection and, 58; monologue closing, 64–66; naming in, 61–63, 67; overview related to, 35; paternity issue in, 58; prologue, 61–63; questions invoked by, 63; storytelling in, 60–61; as theater of justice, 64; wordplay tactics in, 61
First International, 7
Flynn, Elizabeth Gurley, 112–113, 123
force feeding: of Leigh, 99–100; of Lenton, 96–97; of Marion, 97; medical logs and, 100–102, *101*, 280n35; methods of barbarism and, 96–97, *98*; Pethick-Lawrence on, 97
Ford, Ford Maddox, 74
Fournier, Mr., 55
Frauenarbeit und Hauswirtschaft (Braun), 8
freedom, chance and, 189

Freewoman (weekly): "Discussion Circle" in, 14, *15*; letters to editor in, 13–14; motherhood endowment and, 12–15; questionnaire published in, 13; topics in, 12
Freytag, Gustav, 87
Fried, Michael, 160, 286n34
From an Ethnographic Museum series (Höch): Lavin and, 161; *Love in the Bush* in, 163–164, *164*; mixed-race body and, 146; *Monument 1* in, 161; *Ohne Titel* in, *159*, 160, 162–163; *Picture Book* related to, 173; theatricality and, 170
Frontière humaine (Cahun): blurring of boundaries in, 209, *210*; constraint and, 212; dismemberment and, 209, 291n48; photographic trick effects of, 211; surrealist ghostliness of, 291n48
fury, feminist political action and, 4–5
futurism, 187

G. (author), 114
gambling tomorrow: Cahun and, 197–200; *Nadja* and, 195–197
Garner, Margaret, 137
Garrity, Jane, 271n4
Gärtner, Margarete, 151
Gawthorpe, Mary: assault of, 14–15; questionnaire by, 13
Gender Trouble (Butler), 198
generational model of rights, 6
genocide: birth control movement and, 139–143; Convention on the Prevention and Punishment of the Crime of Genocide, 140; human rights and, 139; lynching and, 140–141
"Gentlebread" (*Picture Book*), 177–178
Georges (lynched black men), 129–130
Gerber, Henry, 23
German Ficte-Bund leaflet, 151
Gilroy, Paul, 108
Giorni, Secondo, 110
Gladstone, Herbert, 95
Goldman, Emma: birth control and, 110, 114–115; Hirschfeld and, 22–23
Gorden, Frances, 97

Gould, William, 136
"Government's Methods of Barbarism, The" (*Votes for Women*), 96, 98
Grandmother Moorhead's Aromatic Kitchen (Carrington), 258
Grewal, Inderpal, 232–233
Grimké, Angelina Weld: Burrill and, 134; "The Closing Door" by, 130–135, 137–139; *Rachel* by, 128–130
Gurdjieff, George, 257

Habermas, Jürgen, 18
Half-Breed (Höch): Brio on, 164, 166; mouth in, *165*, 167, 169; negative space and, 164–167, *165*, 169; photo used in, 166–167, *168*; suffering in, 164, *165*, 166; sympathy and, 166; theatricality and, 170
Hausmann, Raoul, 158, *159*
Hays, George, 136
Hearing Trumpet, The (Carrington): as archive, 265; background, 27–28, 256; conclusions about, 268; dream-like narration of, 264–265; freezing effect of, 262–263; friends appearing as characters in, 265; obsolescence and, 262; postcolonial literature and, 256; second-generation human rights and, 267; shared ethic of care in, 258; surrealism as commonplace and, 259–260; Weisz-Carrington and, 263, *264*; woman-child and, 260; as zany, 258–259
Hirschfeld, Magnus, 22–23
"History of the Hunger Strike, A" (*Woman Rebel*), 122
Höch, Hannah, 146; amalgamated bodies in works by, 157–158; animal-alien species and, 179–180; censorship and, 177; *The Concept of the Political* by, 169–170; *Cut with the Kitchen Knife* by, 158, *159*, 161–162, 179; on Dada, 178–179; Dada period of, 158, *159*; "Department Store of Love" and, 176–177; ethnographic period of, 157; from flatness to figural, 158, *159*, 160; "Gentlebread" by, 177–178; group identity and, 147; *Half-Breed* by, 164–167, *165*, *168*, 169–170; incommensurate viewpoints and, 162–163; Lavin and, 161; "Little Baby Gamma" by, 173–174; *Love in the Bush* by, 163–164, *164*; Luyken and, 172; on Negro art, 161; *Ohne Titel* by, *159*, 160, 162–163; overview related to, 26. *See also From an Ethnographic Museum* series; *Picture Book*
Hollier, Denis, 197
homosexuality: Billings case and, 200–201; Breton and, 193–194; citizenship and, 191, 225; costume and, 201–202; depopulation and, 191; documenting, 21–24; France in 1920s and, 192–193; identity categories and, 225–226; interwar Europe and, 191–192; *L'Amitié* and, 201; nuclear family and, 191; Ray and, 194; rights groups, 23–24; *Sex and Character* and, 188; surrealism and, 193–195
Homosexuality in Men and Women (Hirschfeld), 22–23
Hong, Grace, 271n4
Hopgood, Stephen, 252, 255
Horror on the Rhine (Morel): background, 149; legal explanation genre in, 152–153; "Outrages Upon Women" in, 153–154
housewifization, 19
housework wages. *See* motherhood endowment
"How to Establish a Birth Control Clinic" (pamphlet), 115–116, *117*
Hugnet, Georges, 147–148
Human Condition, The (Arendt), 90–91
"Human Document, A" (G.), 114
human rights: Cahun and, 221; CRC, 139; epistolary novel and, 111–112; extraterritorial, 10; feminist internationalisms and, 6–16; First International and, 7; gay rights groups and, 23–24; generational model and, 6; governance of, 6–16; *Inventing Human Rights*, 111; language and, 7, 269; *The Last Utopia* and, 255; League for Human Rights, 23; methods of barbarism and, 96–97, *98*; motherhood endowment and, 12–16, 173n22; Moyn and, 7–8, 255; narratives, alternative, and, 5–6; *News for*

Human Rights, 23; only and, 268–269; overview related to, 26–27; public/private split and, 10–11; revolution theories and, 8–10; second-generation, 267; socialism related to feminism and, 8–10; Society for Human Rights, 23; ways to narrate, 6–7; *We Charge Genocide* and, 139; women's rights as, 10–11. *See also* Universal Declaration of Human Rights
Human Rights and the End of Empire (Simpson), 255
Humphrey, John, 230
hunger strike: Edelsohn and, 122–123; as long middle of resistance, 99; medical logs and, 100–102, *101*, 280n35; methods of barbarism and, 96–97, *98*; Pethick-Lawrence on, 97; as Russian method, 95. *See also Leigh v. Gladstone*
Hunt, Lynn, 3, 111
Huot, Marie: population control and, 105; production of people analogy of, 105–106; strike of wombs and, 105, 281n7

identity: categories, 225–226; feminist scholarship focus on, 2, 271n4; group, 147–148
"If We Must Die" (McKay), 127, *128*
"In Defense of Assassination" (*Woman Rebel*), 122
Index of Women Suffragettes Arrested, 71
infanticide, 135–137
injury, feminist scholarship focus on, 2, 271n4
Institute of Sexual Science, 174
Intercollegiate Model Assembly, 237
International Convention for the Suppression of the Traffic in Women and Girls, 237, 294n22
intimate theory: of avant-garde, 16–21; social reproduction theory and, 19–20
Inventing Human Rights (Hunt), 111
Ishay, Micheline, 7

James, Henry, 74
Jameson, Fredric, 20
Jane (a slave) v. The State, 137
Jeanne, Marie, 44

Jenneret, Georges, 33–34
Jews, *Sex and Character* and, 188
Johnson, Bascom, 238
Johnson, Paul, 225
Joseph-Henri, Madame, 245

Kenney, Annie: event lists and, 78–79; on living in now, 78; metamorphosis of, 77
Kipling, Rudyard, 135
Kline, Katy, 198
Krauss, Rosalind, 162, 198

Lacaille, Eugène, 49
L'Amité (journal), 201
Laqueur, Thomas, 150
L'art di non fare figli (Giorni), 110
Last Utopia, The (Moyn), 255
Latimer, Tirza True, 201
Laugh a Defiance (Richardson): high-toned style of, 80; self-realization in, 80; table of contents, 79–80, *82*
Laval, Emilie, 245
Lavin, Maud, 161
Law of 1920, 190–191
Law to Prevent Hereditarily Sick Offspring, 171
League de la régénération humaine, 106, 110
League for Human Rights, 23
League of Nations News, 237
League of Rhenish Women (RFL), 150
Lee, Steven S., 256
Leigh, Mary: aims of, 101–102; arrest of, 95; consent compared to refusal and, 100; contradictory character of, 95; force feeding and, 99–100
Leigh v. Gladstone: contractual law and, 97; long middle of resistance and, 99; medical logs and, 100–102, *101*, 280n35; or right to refuse, 94–102
Lemkin, Raphael, 139
Lenin, Vladimir, 8–9
Lenton, Lilian, 96–97
"Lettre à Gaston Ferdière" (Cahun), 291n56
"Lettre au Paul Levy" (Cahun), 291n56
Levy, Paul, 220–221, 291n56
Lewis, Wyndham, 93

Lineal, Charlotte, 245
"Little Baby Gamma" (*Picture Book*), 173–174
Liu, Lydia, 252
Loisne, Charles Menche de, 45–48
long middle: hunger strike and, 99; *Leigh v. Gladstone* and, 99; of resistance, 99; *Sanctuary for Furies* and, 270; *The Sentinel* and, 92–93; of suffrage, militant, 71–72; of women's rights, 21–22
"Looking Glass, The" (*Crisis*), 126–127, *128*
Love in the Bush (Höch), 163–164, *164*
Lubin, Léopold, 46
Lumina Sophie. *See* Surprise
Luxemburg, Rosa, 9
Luyken, Gunda, 172
lynching: antilynching drama, 128–130; "Chicago and Its Eight Reasons" and, 125, *127*; Georges and, 129–130; "If We Must Die" and, 127, *128*; "The Looking Glass" and, 126–127, *128*; national borders and, 140–141; *Rachel* and, 128–130; *We Charge Genocide* and, 140–141
Lyon, Janet, 73, 259

Macco, Hans, 171–172
Magnard, Francis, 37–38
Mahmood, Saba, 243
Makela, Maria, 163
Malherbe, Susanne. *See* Moore, Marcel
Malik, Charles, 224, 231
Manesta, Evelyn, 68, *70*
"Manifesto for an Independent Revolutionary Art" (Breton & Rivera), 213–214
Ray, Man: blurring of portrait by, 209–210; Casati portrait as mistake, 185; Dada and surrealism related to, 186–187; homosexuality and, 194
Marchais, Joséphine, 31
"Marie Jeanne's Hands" (Rimbaud), 44–45
Marinetti, F. T., 187
Marion, Kitty: force feeding of, 97; surveillance photographs and, 68, 277n1
Marquise Casati (Ray): blurring effect in, 185–186, *186*; as mistake, 185; as premeditated, 186

Marsden, Dora: assault of, 14–15; "The Drudge" by, 12; questionnaire by, 13
Marsh, Charlie, 95
Martinique Insurrection: Codé and, 46, 47; colonial insurgency and, 45–55; Cyrille and, 50, 52–56; events leading to, 45–47; *Fire's Daughters* and, 58; Fournier and, 55; French Empire fall sparking, 47; immigrant labor and, 46–47; juridical human and, 57; Lacaille and, 49; legal positivism and, 56; Loisne account of, 45–48; overview, 24–25; race war and, 49; St. Pée and, 53–56; Surprise and, 48, *50*, 51–52, 55; theories of right related to, 55; unreliable reports of, 48; witness testimony on, 51, 276n39
Marx, Karl: *The Civil War in France* by, 38–39; *The Communist Manifesto* by, 93; Paris Commune and, 38–39; social experiment and, 253; on theoretical person, 241
mask, 198, 250
Masses, The (publication), 111
McKay, Claude, 127, *128*, 149
Mein Leben für Euch! (Beveridge), 144
Memories of a Militant (Kenney): event lists and, 78–79; metamorphosis in, 77; wavering arc in, 78
Ménil, René, 247
methodology, 21–24
Mexico: Carrington in, 257; Cold War and, 267
Michel, Louise, 22–23
Mies, Maria, 19
"Militants in England, The" (*Woman Rebel*), 121–122
Militant Suffragette Movement, The (Raeburn), 81, 84, *85*
Montagnac, Lieutenant-Colonel de, 34
Moore, Marcel (née Susanne Malherbe): anti-Nazi propaganda leaflets of, 216–218, 291n56; Cahun and, 201–202, 228; manuscript of, 227–229, *228*; soldier without name and, 217
Morel, E. D.: *Daily Herald* and, 148–149; *Horror on the Rhine* by, 149, 152–154; legal

INDEX 325

explanation genre and, 152–153; native rights in central Africa and, 148; "Outrages Upon Women" by, 153–154
Moretti, Franco, 75
Morgan, Jennifer L., 135–136
Morgan, John H., 136
Mosse, George, 188
motherhood endowment: debates related to, 12; "The Drudge" and, 12; *The Egoist* and, 15–16; extended consideration of, 173n22; *Freewoman* and, 12–15; human rights and, 12–16, 173n22
Moyn, Samuel, 7–8, 252, 255
Murphy, Michelle, 117–118
Mussolini, Benito, 187

Nadja (Breton), 195–197, 217–218
Nardal, Paulette: background on, 233; civilizing process and, 243; daily life of *Woman in the City* and, 241–248; Division on Non-Self-Governing Territories and, 241–242; localized practices and, 252; overview related to, 27; on UN, 242; universalist perspective of, 243–244
narrative: autobiography and, 77; "The Closing Door," 135; *The Hearing Trumpet*, 264–265; human rights and, 5–6; realist model of, 2–3
National Fascist Party (PNF), 187
natural law, positive law related to, 56–57
"Navel" (Arp), 260
"Nélissa and the Three Monsters" (Maguy): committee meeting related to, 251–252; first ending of, 248–249; legal personhood and, 250–251; public testimony as tactic in, 250; second ending of, 250; style of, 248; wordplay in, 249–250
neo-Malthusianism, 110
News for Human Rights (journal), 23
Nigeria, 254
Night and Day (Woolf), 74

Ohne Titel (Höch), *159*, 160, *162*–163
"Opinion" (Du Bois), 125, *126*
Other Germans (Campt), 172
"Outrages Upon Women" (Morel), 153–154

Pankhurst, Sylvia: life events list of, 80–81; McKay and, 149; *Suffragette Movement* and, 80–81, *82*
Pannekoek, Anton, 9
Papavoine, Eulalie, 31, *41*
Paris Commune: Eugène Appert and, 40–42, *41, 43*; avant-garde and, 18; Marx and, 38–39; as social experiment, 31–32; Versailles arrests and, 40–42, *41, 43*; working existence and, 39–40
Parker, Fanny, 97
parliamentary report, 150–151
Pavlov, Alexei: as long-winded, 230; right to life and, 231
Paz, Octavio, 257
Peace, Rachel, 100, *101*
Pendleton, E. M., 136
Péret, Benjamin, 194
Pétain, Marshal, 191
Pethick-Lawrence, F. W., 97–98
pétroleuse (female arsonists): appearances of, 31; caricatures of, 32–33; Jenneret and, 33–34; Magnard on, 37; "Marie Jeanne's Hands" and, 44–45; nameless others, 33–34; as non-traditional, 37; overview, 24–25; Pont-Jest on, 32; Role of Women During the Battle of the Commune and, 36, *36*; as unnatural, 35
photomontage, severing process and, 162
Picasso, Pablo, 160
Picture Book (Höch): animal-alien species and, 172–173, 179–180; censorship and, 177; "Department Store of Love" in, 176–177; end of, *180*, 180–181; "Gentlebread" in, 177–178; "Little Baby Gamma" in, 173–174; taxonomy and, 180–181
PNF. *See* National Fascist Party
Poetry of the Revolution (Puchner), 170
Poggioli, Renato: avant-garde and, 16–18, 212–213; deformation and, 212–213
Pont-Jest, René de, 32
positive law: human as a legal category and, 57; natural law compared to, 56–57; transition to, 56–57
Pound, Ezra: avant-garde and, 20; vorticism and, 93

Poupées (Bellmer), 208–209
Prévert, Jacques, 194
Prima, Diane di, 268
"Prison des Chantiers à Versailles" (Appert, Eugène), 40, 42, *43*
Puchner, Martin, 170

Queneau, Raymond, 194

Race Problems in the Third Reich (Macco), 171
Race Suicide in the United States (Thompson), 132
Rachel (Grimké), 128–130
racism, sexual deviance and, 188
Raduzveit, Friedrich, 23
Raeburn, Antonia, 81, 84, *85*
Raney, Reb, 113
Recherches sur la sexualité (publication), 193–194
Reichszentrale zur bekämpfung der Homosexualität und Abortion, 192
Reitman, Ben, 114–115
Report on Alleged German Outrages in Belgium. See Bryce report
reproductive justice, 138, 284n70
Rétiffe, Elizabeth, 31
revolution: "Actions of the Revolutionary Party," 83; avant-garde and, 20–21; Lenin and, 8–9; "Manifesto for an Independent Revolutionary Art," 213–214; means and ends of, 72, 278n4; only and, 268–269; *Poetry of the Revolution*, 170; revolutionary picaresque, 86–94; theories of, 8–10; *Votes for Women* column on, 81, 83–84, *84*, *85*
"Revolutionaries, The" (*Votes for Women*), 83
"Revolutionary Birth-Control" (Chamberlain), *111*
Revolutionary Letters (Prima), 268
RFL. See League of Rhenish Women
Rhineland bastard, 144–145; Beveridge and, 144–145; black shame on Rhine and, 148–157; Bryce report and, 154–155; *Colored Frenchmen* and, 150; *The Concept of the Political* and, 169–170; English-speaking socialist circles and, 149; fact and, 152–153; German Ficte-Bund leaflet and, 151; German literature produced about, 149; *Horror on the Rhine* and, 149, 152–154; humanity and, 145–146, 155–157; legal explanation genre and, 152–153; "Little Baby Gamma" and, 173–174; *Love in the Bush* related to, 163–164, *164*; Macco and, 171–172; McKay and, 149; overview, 26; *Picture Book* and, 172–174; police reports and, 153–154; public genres and, 146–147; RFL and, 150; sterilization in, 171–172; transnational public and, 156–157; Treaty of Versailles and, 145; war crime pamphlets and, 145
Richardson, Mary Raleigh: arrest record of, 68, 71, *71*; event lists and, 79–80, *82*; high-toned style of, 80; self-realization of, 80
rights. *See* human rights; women's rights
Rimbaud, Arthur, 44–45, 218
Rising Tide of Color, The (Stoddard), 132
Rivera, Diego, 213–214
Rivière, Joan, 198, 290n28
Roberts, Dorothy, 138
Robin, Paul, 106, 110
Robins, Elizabeth, 74
Role of Women During the Battle of the Paris Commune, 36, *36*
Romulo, Carlos, 232
Roosevelt, Eleanor, 230
Roptus, Marie-Philomène. *See* Surprise
Ross, Kristin, 39
Ruptures of American Capital, The (Hong), 271n4
Russian method, 95

Sabotage (Flynn), 112–113, 123
St. Pée, Jean David, 53–56
Salle de Mutualité meetings, 245
Salomé (Wilde), 200–201
Sanctuary for Furies (Carrington), 265, *266*, 267, 270
San Francisco Charter, 231–232
Sanger, Margaret: birth control and, 119; *Family Limitation* by, 115, *116*, 118; slave language and, 124

scavenger ideology, 188
scene of beholding, 160, 286n34
Schehr, Lawrence R., 193
Schmitt, Carl, 169–170
Sentinel, The (West): bildungsroman and, 86–87, 88; compulsion and, 89–90; end of, 91–92; first section of, 86–87, 88; Freytag and, 87; ghost and, 93–94; long middle and, 92–93; political action and, 91–92; revolutionary picaresque and, 86–94; rising and falling action in, 87–90, *88*; style of, 86; vorticism and, 93
Sex and Character (Weineger), 188
sex-trafficking. *See* anti-sex-trafficking legislation
sexual deviance: Casati and, 187; interwar Europe and, 191–192; racism and, 188
Sexual Inversion (Ellis), 132
Shaw, Jennifer, 198
Shawcross, Hartley, 238, 240
Sherman, Cindy, 226
Short, Jane, 100, *101*
Simpson, A. W. Brian, 255
SisterSong Women of Color Reproductive Collective, 284n70
Slaughter, Joseph, 3
Snowden, Philip, 96
socialism: end of, 256; feminism compared to, 8–10; First International and, 7; Lee and, 256
social reproduction theory: development of, 27–28; intimate theory and, 19–20. *See also Hearing Trumpet, The*
Society for Human Rights, 23
Solomon, Mrs. Saul, 97
Some Do Not (Ford), 74
Somers, Margaret, 271n4
space of appearance, 92
Special Committee for Non-Self-Governing Territories, 234–236
Step-Daughters of England (Garrity), 271n4
sterilization, 171–172
Stoddard, Lothrop, 132
Stopes, Marie, 115
strike of wombs, 105, 281n7
structural adjustment, 254

Suétens, Léontine, 31
suffrage, militant: action compared to demand and, 91–92; "Actions of the Revolutionary Party" and, 83; *Ann Veronica* and, 74; "At Bow Street on Wednesday" and, 84; autobiography and, 75–81; avant-garde formation and, 73; bildungsroman and, 75, 76; *The Bostonians* and, 74; Cat and Mouse Act and, 68, 71; conclusions, 102; *The Convert* and, 74; historical materials on, 71, 278n2; *Index of Women Suffragettes Arrested*, 71; *Laugh a Defiance* and, 79–80, 82; *Leigh v. Gladstone*, 94–102; long middle of, 71–72; *Memories of a Militant* and, 78–79; *The Militant Suffragette Movement* and, 81, 84, 85; mugshots, 68, *69–70*, 277n1; narrative chronology and, 77; *Night and Day* and, 74; novels and, 73–75; overview, 25–26; political action and, 91–92; "The Revolutionaries" and, 83; *The Sentinel* and, 86–94; *Some Do Not* and, 74; *Suffragette Sally* and, 74; tactics compared to demands and, 72; vorticism and, 93; writings and, 73–85; Ziarek and, 72
Suffragette Movement (Pankhurst), 80–81, 82
Suffragette Sally (Wannop. Colmore), 74
Suleiman, Susan Rubin, 296n11
Surprise (Martinican woman, also called Lumina Sophie), 48, *50*, 51–52, 55
surrealism: autobiography and, 208; chance and, 189; as commonplace, 259–260; *Daisies* and, 226–227, *227*; esoteric avant-garde and, 257–258; Exquisite Corpse and, 256–257; female form and, 188; homosexuality and, 193–195; identity categories and, 225–226; Man and, 186–187; Trotsky and, 213–214; woman-child and, 260
sympathy, 111–112, 166

tactics: birth control movement and, 118–124; Certeau and, 119; *Woman Rebel* and, 119–124, *120*
Tamagne, Florence, 191
Tanner, Kathleen, 99

Taylor, Diana, 64
Theory of the Avant-Garde, The (Poggiol), 16–18
They That Sit in Darkness (Burrill), 134
Thompson, Warren S., 132
Tocqueville, Alexis de, 34
Treaty of Versailles: *The Concept of the Political* and, 169–170; Rhineland and, 145
Tropiques (Césaire & Ménil), 247
Trotsky, Leon, 213–214
Tzara, Tristan, 147

UDHR. *See* Universal Declaration of Human Rights
UN. *See* United Nations
Unik, Pierre, 194
United Nations News, 237
United Nations (UN): anti-sex-trafficking legislation and, 237–239; Division on Non-Self-Governing Territories, 241–242; Nardal on, 242; "Nélissa and the Three Monsters" and, 251–252; San Francisco Charter and, 231–232; Special Committee for Non-Self-Governing Territories, 234–236; Trusteeship System of, 232. *See also* committee meeting, of UN
Universal Declaration of Human Rights (UDHR): Cahun and, 221; counterarchive of rights leading to, 4; family and, 224–225
Unnatural Selections (English), 127–128

Varo, Remedios: esoteric avant-garde and, 257–258; Exquisite Corpse and, 256–257; Gurdjieff and, 257; second-generation human rights and, 267
Vasak, Karel, 6
Vieux, Mr., 238–240
vorticism, 93
Votes for Women (newspaper): methods of barbarism and, 96, *98*; revolution column in, 81, 83–84, *84, 85*

Wages for Housework Movement, 268
Wannop. Colmore, Valentine, 74
Warner, Michael, 293n19

We Charge Genocide (CRC): evidence lists in, 141–142; human rights and, 139; internationalist juridical scope of, 143; lynching and, 140–141; as media event, 139; petitioners of, 140; tactic of, 142–143
weekly column: "Actions of the Revolutionary Party," 83; "At Bow Street on Wednesday," *84*; "The Revolutionaries," 83; timeline and, 84–85; *Votes for Women*, 81, 83–84, *84, 85*
Weineger, Otto, 188
Weisz-Carrington, Pablo, 263, *264*
Wells, H. G., 13, 74
West, Rebecca (née Cicely Isabel Fairfield): bildungsroman and, 86–87, *88*; ghost and, 93–94; political action and, 92; revolutionary picaresque and, 86–94; vorticism and, 93; writing styles of, 86. *See also Sentinel, The*
What Is to Be Done? (Lenin), 8–9
White, Hayden, 84
White, Walter, 125, *127*
Why and How the Poor Should Not Have Many Children (Goldman and Reitman), 114–115
Wilde, Oscar, 200–201
Wilson, Aimee Armande, 111
Wise Parenthood (Stopes), 115
"Without Benefit of Clergy" (Kipling), 135
Woman in the City (periodical): civilizing process and, 243; committees and, 233–234, 244–245; contents of, 233, 243; Creole folktales and, 247–252; daily life of, 241–248; editorials, 246–247; grassroots mobilization and, 244–245; "Nélissa and the Three Monsters" in, 248–251; overview about, 27; Salle de Mutualité meetings and, 245; universalist perspective of, 243–244; Women's Assembly and, 242–243
"Womanliness as a Masquerade" (Rivière), 198
Woman Rebel (journal): "Becky and the Respectables" in, 122; birth control movement and, 119–124, *120*; Edelsohn and, 122–123; historical lessons in, 121; "A

History of the Hunger Strike" in, 122; imagination and, 121–123; imperative tense of, 121; "In Defense of Assassination" in, 122; "The Militants in England" in, 121–122; mobile action and, 123; readership of, 119–120; *Sabotage* and, 123; slave language and, 124; subtitle of, 119

women. *See specific topics*

Women's Assembly (Martinique), 242–243

women's rights: avant-gardes and, 3–4; Carrington and, 267; coalitional entanglement and, 1–2; as human rights, 10–11; language and, 269; long middle of, 21–22; only and, 268–269; public/private split and, 10–11; reproductive rights rulings, 106–107; witness and realist genres of, 2–3. *See also specific topics*

Woodlock, Patricia, 95

Woolf, Virginia, 74

working existence, 39–40

Wynter, Sylvia, 295n42

Yotte, Amelie, 245, 246

Zetkin, Clara, 8, 109

Ziarek, Ewa Płonowska, 72

MODERNIST LATITUDES

Barry McCrea, *In the Company of Strangers: Family and Narrative in Dickens, Conan Doyle, Joyce, and Proust*, 2011

Jessica Berman, *Modernist Commitments: Ethics, Politics, and Transnational Modernism*, 2011

Jennifer Scappettone, *Killing the Moonlight: Modernism in Venice*, 2014

Nico Israel, *Spirals: The Whirled Image in Twentieth-Century Literature and Art*, 2015

Carrie Noland, *Voices of Negritude in Modernist Print: Aesthetic Subjectivity, Diaspora, and the Lyric Regime*, 2015

Susan Stanford Friedman, *Planetary Modernisms: Provocations on Modernity Across Time*, 2015

Steven S. Lee, *The Ethnic Avant-Garde: Minority Cultures and World Revolution*, 2015

Thomas S. Davis, *The Extinct Scene: Late Modernism and Everyday Life*, 2016

Carrie J. Preston, *Learning to Kneel: Noh, Modernism, and Journeys in Teaching*, 2016

Gayle Rogers, *Incomparable Empires: Modernism and the Translation of Spanish and American Literature*, 2016

Donal Harris, *On Company Time: American Modernism in the Big Magazines*, 2016

Celia Marshik, *At the Mercy of Their Clothes: Modernism, the Middlebrow, and British Garment Culture*, 2016

Christopher Reed, *Bachelor Japanists: Japanese Aesthetics and Western Masculinities*, 2016

Eric Hayot and Rebecca L. Walkowitz, eds., *A New Vocabulary for Global Modernism*, 2016

Eric Bulson, *Little Magazine, World Form*, 2016

Aarthi Vadde, *Chimeras of Form: Modernist Internationalism Beyond Europe, 1914–2014*, 2016

Ben Conisbee Baer, *Indigenous Vanguards: Education, National Liberation, and the Limits of Modernism*, 2019

Claire Seiler, *Midcentury Suspension: Literature and Feeling in the Wake of World War II*, 2020

GPSR Authorized Representative: Easy Access System Europe, Mustamäe tee 50, 10621 Tallinn, Estonia, gpsr.requests@easproject.com

www.ingramcontent.com/pod-product-compliance
Lightning Source LLC
Chambersburg PA
CBHW021933290426
44108CB00012B/824